SELECTED MODELS OF DEVELOPMENTAL EDUCATION PROGRAMS IN HIGHER EDUCATION

Edited by
Vernon L. Farmer
Wilton A. Barham

University Press of America, Inc.
Lanham · New York · Oxford

Library of Congress Cataloging-in-Publication Data

Selected models of developmental education programs in higher
education / edited by Vernon L. Farmer, Wilton A. Barham.
p.   cm
Includes bibliographical references and index.
1. Developmental studies programs—United States.
2. Remedial teaching—United States. I. Farmer, Vernon L.
II. Barham, Wilton A.
LB2331.2 .S45   2001   378.1'25—dc21   2001027160 CIP

ISBN 0-7618-1713-1 (cloth: alk. paper)
ISBN 0-7618-1991-6 (pbk. : alk. paper)

♾™ The paper used in this publication meets the minimum
requirements of American National Standard for Information
Sciences—Permanence of Paper for Printed Library Materials,
ANSI Z39.48—1984

Contents

Preface

I am especially grateful for the thoughtful deliberation and keen insight that characterize the scholarly work of the authors who contributed to this book. The selected developmental education models are based on defendable theories about how students grow and develop at all levels of the learning continuum. These models emphasize the theories and concepts that underlie developmental education as a field of practice and research with a theoretical foundation in developmental psychology and learning theory. These models consist of methods and techniques for implementing developmental education activities and ways of creating environments intended to improve developmental students' learning outcomes. These models include a rationale, a theory that justifies the models and an explanation of how the models are designed. The rationale is supported by empirical evidence that the models work. These models were selected because they represent varied frames of reference toward educational goals and objectives. Some of the theory-based models presented are more appropriate to some educational goals and objectives than to others. For example, some models are more appropriate for the mastery of subject matter, including the basic skills of reading, writing, and mathematics. Other models are specially tailored to help students develop metacognitive skills and grow in self-awareness and strength of self-confidence; still others are useful for helping higher education institutions develop institutional assessment models for developmental education program evaluation. While some models are quite narrow in their focus, others are more comprehensive and serve multiple purposes in developmental education.

Selected Models of Developmental Education Programs in Higher Education is organized into five parts consisting of twenty-one chapters. *Part I: Introduction* is composed of two chapters. In Chapter One, Vernon

L. Farmer and Wilton A. Barham provide a viewpoint on modeling in developmental education. In Chapter Two, Hunter R. Boylan develops a demographic profile of developmental students in developmental education programs in higher education institutions.

Part II: Models of Affective and Cognitive Support Services includes six chapters. In Chapter Three, Nelson DuBois proposes a developmental information processing model designed to teach students metacognitive skills and help them become self-regulated learners. In Chapter Four, Cheryl B. Stratton, Nannette E. Commander, Carol A. Callahan, and Brenda D. Smith introduce a model that expands learning assistance to all students. In Chapter Five, William Collins describes a comprehensive model of affective and cognitive support that includes advising, academic assistance, and personal support for college students. In Chapter Six, Martha Maxwell discusses a counseling model that is designed to meet developmental learners' personal, academic, and career development needs. In Chapter Seven, Thomas J. Grites describes an academic advising model for developmental college students. In Chapter Eight, Augusta A. Clark, Andolyn B. Harrison, and A. Phillip Butler propose an alternative assessment model for developmental students' admissions and matriculation.

Part III: Models of Curriculum and Instruction consists of six chapters. In Chapter Nine, Wilton A. Barham discusses how supplemental learning can be integrated into a comprehensive developmental education model. In Chapter Ten, Olatunde A. Ogunyemi develops a systems model for designing courses for developmental studies. In Chapter Eleven, Evelyn Shepherd-Wynn, Lorraine Page Cadet, and Ernesta Parker Pendleton propose a collaborative writing model designed for teaching composition to college students. In Chapter Twelve, Evelyn Shepherd-Wynn, Ada Harrington Belton, Peggy R. Porter, and Loretta Walton Jaggers design a whole language reading model for teaching developmental college readers. In Chapter Thirteen, B. Runi Mukerji and Kathleen G. Velsor introduce a model that describes how educational technology can be used to enhance developmental college students' learning outcomes in the classroom. In Chapter Fourteen, Gabriel O. Fagbeyiro in his model examines the effects of learner characteristics and computer feedback strategies on learning achievement of students in developmental courses.

Part IV: Models of Assessment and Evaluation is comprised of six chapters. In Chapter Fifteen, Dorothy Bray discusses a comprehensive assessment learning model designed to help colleges and universities meet the needs of developmental learners. In Chapter Sixteen, Darrel A. Clowes describes a four-stage model for evaluating remedial, compensatory, and developmental education programs in higher education. In Chapter Seventeen, Leonard B. Bliss proposes using an instructional model for student assessment. In Chapter Eighteen, Darlene A. Thurston and V. Carolyn Craig propose an assessment and evaluation model designed for developmental education programs. In Chapter Nineteen, Clara Wilson-Cook discusses a developmental students' persistence model for examining reinstated students' characteristics to improve retention. In Chapter Twenty, Vernon L. Farmer, Neari F. Warner, and Raymond A. Hicks develop a perspective to help higher education institutions design institutional assessment models for developmental program evaluation.

Part V: Integrating Developmental Programs in a Comprehensive Developmental Education Model consists of the final chapter in *Selected Models of Developmental Education Programs in Higher Education*. In Chapter Twenty-one, Vernon L. Farmer and Wilton A. Barham provide a framework for integrating developmental programs into a comprehensive developmental education model.

Finally, the selected developmental education models reflect the theoretical underpinnings and concepts of developmental education as a field of practice and research. Therefore, *Selected Models of Developmental Education Programs in Higher Education* should serve as a valuable resource for scholars, researchers, educators, and practitioners seeking to improve developmental education programs in order to enhance students' learning outcomes.

Vernon L. Farmer

Acknowledgments

An edited book such as *Selected Models of Developmental Education Programs in Higher Education* depends on the work, the thoughts and ideas, and the critical input of the contributing authors and many other individuals. This makes it nearly impossible to recognize all of those involved publicly. However, as editors we wish to thank all of them, particularly the chapter authors, for their scholarly contributions to this book. We are also indebted to Helen Hudson, Peter Cooper, Beverly Baum, and Lois Raimond at University Press of America who, when we agreed to undertake this project almost five years ago, kept after us until we finally delivered. Many thanks to Janet Cooper for her invaluable expertise in preparing the final copy of the manuscript for publication. We are grateful to Ernesta Parker Pendleton, a terrifically insightful, sensitive individual, for her editing skills. Appreciation is also extended to our colleagues at Grambling State University. We are especially indebted to Evelyn Shepherd-Wynn for her editing and technical expertise and for her dedication throughout the fruition of this book; Carmen Giles Copes for helping to improve the visual illustration of the models; and our colleagues in the College of Education for their ideas and suggestions during this research project. We would also like to thank our graduate students, Ericka Battle, Paul Ifeanyi, and Xanthe Seals, for helping to compile the index. Finally, a small portion of the funding for this research venture was made available by Title III's Research Excellence Fund. Therefore, special thanks is extended to Joe Copes and Olatunde Ogunyemi.

Acknowledgment is given to the following sources for permission to reprint minor or major portions of selected chapters:

Clowes, D. A. (1980). More than a definitional problem: Remedial, compensatory, and developmental education. *Journal of Developmental Education, 4*(1), 8-10. Copyright ©1980 by National Center for Developmental Education, Appalachian State University, Boone, NC.

Clowes, D. A. (1984). The evaluation of remedial/developmental programs: A stage model of program evaluation. *Journal of Developmental Education, 8*(1), 14-15, 27-30. Copyright ©1984 by National Center for Developmental Education, Appalachian State University, Boone, NC.

Commander, N. E., Stratton, C.B., Callahan, C. A., & Smith, B. D. (1996). A learning assistance model for expanding academic support. *Journal of Developmental Education, 20*(2), 8-16. Copyright ©1996 by National Center for Developmental Education, Appalachian State University, Boone, NC.

Farmer, V. L. (1992). Developing a perspective for assessment of effectiveness in developmental education. *Educational Research Quarterly, 16*(1), 25-33. Copyright ©1992 by Grambling State University, Grambling, LA.

Part I:
Introduction

Chapter 1

ॐ

Prologue: A Viewpoint On Modeling

Vernon L. Farmer and Wilton A. Barham

How faculty view their roles as professional educators in relationship to developmental education is important to the success of developmental learners. Faculty are responsible for numerous types of instruction, for helping students grow metacognitively and in strength of self-confidence as well as in many other areas. These responsibilities can be placed into several categories: responsibility for the personal growth of students, responsibility for their social development, responsibility for their cognitive development, and responsibility for their mastery of the basic skills (reading, writing, and mathematics) that are essential to college success. To perform these multiple responsibilities, educators often employ developmental education models to enhance the learning outcomes of developmental students in higher education. To carry out these multiple responsibilities, educators draw upon these models to organize and deliver learning experiences to developmental learners.

Modeling is increasingly being employed in the social sciences including education. Educators have adapted this approach from economists who are known for model building. In modeling, economists describe the relationship among specific variables of interest. Then by analyzing data describing past events, they predict what should have occurred and determine whether their model was accurate in predicting what happened (Krathwohl, 1993). Developmental educators employ modeling to predict students' learning outcomes as a function of developmental education models which are assumed to affect academic performance. Educational researchers test these models by analyzing data on the variables of interest to determine the effectiveness of developmental education programs (McCray & Farmer, 1999).

In the attempt to understand the intellectual and social growth of developmental learners, modeling is beneficial to educators in several ways: (1) model value is tested by prediction and (2) model value is tested by its usefulness in organizing and describing phenomena and events (Krathwohl, 1993). The models in *Selected Models of Developmental Education Programs in Higher Education* demonstrate their usefulness in both ways: some are tested by prediction and some are proposed for their utility in understanding the nature and needs of developmental students through the establishment of reasonable theories. We do agree with Krathwohl (1993) that "theories, like models, describe the way in which variables are related in certain situations" (p. 34). Because theories tend to integrate previously disparate facts and findings, they are viewed by many researchers in varied professions as a useful approach to model building. These selected models promote the integration of teaching and learning with the support systems essential to developmental students' success. The theory-based models that are advanced in subsequent chapters represent the speculation, acute observation and research of the contributing authors. They describe how these models can be used to improve developmental college students' learning outcomes.

Finally, developmental educators concerned with specialized areas in developmental education should benefit significantly from *Selected Models of Developmental Education Programs in Higher Education*. Although these selected developmental education models focus primarily on the higher education system, they should also prove useful to K-12 educators as they strive to meet the needs of developmental learners in the their school system.

Chapter 2

ℰᴑᴥ

Developmental Students: Why Are They Here and Who Are They?

Hunter R. Boylan

In spite of an abundance of literature and research, confusion still remains when the discussion turns to students who take remedial courses, participate in developmental education programs, or seek services from learning assistance centers. College professors ask, "Why do I have to teach underprepared students?" Legislators ask, "Why do we have to pay to teach skills in college that should have been taught in high school?" Students ask, "Why do I have to take remedial English? I got a B in my high school English course." The answers to all these questions are that some students either do not take college preparatory courses in the first place, fail to learn all they can the first time they have the chance, or do not enter college immediately after high school learning takes place.

The fact that citizens have already paid to have college preparatory courses taught in the high schools does not mean that every student who eventually goes to college gets the full benefit of those courses. Some students, by virtue of their social or economic status, their life goals, or even the color of their skin, are not advised to take a full load of college preparatory courses. They are often encouraged to take vocational and technical courses instead. Some students deliberately take as few high level college preparatory courses as possible in order to earn higher grades or to avoid more difficult work. Some students might want more rigorous courses but do not have access to a full range of college preparatory courses at their particular high school.

Sometimes college preparatory courses are poorly taught or taught with inadequate equipment. Sometimes they are taught by teachers without a full mastery of the subject matter. Sometimes what passes for college preparatory work at one high school is comparable to the basic curriculum at another school. Often, what is labeled as a college preparatory course falls far short of actually preparing students for college.

College preparatory courses are, indeed, offered in high school throughout America at the taxpayer's expense. That does not mean, however, that they are well taught or that they are truly preparatory level courses. Nor does it mean that everyone takes them.

According to a 1996 issue of *U.S. News and World Report*, only 47% of today's high school students take a core of academic subjects. Yet a large number of the 53% of high school graduates who do not take a core of academic subjects still go on to college. Just because a student applies to a college does not mean that the student has been fully prepared for college.

Furthermore, many students do not get all the possible benefits even if they take a full load of well taught college preparatory courses. In many cases, there is still a gap in preparation even after students have taken what school officials consider to be the appropriate courses to prepare them for college.

Most students would not feel inadequate if they left high school with a B- average in college preparatory courses. Many parents would be quite proud if their children graduated high school with a 2.65 grade point average and finished in the top 25% of their graduating classes. Many college professors think they would be happy to teach English to students who obtained a B in the course in high school.

The fact remains, however, that many students who earn B's and C's in college preparatory courses arrive in college underprepared in one or more basic skill areas. Sometimes these students read and comprehend well but do so slowly. Often these students have a basic mastery of English grammar and spelling but still have difficulty understanding more complex concepts like rhetoric and exposition. Frequently, students who took advanced Algebra in high school still have difficulty with college calculus.

This should not be surprising. After all, college is supposed to be harder than high school. The quality of thought, the level of analysis, the amount and quality of reading and writing, and the level of mathematical competence required for success are all expected to be greater in college. A student who earned a C in high school English might be expected to have some difficulty in college composition. The student who earned a B- in second year Algebra might be expected to have some difficulty in college Calculus.

There are also students who earn A's in high school courses and still have difficulty when they attend some of the nation's more rigorous or selective institutions. This, too, should be expected. It should not be surprising that many students have difficulty with college level work. College courses are supposed to be harder than high school courses. What is surprising is that this seems to come as such a surprise to so many legislators and college faculty.

In addition, there are also those who take remedial courses or developmental courses and participate in learning assistance programs for reasons other than academic and nonacademic reasons. Many honor students choose to take study skills courses so that they will be better able to cope with graduate and professional schools. It is not uncommon for senior premedical students to take reading development courses to help them handle the huge amounts of reading required in medical school. Many students with high grade point averages participate in tutoring programs to help them get better grades in difficult courses outside of their major field.

So far, only traditional age students who entered college immediately after graduating from high school have been discussed. What about those who entered the military upon high school graduation and return to college having been away from study routines for four years or more? What about those who, at age 35, find themselves victims of corporate or industrial "downsizing" and have to return to the local community college to learn skills for a new job? What about the recently divorced or widowed homemakers who must suddenly fend for themselves and their children and seek a college education as a means of supporting themselves and their families?

Few reasonable people would expect all these students of different ages, different backgrounds, and different life situations to arrive in college fully prepared to write essays, analyze literature, do research papers, and solve Calculus problems. Yet there remain countless educators, politicians, and administrators who ask why so many students need to take remedial courses, be tutored, or participate in learning assistance centers.

The fact of the matter is that not everyone who enters college is a recent high school graduate who completed college preparatory courses with A's and B's. Perhaps if they were, we would not need remedial courses, developmental education services, or learning assistance centers. But the chances of this happening in the near future are not good. The reality today, just as it has been throughout much of the history of American higher education, is that a large number of students who arrive on college campuses do not bring appropriate prerequisite skills with them (Boylan & White, 1988).

Will We Always Need Remediation?

The quality of academic preparedness among students graduating from high school is not likely to improve at any point in the near future sufficiently to reduce the need for college level remediation and academic development. In spite of a decade's worth of school reform efforts, the average SAT scores of entering freshmen have shown little improvement. In 1987, these scores averaged 1008 for the two sections most commonly used in college admission (American Council on Education, 1996). For 1989, the National Center for Education Statistics report that approximately 25% of all freshman entering college enrolled in one or more remedial courses (NCES, 1991).

In 1996, the entering SAT scores of college freshmen averaged 1013 for these same two sections (American Council on Education, 1996). Boylan (1995) estimated that approximately 30% of those students took one or more remedial courses upon entering college in the early 1990s.

In essence, today's high school graduates appear to be neither better prepared nor worse prepared for college than those of years past. Their SAT scores have improved only slightly and their need for remedial courses once they arrive in college has been relatively constant during the past ten years. There is little evidence available to suggest that this situation will change quickly.

Some states' reform efforts may, indeed, have generated substantial increases in the SAT scores of high school graduates. South Carolina, for instance, managed to raise its average SAT scores by 43 points during the late 1980s (Hodgkinson, 1993). This however does not seem to have resulted in a subsequent improvement in the academic preparedness of South Carolina's entering college students, huge numbers of whom still had to take remedial courses in the early 1990s (South Carolina Commission on Higher Education, 1992).

Other states have had similar experiences. Slight or even substantial gains in SAT scores among high school graduates have rarely resulted in a reduced need for remediation once these students reach college. This has kept the amount of remediation offered in American higher education relatively constant for at least a decade. In 1983, the National Center for Education Statistics reported that approximately 75% of American Colleges and Universities offered remedial courses (National Center for Education Statistics, 1983). A decade later, the National Study of Developmental Education (Boylan, Bonham, & Bliss, 1992) reported that this figure had not changed. Seventy five percent of American colleges and universities still offered remedial courses.

Interestingly enough, this figure of 75% seems to have been a constant throughout most of the 20th century. Maxwell (1985) reported that, in 1915 according to the U.S. Commissioner of Education, 75% of the nation's colleges and universities "had preparatory department, suggesting that a gap remained between high school preparation and the expectations of colleges" (p. 8). Almost eighty years later, in 1993, the percentage of colleges offering remedial or preparatory courses remained the same (Boylan, Bonham, & Bliss, 1992).

It would appear unrealistic to expect school improvement and reform efforts to make a significant difference any time in the near future. It is worth noting, for instance, that the schools so many people are complaining about today have already undergone more than a decade of improvement and reform efforts since the publication of "A Nation at Risk" (1983). While some improvement has, indeed taken place, this improvement has not led to a decline in the amount of remediation required for students to be successful in college.

Who Are the Developmental Students?

Like the poor, it is likely that developmental students will always be with us. It would be advisable, therefore, to spend more time attempting to understand who they are and what they need and less time complaining about the fact that they continue to exist. History suggests that neither complaints nor school reform efforts will cause them to go away.

It would also be useful to note that a substantial number of students who enter college underprepared are still able to be successful through developmental education. Results from the National Study of Developmental Education (Boylan & Bonham, 1992) suggest that those underprepared students who participate in some form of remedial or developmental education are only slightly less likely to be retained and to graduate than their better prepared peers in universities. The same study indicates that community college students who experience developmental education are more likely to graduate than the average community college student.

It is of primary importance to recognize, therefore, that students who participate in remedial and developmental courses and services improve their chances for college success. With help, developmental students have every chance of becoming college graduates and making a positive contribution to the economy and the society at large. Other than that, it is difficult to make generalizations about those who participate in developmental education. Developmental students are an exceedingly diverse group of learners.

According to the American Council of Education (Knopp, 1996), approximately 13 percent of all undergraduates, about 1.6 million students, reported that they took at least one remedial course in 1992-93. When those who receive tutoring, counseling, or individualized instruction through learning assistance and educational opportunity programs are included, this number increases to over 2,200,000 (Boylan, 1995). Developmental students, then, are a very large constituency in American higher education.

What Are the Demographics of Developmental Students?

Ethnicity

Contrary to popular opinion, the vast majority of those who participate in remedial and developmental courses and services are white. According to the National Study of Developmental Education (Boylan, 1994), white students comprised 67% of students taking remedial courses at two year institutions and 59% of those taking courses at four year institutions. Among the minority students, the largest group participating in remedial courses was African Americans. At two year institutions, they represented 23% of those taking remedial courses and at four year institutions, they represented 30% (Boylan, 1994).

It is erroneous to assume, therefore, that any significant number of those who participate in remedial courses are minority students who are beneficiaries of affirmative action. According to the National Council on Education, only 19% of all African American, Hispanic American, Asian American and Native American students in higher education reported taking remedial or developmental courses during their undergraduate years (Knopp, 1996). The overwhelming majority of students of color, therefore, are not participating in remedial or developmental courses and services in American higher education.

Although African Americans are the largest minority group in developmental education, another 6% are Hispanic, just over 1% are Native American Indians, and 3% are Asian Americans. Altogether, therefore, students of color represent only 33% of the population of students participating in remedial/developmental programs.

Age

Developmental students tend to be within the traditional age bracket for college students. The average age of developmental students is 21 years old. At 4-year institutions, the average is 19 years old and at 2-year institutions the average age is 23 years old (Boylan, Bonham, Bliss, 1994a).

These figures sustain the popular wisdom that developmental students at community colleges, like most community college students, tend to be older than the traditional age college student. At community colleges, the age range for those participating in remedial courses was 16 to 55 (Boylan, Bonham, & Bliss, 1994a).

At four year institutions, however, developmental students fall well within the traditional age group for college students. This probably reflects the tendency of academic advisors at 4-year institutions to urge incoming students to take their remedial courses immediately. In fact, many 4-year institutions require students to take whatever remedial courses are necessary during the freshman year. This may also reflect the fact that mandatory placement in remediation is more common in 4-year institutions than in 2-year institutions (Boylan, Bonham, & Bliss, 1992).

Given all this, it is reasonable to say that those participating in remedial and developmental courses and services at 4-year colleges and universities are about the same age as other students at such institutions. At community and technical colleges, those participating in developmental education are older but their average age is still typical of 2-year college students. Nevertheless, the vast majority of developmental students fall within the so-called "traditional" college age range of 19 to 23 years old.

Gender

A slight majority of developmental students are women. This is true at both 2-year and 4-year campuses. At 2-year institutions, 53% of the developmental students are women. At 4-year institutions, 54% of developmental students are women.

The fact that women are slightly more prevalent in developmental programs than men seems to be in keeping with national figures. According to the Chronicle of Higher Education ("The Nation," 1993), female students represent a slight majority throughout American higher education.

The performance of female students participating in remedial and developmental courses and services does not differ significantly from men. According to the National Study of Developmental Education (Boylan, Bonham, & Bliss, 1992), there were no statistically significant differences in the performance of male and female developmental students as measured by grades in developmental courses, grades point average upon graduation or departure, or rates of retention. Gender, therefore, does not appear to have an impact on the performance of students participating in remedial or developmental courses and services.

Admission Status

Although almost all students participating in remedial or developmental courses and services were placed there because their institutions considered them to be underprepared, the majority of these students were regularly admitted. At 2-year institutions, 93% of those taking remedial or developmental courses had been admitted without restrictions (Boylan, Bonham, & Bliss, 1994a). Because 2-year institutions usually follow an open admissions policy, this is not surprising. Non-selective admission procedures might be expected to yield a large number of students who are not fully prepared for college. On the other hand, the fact that those who end up in remedial courses and developmental programs at 2-year institutions were regularly admitted suggests that someone considered them to be college material at that particular institution.

According to the National Study of Developmental Education, 57% of those participating in remedial and developmental programs at 4-year institutions were admitted without restrictions (Boylan, Bonham, & Bliss, 1994a). Many of the institutions in this sample were at least moderately selective in their admission practices.

It appears that 4-year institutions admit a fairly large number of students who, upon application, are not considered to be in need of any special help in order to succeed. It is only after these students arrive that they are found to be lacking in one or more of the basic skills. Less than half of those students participating in remedial or developmental courses and services are originally admitted with restrictions or conditions placed upon their enrollment.

In short, insofar as their admissions credentials are concerned, the majority of developmental students come from the typical pool of those admitted to any given institution. This is true of moderately selective institutions as well as open admission institutions.

Degree Seeking Status

It has often been argued that student retention or graduation are poor measures of the effectiveness of remedial and developmental education in community colleges. This is because students at these institutions are frequently there to attain short term goals other than obtaining an associate's degree.

This is a reasonable argument. In fact, Cohen and Brawer's (1989) mission of the 2-year college has declined substantially in the past few decades. Today, fewer students are attending community colleges for the purpose of obtaining an associate's degree and transferring to a university. Instead, a great many community college students are seeking to upgrade job skills, qualify for promotion, or learn for leisure and recreational purposes.

Analysis of data from the national Study of Developmental Education (Boylan, Bonham, & Bliss, 1994a), however, suggested that those participating in remedial courses at community colleges are overwhelmingly degree oriented. Of those students participating in community college remediation, 77% had expressed the intention of obtaining an associate's degree. In this regard, developmental students are considerably different from their peers at 2-year institutions.

At universities, on the other hand, those participating in remedial and developmental programs were almost always degree-seeking students. Moreover, 98% of those taking remedial courses at 4-year colleges and universities had expressed the intention of attaining a baccalaureate degree (Boylan, Bonham, & Bliss, 1994a).

Developmental students at 2-year institutions, therefore, appear to be different from most 2-year college students in terms of their degree aspirations. They are more degree oriented. At 4-year institutions, developmental students are overwhelmingly degree oriented, just like most of their peers.

Full-time Versus Part-time

As might be expected, developmental students at 2-year institutions were more likely to be studying on a part-time basis than developmental students at 4-year institutions. Among those participating in remedial and developmental programs at community and technical colleges, 32% were part time students. Only 8% of developmental students attending 4-year institutions were engaged in part-time study (Boylan, Bonham, & Bliss, 1994a).

What is interesting to note, however, is that developmental students are considerably more likely to be enrolled in full-time study than the American higher education population at large. This is true at both 2-year and 4-year institutions.

According to the *Chronicle of Higher Education* ("The Nation," 1993), about half of all those enrolled at 4-year institutions are part-time students. At 2-year institutions, about two thirds of those enrolled are part-time.

For reasons that have not yet been fully explained, those participating in remedial developmental education are more likely to be full-time students than the college population at large. One possible explanation for this is that part-time students, particularly at 4-year institutions, are often exempt from assessment and placement testing. Consequently, only those students enrolled full-time are assessed and, as a result, placed in remedial or developmental courses. Also, 4-year institutions are much more likely to require mandatory placement as a result of assessment than are 2-year institutions (Boylan, Bonham, & Bliss, 1992). These factors would contribute to the finding that developmental students are more likely to be enrolled on a full-time basis than other students at 4-year institutions. The reason they are more often engaged in full-time study than their peers at 2-year colleges has yet to be explained.

Hours of Work

The most obvious reason why so many developmental students at 2-year colleges attend on a part-time basis is that they work during some other part of their time. Knopp (1996) reported that only about 20% of those taking remedial or developmental courses do not work at all. The remainder works from 1 to over 35 hour per week.

According to Knopp (1996), about 14% of all those taking remedial or developmental courses work 1 to 15 hours per week. Another 28% work from 10 to 34 hours per week. The largest single group of working developmental students is on the job for 35 hours or more each week. A total of 38% of all those taking remedial or developmental courses report working at least 35 hours per week. Well over a third of all developmental students, therefore, work hours that are at least the equivalent of a full-time job. Many of these work several jobs.

Marital Status

At 2-year institutions, 22% of developmental students are married, while only 6% of those at 4-year institutions are married (Boylan, Bonham, & Bliss, 1994a). Although no comparative data exists by institutional type, Knopp (1996) reported that the percentages of married and unmarried students among developmental and non-developmental students are almost exactly the same. The figures cited here, therefore, are generally consistent with national rates.

Because the vast majority of developmental students at 4-year institutions are 18 to 20 years old, perhaps it is not surprising that so few of them are married. The fact that more than one in five developmental students at 2-year colleges is married does not seem particularly surprising. Again, age might contribute to this. The developmental students at 2-year colleges are typically 21 to 30 years old. Obviously, a larger percentage of this age group might be expected to be married. On this dimension, developmental students are probably no different from others enrolled in American higher education institutions.

Financial Aid

An interesting pattern is apparent for the financial aid status of those participating in developmental education at 2-year and 4-year institutions. At community and technical colleges, the developmental students are somewhat less likely than other students to have received financial aid. Among developmental students at 2-year institutions, only 40% report that they have received financial aid awards (Boylan, Bonham, & Bliss, 1995). Among all 2-year college students, however, 44.5% received financial aid ("The Nation," 1993).

At 4-year institutions, this situation is reversed. Among those participating in remedial and developmental programs at 4-year institutions, 75% reported receiving financial aid (Boylan, Bonham, & Bliss, 1994a). However, only 60% of all students enrolled at these institutions receive financial aid. The likelihood of developmental students receiving financial aid awards at 4-year institutions, however, is greater than the nondevelopmental students.

There is a well known correlation between SAT and ACT scores and family income. As family income increases, so do assessment test scores. As income declines, assessment test scores also decline. It is likely, therefore, that many students with low college assessment test scores are also from low income backgrounds. This is supported by the American Council on Education (Knopp, 1996), which reported that well over 50% of those taking remedial or developmental courses come from families with incomes of $20,000 a year or less. Those from families with incomes over $50,000 a year comprise only about 7% of developmental students.

This is the obvious explanation for the higher number of financial aid recipients among developmental students at 4-year institutions. It is difficult to determine why developmental students at community and technical colleges are less likely than their peers to receive financial aid since they appear to have at least a similarly high financial need.

Class Level

The majority of students taking remedial or developmental courses are freshmen. This is supported by the American Council on Education which reported that 56% of those taking one or more remedial courses were in their first year of college (Knopp, 1996). This should be expected because, at both 2-year and 4-year institutions, advisors encourage students to take any necessary remedial courses as soon as possible. This simply makes good sense. When a student is lacking in a particular basic skill, it is a good idea to develop that skill before attempting courses that require the skill.

What is surprising, however, is that a fairly large number of students enroll in remedial or developmental courses after their freshman year. A total of 33% of those taking remedial or developmental courses are sophomores or juniors. Seniors account for 9% of those taking developmental courses (Knopp, 1996).

Apparently, a rather substantial number of students who need remediation do not receive it until their second or third year in college. A few students even find themselves in remediation during their senior years. There is also no particular pattern to the types of remediation needed. The percentage of students needing remedial mathematics, reading, writing, or study skills late in their college careers is about even (Knopp, 1996).

It is true that the majority of students needing remediation participate in it during their freshmen year. A large percentage of those in remedial or developmental courses, however, are upperclassmen.

Second Language Students

English as a second language is generally considered to be a remedial course. Many institutions, particularly 2-year colleges, however, use remedial English courses as a primary source of assistance to those students for whom English is a second language. When both English as a second language courses and remedial English are considered together, a substantial number of those enrolled in remediation are non-native speakers of English.

According to the American Council on Education (Knopp, 1996), 21% of students enrolled in developmental education speak English as a second language. Of these, 33% enroll in remedial reading courses and 35% enroll in remedial English courses. Non-native speakers of English also comprise about 15% of those enrolled in remedial mathematics.

English is a second language for slightly more than one of five developmental students. Consequently, the population of developmental students includes a substantial number of recent or first generation immigrants to the United States. Observation suggests that, depending upon the region of the United States, they are most likely to have immigrated from South or Central America or from South Asia.

What Is the Academic Background of Developmental Students?

Thus far, we have considered the demographic background of those who find themselves in developmental education. Now, what about the academic background of developmental students?

Both the National Study of Developmental Education (Boylan, Bonham, & Bliss, 1992) and the American Council on Education (Knopp, 1996) collected academic background data on developmental students. The National Study of Developmental Education obtained data on high school grade point averages, cumulative grade point averages in college, and retention rates for developmental students while the American Council on Education obtained data on the SAT scores of students enrolled in remedial courses. However, some of the findings run counter to conventional wisdom.

SAT Scores

SAT scores are rarely required as part of the admission process at 2-year institutions. A large number of students seeking admission to community and technical colleges never took the SAT or, if they did take it, it was more than five years ago. Because the producer of the SAT, the Educational Testing Service, only keeps records of test scores for five years, scores are not attainable for students who took it five or more years previously. Consequently, SAT scores for those attending 2-year colleges are seldom available. However, these scores are required for admission by a very large number of 4-year institutions. Therefore, the findings discussed here refer specifically to 4-year institutions.

Boylan, Bonham, & Bliss (1994a) found that the average combined SAT score for all developmental students in a 4-year institutions was 674. There was, however, a substantial breadth of scores among developmental students, ranging from the low 400s to over 1300. Knopp (1996) found that half of those taking one or more remedial courses had combined SAT scores under 800. However, she also found that 19% of those participating in remediation had SAT scores of 1001 or higher. In fact, about 4% of those taking remedial courses had combined SAT scores of 1201 or higher.

A combined score of 1000 on the two sections of the SAT most commonly used for admission purposes is considered average. According to Knopp (1996) about 70% of developmental students have SAT scores considered to be below average. Almost 20% however, have SAT scores considered to be average or well above average.

There are two implications to be drawn from this. One is that the majority of developmental students have SAT scores placing them below the national average. This is, perhaps, to be expected. Many developmental students have basic skill shortcomings ranging from modest to extremely serious. It is not surprising, therefore, to find that they have relatively low scores on standardized measures of achievement.

On the other hand, about one in five developmental students have SAT scores that are average to well above average. Developmental students, therefore, are not just those with below average academic skills. Some of our very best students at 4-year institutions also find themselves in need of remediation. This should come as a surprise to many who have never taught developmental students.

High School Grades

The National Study of Developmental Education (Boylan, Bonham, & Bliss, 1994a) collected high school transcripts for over 5,500 college students enrolled in developmental programs. Analysis of these transcripts indicated that the average high school grade point average for those participating in developmental education in 2-year colleges was 2.40. At 4-year institutions, the average high school grade point average was 2.58.

This suggests that most developmental students did not do that poorly in high school. A 2.40 average is the equivalent of a high C average and a 2.58 is the equivalent of a low B average. Although typical developmental students are not at the top of their high school graduating classes, neither are they at the bottom. In general, they are average high school students.

Interestingly enough, the high school grade point averages of first year community and technical college developmental students and developmental students at less selective 4-year institutions are not very different. Both groups have high school grade point averages in the high C range. This suggests that, at the lower range of the college admission spectrum, 2-year colleges and less selective 4-year institutions are actually competing for the same type of students.

Collegiate Grades

The National Study of Developmental Education (Boylan, Bonham, & Bliss, 1994a) also collected college transcripts for over 5,500 developmental students. Analysis of these transcripts indicated that, although developmental students, on the average, do not attain high grades, they at least do well enough to persist and graduate from college.

At 2-year institutions, the average grade point average for developmental students upon completion or departure was 2.28. At 4-year institutions, the average grade point average was 2.11.

Obviously, those who participate in remedial and developmental courses are not likely to be honor students. Their grades at both 2-year and 4-year schools average out to just above a C. However, a C represents good academic standing at practically all higher education institutions in the United States. This suggests that even those who need remediation are capable of success in college.

At 2-year institutions, 74% of students participating in remedial or developmental courses remained in college for at least one year. For 4-year institutions, this figure was 67% (Boylan, Bonham, & Bliss, 1994a). First year retention rates for developmental students, therefore, are reasonably high. In fact, they are considerably higher than average for 2-year college students. Furthermore, the vast majority of those who left any type of postsecondary institution after their first year but before graduating did so in good academic standing. In other words, the majority did not leave because of academic difficulties. Developmental students, therefore, although unlikely to be the best and the brightest of students, still have every chance to be successful in college.

What Do We Know About Developmental Students?

If we define developmental students as any of those who take remedial or developmental courses or participate in learning assistance, the most obvious thing we know about them is they are plentiful. Depending on how their numbers are calculated, they represent anywhere from 15% to 30% of the college student population. In some regions of the country, they represent over 40% of those attending college (Abraham, 1991).

As Abraham Lincoln was once reported to say, "The Lord must have loved common man... He made so many of them." In many respects, developmental students are the commoners of higher education.

They are not likely to attend Ivy League institutions, major research universities, or elite private colleges. They are found in abundance, however, at community colleges and less selective state universities.

Developmental students include about equal numbers of men and women. They are mostly white but also include large numbers of African-American students, a reasonable contingent of Hispanic students, and a fair portion of recent and first generation immigrants. Most of them come from low income backgrounds but a substantial number also come from middle to high income backgrounds. A large number of them are part-time students who work anywhere from 10 to 40 hours a week.

Although developmental students occasionally go on to join the Dean's List, become honor students, or holders of Phi Beta Kappa keys, most are average students. Almost 40% of them eventually attain college degrees (Boylan, Bonham, & Bliss, 1992).

This, by the way, is consistent with the national average. About 40% of all those who go to college eventually graduate (Tinto, 1987). Practically all developmental students are capable of succeeding in and graduating from college.

Yes, they probably are the commoners of American higher education. But they are also more like average Americans than anyone else.

They are the single parents who struggle to make day care arrangements allowing them to attend classes. They are the hourly laborers who hope that taking classes or getting a degree will serve as a stepping stone to better employment. They are the children of the poor and sometimes they are the parents of poor children. They are the displaced workers who use college courses to retrain for new jobs. They are the middle class young adults who seldom paid attention in their college preparatory high school courses. They are the traditional age students who failed to take the courses they should have in high school. They are the older adult students who took the right courses but put fifteen years between high school graduation and college.

Who are the developmental students? They are a lot like the rest of us.

Conclusion

Given the profile of developmental students, it is difficult to understand recent efforts by politicians in many states and cities to disparage them and the programs serving their needs. It is difficult to understand why these politicians consider it wise to disparage their constituents and argue for the reduction of services they need.

Developmental students are not part of some monolithic subset of students who "don't belong in college." Although many of them score below average on standardized tests of achievement, some of them are average or above average as measured by these same instruments. In fact that many developmental students enter college underprepared does not predestine them to failure. Those who participate in developmental programs are only slightly less likely to succeed than their better prepared peers to do not participate. In fact, they are somewhat more likely to succeed than their better prepared peers at community colleges (Boylan, Bonham, & Bliss, 1992).

Developmental students are not the "welfare mothers" of higher education as some have described them. for the most part, they are part of the middle class or they are among the working poor. As noted earlier in this chapter, more than three quarters of developmental students hold jobs and more than a third are working full-time while they attend college. They are already making a contribution to society and, if they attain their educational goals, they are likely to make an even greater contribution.

Developmental students do not even represent a significant cost burden for American higher education. A recent report from the Brookings Institute (Breneman, 1998) revealed that the total public expenditure for developmental education in colleges and universities is about one billion dollars or less than 1% of the public higher education budget.

A follow up to this report goes on to state that:

> The fact that remedial education draws political fire far in excess of any reasonable view of its budgetary costs suggests that other factors are driving the criticism. As a minimum (future discussion)...should focus on those non-financial factors, not confusing the debate with inaccurate claims that the nation, or the state, cannot afford the direct economic costs of providing remedial instruction to those who need it? (Breneman & Haarlow, 1998, p. 40)

Developmental students are not consuming an unfair share of higher education resources. When measured against total expenditures for higher education, the costs of developmental education are insignificant. Furthermore, when compared to the costs of not providing developmental education as measured by "dead end jobs, employment, welfare, criminal activity, together with the social costs accompanying these paths, (it) is surely a good investment" (Breneman & Haarlow, 1998, p. 39).

Developmental students represent a cross section of the population of the United States. They are the upper class, the middle class, and the working poor. They come from all races and all cultures. They attend college in the hope that it will improve their lives and the lives of their children. If they are successful, they will be stronger contributors to the nation's tax base instead of consumers of tax revenues. They will be better parents and wiser voters. In short, developmental students have the same backgrounds, the same potential, and the same hopes and dreams as the rest of us. They simply have to work a little harder and need a little more help to reach their potential and attain their hopes and dreams than those few of those us who found it easy to be successful in college.

Part II:
Models of Affective and Cognitive Support

Chapter 3

A Developmental Information Processing Model: Metacognition and Self-Regulated Learning

Nelson DuBois

Introduction

B etween a third and a half of all first year college students lack the basic reading, writing, or mathematics skills needed to perform successfully in college (Abraham, 1987). Additionally, a number of students possess the basic skills but lack effective self-regulatory strategies to manage their learning and motivation. Clearly the problem is massive.

Successful retention of minority students is particularly urgent. As we start the 21st century the demands for a highly educated culturally diverse population are self-evident. Unfortunately, many members of minority groups are the least prepared to benefit from higher education experiences. For example, Noel, Levitz, and Saluri (1985) have identified the following seven factors that contribute to college retention problems of minority students: (1) boredom, (2) uncertainty about what to study, (3) problems of adjustment, (4) college/student incompatibility, (5) inappropriate expectations of college, (6) academic unpreparedness, and (7) curricular and pedagogical ineffectiveness.

To further explain the adjustment difficulties of minority students, Fingeret (1983) suggests that many students from different cultures have experienced an "oral culture" which values common sense in contrast to a "literate at culture" which emphasizes deductive science, prediction, abstract universal knowledge and formal logic. According to Fingeret, those experiences contribute to the student's lack of preparedness for college. In contrast, Claxton (1990) argues that the research does not support the contention that minority students have different learning styles. Rather, Claxton proposes that if the dominant teaching mode of information-presenting were changed to problem posing, the success rate of all students should improve. From Claxton's perspective, the problem is the instruction the student receives.

Diverging from the previous two perspectives, Knott (1991) suggests that, while the student's cultural background clearly influences learning preferences, successful academic achievement can only occur when the student adapts to the academic demands of the institution. According to Knott, education is more than just learning content; it is also a process of changing the student and the student's orientation to the world. Regardless of the explanation of the problem, academic success is closely related to the degree to which the institution helps the students *match* or *fit* the institutional goals (Tinto-cited in Spann, 1990). To accomplish these goals, Miles (1990) proposes that we need to help students learn how to process information effectively. As Miles suggests, learning effectiveness is directly related to learner expectations about themselves and the task. While numerous programs have been employed to help the student adapt to college (e.g., individualized programs, learning support services, study skill courses, developmental studies programs, summer bridge programs), a strong focus of most programs is to help the students become more proficient learners.

The major perspective of this chapter is that students can potentially employ effective strategies to overcome real or imagined internal and external obstacles associated with poor learning. This self-regulatory perspective is refreshing. It suggests that the student must understand, believe and take responsibility for the following maxim: *Effective effort leads to success; ineffective effort leads to failure or poor performance.* Effective effort originates from smart choices and effective strategies, not high ability. It also suggests that learning and motivation are potentially under the control of the student through the application of effective strategies. Unfortunately, non-self-regulated students tend to view bad situations as "reasons" to perform poorly and to avoid effective effort rather than to strategically adapt to the situation. Thus they tend to "attribute" their poor performance to internal factors which they perceive they can't control (i.e., I lack ability, I'm bored, I can't do this) or external factors which they perceive they can't control (i.e., the test was unfair, this course is too hard, the class is too large) (Seligman, 1975; Weiner, 1979; 1990).

On a positive note, researchers have demonstrated that students who believe their low academic performance is due to low ability can be retrained to attribute success to effective effort. Two conditions must occur for students to change their unproductive attributions. First, they need to be taught effective learning strategies and observe that the strategies work. Secondly, they need to learn to attribute their success to the strategy, not to their ability (Carr & Borkowski, 1989; Carr, Borkowski, & Maxwell, 1991).

The question posed in this chapter, therefore, is how can professionals help students become self-regulated learners in spite of possible inadequate prior experiences, likely non-supportive past environments and likely unproductive beliefs, attitudes and strategies to learn effectively? First, professionals need to help students understand that effective strategies, do indeed, make a difference. Second, the professionals must help the students understand that the effective effort is worthwhile. Third, the professionals need to help the students understand they can employ effective learning and motivational strategies to perform at a high level of proficiency. The purpose of this chapter is to propose, and then expand upon, the following assumptions: *The degree to which a student employs self-regulated learning and motivational strategies necessary to convert information into coherent accessible knowledge is the degree to which the student will experience academic success.*

These assumptions make no distinctions between developmental and non-developmental students with respect to what the student needs to do to perform successfully. The differences between effective and ineffective information processing, however, are clearly related to the motivation and information processing strategies the learner applies to the task. *Self regulation* refers to the strategies the learner employs to control the learning and motivational dimensions necessary for effective information processing. *Motivation* includes the students' beliefs about values, goals, volition, and the attributions they employ to "explain" their performance. *Information* generally refers to spoken or written language. *Converting information into coherent accessible knowledge* refers to the strategies the student employs to identify, understand, represent, and "store" the information in long term memory. *Coherent* means the student constructs meaningful connections between and among the topics and supporting details and prior knowledge. *Accessible* means the student "stores" the information in a manner that facilitates the retrieval of information when required. Lastly, *knowledge* means the student can use the information in new settings when required.

Three principles underlie these assumptions:

1) **The ultimate control of academic motivation and learning resides with the student.** Essentially the student must acquire strategies to control academic motivation as well as all the dimensions associated with processing information effectively.

2) With respect to learning, **the degree to which the student applies strategies to construct computationally efficient notes and use the notes properly is the degree to which the student will experience academic success.** Clearly, the research indicates students must learn to replace the highly reproductive strategies associated with rereading and rehearsal of information in the same sequence it is presented with more constructive strategies designed to acquire coherent understanding of the content.

3) **The review strategies the student chooses should correspond to the performance conditions of the exam.** Well-prepared students are rarely fooled by the content or emphasis of exams. Their review strategies match their predictions. For example, knowing that a professor includes diagrams on an exam, effective students prepare "smart" diagrams to review. Knowing that the professor includes a lot of problems on the exam, effective students practice classifying problems from the chapter. Knowing that the instructor asks a lot of compare/contrast questions, effective students generate compare and contrast questions during review and then elaborate on the content.

What are the implications of the these principles? Consider the factors identified by Noel, et al., as reasons for academic difficulties experienced by developmental students (e.g., boredom, uncertainty about future, unpreparedness, etc.). From a self-regulatory perspective on student learning, these are NOT "reasons" for doing poorly. These are unproductive beliefs and attitudes that directly lead to poor academic performance. The student's role is to strategically overcome, circumvent or eliminate these unproductive beliefs and attitudes through effective strategy deployment.

The Self-Regulated Learner:
An Information Processing Perspective

To fully understand the role of helping students become self-regulated learners, it is necessary to understand the factors involved in effective information processing. Much research has been conducted over the past twenty years about how students prepare, process, store and use information. The model in Figure 1 presents a synthesis of many of the current perspectives on information processing. The model consists of two major dimensions: (1) self management and (2) information processing. Self management refers to the strategies the learner employs to plan, choose, orchestrate multiple strategies, monitor, and evaluate strategies. It also refers to those factors involved in self-motivation, maintenance of effort, and time management (Borkowski, Carr, Rellinger, & Pressley, 1990; Corno, 1986; Pintrich & De Groot, 1990; Zimmerman & Martinez-Pons, 1986; Zimmerman, 1989; Zimmerman & Schunk, 1994). Self-management also includes such motivational dimensions as self-efficacy, values, goals, volition and attributions. The information processing dimensions include selective attention, encoding, representation, test appropriate review strategies, rehearsal and retrieval. Performance refers to achievement in various testing conditions.

Figure 1. Self-regulated Learning

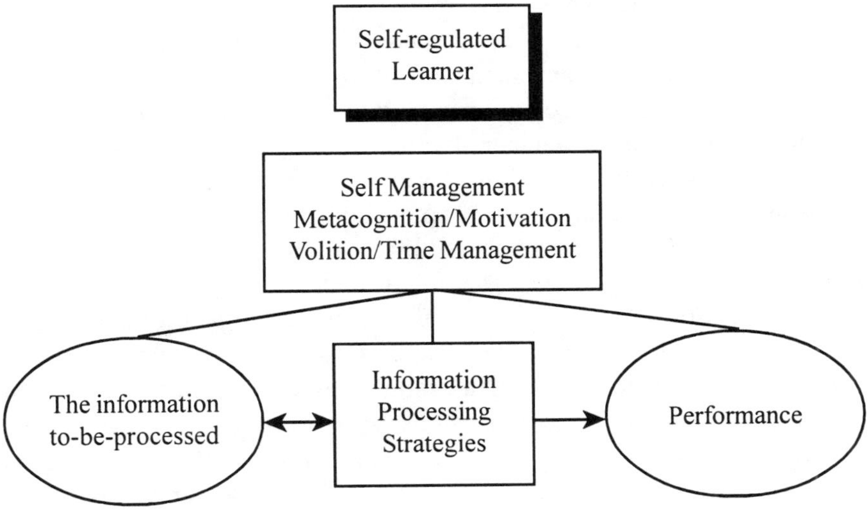

Figure 2. Metacognition

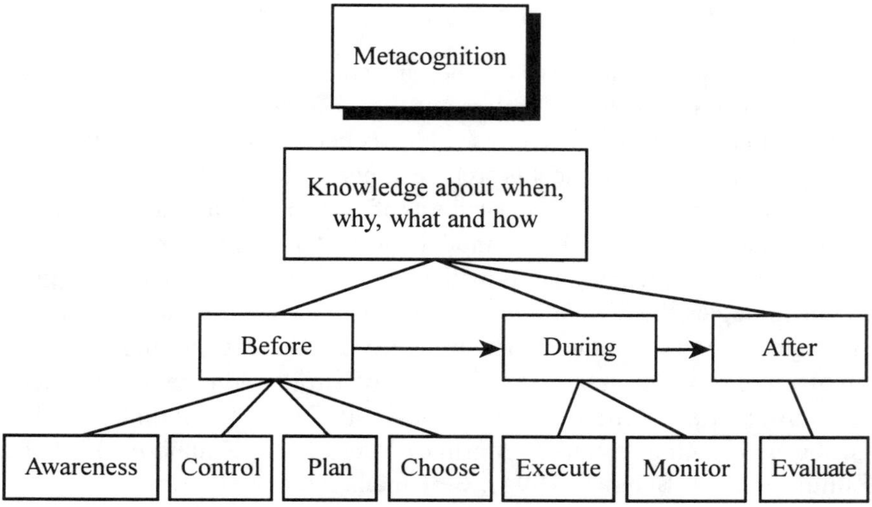

Personal Control

Metacognition

Metacognition refers to the awareness students have about when, why, and how to employ strategies to process the information (Flavell, 1985; Pressley, Borkowski, & O'Sullivan, 1984; Pressley, Borkowski & Schneider, 1989). Essentially self-regulated learners choose to be successful. Then they take action. See Figure 2 for an overview of the major decisions students make about their self-management and information processing tasks.

Students high in metacognition know when, why, and how to implement strategies. They control their motivation, manage obstacles, and avoid daydreaming. Because they know how to study, they plan effectively. They make smart choices about when to study, how much to study, and how to study. When they study they successfully orchestrate self-management and information processing strategies. They also manage their time reasonably well. As they study, they carefully monitor their performance. Finally, after they receive feedback about their test performance, they take corrective action to repair faulty strategies. In contrast, students low in metacognition fail on one or more of these dimensions.

To change incorrect studying practices, the student must understand the factors involved in information processing. This includes strategies to self-observe study strategies, evaluate those strategies, and then react negatively to the poor performance. This negative self-reaction is viewed as a necessary condition for self-change (Bandura, 1991). According to Zimmerman, Greenberg and Weinstein (1994), the essential feature of an information processing perspective is a negative feedback loop. This is defined as a situation in which the learner identifies task goals, initiates an action, compares the results of the action with the initial goal, and then takes corrective actions to meet the goals.

Academic Motivation

Academic motivation includes the expectancies, incentives, volitions and attributions the students feel about processing information (Zimmerman, Bandura, & Martinez-Pons, 1992). See Figure 3 for an overview of the dimensions of academic motivation. Self-regulated learners control the four dimensions of motivation identified in Figure 3 (Zimmerman, 1986; 1989). They don't wait for the motivation to occur; they carefully develop the motivation through effective strategy employment.

Expectancy. Self regulated students believe they are capable of a high level of achievement. Ideally, they believe they are capable because they are capable of using effective strategies (Dweck, 1986; Elliot & Dweck, 1988; Schunk, 1994). Essentially they validate their capabilities through effective strategy employment. They know the strategies work. They know they are capable of using the strategies. And they know they will employ the strategies appropriately.

Incentive. Prior to taking action the student has to have a reason (goal) for the action (Nicholls, 1984, 1989; Nolen, 1988, 1996; Pintrich & Garcia, 1991). Self-regulated students want to succeed, believe they are capable of

Figure 3. Dimensions of Academic Motivation

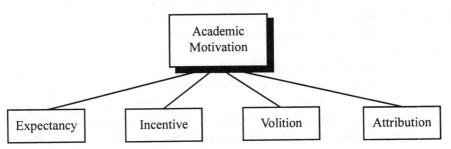

succeeding, and then assume the responsibility for succeeding (Bandura, 1986). People are more likely to develop productive goals when they realize effective strategy deployment will lead to success.

With respect to the formation of goals, the research suggests that smaller achievable goals have a greater effect on performance than vague goals. Likewise, proximal goals are likely to have a greater effect than distal goals on performance and on task interest (Mossholder, 1980). In contrast, when the learner already possesses a high degree of interest in the subject, apparently moderately distal goals may have a stronger effect on persistence than proximal goals (Kanfer & Grimm, 1978).

Volition. When the student decides to take action, the student needs to employ strategies to maintain the action. Volition refers to those strategies a person uses to sustain effective effort (Corno, 1994). Sustained effective effort includes strategies to maintain attention, employ effective information processing activities, monitor the effectiveness of those actions, overcome internal and external obstacles that are likely to interfere with the attainment of the goal, and perceive the studying activities as reasonably pleasant. Essentially volition includes all those strategies students employ to sustain their effort in spite of internal and external obstacles (Corno, 1995). For example, Heckhausen and Kuhl (1985) define volition as a psychological state that leads to the conversion of goals into sustained action; a predisposition to use available resources to manage and maintain intentions. Clearly many aspects of volition are closely related to sound time management principles—the deliberate use of strategies to direct and control achievement efforts (Zimmermann, 1990).

Attributions. While the student's motivational state prior to studying and during studying are key factors that contribute to the student's overall performance, the student's perceptions of the results of studying will greatly influence future efforts (Dweck, 1986; Garcia & Pintrich, 1994; Schunk, 1991). Ideally, we want students to attribute their success (defined as "mastery" of the content) to effective effort. In contrast, we want students to attribute poor or failing performance to ineffective effort. This implies that the student knows how to identify patterns of errors and can take action to change the pattern.

In either case, the ***effective effort*** attribution is likely to lead to effective future performance. On the other hand, if the student believes that success or failure is due to high or low abilities, the student is likely to remove the responsibility for employing effective strategies in the future. Since this student believes that ability determines success or lack of success, the student remains intellectually impotent for future learning. Obviously, as long as the student maintains this unproductive belief, the student is correct—there is nothing the student can do to change. Unfortunately, some high ability students believe that trying hard is an indication they lack ability, thus they avoid the effort. Further, poor performance following little or no effort helps to maintain the unproductive belief: "I could have done well if I tried."

The Information-to-be-processed

Studying is a verbal activity. Tests essentially evaluate how well students select, interpret, convert spoken or written information into knowledge, retain the knowledge, and use the knowledge in new situations. Students can experience two difficulties with the manner in which verbal information is presented. First, verbal information is inherently linear. Because of linear verbal presentations, the student needs strategies to connect concepts separated by the linear presentations. Second, often the linear presentations are difficult to process because the author or lecturer presents the information

Figure 4a. Linear Outline Facial Expressions

Smile develops first:	2-3 months smile in response to adult face
Anger expression:	8 months following something unfavorable (remove cookie)
Surprise:	4 months usual situation
Fear:	5-7 months loud noises
Shyness:	6-8 months unfamiliar person enters room
Laugh:	4-5 months silly face
Laugh:	1 year at something they cause
Guilt:	during 2nd year at some bad behavior

in an inconsiderate mode for effective information processing. The student needs to employ strategies to adapt to inconsiderate presentations.

Linear Presentations

Lectures and texts present information sequentially. Given a lecture, initially a student must process the information in the same order it is presented. For auditory learning, the student has no control over the rate of presentation. Further, unless the student is highly sophisticated, the student records the information in the same sequence as presented and then rehearses the information in the same sequence as presented in the lecture.

In contrast, visual information is recorded on paper, thus the information processor can control the rate of presentation by slowing down the reading rate, stopping, or strategically referring back to prior information in the text. Thus, effective students strategically use texts to construct meaningful connections. In contrast, just as with the lecture, ineffective students process the information in the same sequence as presented, record the information in the same sequence, and then rehearse the information in the same sequence as presented. This linear, reproductive approach to information processing is devastating for learning complex content.

To demonstrate the difference between rehearsal and making internal connections, refer to Figures 4a and 4b. The outline in Figure 4a was reproduced in the same sequence it was presented in the text. If we asked ineffective students to study the outline in Figure 4a, most students would

Figure 4b. Sequence Matrix: Facial Expression

	Facial Expression						
	smile	surprise	laugh	fear	shyness	anger	laugh	guilt

age in months:	2-3	4		5-7	6-8	8	12	24
response inducement	adult face	unusual situation	silly adult face	loud noise	new person	take away cookies	at event they cause	bad behavior

simply reread and rehearse the information until they felt they could reproduce it on a test. The outline makes it extremely difficult to compare and contrast coordinate topics or trace the development of supporting detail. Given an outline, students simply would not look for patterns.

Now consider Figure 4b. Figure 4b presents the information as a sequence matrix. The facial expressions are ordered by the age of occurrence of the facial expression. Furthermore, comparable supporting detail information is presented in horizontal rows across the page. The reader simply looks across the row to make connections between or among the topics and supporting detail. A careful inspection of this matrix will lead the reader to the following conclusions: (1) The first three facial expressions are characterized as positive responses. (2) The next three responses are negative. (3) The first six responses are caused by external stimuli. (4) In contrast, the latter two facial expressions are caused by internal factors. (5) The positive and negative patterns reoccur during the second year. The learner is now in a position to speculate about the reasons for the coordinate patterns. Furthermore, because the learner has discovered these patterns, the learner can remember the patterns much more easily.

Since the same amount of effort is required to record notes in an outline format as in a matrix format, we need to help our students understand the significance of recording computationally efficient notes—notes that lead to effective information processing during review.

Inconsiderateness of the Presentation

Practically all the information students need to know for an exam is presented linearly through spoken or written language. For a lecture, aside from the difficulties associated with processing linear information, other important lecture characteristics that influence the information processing capabilities of the student include the degree of familiarity of information, the organization of the lecture, the speed of delivery, the use of visual presentations to augment the lecture, the degree to which the lecture parallels the text content, the number of units of information presented in different time segments of the lecture, the degree to which the lecturer signals important relationships, and the capabilities of the student to record effective notes. One of the implications of inconsiderate lectures is that students need to acquire strategies to adapt to the inconsiderate presentations (Kiewra, 1988).

Students also experience a great deal of difficulty processing information from texts. Unfortunately, many texts are poorly written. Pressley, Yokoi, vanMeter, Van Etten and Freebern (1997) have identified the following problems with texts that interfere with effective information processing. Many texts are encyclopedic in scope. They are filled with misinformation. They are poorly organized and the sentences fail to help the reader make important connections among the topics and supporting details. Often they include superfluous illustrations. Frequently the reading level of the text is mismatched for students. And the writing is boring.

The argument made in this chapter, however, is that while many instructional situations are far from ideal, the student can employ self-regulatory strategies to adapt successfully to these situations. Indeed, successful students do adapt to these difficulties. Thus, it is imperative that any professional working with developmental students should understand the principles associated with self-regulated learning. Secondly, as professionals we need to instruct our students how to employ effective strategies to overcome less than adequate instructional situations and become self-regulated learners.

Information Processing Dimensions

The processes needed to convert the information into knowledge consist of, but are not limited to, attention, perception, rehearsal, encoding, and test appropriate review.

Attention. Attention refers to those processes that allocate and maintain the student's cognitive effort to process the information or to maintain the effort to think about knowledge retrieved from long term memory. An effective student possesses three critical attentional characteristics that the ineffective student lacks. First, the effective student often *knows what is important prior to processing the information* (selective attention) (Broadbent, 1958). Because the effective student knows what is important the student allocates different amounts of attention to the important, information once it is initially processed (Shriffrin & Schneider, 1977).

Secondly, the effective student quickly *perceives how the concepts within the lecture or text are interrelated* or are potentially interrelated (Mandler, 1984; Marshall, 1995; Mayer, 1989; Rumelhart & Ortony, 1977; Tennyson & Cochiarella, 1986). Given a linear text, the effective student actively identifies interrelationships between the topics and supporting details. In contrast, the ineffective student merely processes the topics and supporting details in the same sequence as it is presented. Essentially the ineffective student uses an unfocused linear, indiscriminate, rote and reproductive information processing style to process the information. Obviously this indiscriminate linear processing interferes with acquiring coherent knowledge.

Lastly, once the effective student identifies the pattern, the effective student also *knows what is not important*. This knowledge enables the student to inhibit unnecessary attention in working memory for unimportant content (Dempster, 1992). Thus, the effective student maintains more processing space in working memory to make more significant connections. In contrast, because the ineffective student fails to distinguish between important and unimportant information, the ineffective student fails to allocate as much time to the critical content. The ineffective student either fails to filter out the unconnected and unimportant information or fails to process the important information. In either case, the information available in working memory for the ineffective student is inappropriate and is likely to interfere with acquiring coherent knowledge (Gernsbacher & Faust, 1991).

Perception. Perception refers to the processes we employ to acquire meaning from what is attended to in the sensory register. Essentially this requires the identification of important details and patterns presented in the lecture or text. Thus, during working memory, the students construct new knowledge from the perceived information.

Rehearsal. Rehearsal is essentially the repetition of the information in the same sequence it is presented. Overwhelmingly, the research suggests that rehearsal is an extremely poor strategy to make the information available in long term memory, particularly if the student is to develop a meaningful coherent understanding of the relationships among the topics and supporting details. Unfortunately, rehearsal is the preferred studying method for many students.

Encoding. Encoding refers to any activity the student uses to form durable mental representations based on the critical features of the learning task. Encoding is efficient when the learner constructs a lot of meaningful connections; it is ineffective when the connections are fragmented, incomplete, and disorganized.

Research on long term memory (LTM) suggests that information is stored in interconnected information packets (Rumelhart & Ortony, 1977). These packets, or schemas, consist of slots that include topics, supporting details, significant relationships to other schemas, and procedures for using the schemas in new situations (Jonassen, Beissner & Yacci, 1993; Marshall, 1995). Well-organized schemas help the individual recognize new experiences, pay selective attention to relevant information, facilitate rapid access of the relevant information in LTM, and guide the individual's problem solving strategies. Poorly stored information, on the other hand, often remains inert and isn't available for problem solving.

Marshall (1995) proposes that well-developed schemas include four knowledge functions: identification, elaboration, planning, and execution. *Identification knowledge* helps the individual identify patterns that lead to the initial recognition of a situation, event or experience. *Elaborative knowledge* is essentially abstracted information that enables the individual to create a mental model about the current problem. The individual's understanding of an experience results from ways in which the details and connections of the schema are mapped onto the experience. *Planning knowledge* refers to the way in which schemas guide plans and set up goals. *Execution knowledge* include all the techniques that lead to action. Thus, organized knowledge leads to effective information processing; disorganized or fragmented knowledge leads to ineffective information processing.

Recently researchers have begun to investigate how learners can make meaningful connections. For example, Mayer (1989) suggests that learners should always attempt to acquire a coherent understanding of the information-to-be-processed. To do this, the learner needs to construct internal connections between and among the topics and supporting details of a domain to produce coherent explanations of the content. Further, the student needs to employ strategies to integrate the newly acquired with existing prior knowledge. To demonstrate these differences, consider how a reader of this chapter might construct internal and external connections.

To make ***internal connections*** of this content, a reader would have to identify the characteristics of the information stores and understand how the processes select and transfer information across the information stores. Additionally, the reader would have to understand which processes occur within or between different stores. Thus, effective readers often *rearrange* information as necessary to make more meaningful connections.

Continuing with the same example, to make ***external connections*** an effective reader often relates newly acquired information to prior knowledge. For example, a reader of this part of the chapter might generate an analogy between how people process information and how computers process, store and use information. By noting the similarities between the brain and the computer, the reader brings relevant prior knowledge to the task. The more correct elaborations the student generates during processing, the better they are likely to retain the knowledge and transfer it to new situations (Pressley, McDaniel, Turnure, Wood & Ahmad, 1987).

Test Appropriate Practice

Test appropriate practice refer to strategies students employ that directly correspond to the demands of the test (McDaniel & Einstein, 1989). For example, if a professor provides a definition of a concept and then provides an example, during review the student needs to determine why the example is an instance of the definition. Further, the student needs to determine how the example is similar to, and different from, related concepts. Finally, the student needs to learn a range of applications of the concept. By not applying conceptual learning strategies during review, many students fail to convert propositional information presented in lectures and texts into conceptual knowledge. Thus, given new examples of the concept on the test, students fail to recognize the example as an instance of the concept.

This same situation occurs in procedural knowledge courses (e.g., math, physics, chemistry). Instructors often demonstrate procedures, have students practice the procedures for homework, and then quiz the students on the procedures. Unfortunately, this practice often results in reasonably good performance on the homework and quizzes but results in extremely poor performance on major tests. Because the problems for homework and quizzes are usually preclassified, the students fail to acquire the important conditional knowledge associated with recognizing new examples. Thus, the review conditions fail to match the performance conditions. Lacking systematic conditional knowledge, the students fail to classify the problems on the test. Of course, disastrous consequences follow.

Information Stores

Sensory Registers

The sensory register holds an exact copy of the stimulus for about 1 second for visual information and about 4 seconds for auditory information (Moates & Schumacher, 1980). If a student fails to quickly act upon the information in the sensory register, no further processing takes place. Thus, a fleeting daydream permanently interferes with effective processing. Although the capacity of the sensory register is virtually unlimited, the learner must quickly employ strategies to transfer the information from the sensory register into working memory.

Working Memory

Working memory is viewed as the "workbench" of cognition. It is here that the learner discriminates important information from unimportant information. Essentially the learner has four choices in working memory: ignore the information, retain it for a brief period by rehearsing it, think about it, or transfer the information into long term memory.

Unfortunately, one of the severely limiting characteristics of working memory is that this "workbench" has a limited capacity. All cognitive activities occupy processing space in working memory. For example, to simply rehearse a series of digits presented at one second intervals requires considerable effort. An average adult is limited to about 5-9 bits of information they can hold in working memory (McGraw, 1987). Unfortunately, thinking about complex information takes up additional space in working memory. The average adult can only hold 3-5 units of information in working memory when thinking about complex content. Thinking is "informationally expensive."

Consider note taking as an example. Some of the cognitive operations involved in note taking include selective attention, pattern recognition, rehearsal of selected phrases until the notes are recorded, comprehending the propositions, and thinking about the lecture. All of these cognitive operations occur simultaneously or almost in sequence. Obviously effective note taking requires numerous sophisticated and orchestrated strategies to hold the information in working memory and then to record the information. Thus, a student lacking effective note taking strategies is clearly at a major disadvantage in note taking situations.

Long Term Memory

Long term memory is the permanent store of information. Ideally students should "store" the information in long term memory as connected schemas or conceptual mental models (Mayer, 1989; Marshall, 1995). A schema is a mental structure centered on events, situations, objects or problems. It organizes past experiences in such a way that the information is recorded as a coherent whole (Marshall, 1995). A conceptual model includes the major objects and actions in a system being studied as well as the causal relations among them (Mayer, 1989). In either case, schemas and conceptual mental models serve the same functions—to facilitate the retrieval of integrated chunks of knowledge to be used in transfer situations.

Unfortunately, students rarely study to acquire coherent understanding.

Rather, most students prefer to reread, recite, and reproduce the information in the same order it is presented to them. This pattern is particularly prevalent for poorly motivated students. The rereading, rehearsal and reproducing information (3 R's) strategies that the ineffective student employs results in fragmented, incomplete, and often incoherent knowledge structures. Lacking coherent knowledge, the student fails to use the newly acquired information in problem solving situations.

An Integrated Information Processing System for Studying

The purpose of this section of the chapter is to introduce four major principles associated with effective information processing and to demonstrate strategies students can employ to implement the principles. These strategies have been employed in the learning strategy course at the State University of New York at Oneonta. Research on the effectiveness of the course has been very favorable. For example, students randomly assigned to the study skills course successfully completed approximately three more credits in the semester they took the study skills course (p<.00001) compared to students who didn't take the study skills course.

Principle #1: Successful strategy implementation is directly related to the degree to which the student *orchestrates* repertoires of strategies to process information effectively.

The key to this principle is strategy orchestration. Strategy orchestration refers to the knowledge the student has about integrating strategies. For example, in strategy orchestration the product the student produces in an earlier learning phase becomes the input for a later phase. Refer to Figure 5 for an overview of the major processes involved in converting information into coherent accessible knowledge.

As Figure 5 suggests, an effective learner knows how to identify important information and to identify significant connections within, between, and among topics and supporting details. Next, the student records sets of informationally and computationally efficient notes. Informationally efficient notes refer to a complete set of notes. Computationally efficient notes refer to notes that the student can use to make meaningful connections (Larkin & Simon, 1987). During early review the student uses the notes to acquire schemas, to acquire mental models, to elaborate on the information, and to pose important questions.

To understand how an integrated system works, consider any studying

Figure 5. Major Principles of Effective Information Processing

```
              ┌──────────────────────────┐
              │  Major Principles of      │
              │  Effective Information    │
              │  Processing               │
              └──────────────────────────┘
```

Identification and Interpretation of connected information	→	Representation of connected information	→	Initial construction of integrated schematic knowledge and mental models	→	Converts information into potentially activated knowledge

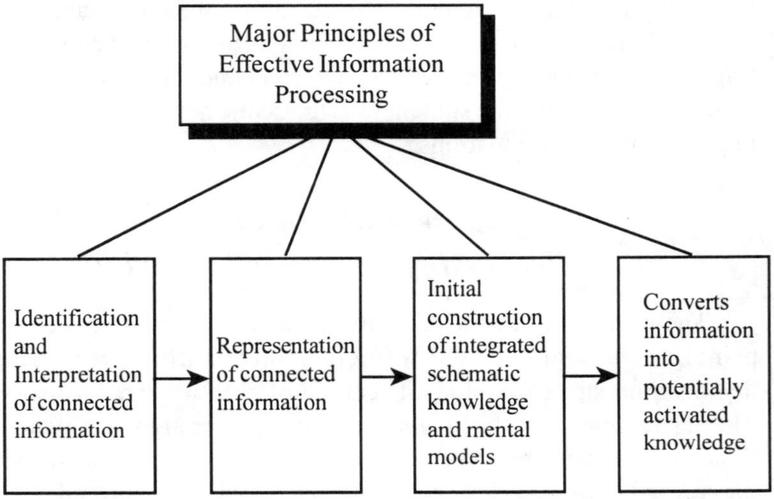

Major activity	Selects important information & identifies relationships	Constructs informationally and computationally efficient notes	Make connections: Describes/explains/ compares & contrasts	Practice conditions match test conditions

episode a student pursues. For instance, assume a student starts to read a section of a chapter. An effective reader identifies important information, identifies critical connections among the topics and supporting details, and marks the section. Essentially the student uses the reading activities and the marking activities to prepare the text for note taking. For example, if notes should record important connections between topics and supporting details, then the student marks the text to highlight those connections. If notes should only include important phrases, then the student only marks the phrases. Thus the student uses the marked paragraphs to guide the construction of a set of computationally efficient notes.

Given a set of computationally efficient notes, the student uses the notes (an output from the marked text) as the input to make meaningful connections during review. During review the student then uses the notes to generate smart questions that should correspond to the test demands. Thus, ultimately the marked text serves the purpose of generating smart questions during review.

Now contrast the above approach with a single isolated learning strategy approach. The purposes of marking a text in this system might be to identify important content and to understand it. A student most likely would employ a high lighter for this purpose. For the single isolated learning strategy system the product the student produces is the end product. In contrast, in an integrated learning strategy system, students would not use a high lighter because the student could not record important comments in the margin to be included in the notes. Further, the student could not use a high lighter to enumerate points in the paragraphs or to make connections among the paragraphs. The differences between strategy orchestration and individual strategy deployment are striking.

To teach strategy orchestration, we carefully describe each strategy. We demonstrate how to employ the strategy, as well as why and when to employ the strategy. We also indicate how the product of the strategy is used in the next information processing phase. During this instructional phase, it is important to help the student understand that they possess the capabilities to perform the strategy (Bandura, 1991) and that the effort is worthwhile. We then provide students with practice exercises. Often the students initially practice the strategies in small groups or with a partner. Then they apply the strategy in another course they are taking. Finally, they combine the strategy with other strategies. Additionally, we often encourage our students to teach their friends how to apply the strategies.

Principle #2: The degree to which the student knows when, why, and how to implement strategies, coupled with a desire to do so, is the degree to which the student should experience academic success.

Effective students know when, why, and how to implement effective self-management and information processing strategies. And they take action on their knowledge. In contrast, ineffective students, with the exception of those students who obviously lack prerequisite skills or knowledge, either don't know effective strategies, don't care to master course content (which is the direct result of ineffective motivational strategies), or fail to employ the strategies.

Thus, it is important for students to understand that many college instructors are not trained in teaching. It is also important to indicate that many instructional situations are less than ideal (e.g., large classes, poorly written texts, and disorganized lectures). Given less than ideal situations, however, students must understand that poor instructional situations do not automatically have to lead to bad outcomes. On the contrary, students need to understand that many students do fine in college in spite of poor or extremely poor teaching. The difference is NOT in the instruction; the difference is the strategies the students use to adapt to the poor instruction. Bad decisions and poor strategies (i.e., ineffective effort) lead to ineffective outcomes. Good decisions and good strategies (i.e., effective effort), on the other hand, lead to effective outcomes.

Expectancies

The student must expect that effective strategy execution leads to successful goal attainment (Schunk, 1994; Schunk & Swartz, 1993). The student needs to expect that the strategy works and that the student possesses the skills necessary to learn the strategy and use it. Thus, incentives, expectancies, and strategy choice are closely interrelated. We provide the students with numerous activities to help them develop realistic expectancies about themselves and the strategies we introduce.

Personal Challenge (Incentives)

Regardless of the types of learning task facing the student, the student should employ strategies to make the task a challenge (Nicholls, 1984). The student should understand that having long term goals IS NOT NECESSARY to do well. In contrast, setting short term proximal goals and sticking to those goals will help the student measure progress towards the goal (Nolen, 1996). During this phase of the course we help the students identify reasonable and attainable goals.

Volition and Time Management

To help the students acquire effective time management strategies, we spend considerable effort on this unit. Students are required to fill out a time management sheet (6:00 A.M.-10:00 PM) and monitor their daily performance. We have students record their daily commitments, fun activities and studying activities. For studying we want the students to include products for many of their activities (e.g., mark pages 28-40 in biology text; take matrix notes on pages 53-60). Students are required to employ the following five strategies when they generate their time management sheets.

1. Use the daytime hours, particular the morning hours, for studying.

2. Distribute studying time. It is usually better to study content for two three-hour segments than one six-hour segment.

3. Be ready three days in advance for all major tests.

4. Monitor their studying effectiveness during each studying episode, at the end of the day, and at the end of the week.

5. Identify potential obstacles and plan to avoid the obstacles.

The time management unit continues throughout the course. Particular emphasis is placed on having the student constantly monitor the quality and quantity of studying time spent for each subject. Indeed, monitoring and evaluation receive a strong emphasis in our course. The research indicates that college students do not monitor their learning very well (Butler & Winne, 1995; Pressley, Ghatala, Woloshyn, & Pirie,1990; Schommer, 1993). Butler and Winne postulate four reasons for this difficulty. First, the student might misclassify the task and adopt incorrect goals. Thus the student is unable to generate corrective feedback information, nor does the student discover, until it is too late, how to change the inappropriate strategy. For instance, the professor might announce in class that definitions are important to know. The student interprets this to mean that memorization of the definitions is all that is needed to do well. Unfortunately, the professor administers a conceptual test where the students must recognize new examples. Thus, because the student misinterprets the professor's statement about definitions, the student studies incorrectly and does poorly on the exam. Second, the student may predict the correct cues, but not really understand what is expected during the testing conditions. For example, for an essay test the student might fail to predict his/her ability to retrieve organized bodies of information during the testing condition. Third, in some instances the task demands of studying are intense. The student might become overwhelmed by the cognitive demands of the task. In this instance, the student is unlikely to monitor studying effectiveness. According to Butler and Winne (1995), the student is more likely to monitor learning effectiveness when the student chunks the information or acquires automated procedures. In these two cases, the demands on working memory are considerably reduced. Finally, the student may lack the motivation to monitor learning or change the quality of effort necessary to do well.

Attributions

Attributional analysis is another major component of the motivational section of the course. Our intention is to help students understand that effective effort leads to success and ineffective effort leads to poor performance or failure. To do this we help students understand that the "reasons" students usually give for their poor performance most often serve as excuses to avoid studying. For example, the such attributions as: I lack the ability, I'm not sure about my future goals, I'm not in the mood, I don't like to study, I'm not a good test taker, I have a personal problem, the class is too large, and things distract me when I study are most often excuses. We have developed assignments in class to address every common attribution students tend to employ as excuses.

Another instructional strategy we employ, sometimes with great success, is to discuss and even demonstrate ineffective studying strategies. Our goal is to help students contrast ineffective strategies with more effective strategies. This metacognitive training often keeps the students' interest. For example, we ask the student to purposefully choose a time and location to study that is likely to lead to constant interruptions. Often hilarious discussions ensue. We then ask our students to purposefully create situations in which they know they will daydream. They generate such strategies as reading in bed, sitting in the back of the classroom, and thinking about other things as soon as they start to read.

In one informal classroom study, we found that most students reported daydreaming after reading four to five pages in a text. To help the students understand the conditions that contribute to daydreaming we instruct them to daydream the next time they play sports. Daydream when the ball is thrown. Daydream at the foul line. Daydream when you are up at the plate. We ask the students to explain why they don't daydream, indeed, why they can't daydream in these instances. Now the analogy can be made to reading. Marking a text to produce a quality set of notes requires attention. It is impossible to selectively mark a text and record quality notes while daydreaming, just as it is impossible for a player to daydream when the ball is thrown.

Given these analogies the students discover strategies to combat daydreaming. Selecting important information and marking texts are simply incompatible with daydreaming. Since they know they start to daydream after four to five pages, they discover they can combine that knowledge to generate a potential solution. Just read, mark and take notes on four to five pages of content for short segments of time three-four times a day.

In each of the above examples we provide the class with ridiculous examples of students being interrupted, daydreaming, and actually getting themselves in poor moods to study. In fact, we have students list strategies to get themselves in a *bad mood*. Throughout this phase of the course our goal is to help our students acquire an awareness that they can control their own motivation and learning efficiency. In the system we employ, lack of motivation is directly related to the choices they make. Many students fail to understand this principle. Essentially they need to replace these unproductive choices, motivations, and strategies with productive choices, motivations and strategies. Thus we relate our motivational intervention to learning strategy choices (Nolen, in press). Many researchers have recently concluded that one of the major conditions of positive self-efficacy is the student's knowledge about appropriate task strategies (Bandura, 1986; Locke, Frederick, Lee, & Bobko, 1984; Locke & Latham, 1990). Throughout this phase of the course, therefore, we try to help our students value deep-processing strategies (Nolen & Haladyna, 1990) that will lead to effective learning outcomes.

Finally, throughout the motivational units we constantly emphasize that the students can potentially control their desire, intention, focus, and sustainment. They need to describe their unproductive strategies for each phase, identify obstacles that are likely to keep them from achieving success, and finally generate strategies to maintain their *desire, intention, focus*, and *sustainment*. Finally, they need to substitute the effective strategies for the ineffective strategies. We often have the students visualize success. To keep reminding the students of the value of self-motivation we have created a powerful first letter mnemonic: DIFS makes the difference. Also to make this section more enticing, we employ many group activities in this phase of the course.

Preparing Information for Review:

Principle #3: During reading, listening and note taking the student should constantly attempt to identify important relationships among the topics and supporting detail to acquire a coherent understanding of the content.

This principle applies to listening, reading, note taking, and any of the plethora of review strategies the student employs for any type of content. In fact, this principle governs all the information processing strategies. To do this, the student needs to identify potentially coherent patterns during the lecture or reading assignment, construct computationally efficient notes, and then generate smart questions during review. A computationally efficient representation refers to any note taking system that helps the student to easily identify meaningful connections within, between or among the topics, subtopics, and supporting detail (Larkin & Simon, 1987; Robinson & Kiewra, 1995). Because of spatial limitations in this chapter, procedural knowledge courses are omitted from discussion. While the same general principles apply in these types of courses, some specialized strategies are also required.

Refer back to Figure 4a and Figure 4b to compare computationally efficient and inefficient representations. You will recall in Figure 4a that information about the facial expressions was presented in an outline form. As you will recall a learner would find it virtually impossible to identify significant patterns between the cause of the facial expression and the age of onset of the facial expression using an outline. Indeed, the outline separates the critical information. In contrast, when a student uses a matrix (Figure 4b) the student can easily identify significant patterns, find information quickly, and discover if information is missing. Further Figure 4b is less cluttered.

In the early phases of learning, therefore, a student looks for significant patterns of information and constructs computationally efficient notes. Four strategies are described in this section that will help students identify and record computationally efficient notes. These include the identification of alert words, knowledge patterns, repeatables, and the choice of a note taking system or systems.

Alert Words

Given a text or a lecture, one of the first steps is to identify the best note taking structure for the content. To keep the note taking system quite simple, the student can represent almost all knowledge using one of two patterns: a hierarchy or sequence. The student identifies these patterns by identifying three different types of *alert words* that "signal" the appropriate note taking pattern(s). Figure 6 includes examples of the three different types of alert words.

Alert words inform readers or listeners about the most likely relationships between the topics and subtopics. For example, consider the *outer framework alert words*. These words inform the reader or listener about the overall structure of the notes (e.g., Is it a hierarchy or sequence?). For example, words such as *types, parts, and levels* suggest a hierarchical relationship. These words most frequently are found in the beginning of a paragraph or section. In contrast, words such as *phases, stages, first, cause-*

Figure 6. Examples of Alert Words

	Outer Framework	Inner Framework	Extended Framework
hierarchies	types	usually	behavioral views
	parts	some	short term memory
	classes	although	capitalistic system
	levels	normal	autotrophic nutrition
	components	similar	inheritable mutations
	dimensions	however	zone defense
	elements	most	lower income
	characteristics	an exception	families
	properties	advantages	declarative
		contrast	knowledge
			direct current
			demand pull inflation
			inductive reasoning
sequences	leads to		effective students
	origins		Baroque style
	first		healthy heart
	stage		Expressionist
	phase		movement
	process		modern societies
	development		characteristics of
	methods		mature ecosystems
	cycle		
	cause-effect		
	action verb		
	nouns implying		
	process/change		

effect, and *photosynthesis* suggest a sequence. These words are also often found in the beginning of a paragraph. Once the student identifies the critical words indicative of the overall structure for the notes, the student constructs the hierarchical or sequential map. See Figure 7a & 7b for examples.

Inner framework alert words, in contrast, provide additional information about the relationships between the topic and subtopic, or about the topic and some repeatable categories of information (See Figure 8a). For example, consider the word *usually*. If a lecturer announces that "Usually students should use matrix notes" a note taker would instantly record two boxes, one for matrix notes, and one for another type of notes. When should matrix notes be used and when should the other type of notes be used? Now consider a textbook that is analyzing the similarities between the Far Right's viewpoint on big business with the Populist's viewpoint. Notice in this instance the author suggests the viewpoints are *similar*. Instantly a note taker would know that two topics are compared with respect to similarities and *differences*! Also, since the author discussed big business, the note taker would predict there might be differences for small businesses. Finally, consider the word ***advantages***. Assume a coach at a clinic starts to discuss the advantages of a zone defense. Immediately a note taker would know that at least two types of defenses will be discussed with respect to advantages and ***disadvantages***. Remember, the purpose of studying is to acquire a coherent understanding of the topic. If advantages are important, so are

Figure 7a. Sample Hierarchical Map

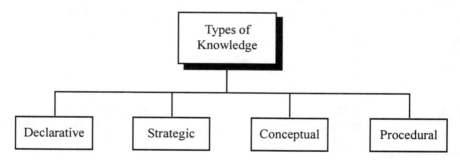

Figure 7b. Sample Sequence Map

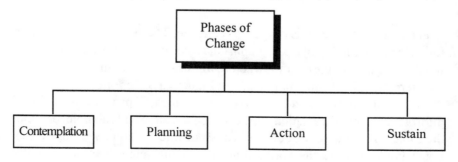

disadvantages. Inner framework alert words are often found in the middle of paragraphs in which the author wants the reader to connect supporting detail information. See Figure 8a for several examples of these words. Notice that *usually, although* and *contrast* suggest a comparison among at least two groups, *similar* automatically implies *different*, and that *advantages* implies *disadvantages*.

Thus the reader or listener actively predicts potential connections that are only implied in the presentation. The same outcome occurs when the student identifies *extended framework alert words* (See Figure 8b). These words inform the student about potentially new topics that are likely located in another section of the chapter. For example, consider the phrase *short term memory*. To acquire a coherent understanding of the topic, the student automatically predicts that at least one other type of memory is important (e.g., probably *long term memory*). The passage about long term memory may be found in the same section of the text, in the next section of the text, or perhaps in another chapter. In any case, when a student actively listens for or reads to make connections, information processing efficiency increases significantly. For example, Palinscar and Brown (1984) have found that teaching students to predict future content leads to effective information processing.

Now consider the phrase *the characteristics of a mature ecosystem*. This phrase should present the student with a little difficulty. This is because

Figure 8a. Examples of Inner Alert Words

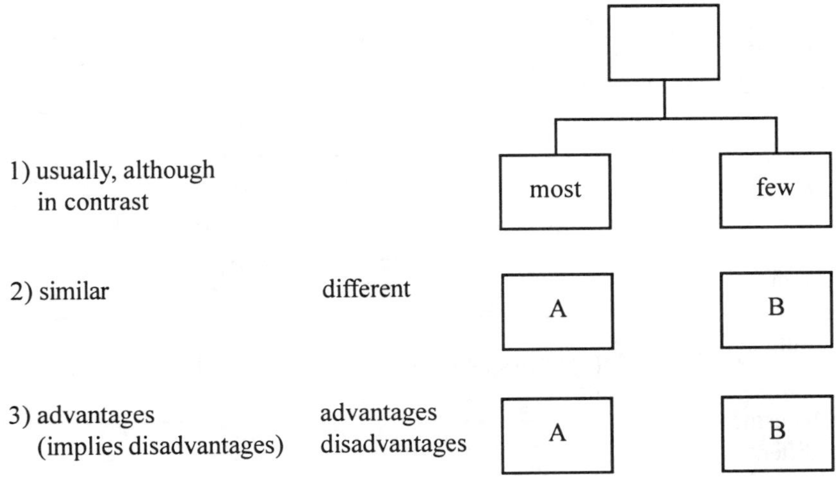

1) usually, although
   in contrast

2) similar   different

3) advantages   advantages
   (implies disadvantages)   disadvantages

	most		few
	A		B
	A		B

characteristics is generally represented as a hierarchy (see Figure 9a). The phrase *mature ecosystem,* however, clearly infers an immature ecosystem also exists. And clearly an immature ecosystem occurs before a mature ecosystem existed. Thus the student should record a sequential map to organize the notes (See Figure 9b). In this example, the students would want to trace how the characteristics of an immature ecosystem evolved into a mature ecosystem. See Figure 9 for the outer structure of the notes.

The common feature of alert words is that they inform the student about the potential pattern of the notes. With this system the student can identify connections that are clearly difficult if not impossible to identify using more traditional note taking systems.

Figure 8b. Extended Framework Alert Words

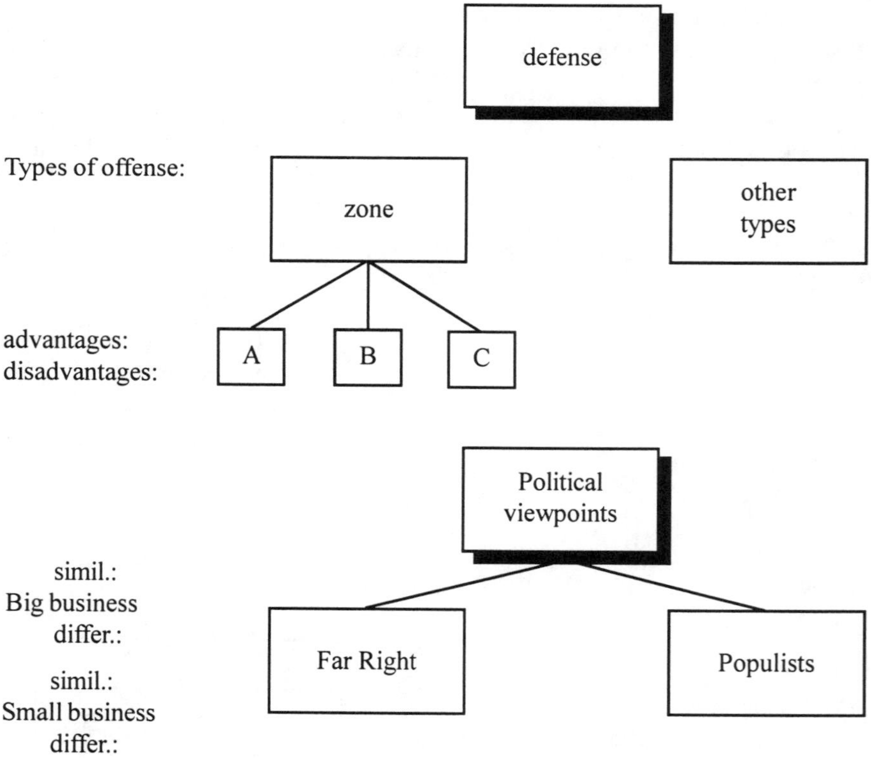

Figure 9a. Hierarchical Structure

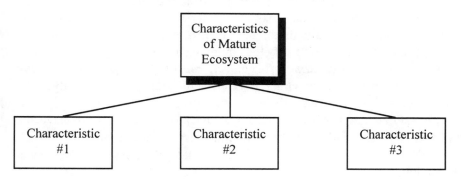

Figure 9b: Hierarchy Converted to Sequence

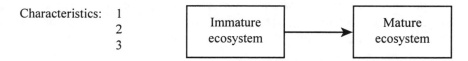

Repeatables

Students often have a difficult time identifying important information in a lecture or chapter. To help students with this task, we introduce the *repeatables strategy*. This strategy is very powerful and can be used in any course. All disciplines have a basic structure. All topics at the same level of abstraction consist of the same categories of supporting detail. Obviously if the student knows this information prior to listening to lectures or reading texts, the student can select the important supporting details for each topic. Unfortunately, rarely do texts or instructors provide students with this critical information, thus the students record incomplete notes.

To demonstrate the *repeatables* strategy, consider a history course. History is the study of events. To fully understand a historical event a student must understand the repeatable body of facts about the event. For example, all events consist of *who, what, when*, and *where* information. To *describe* an event the student must answer these questions about the event. All events also consist of *how, why*, and so *what* (e.g., what is the significance of the event?) information. To *explain* an event the student must answer these questions about the event. As consistent as the sun rises, these seven repeatable questions form the basis for understanding any event. Now if the student had to study a common set of historical events (e.g., explorers), then the student would identify the common subset of repeatables for each explorer (e.g., *date, name of explorer, reason for explanation, route followed, result*, and *so what*). Further, if the student has to analyze the cause and effects of events, the student can employ a repeatable analysis of events. For example, we present the idea that all events potentially have one or more of the following generic causes: political, economic, social, intellectual (including religious beliefs, and natural causes (e.g., the plague, London fire).

Now consider a transmission system in biology (i.e., circulatory, nervous, digestive, hormonal). Without an exception, all transmission systems consist of the same generic repeatable categories. Systems have a *purpose*, a *beginning*, a *medium* or *mediums*, a *process* to initiate the move, and some *outcome*. Additionally potential *dysfunctions can occur* at any phase in the process. When the something (e.g., a hormone) reaches its terminal location, another set of activities must occur.

Students are taught to identify the repeatables three ways. First, a student can simply think about the topic. What must the topic include? A student, with little or no prior knowledge, could have discovered most of the repeatables for the history, explorer, and transmission system examples. Second, quite frequently a lecturer or author will announce the repeatables. For example, a lecturer might start the lecture by announcing: "We will compare and contrast the three styles of music on the rhythm, melody,

Figure 10. Embedded Repeatable

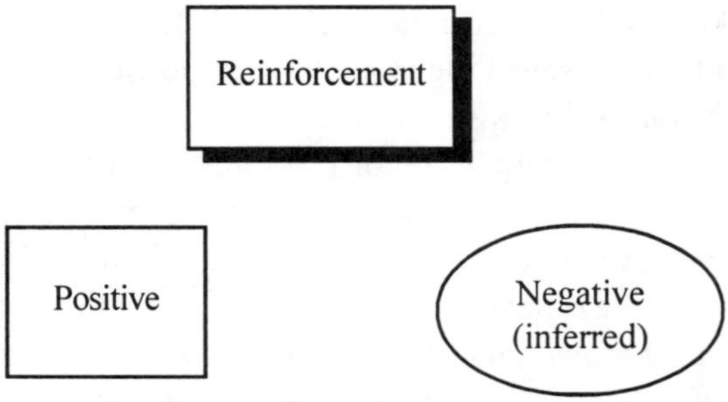

def.:
ex.:

Figure 11. Examples of Repeatables

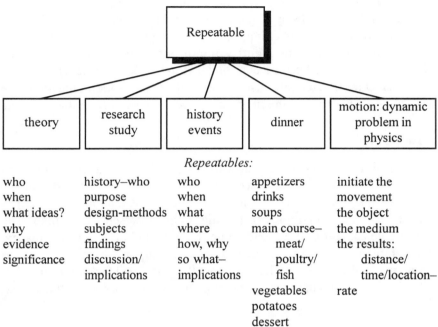

theory	research study	history events	dinner	motion: dynamic problem in physics

Repeatables:

who	history–who	who	appetizers	initiate the
when	purpose	when	drinks	movement
what ideas?	design-methods	what	soups	the object
why	subjects	where	main course–	the medium
evidence	findings	how, why	meat/	the results:
significance	discussion/	so what–	poultry/	distance/
	implications	implications	fish	time/location–
			vegetables	rate
			potatoes	
			dessert	

dynamics, and harmony techniques the composers employed." In this case, the repeatables are announced up front.

Finally, in many instances the repeatables are embedded in the lecture or text and only become apparent as the text or lecture evolves. For example, the lecturer might say:" Let's define *positive reinforcement*." A sophisticated student immediately knows at least one other type of reinforcement exists— probably *negative reinforcement*. Further, the student should quickly realize the generic definition of *reinforcement* is important. See Figure 10 for an example of how the student should structure the notes.

Notice, even though the lecturer doesn't announce that examples are provided, the student understands that *examples* are always needed to fully understand the definition. Thus, if the lecturer fails to provide examples, the student should ask the professor for examples. In a traditional note taking system, the student doesn't know what is missing. With a matrix, the student immediately knows which information is missing—a blank in the matrix is self-evident. Now assume the lecturer announces that each type of *operant* can have negative effects on a person. Thus *effects* becomes a generic repeatable—*negative* and *positive* effects are two subrepeatables. Refer to Figure 11 for some examples of more common repeatables.

As can be seen from a demonstration of the above examples, the purposes of reading, listening, surveying a text, and taking notes are essentially the same: to identify important relationships among the information presented in the lecture and text and to record these relationships on paper. Once the student constructs the outer framework for the notes, the student is ready to record the supporting detail. Matrices serve this function.

Matrices

Essentially a matrix is a downward extension of a hierarchical or sequential map. Matrices consist of three parts: topics (the maps), repeatable categories, and details. The topics are found across the top of the matrix. These are the major topics in the hierarchical or sequential map. The repeatable categories are found along the left hand margin of the matrix. Repeatable categories refer the characteristics upon which each topic is compared and contrasted. The details are the associated facts for each topic. The facts, recorded in phrases, are found in the intersections of the matrix.

Figure 12. Example of a Matrix

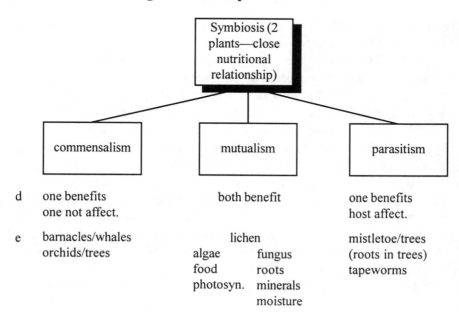

Figure 13. How to Construct a Matrix

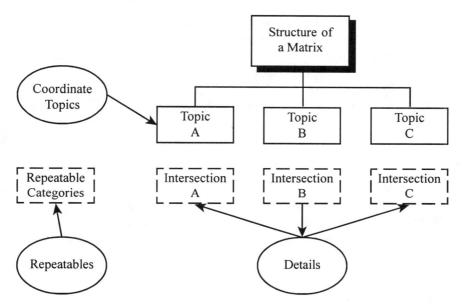

Refer to Figure 4b or Figure 12 for an example. Notice that the generic definition of symbiosis is located at the top of the matrix—all three types of symbiosis possess those generic characteristics. Also notice that each part of the definitions are written so that the student can easily make horizontal connections between or among the definitions. Figure 13 demonstrates how to construct a matrix.

The advantage of a matrix is that it presents information in tabular form. The columns of information include all the important repeatable categories of information for one topic. The rows of information include all the repeatable categories of information for one category across all the topics. Thus a learner can look down a column to identify within-topic connections and across the rows to identify across-category connections. By looking across the row the student can compare and contrast similar topics as well as note sequential information about the topics. Other note taking systems fail to provide this extremely important advantage.

Review

Principle #4: During review, the student converts the information recorded in the maps and matrices into coherent accessible knowledge.

During review the students should use their notes to make meaningful connections by asking smart questions. Review consists of four phases. See Figure 14 for an overview of the model of review we employ in the course. As mentioned earlier, the purpose of review is to acquire a coherent understanding of the content.

Phase 1: Inspect notes for computational efficiency:

To make meaningful connections the students must have notes that are computationally efficient. The students ask a simple question. Can they use their notes to acquire a coherent understanding of the content? If the notes are not in the appropriate format, the student corrects or rewrites the notes for review.

Phase 2: Make coherent connections:

In the second phase the student makes the appropriate connections. It is during this phase that the students systematically answer questions about *definitions, examples, descriptions*, and *explanations*. Essentially the student needs to master the vocabulary in the discipline. Simultaneously the students generate systematic questions about the description of the topics. We have adapted some of our strategies from King (1989, 1991, 1992). King developed a system to help the students elaborate on the content to-be-learned by asking smart questions. King found that students who elaborate retain much more knowledge than those who simply rehearse the information-to-be-learned. For example, given an event in history, can the student answer *who, what, when* and *where* questions about the event? Given that the student can describe the topic, the next strategy is to generate questions about explanations. For instance, given the same event, can the student answer the *how, why* and *so what* questions about the event? By the end of this phase the student should be able to answer any of the important questions about the topic and supporting details. Obviously the student can use the repeatables to generate systematic questions about the topics.

Figure 14. Generic Phases of Review

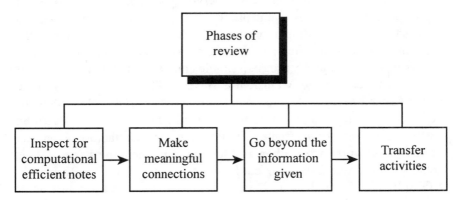

Phase 3: Going beyond the information given:

Effective review does not just consist of reproducing information for factual tests. During the third phase the students actively make connections between and among the topics and supporting details. It is during this phase that the students compare and contrast topics, derive analogies from prior knowledge, determine the significance and importance of the content, make judgments about the content, and summarize the chapter. Just as in the second phase, the student employs a series of systematic questions to elaborate the content.

Phase 4: Practices for new situations:

Finally, during the fourth phase, if necessary, the student is shown how to practice the newly acquired knowledge in new situations. Cooperative learning strategies are encouraged in which students systematically identify a range of applications for the content. Units on cooperative learning and studying for conceptual and procedural knowledge content are included in this phase of the course.

Transfer: The Final Key Element in Strategy Instruction

Simpson, Hynd, Nist and Burrell (1997) note that college learning assistance programs offer a wide range of intervention programs. Some of the more frequent programs have included: laboratories where self-paced instruction is provided, drop-in learning services, workshops, developmental studies programs, summer bridge programs, supplemental instruction, and courses focusing on reading improvement or learning strategies. While the research is scant on the effectiveness of these various intervention models, what is apparent is that any program should emphasize the transfer value of the demonstrated strategy (Weinstein & Mayer, 1985). It is clear that generic strategies can be taught (McKeachie, Pintrich & Lin, 1985). Regardless of the type of program employed to teach the strategy, whenever a learning strategy is taught, the instructor should consider four factors. First, the **student must know why, when and how** to implement the strategy. This metacognitive training should occur for every strategy (Pressley, Borkowski & O'Sullivan, 1984). Second, in order for transfer to occur the instructor should **require the students to be metacognitive** about their strategies. They need to reflect upon the processes involved in the strategy and they must understand the products the strategies will produce. For example, instructors should require students to justify their choice of strategy in different instructional contexts. To be metacognitive about a strategy, the student should possess the relevant declarative, conditional, and procedural knowledge about the strategy (Paris, Lipson & Wixson, 1983). Declarative knowledge is defined as the understanding of the purpose or intent of the strategy. Conditional knowledge is defined as understanding the conditions when the strategy should be used whereas procedural knowledge refers to the knowledge the student should possess about how to perform the strategy. Third, the instructor should **provide a systematic range of practice examples** for the students. To do this the instructor should identify the specific characteristics of the situation which inform the learner about which strategy to choose.

Lastly, the instructor must **evaluate the effectiveness of the strategy**. Professionals can measure the effectiveness of a strategy by measuring four outcomes:

1. Do the students perceive value in the strategies taught in the course?

2. Do students believe they can employ the strategies in appropriate contexts?

3. Do the students actually employ the strategies appropriately in those contexts?

4. Do the strategies have the effect they are supposed to have?

Summary

This chapter takes the position that a major objective in working with students likely to experience difficulty in college is to provide them with the necessary training to become self-regulated learners. A self-regulated learner knows when, why, and how to apply self-motivational strategies and information processing strategies to convert information into coherent accessible knowledge. The self-regulated learner controls both the motivational, affective, and cognitive dimensions of learning.

The self-regulated learner expects to do well, desires and intends to do well, controls likely internal and external obstacles that interfere with effective learning, persists at a task until it is successfully completed, and attributes the success to effective effort. Additionally, the self-regulated learner strategically selects and interprets the meaning of important content, records computationally efficient notes, and reviews the content to make durable connections between and among the important topics and supporting details. During all phases of learning the self-regulated learner monitors the effectiveness of the motivational, affective, and learning strategies.

Chapter 4

ಬೀಲ

A Model to Provide Learning Assistance for All Students

Cheryl B Stratton, Nannette E. Commander,
Carol A. Callahan, and Brenda D. Smith

College support for student success and retention must be a dynamic process. Growing the mission of developmental education means change in the programs, practices, and commitment of educators. The need to address low retention rates can be seen in reports such as Tinto's (1993) which found that of the nearly 2.4 million students entering higher education for the first time, over 1.5 million will leave their first institution before receiving a degree. Also, data from the two and four-year institutions that reported to the American College Testing Program (1992) show first year attrition rates as 67.7 and 53.3 percent respectively.

Past retention efforts have emphasized developmental or remedial courses. The Survey on Remedial Education in Higher Education Institutions by the U.S. Department of Education reports that 78% of higher education institutions that enroll freshmen offered at least one remedial reading, writing, or mathematics course in fall 1995. Twenty-nine percent of first-time freshmen enrolled in at least one remedial reading, writing, or mathematics course (Arendale, 1996). These efforts in higher education have often focused heavily on learning support programs that offer developmental classes for students identified as high-risk or tutorial centers for students experiencing academic difficulties. However, Noel, Levitz, Saluri and Associates (1985) examined academic records and discovered that entry profiles did not necessarily predict many of those students who leave college. Although developmental classes and tutorial centers provide significant academic support, attrition cannot be addressed effectively by serving only those students who show either predisposed learning weaknesses or learning problems. Students, other than those identified as high risk, also need assistance in adapting to the culture of college.

Some colleges have recognized that their students have trouble becoming independent learners and mastering the strategies that will make them successful (Simpson, Hynd, Nist, & Burrell, 1997). The University of California system accepts only the top 12.5% of their high school graduates but requires a writing course of more than half of the entering freshmen at the Berkeley campus (Callas, 1985; Maxwell, 1979; Roueche, 1985). Stanford University's Learning Center, established in 1972, continues to offer assistance to over half of the university's incoming freshmen (Henry, 1986; Roueche, 1985).

It is clear from past research that developmental education in an expanded mission is needed and can be effective. In their report, "Program Components and Their Relationship to Student Performance" Boylan, Bliss and Bonham (1997) reported several program components that show statistically significant relationships to student success. Centralized developmental programs report more student success than decentralized programs. Mandatory placement into developmental programs proved to be positively correlated with larger retention rates at 4-year institutions. Advising and counseling services were essential to student success as seen in pass rates of these students. Tutoring was reported at most programs of developmental education, and the most effective was tutoring with tutor training. Although the survey did not find enough programs including such things as peer mentoring or paired courses to report on them, Boylan concluded that there are certainly other components that have positive effects on students. Kulik, Kulik, and Schwalb (1993) also report statistically significant improvements in grades among students participating in intervention programs.

High rates of student departure demonstrate a need for academic support not only for a select population but a larger population of students who need a wide range of academic assistance. In spite of high admission standards, some of the most academically rigorous institutions in the nation deem it important to provide assistance to all their students. Institutions are recognizing that offering a more comprehensive learning program that provides assistance to all students, including those who are regularly admitted, is a wise investment. The success rates of these successful intervention programs demand the serious reexamination of traditional developmental strategies. It is clear from past research that developmental education in an expanded mission is needed and can be effective.

Our University

At our university—Georgia State University, an urban institution with 25,000 students—the Division of Developmental Studies was established in 1974 to serve two primary purposes: as an academic intervention program to provide access for the marginally-prepared student and as the guardian of standards for the institution. The primary responsibility of the Division was the administration of the developmental course work to those students accepted to the university on a conditional basis. As a traditional division of Developmental Studies, courses were offered in mathematics, composition and reading as well as a seminar course which included orientation to the university and study skills. Students were called high risk because they were identified, through a university formula of high school average and SAT scores, with academic weaknesses and learning problems.

What We Were

- Traditional Division of Developmental Studies
- Academic Intervention—Remedial Classes
- Mathematics, Composition, Reading, and Orientation Seminar
- Tutorial Assistance

Our Students

- were called high risk
- were identified with academic weakness
- had learning problems
- often had already failed a class
- had an average age of 28

Between 1976 and 1993 the division acquired additional responsibilities

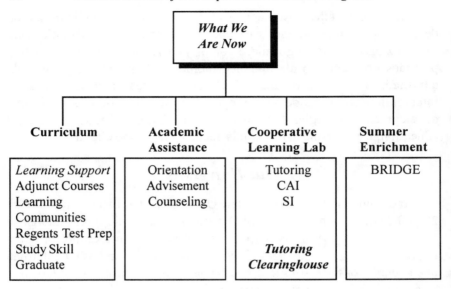

for administering a learning laboratory, a Summer Enrichment Program, an office of academic assistance, and remedial instruction for students experiencing difficulty with the State-mandated test of competence in composition and reading. The learning lab offers tutorial assistance for drop-in developmental students with computer programs (CAI) available for student use in the nearby computer lab. The summer enrichment program (BRIDGE), a month long pre-college program, emphasizes orientation and retention. The office of academic assistance presents orientation programs and does advising and counseling. The department also teaches 6-week classes for students who need help passing the Regent's Exam, a state-mandated test of competence in composition and reading for rising juniors.

In 1993, the Board of Regents for the state of Georgia recommended that the role of developmental programs be expanded to serve a wider population of students. The new population would include those students who meet system-defined standards for admissions but who, nevertheless, need academic assistance in meeting the challenge of the core curriculum. In 1995, the division was reorganized into a department within the College of Arts and Sciences and given the new name "Learning Support Program" to reflect our expansion into services for regularly admitted students who need learning assistance with content area courses. Today, the department emphasizes student success and university retention. It has expanded into areas well beyond developmental education. The most recent programs are described in this chapter.

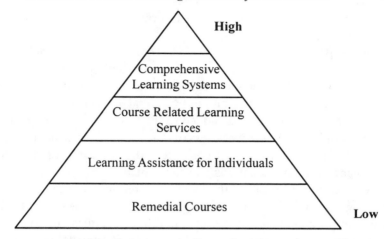

Keimig's Heirarchy of Learning Improvement Programs

In the area of curriculum, the department offers learning support classes for underprepared students, preparation classes for students taking the state mandated test of competence in reading and composition, orientation seminar courses, adjunct courses paired with core academic courses and graduate courses for students who wish to study the teaching of post secondary mathematics, reading or composition. The cooperative learning lab continues to offer the previous services and now also trains tutors, coordinates Supplemental Instruction and acts as a tutorial clearing house for students who want to be private tutors.

An examination of Keimig's (1983) research on effectiveness of learning programs helps to put our change of mission into perspective. She developed a "Hierarchy of Learning Programs" that used four levels to rank four types of learning programs in ascending order of effectiveness for impact on Grade Point Average (GPA) and retention. Learning support programs are differentiated on the basis of two criteria: the comprehensiveness of the program and the degree to which the program is institutionalized in the overall academic delivery. Keimig's hierarchy begins with a Level I designation for programs with only remedial/developmental classes for students identified with academic weaknesses. Typically such students must complete their developmental course work prior to enrolling in the core curriculum courses. Results from a survey conducted by the National Center for Education Statistics indicate that 82% of all public and private institutions offer at least one developmental course (Abraham, 1987). The

Developmental Studies Program at Georgia State University began with only Level I.

Ranked as Level II by Keimig (1983) are programs that include tutorial assistance for individual students. In the early 1970s, peer tutoring programs began in California community colleges, and they eventually led to formal learning centers in many institutions by the end of that decade (Wyatt, 1992). In 1992, a tutorial center was added to the Division. Although successful for many individuals, the weakness of tutorial services is that participation often takes place after a failure has occurred. Also, tutoring often does not take place on a consistent basis because of its "drop-in" nature, and the students who need tutoring the most are often inclined to use it the least (Keimig, 1983). Keimig (1983) designates a Level III, the next to the highest rating, to programs that deliver course-related services but do not require the content professors to change their instructional delivery style. The department offered programs that fit Level I and II. But learning support efforts that would meet Keimig's Level III were still needed. This chapter describes how the learning support program expanded to include Level III services including the Summer Enrichment Program, (BRIDGE), Supplemental Instruction, and adjunct or co-courses.

Expanded Avenues of Academic Support

BRIDGE

In 1984, the Summer Enrichment Program, "BRIDGE," at Georgia State University was designed with the goals of recruitment and retention of African-American students. Recruitment activities included informing local school counselors about the BRIDGE Program, visiting high schools and talking to students during the academic year before BRIDGE. Initially, the Program focused on enrichment activities which would orient students to college life and the Georgia State University campus; improve student's attitudes (e.g., to improve their self-confidence, to reduce academic anxiety, clarify career goals) toward entering college; and encourage the development of group cohesion and peer support systems. The month long session also included academic components of composition, reading and mathematics which were blended with enrichment activities to enable students with marked improvement to move to a higher level in their required composition or reading developmental courses.

By 1993, the goal changed somewhat. The student pool came from students who had already been admitted to the university, so BRIDGE did

Table 1. Recruitment Statistics for the 1996 BRIDGE Program

Letters Mailed To Students	140
Applications Received	43
Males	13
Females	30
Acceptance Letters Sent	43
Males	13
Females	30
Students Who Began Program	27
Males	8
Females	19
Students Who Completed Program	27
Males	8
Females	19
Students Who Registered For Fall Classes	26
Males	7
Females	19

not play as large a role as it did in the early years toward recruitment. Many students who have been accepted to a university, however, choose not to attend. Offering these students a free BRIDGE Program during the summer did help them confirm their choice as Georgia State. (Table 1). The major goal then was retention—and retention efforts that reflected the most current research specifically involving African American students. In addition to the content developed over the first 10 years, the curriculum began to focus on issues most important to African-American students.

The Program incorporates many of the past successes into a meaningful experience for students. Through a theme of how knowledge of the students' African American Heritage can help students succeed, the BRIDGE Program prepares students for their college course work, provides students an opportunity to bond to the university, promotes group cohesion, and helps them become acquainted with the ramifications of the university experience. Looking at historical and current events, students use research about their culture's difficulties and successes to better cope with the new experiences at the university. Among the orientation objectives are for students to become oriented to the GSU campus; improve their self-confidence, reduce anxiety; build a collegial atmosphere, create a peer support system; gain access to various university staff and resources; acquire university computer accounts and learn to access the university computer; learn to use the GSU Library; learn to use Word Processing, access the Internet, and send e-mail; learn how to use the library and the OLLI (On Line Library Information System); and learn to use the graphing calculator. Students study historical and current issues, particularly as they relate to the Civil Rights Movement through a variety of media; participate in discussions, formulate and express their opinions; analyze, and synthesize historic issues and compare them to current issues orally and in writing; write about experiences, both real and vicarious; travel to historic sites like the Civil Rights Institute, the 16th Street Baptist Church and the Jazz Hall of Fame in Birmingham; interview and write reports; strengthen specific academic skills in reading, composition and mathematics; recognize realistic academic and career goals and find ways to achieve these goals; improve attitudes toward mathematics; improve their problem solving skills; and improve general study skills.

The BRIDGE Program provides its participants with unique academic, social, and personal enrichment experiences. As a method of easing the transition of African- American students to the university, BRIDGE has shown to be successful by the positive responses reported from the students. They express feelings of belonging and comraderie and feel their new knowledge of the university will help them succeed. They see BRIDGE as a major asset toward accomplishing their goals at the university.

Many of the other objectives of the Program are accomplished each year. This is evidenced by the successful completion in 1996 of all 27 students of the Seminar component which allowed these student to be exempted from this course in the fall quarter. Also, all 27 students moved up in reading. Students' leadership abilities usually emerge. They demonstrate talents and desires to achieve that are above normal. Students express positive feelings about starting the fall quarter and they feel a step ahead of other freshmen. Some students learn for the first time that they are not as strong academically as they had thought. For those willing to reflect upon the possible reasons for their unrealistic views, the summer program serves as a stimulus for them to work harder. As Hovland (Kluepfel, 1994) says, "a clear message is sent to students that 'college is serious business'" (p.28). Students learn who to see, where to go, what to ask, and why things (like organizational policies) exist. Through the rigor of the academic components of BRIDGE,

Table 2. Georgia State University Summer Enrichment Program:
The BRIDGE: Program Completers

	1987	1988	1989	1990	1991	1992	1993	1994	1995
Completed BRIDGE Program	80%	84%	87%	82%	98%	98%	99%	97%	89%
Completed LSP*	71%	68%	80%	75%	64%	86%	72%	80%	29%
Retained four or more quarters*	69%	81%	85%	89%	95%	90%	83%	79%	nn/a
All African American students retained four or more quarters	n/a	n/a	n/a	72%	69%	62%	72%	n/a	n/a

*Does not include students in the BRIDGE program who never enrolled at Georgia State University. **After only two quarters. ***Data not yet available.

students begin to understand some of the academic realities they will be experiencing in the university. Each academic area (language arts, mathematics, and seminar) provides well-planned, thoughtful instruction which successfully blends the objectives of orientation and academic enrichment.

Faculty and staff are extremely motivated and work harmoniously to promote student unity and comraderie. Their planning and implementation of the Program is excellent. Faculty growth is a significant outgrowth of the Program. Faculty have opportunities to plan activities that they would not usually be able to use in regular academic courses.

Two Peer Advisors provide positive role models. These advisors attend BRIDGE sessions with the students and mentor as much as possible. They worked closely with the director and the instructors to provide orientation, academic, and administrative assistance.

The real evaluation of the Program may be found in the follow-up statistics on the retention and success of the BRIDGE students. Data from the past BRIDGE programs shows that retention of BRIDGE students is above that of other African American students (Table 2). There appears to be long-lasting positive effects of the BRIDGE Program. Hovland (Kluepfel,

1994) says about summer bridge programs, "the earlier various campus programs begin and the longer they last, the more successful they are likely to be in achieving retention goals" (p. 28).

Supplemental Instruction

Supplemental Instruction (SI), was originally developed to help medical students at the University of Missouri-Kansas City (Martin, 1980). It has since been adopted for students at all levels by providing voluntary, small group sessions that focus on the integration of learning strategies with material from a content area course. SI has all of the components found to increase learning by the *Harvard Assessment Seminars* (Martin & Arendale, 1990): quizzes, tests, oral exams, and group study. Because it is directly related to course content, SI averts some of the problems of nontransferability when study skills are taught in isolation (Stahl, Simpson, & Hayes, 1992).

Not only does SI offer an opportunity for academic improvement, it also can serve another anti-attrition purpose by helping students bond to each other and to the institution. Tinto (1993) stresses that group interaction and reliance on each other for knowledge and success is important for students to build a sense of community. The SI sessions, consisting of small group work and opportunity for collaborative learning, foster this sense of community. Additionally, ongoing research on SI and affect (Visor, Johnson & Cole 1992; Visor, Johnson, Schollaet, Majab, & Davenport, 1995) indicates a possible relationship between SI and affective variables such as self-efficacy, self-esteem, and locus of control. The possibility of a reciprocal relationship between affect and SI (Visor et.al, 1992) increases the relevance of the effect of SI on persistence and performance.

"Student Leaders" are trained with a curriculum (Table 3) which helps them act as coaches and model students and they attend all classes and take all notes. The student leader becomes the facilitator encouraging students to collaboratively decide what they need to know in order to be successful in the course. The strategies employed by the leader then follow from these decisions and the direction of the course. The curriculum of SI focuses on strategies necessary to pass the course. Reading the text, memorizing, and predicting test questions may all be addressed. Other activities involved in the SI sessions are to build a complete set of notes, analyze test results, and design practice tests. This differs from typical Teaching Assistant (TA) breakout sessions where the TA is a "mini-professor" and viewed as the expert in content. The SI leader remains on the student side of the desk and functions as peer leader.

Supplemental Instruction was a logical addition to Georgia State University's Department of Learning Support as part of the move toward serving a wider population because it has a non-remedial focus and includes Aregular" students. Rather than targeting "high-risk" students, SI targets "high-risk" courses, or those courses having a 30% or higher D or F [or W] final course grades and withdrawals. At Georgia State some core-curriculum courses at or approaching "high-risk" include introductory courses in History, Political Science, Biology, Algebra, Accounting, and English. Delivery systems for these courses often feature auditorium-sized populations, and some courses serve as 'gatekeepers' leading to majors and professional programs.

A SI consultant from the University of Missouri-Kansas City came to GSU to provide information about the system. Our Learning Support Instructional Services Coordinator received SI Supervisor training. The firstSI pilot was offered in the fall of 1993. Two SI sessions were attached to two sections of Political Science, and the results generally equaled those reported by UMKC. Table 4 compares grades of Political Science students who attended one or two sessions (Some SI), and three or more sessions (High SI) with students who did not attend SI (NO SI). Comparisons were also made between former Developmental Studies students and regularly admitted students. SAT scores and other predictors of success were observed. Those who attended SI sessions three or more times achieved an average grade of 2.7 as opposed to an average 1.9 for those who did not attend. More importantly, even students with a low predicted success rate (Predicted Grade Point Average based on a formula including SAT & other factors) out performed their peers with a higher predicted success rate. Funding was increased based on these results. Tables 5, 6, and 7 show similar results in course grade averages for students taking American history, accounting, and biology over several quarters. SI sessions have now been offered to accompany a total of 28 course sections. Out of the 5103 students offered SI, 33% participated in sessions.

Table 3. Curriculum for Supplemental Instruction Leaders

Learning Theory
    Bloom's Taxonomy
    Piaget
    Dale's Cone of Experience
    Keimig's Hierarchy of Learning Improvement
    Tinto's Student Retention Model
    Schema
    Metacognition

Group Theory
    Leadership
    Stages of the Development of Learning Groups
    Development of Productive Learning Groups
    Affect and Group Membership

Study Skills
    SQ3R
    Cornell Notetaking System
    Test Preparation
    Test Taking
    Test Anxiety
    Time Management
    Mnemonic Devices
    Marking Text
    Vocabulary
    Matrices
    Incomplete Outline and Other Impromptu Quizzes

SI Program Management
    Marketing
    Preparation
    Paper Work
    Ethics and Sensitive Information
    Evaluation

**Table 4. Success of Participants vs. Non-participants in SI
Fall Quarter 1993 Pilot in Political Science 101**

Regularly Admitted Students	Course Grade Average	SAT Composite Average	**Former DS Students**	Course Grade Average	SAT Composite Average
High SI*	2.7 (n=52)	900	High SI	2.8 (n=6)	767
Some SI**	2.4 (n=40)	845	Some SI	1.8 (n=11)	799
Total SI	2.6 (n=92)	872	Total SI	2.1 (n=17)	783
No SI	1.9 (n=169)	918	No SI	1.7 (n=29)	815

*High SI – 3 or more sessions   **Some SI – 1 to 2 sessions

Table 5. SI for American History

Academic Quarter	Attended SI		Did not attend SI
	3+ times	1+ times	
Spring 1994	3.6 (n=8)	2.9 (n=14)	1.8 (n=45)
Winter 1997	3.3 (n=13)	n/a	1.7 (n=200)

Table 6. Accounting

Academic Quarter	Attended SI		Did not attend SI
	3+ times	1+ times	
Spring 1994	2.5 (n=4)	2.5 (n=22)	1.6 (n=88)
Fall 1994	2.3 (n=17)	2.1 (n=36)	2.1 (n=52)
Winter 1995	2.5 (n=17)	2.3 (n=30)	1.1 (n=45)
Spring 1995	3.0 (n=5)	3.1 (n=8)	2.4 (n=29)
Fall 1995	2.3 (n=19)	2.2 (n=26)	1.8 (n=92)

Table 7. Biology

Academic Quarter	Attended SI		Did not attend SI
	3+ times	1+ times	
Fall 1994	2.9 (n=13)	2.8 (n=31)	2.4 (n=125)
	3.2 (n=5)	3.1 (n=7)	2.3 (n=28)
Spring 1995	n/a	2.8 (n=8)	2.3 (n=59)
	n/a	3.0 (n=103)	2.4 (n=45)
Winter 1996	2.4 (n=5)	1.8 (n=9)	2.6 (n=158)
Fall 1996	3.0 (n=41)	2.5 (n=49)	2.5 (n=44)
Winter 1997	2.9 (n=39)	2.5 (n=52)	1.9 (n=49)

Adjunct Course Offerings

Adjunct or co-courses may be viewed as a variation on traditional SI. Adjunct courses offer learning strategies instruction with direct application to students who are co-registered in content courses such as history, mathematics, political science, or psychology. After 6 years of experience teaching adjunct courses at California State University, Dimon (1988), noted that adjunct courses work because "they have a definable purpose, function as a support group, challenge students, promote participation, are flexible, and do what they say they do" (p. 33). Like SI, adjunct courses focus on helping students pass a particular content course. Unlike SI, students must register for the course, rather than just show up for sessions. Also, adjunct course students usually take additional quizzes and exams based on the adjunct course curriculum for which they receive an institutional course grade.

Reading adjunct courses. The first adjunct course is offered to upper level developmental studies students conditionally accepted to the university with a required course in reading. Prior to the development of this adjunct course, students in developmental studies with a reading requirement had to successfully complete a reading course before registering for any content area course. To be eligible to enroll in the adjunct course, students in the developmental program were required to have at least a 340 on the verbal section of the Scholastic Aptitude Test (SAT) as well as be placed in the exit level of a two-course developmental studies reading program sequence. Students who met the requirements could choose to enroll in the adjunct course in place of their developmental studies reading requirement. Participants received five quarter hours "institutional credit" for the adjunct course, and they received five quarter hours credit toward their degree for the American History course.

The pilot adjunct course was paired with an introductory American history course for several reasons. It was a course in which many students experienced difficulties, and the chair of the Department of History was very receptive to our project. The five hour adjunct course , entitled, "Learning Strategies for History" (LSH 072), was offered in the time block prior to the five hour history course two days a week for a 10-week quarter. Unless students self-identified, the history professors did not know which students were enrolled in the LSH adjunct course.

There are three instructional components employed when integrating and applying learning strategies to content area courses: 1) Learning

Strategies, 2) Increase in Metacognitive Awareness, and 3) Structure of the Discipline. The curriculum of LSH focused on these three main instructional components. First, instruction centered on typical study and learning strategies such as time management, text annotation, outlining, note taking, reading comprehension, memory, and test wiseness. Second, efforts were made to increase students' metacognitive awareness through learning logs, weekly observations of student behaviors, and learning styles inventories. Finally, historiography—or ways of reading, writing, and thinking that give structure to the study of history—provided information on time lines, map usage, interpretation and interrelation of events and where they took place, generalization about the meaning of events, and significance and application of specific historical terms. Overall, the curriculum of the LSH emphasized integration and application of learning strategies to the content area course material with modeling as the essential teaching technique.

The adjunct course, "Learning Strategies in History," has now been offered 7 quarters for developmental students. Because of registration difficulties, the first quarter LSH students were co-registered in eight different sections of American history, and this severely limited direct instructional opportunities. The second quarter the LSH students were co-registered in three different sections of American history. The third, fourth, and fifth quarter the LSH students were co-registered in only one section of Americanhistory. These varied experiences taught us that adjunct courses should be paired with as few content courses as possible(Commander & Smith, 1995).

Table 8 compares performance of students during the first five quarters. Comparisons were made for the groups: regularly admitted students enrolled in American history and the developmental studies students enrolled in Learning Support not paired with one history teacher. The LSH students' mean grade in American history was 1.78 (SD = .81) on a 4.0 scale, whereas the mean grade for non-LSH students was 2.14 (SD = .95). Of the LSH student who completed the quarter, 88.2% had a passing grade (A, B, C, C) in American history: 91.4% of non-LSH students who completed the course had a passing grade. An independent t-test indicated that the difference in the means of these two groups was not significant (t(349) = 2.51, p > .05). This means that both groups could have come from populations with identicalmeans. In other words, the LSH students did statistically as well as the regularly admitted students.

If success is defined as completing the content course with a passing grade, the 74.8% pass rate qualifies the history course as high risk. However,

Table 8. Success of LSH and Non-LSH
students in American history

	American history Only[1] % Passed	LSH and American history[2] % Passed
Fall '93	87.98 (8 different Am. hist. teachers)	84.62
Winter '94	92.59 (3 different Am. hist. teachers)	89.47
Fall '94	90.54 (1 Am. hist. teacher)	90.91
Winter '95	86.84 (1 Am. hist. teacher)	83.33
Fall '95	83.93 (1 Am. hist. teacher)	84.21

[1] Students in American history Only were regularly admitted Freshmen-Seniors.
[2] Students in LSH and American history were pre-Freshmen, placed in Developmental Studies, who would not have been eligible to enroll in American history.

the 81% pass rate for history with learning support indicates the adjunct course did make a difference in student success.

Similar comparisons were made of students in the groups: regularly admitted students enrolled in American history and developmental students enrolled in learning support paired with one history teacher (LSH). The LSH students' mean grade in American history was 1.85 (SD = .91) on a 4.0 scale, whereas the mean grade for non-LSH students was 1.97 (SD = .96). Of the LSH students who completed the quarter, 88.7% had a passing grade (A, B, C, D) in American history; 86.9% of non-LSH students who completed the course had a passing grade. An independent t-test indicated that the difference in the means of these two groups was again not significant ($t(281) = .87$, $p > .05$) This means that both groups could have come from populations with identical means. In other words, the LSH students did statistically as well as the regularly admitted students.

If success is defined as completing the content course with a passing grade, the 78.9% pass rate qualifies this history course as high risk. However, the 85.5% pass rate for history with learning support indicates the adjunct course did make a difference in student success.

When comparing the LSH students to the American history only students, it is important to consider that the LSH students would not have even been permitted, according to university admission standards, to enroll in American history. Another consideration when comparing the percentage of passing rates is that most students enrolled in American history are not entering freshmen. Therefore, they have the benefit of prior course experience.

Math adjunct courses. The second adjunct course is paired with college algebra. As at most universities, this beginning level algebra course at GSU is required of many degree programs. It is considered a very "high-risk" core curriculum course, since failure and withdrawal rates sometimes reach as high as 50% (Stone, 1995).

The population of the math adjunct course differs from the reading adjunct course in that it is not limited to developmental students. This class is advertised to all students and volunteers came from 3 groups: (a) former developmental mathematics students who felt the need for further academic support, (b) students who had previously made F or W in college algebra, and (c) other students interested in assistance. Although others (Simpson, Holschah, Nist & Hynd, 1994) used non-credit adjunct courses with muchsuccess, this adjunct course was designed as a 3 hour "institutional credit" course.

The course emphasizes the processes of learning mathematics, learning study skills specific to mathematics, and understanding instructions on the use of the graphing calculator using the content of college algebra. Pre- and post-instruction math attitudes survey (Hart & Najee-ullah, 1995) are given to determine change. Students are asked to balance their study of algebra content with their exploration of skills and methods that would help them become better math students. Collaboration is emphasized as a learning technique. Students form their own groups, exchange phone numbers and arrange study sessions. Students learn time management skills sometimes using daily and weekly logs. The classes learn relaxation and anxiety reduction techniques and keep journals. There are discussions of other topics specific to mathematics, such as how to start a problem and how to recognize patterns. Students work actively to find their personal learning style.

The first adjunct math pilot classes ran during the spring quarter of 1995. In our first pilot, students enrolled in a specific paired college algebraclass with one professor, and co-registered for the adjunct course entitled, "Learning Strategies in Algebra" (LS 094).

Although students were not randomly assigned, final grades in the college algebra classes were used to compare students taking the LS 094 course

MATHEMATICS ADJUNCT COURSE

Mathematics as a pump not a filter

Learning Support co-course for College Algebra

Population - voluntary   **Paired Classes**
former DS students   3hrs institutional credit
students with F/W in College Algebra
    previously
others

INSTRUCTIONAL FOCUS

content based
problem solving   collaborative
mastery learning   study skills
attitudes   technology
time management   relaxation
pattern recognition   journals

along with college algebra to students taking only college algebra. Students who participated in the adjunct course along with college algebra demonstrated equal or greater mathematics proficiency by satisfactorily completing the college algebra course with equal or higher scores than students who did not take the co-course (Stratton, 1996). Table 9 shows final grades and averages.

All students who completed the adjunct course passed college algebra. The LS students' average grade in college algebra was 2.25 (SD = 1.05) on a 4.0 scale, while the average for non-LS students was 1.57 (SD = 1.31). Of the LS 094 students who completed the quarter, 100% had a passing grade (A, B, C, D) in College Algebra but only 80% of non-LS students who completed the course had a passing grade. On the average, students who participated in the adjunct course earned a higher score by 7 percentage points or by more than one-half letter grade higher in college algebra than did the students who did not participate in LS 094. An independent t-test indicates that the difference in the means of these two groups is significant (t (72) = -2.45, p < .05). These grade comparisons show that students

Table 9. Success of LS094 and Non-LS094
Students in College Algebra

College Algebra Grade	LS094	non-LS094
A	3	3
B	8	10
C	11	13
D	3	6
F	0	8
W	2	7
grade averages	2.25	1.57
% passed (of completions)	100	80
% passed including Ws	92.5	68

taking the LS 094 course fared better on average in college algebra than students not taking LS 094. Thus, the adjunct course did make a difference in student success.

Since the completion of the first pilot, the adjunct course has been taught each quarter by a variety of professors with varying results. Some of the variations were the result of not pairing the adjunct course with one college algebra teacher. It is strongly recommended that for pilot classes the adjunct course should be paired with a core course taught by one teacher. However, in an effort to make these adjunct courses accessible to more students it may be necessary to open the class to students in different college algebra classes. These courses can be successful also. In the most recent adjunct course there were 19 students representing 16 different teachers. Eighteen of these students were successful in college algebra when paired with Learning Support for College Algebra.

Other Adjunct Courses. The third area in which the department is currently offering adjunct courses is English Composition. Pilot courses are being taught and preliminary reports show similar results. Other core courses that are targeted for pilot courses include psychology, statistics, and economics.

Learning Communities

Research indicates that students gain more from their educational experience the more they are involved (Astin, 1993; Pascarella & Terenzini, 1991; Tinto, 1987). A retention effort that promotes student involvement is participation in Learning Communities by beginning college students. While Learning Communities may vary in form and content, they generally link classes around an interdisciplinary theme and enroll a common cohort of students. Research by Tinto (1996) and others indicates that Learning Communities help first-year students make the transition into both the academic and social life of college, enhance student achievement, and improve student persistence.

Learning Communities involve significant restructuring of curricula so that students have opportunities for deeper understanding and integration of material they are learning. Participants are encouraged to interact with one another and their teachers as colleagues in the learning enterprise. Emphasis is on cooperative and active learning with interdisciplinary themes. Weekly meetings of instructors encourage reflective practices and collaborative teaching techniques.

Learning Communities recognize the importance of a community-based model of education that encourages learning through collaboration. The community-based model of education supports faculty working together and reflecting on their roles as teachers and members of a team seeking to improve student learning. The Learning Communities' effort is distinctive in its focus on structural barriers to educational excellence, pointing to the structural characteristics of many colleges and universities that are major impediments to effective teaching and learning.

The Washington State Center For Improving The Quality Of Undergraduate Education, a clearinghouse on Learning Communities, reports there are currently a hundred Learning Community Programs in 25 states (Levine & Tompkins, 1996). A Learning Communities Program at Georgia State University (GSU) is in the planning stages. In GSU's urban setting where students have demanding obligations outside of class, it is exciting that Learning Communities present an opportunity for restructuring the educational experience to achieve involvement during the short time students are on campus. Research investigating the effects of a Learning Community and the dissemination of the results of this research will encourage activitiethat enhance teaching and learning.

Ten Steps for Expanding Academic Support

One of the activities that the authors of this chapter have become involved in is the dissemination of information regarding the planning and implementation of our experiences in expanding our program. Through presentations and workshops for staff development, we offer ten essential steps in the process of expanding the role of academic support. These steps may guide others interested in designing learning support programs that reach out to students at varying academic levels.

1. **Consider campus uniqueness**. The U.S. Department of Education established a national study of retention programs in 1991. Programs identified by this study at the University of California at Berkeley, Rutgers University, University of South Carolina, and University of s Virginia attest to the diversity of retention efforts with program concepts and designs varying according to the unique demands of different institutions. Programs for commuter schools need to consider the typical stop-out behavior (withdrawing temporarily) of students and lower retention rates compared to residential campuses. The high-risk courses at an institution, the faculty's reception to retention efforts, and class size are only a few of the variables to consider when designing a program to fit institutional needs.

2. **Identify population**. This article describes work with different populations. The adjunct course for History replaces a developmental reading course which is required for students. The adjunct course for math and the Supplemental Instruction learning sessions were *voluntary* and open to any university students. Learning Communities are most likely interdisciplinary and students choose to take these courses as they are linked. BRIDGE is voluntary but open only to Learning Support Programs Students. If pilot programs target developmental students, the success rate of these students may convince others that those same programs would be beneficial to students regularly admitted. Whether it is more appropriate to pilot programs for developmental students or for a wider voluntary population may depend on the needs of the core course department. Another option is to strongly recommend or require some programs for students previously unsuccessful in a core curriculum course. This option must, of course, be carefully coordinated with core curriculum departments.

3. **Identify courses**. Consider guidelines such as those from the University of Missouri at Kansas City: chose sections with large numbers of students; select courses with a 30% or higher D, F, W, rate; target historically difficult courses that are gatekeeper courses leading to a major or professional program. Courses that require much in the way of a particular skill such as reading or mathematics may best be served by adjunct courses in those disciplines. Those that have intensive classroom activity or lab may best be suited to SI learning sessions. Learning Community courses are often identified by professors who want to work together on an interdisciplinary themed project.

4. **Build faculty support**. It is very important to convince some faculty that retention efforts are part of the their responsibilities and that retentionefforts do not compromise academic standards. This task may be achieved more readily when retention goals have specific benefits for the faculty. At our institution academic support programs are presented as methods that allow faculty to award an improved ratio of higher grades. An added benefit to faculty consistently stressed is that these programs create more independent and active students. These students are thus "easier" to teach because they are more responsible and involved in their learning.

5. **Staff courses with seasoned faculty and SI learning sessions with thoroughly trained leaders**. In an interview by Kleupfel (1994) Michael Hovland on retention notes that practitioners tend to think that retention ideas in themselves lead to success. "If I had to choose, I'd have to say that the people running programs are more important than the programs they run" (p. 29).

6. **Market programs at several levels**. Support from faculty, personnel from special campus units such as minority student programs or athletic programs, academic advisors, and counselors can have a profound effect on the success of learning programs. Some specific steps for marketing programs are:

To support SI and Adjunct Courses:

(a) Visit the content course at the beginning of the quarter or semester and discuss specific statistics that support higher GPAs for students who participate in SI sessions or adjunct courses,

(b) Visit exit level developmental courses to encourage students to enroll in content sections with an adjunct or SI attached for support in high-risk courses.

(c) Send letters describing all available programs to students unsuccessful in previous attempts at content area course.

(d) Post notices on the programs throughout campuses.

(e) Describe learning support services to students at orientation programs.

7. Provide feedback to professors throughout the term. Professors need to feel included because their support is essential to success. Supplemental Instruction and adjunct courses provide an opportunity for interaction among academic and developmental educators. Their shared problem solving is identified by Keimig (1983) as the fundamental dynamic in successful learning improvement programs.

8. Involve the administration. Academic support programs cannot operate solely from the "grass roots" level. According to Hovland (Kluepfel, 1994) ideal programs have not only a "bottom up" approach but a "top down" approach as well. Administration is concerned about issues related to retention as well as funding. This concern extends to legislatures (the source of funding) and governing boards. It is less costly to retain students than it is to recruit new ones. At Georgia State University, for example, an increase in retention of only 1% would be the equivalent of recruitment of 17% of the incoming freshman class. Proven retention tools, therefore, become attractive additions to college and university programs. Successful learning support programs also serve as recruitment tool as parents and prospective students become more savvy in their search for the "right" institution.

9. Keep records. Data must be recorded accurately and consistently regarding several aspects of academic support programs (Dimon, 1988). Attendance is a vital issue, as well as grades earned. Most important,

data must be analyzed on post-intervention academic progress for retention purposes.

10. Disseminate information. Describe your learning program in conference presentations and articles. Make faculty and staff on your campus aware of what you are doing and your results. The feedback you receive will help you assess what changes to make or growth to pursue.

A Comprehensive Learning Program

According to Michael Hovland, developer of the National Retention Excellence Awards, successful programs that ultimately impact retention require the addition of support services and changes in thinking and teaching (Kluepfel, 1994). The addition of support services took place at our university as we expanded from only developmental courses to developmental courses and tutorial services, then to our present developmental course work, tutorial, SI, the BRIDGE Program, adjunct courses, and Learning Communities. This expansion represents a movement on Keimig's hierarchy from Level I to Level III.

All too often the situation at many institutions of higher learning is one where support programs constitute one universe and academic departments the other (Kleupfel, 1994). Course-related services, such as those described in this article, allow for the crossing of division lines since learning programs are institutionalized in the overall academic delivery system. Furthermore, faculty gain greater understanding of retention efforts when learning strategies are integrated with content. The result is a comprehensive learning program, integrated with academic content, accessible to all students.

Keimig's (1983) hierarchy of effective learning programs includes a Level IV for programs that monitor students' learning and adjust teaching strategies and learning experiences for each individual. This level can be achieved at our university with the implementation of Learning Communities. With its emphasis on teachers and students as colleagues, Learning Communities can allow for changes in pedagogy based on individual needs.

The Future

Learning Communities is one of the new avenues of support planned for the next academic year. The first goal is to generate interest among faculty in different departments so they might create their own learning communities. A second avenue of support is the expansion of departmental graduate courses to train graduate teaching assistants for the College of Arts and Sciences. Currently, such a course exists for graduate teaching assistants and part-time instructors who wish to teach in the Department of Learning Support Programs. A new course would be developed to target a broader population for the College of Arts and Sciences.

Third, plans are being coordinated for a Freshman Year Experience Orientation course which will be available to all students. Following the example of the University of South Carolina, the hope is to establish an orientation class which will positively affect the rate of retaining students to the university.

Conclusion

The Department of Learning Support Programs at Georgia State University is an evolving example of the expanding horizons available for academic support. The GSU program has grown and diversified as needs have been recognized and opportunities have been created. Our program has met the goals outlined by the National Association of Developmental Education in 1995 by moving beyond developmental courses and offering such programs as SI, adjunct courses, summer enrichments, and freshman orientation classes. Learning communities, graduate courses and freshman orientation courses will bring faculty and students from diverse departments together to provide broader student support and new challenges. The dynamic nature of our department is continuing to provide support for student achievement, course completion, persistence in college and also stimulation for improvement in teaching and curriculum.

Note: Major portions of the above chapter are reprinted with permission from Commander, N. E., Stratton, C. B., Callahan, C. A., and Smith, B. D. (1966). A learning assistance model for expanding academic support. *Journal of Developmental Education*, *20*(2), 8-16. Published by the National Center for Developmental Education, Appalachian State University, Boone, NC 28608.

Chapter 5

ഊരു

A Comprehensive Model of Affective and Cognitive Support Services for Developmental College Students

William Collins

Over the last thirty years American higher education has witnessed a dramatic change in the composition of its student body. The change is essentially one of moving from a rather homogeneous group of young adult students from middle-class and professional family backgrounds to the current status of an incredibly diverse student body estimated as encompassing some 150 different ethnic, economic, and religious groupings and reflecting the growing diversity of American society at large. In addition, some students enter higher education as developmental learners (Beckett, 1995), that is highly motivated and generally the top students in their high schools, but still somewhat at a competitive disadvantage academically relative to their peers. Usually the disadvantage can be attributed to fewer resources, both academic and economic, in their personal and community circumstances. These students have been shown to succeed with appropriate support mechanisms are in place by their institutions (Kulik, et al., 1983; Hardy & Karathnos, 1992; King, 1993). Such diversity brings with it a growing need to assist students in ways that help them to feel a part of the university community as well as a need to assist students in meeting the academic challenges they face. Thus, both affective and cognitive support systems should be in place to help student and institution achieve their goals.

A number of approaches for addressing student cognitive or affective needs are documented across the nation, but few places attempt to address both domains in one program. The current document describes one such effort that has been in existence for some twenty years and which has met with considerable success during that period. The program is a comprehensive model for promoting the affective and cognitive development of students in postsecondary education.

Common Models

Several models of assisting students are known and they can be grouped into four broad categories:

Affective Model

Recognizing that students often face adjustmental difficulties in college, the affective model usually seeks to offer mechanisms by which the student may more readily embrace the nature and requirements of college life (Collins, 1982; Gardner & Jewler, 1992). Extensive advising is often a major component of such efforts, including advice from role-models with backgrounds similar to those of students and who have themselves successfully negotiated the college experience. Role-models may be upperclass students, alumni, or members of the advising/program staff. Group counseling and advising programs are also important and may take the form of intrusive advising (Anderson, 1978), developmental advising (Gordon, 1984), or standard academic advising (Grites, 1977), but with the latter being offered in a more structured or more frequent format; for example, monthly appointments with one's advisor instead of an appointment once-a-semester. Other components of the affective model may include cultural enrichment programs as well as social and recreational activities (Busser, et al., 1992). A major goal of the affective model is to help students feel a kinship with the broader college community, despite what they perceive to be differences between themselves and the more traditional student body. Thus, a welcoming atmosphere is expected to encourage students to take greater ownership of their education and development and utilize their time outside of class more appropriately.

Academic Assistance Model

By definition, developmental students often require assistance in strengthening their academic skills or knowledge base in order to compete successfully in the college environment. Several active approaches are available (Beal & Noel, 1980), but perhaps the most common is the tutorial program in which advanced students who have themselves succeeded with course subject matter provide regularly scheduled opportunities for developmental students to receive assistance in mastering course material. A less effective approach is to offer tutoring on an as needed basis in which developmental students seek tutorial help upon realizing that they are unsure about required academic skills and concepts. The reason the as-needed approach is likely to be less effective is that by the time students realize their difficulty with subject matter and obtain some assistance with it, they are often even further behind with respect to course requirements. Although programs that provide individual tutoring can be helpful, they also tend to be costly as a wide variety of courses must be covered, sometimes serving for only a few enrolled students. Peer tutoring programs that utilize capable undergraduates as tutors is one way to provide assistance while controlling costs.

An alternative to tutoring is the supplemental instruction approach (Martin & Arendale, 1994) in which a knowledgeable resource person holds regularly scheduled, structured meetings with students to clarify subject matter and generally to strengthen students' skills and knowledge. This approach can be particularly effective if the resource person is highly trained, such as a member of a department's instructional staff, though not the course professor. Neither is the Supplemental Instructor to be a teaching assistant who may run a discussion group or lab as in common in large universities. The role of supplemental instruction is to provide an additional resource to developmental students. A resource that recognizes that in addition to clarifying subject matter such as lectures, text readings or problem sets, developmental students may need to learn strategies for studying different kinds of material or strategies for preparing for examinations. Success in college for any student often requires new approaches for meeting the demands and expectations of faculty as well as a heightened commitment for keeping pace with the competitive instincts of other students.

The Supplemental Instruction Program can be an effective means for both sets of requirements. Similar to Supplemental Instruction is the Study Group approach (Coppola & Daniels, 1996) in which students meet regularly among themselves to review subject matter, share insights about course topics and problems, and prepare cooperatively for examinations or other assignments. Study Groups do not necessarily require a knowledgeable resource person to assist the groups' effort. Indeed, the effective Study Group will have a sense of shared responsibility among its members for mastering course material. Resource staff can be available to the study group to serve as motivator or facilitator, but one of the most important outcomes of study groups is the cooperative learning atmosphere that is developed among its members and their consistent investment of time and effort using course subject matter (Johnson & Johnson, 1991).

Academic Skills Model

An alternative to direct academic assistance for developmental students is to encourage their development of effective study skills and habits that are generally useful to being successful in college (Maxwell, 1979; Weinstein, et al, 1988). Such skills usually encompass note-taking strategies, time-management, reading improvement skills, test-preparation techniques, problem-solving strategies, and techniques for storing and retrieving large amounts of information. Good study habits are widely recognized as one of the most important factors in college success regardless of an individual student's level of preparation or standardized test scores. Thus, a focus on the general development of good study habits and strategies for learning can be an effective tool for promoting success in college. Important questions, however, are how and when to offer programs that teach effective study strategies. One answer is to offer such programs as a series of workshops throughout the fall and winter terms allowing students to learn and develop effective strategies at the time when these strategies can be applied immediately to course work. Another approach is to offer programs in study skills in the summer months prior to first-time matriculation as a full-time student at one's intended college. Many schools and colleges offer pre-freshmen programs to bridge the transition from high school to college (Collins, 1981; Gurthrie, 1991) and they do so in part to provide a structured opportunity for developmental students to improve study skills and habits. In addition to a focus on general academic skill development, summer programs also allow for a concentrated experience with college-level demands in such areas as math or English. Although students may complain about having to give up their summer freedom for academic work, summer programs can be invaluable opportunities for helping students to develop an appropriate set of expectations about college requirements.

Extended Orientation

Yet another approach is to provide students with a semester-long course that serves as an extended orientation to college, its requirements and its expectations. Sometimes referred to as University 101 courses (Gardner & Jewler, 1992), their goal is to help students understand the nature of their particular institution as well as the roles of the different people within it, including faculty, staff, and students. Such courses often help students to clarify their own objectives for college while simultaneously helping them to understand the requirements for achieving them.

Comprehensive Model

Institutions of higher learning are themselves incredibly diverse in terms of their course offerings, their missions, and their strengths. The small liberal arts college poses challenges to its students that are distinct from those posed by a technical institute, while the large research university presents yet a different set of challenges. Thus, it is understandable that each kind of institution might offer unique support opportunities for its developmental learners. Yet, no matter the institutional focus, students are apt to benefit most when they sense that a thorough set of initiatives are available to them. That is, a comprehensive program of support can provide the academic assistance, the behavioral modeling, and the occasional prodding developmental learners may need in order to be successful.

The CS Model

The specific components of the comprehensive model may vary according to institution, but in general will include an advising component, an academic assistance component, and a personal support component. The remaining of the chapter describes the components of a Comprehensive Studies (CS) Model established at a large research university (See Figure 1).

Advising

Few entering students can be expected to understand in advance the variety of requirements imposed by their respective institutions. Indeed, requirements change from year-to-year and even faculty sometimes have difficulty keeping up with them. An extensive advising program thus becomes indispensable for helping students to understand requirements and how to meet them. This is particularly true in large institutions in which there may be a number of ways to fulfill a given requirement. Our comprehensive program considers sound academic advice to play a central role in student development and academic progress. The CS model offers a contingent of eight full-time advisors who work with students beginning with a two-day summer orientation program in which academic requirements are reviewed, placement tests taken, and course recommendations and selections are made. During the summer orientation students briefly meet with the staff and offices that will be of assistance to them during the academic year, thus establishing basic familiarity.

The advising connection is maintained during the academic year as students meet individually with their advisors about three times per semester

Figure 1. Model for a Comprehensive Program of Affective and Cognitive Support for Developmental Learners in College

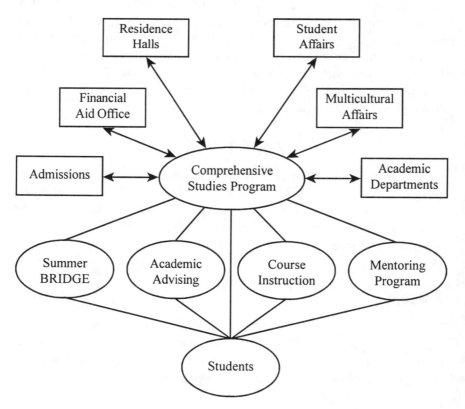

as well as participate voluntarily in group advising and support sessions concerning such topics as study skills, selecting a major, or fulfilling medical school requirements. The Comprehensive program establishes a liaison with other university offices such as the Counseling Center to promote rapid referral when necessary. A Mid-Term Evaluation (MTE) for each course taken by developmental students during freshman and sophomore years is sought from the faculty. This provides useful feedback to advisors about the progress being made by individual students, many of whom are ill-versed in interpreting their standing in college courses which do not provide periodic grade reports as was the case in high school. The MTE is a useful monitoring device that provides a basis for advisors to meet with students about their academic progress in particular courses and to offer suggestions for rectifying problem situations before they become irresolvable. In addition, a computerized information system is in place (CSPIS) to provide computerized access to academic records, to communicate with students via e-mail, and to serve as a file for contacts and notations regarding each student seen in the advising context.

Academic Development and Assistance

Although developmental learners have promise for academic success, the very fact that they are assigned to a special program is indicative of a need for additional academic development. The comprehensive program includes course offerings in a variety of introductory level courses for the purpose of providing additional instructional time, a focus on learning strategies appropriate to the discipline, and modeling of success by other developmental learners.

The additional instructional time is accomplished by a requirement that all "comprehensive program" courses meet for an additional class period each week in comparison to other sections of the same course. This signals to students that more, not less work is expected of those enrolled in "comprehensive" sections. The additional class time is used by instructors to accomplish the second purpose which is to acquaint students with effective strategies for learning course subject matter. Instructors may use the extra period to focus on how to recognize certain kinds of problems, for example, or to help students identify problem-solving steps to follow. Modeling of successful strategies can be achieved by having members of the class solve a problem at the blackboard and explain to the class how it was done and why the approach used was chosen; or students in writing classes might read from papers submitted for grading and comment on them; discussion classes might rotate the assignment of preparing discussion questions or summarizing lecture or reading assignments. More recently, the development of a World-Wide Web Home Page for math sections allows students to access assignments, explanations, and to communicate with faculty from remote sites. These instructional techniques involve students with the subject matter as well as serving to identify effective models of good performance. Many of these same strategies can be used to good benefit in supplemental instruction or tutorial programs, but it is not uncommon for such an approach to be hampered by motivational problems as students see that "real" academic work involves credit and grades, both of which may be missing from supplemental instruction or tutorial programs.

Supportive Programs

It is widely recognized that developmental learners may need support academically and with respect to other college requirements, thus academic assistance and advising programs are routinely offered. Increasingly it has been recognized that the affective domain is also important to student success (Collins, 1982). How one feels about the institution itself as well as how one feels about one's place within the institution can be important motivational factors. The CS program seeks to address this concern in two concrete ways. The first is through a Summer Bridge Program available to promising developmental students identified in the admissions process as "at-risk" with respect to the academic demands of the institution. As its name implies, the Bridge Program is intended to provide an opportunity for students to bridge the transition from high school to college through a rigorous academic summer experience. Participants have a summer opportunity to develop academically and results generally show improvement in such fundamental abilities as math or writing skills. But a by-product of the summer experience is that participants get to know each other as well as get to know the campus, its offices, its faculty and staff. Students learn of the variety of demands that will be made upon them and where they can turn for help if needed. They establish supportive social networks through their summer experience which can help them to negotiate the larger set of social demands that emerge during the regular academic year. In general, summer programs allow developmental learners to become familiar with the institution during a period when staff and students can more readily establish supportive bonds than they can during the academic year when more students and more demands are evident.

Secondly, CS effort includes a mentoring program to promote one-on-one contact between a student and a knowledgeable faculty or staff member. Supportive alumni in the local community can also serve this role. A mentor has to be knowledgeable about the institution, available for individual meetings with the student, and willing to provide advice, encouragement, and sometimes a different perspective than the one that may be of pressing concern to the student at the moment. A key purpose of mentoring is to expand the student's circle of resources and thus build a broader social support network.

Both the Bridge Program and the Mentoring Program serve to create a sense among students that they belong to something larger than themselves and that they are valued members of those communities. This is important because college, particularly the first year at a residential campus, can be a time when one feels alone and isolated from that which is familiar, i.e., one's home community. At our institution the positive benefits that accrue to students who feel they belong to a particular program have been demonstrated in a number of programs. Of particular note is evidence suggesting that minority students who are part of an institutionally sponsored program have higher grade-point-averages and retention rates than do students who are not part of such programs. Matlock et al. (1992) have found a "comprehensive program" effect for minority students in a large research university. Such students seem both to feel better about the institution and to perform better academically than others.

Impact of the Comprehensive Model

The availability of a comprehensive program of academic support serves as a focal point both for institutional offices and for students. The University Admissions Office can more confidently admit students knowing that a wide array of programs and services are available to assist students in their adjustment, while students themselves often decide to enroll in institutions they perceive as supportive.

But we may also wish to compare the academic achievement of students in the comprehensive program to that of other students who do not participate in the comprehensive program. Such an analysis reveals, as expected, that the two groups of students enter college with different characteristics. Those not in the comprehensive program generally have higher standardized test scores, for example, and a higher grade point average from high school. These are traditional criteria used to predict college academic achievement and one might reasonably expect those with the higher scores to outperform those with somewhat lower scores. Our analyses, however, show that the academic achievement of students in the comprehensive program is comparable to that of a randomly selected control group of students who entered college with higher pre-college achievement scores. In fact, the use of analysis of covariance allows for a statistical control on the pre-college achievement differences between the two groups, and suggests the kind of academic achievement that would be expected had both groups of students entered college with comparable standardized test scores and high school grade point averages. These analyses show that the academic achievement of students in the comprehensive program is equal to or better than that of the control group despite differences in test scores or high school grade point averages. Students in the comprehensive program attained a predicted college grade point average of 2.78 while those in the control group attained a predicted grade point average of 2.61.

In addition to objective measures such as grade-point average, anecdotal comments collected by impartial observers are also instructive with respect to understanding the program's impact. As reported in The Michigan Study (Matlock, 1992), a large-scale examination of student expectations and experiences during their college years, students in the comprehensive program expressed such views as the following:

> My comprehensive program advisor has been very important. I usually go in to see her quite often and we just sit down and talk; she's very helpful. She listens to me and when I get discouraged about how hard my classes are, she just cheers me up and tells me: 'You can do it.' And she told me even if you decide that this isn't what you want to do, there're always alternatives.'
>
> In comparison to other counseling available, in the comprehensive program 'there is more of an effort to really understand what students are trying to find out…'

Such anecdotal responses add a human face to the student satisfaction surveys done by the program which consistently show approval ratings in the ninety percent range.

Discussion

Developmental learners in college often come from impoverished economic backgrounds or from predominantly minority communities. Regarding black students, for example, Thomas (1987) has pointed out black student success in higher education is affected by two broad categories of factors: the first category has to do with the personal characteristics of the students themselves; that is, their preparation levels for college work, their conduct in classes, and their motivation or aspirations. The second category of factors affecting black student performance includes institutional characteristics, such as the academic, racial or social climate on the campus; recruitment and retention practices; or the type and availability of financial aid. In fact, some studies have found that many black students lack the appropriate levels of preparation for college level academic success (Berryman, 1983; Davis, 1986). Low preparation for mathematics in particular effectively bars many otherwise promising black students from achieving success in such fields as science or medicine because math functions as an essential gateway course for further work in these fields (Massey, 1992). Yet, Matlock et al. (1992) have found that black students continue to have high aspirations for advanced degrees. These factors which affect black student achievement also apply generally to developmental learners in college.

The different models discussed in this chapter offer distinct forms of support to students with special needs and they all offer benefits. The CS model attempts to combine the essential aspects of academic support into a single program that seeks to develop students' personal characteristics at the same time as it establishes an institutional environment that is supportive of student development and conducive to their academic progress. The fundamental area of impact is with respect to student characteristics, both academic and personal. CS's intensive courses emphasize subject matter as well as the skills needed to achieve success. Those sections in which students follow the prescribed steps and fulfill assignments routinely out-perform other sections of the course. The focus on academic skill development as well as the subject matter itself clearly pays off for these sections. But student personal characteristics also play a role and they are less subject to control. Even in Comprehensive Program courses some students are unsuccessful academically. Such failure is almost always attributable to frequent absences or failure to fulfill course assignment requirements. The reasons for multiple absences or missed assignments are as varied as there are students, but often include comments such as the following: "I was pledging"; or " I had to work"; or "The assignment was more time-consuming than I had anticipated." Other reasons may include over-involvement in student activities or family/home-based problems. In other words, many of the failures we do observe seem to stem from how students attempt to manage time and resources relative to the goals they have.

One response to this problem by the comprehensive program is to assist students to make the transition to college with certain *Academic Socialization* programs. These may consist of seminars, workshops, group counseling activities, or mentoring programs. The intent is to familiarize students with the expectations and requirements of successful college progress. Although such knowledge may be presumed of college students, in reality, it is often lacking, as many of the students we are apt to serve are either first-generation college students or have attended inner-city high schools full of distractions which they have come to accept as normal. For example, metal detectors, hall sweeps and detentions, noise and general disruptive behavior are not uncommon in many urban schools. As Plato's *Allegory of the Cave* suggests, what one is accustomed to seeing, understandably becomes what one thinks of as customary. Student's individual histories follow them to college, but such histories may provide a vision that is not consistent with what college is actually like. The academic socialization effort seeks to acquaint students with realistic views about expectations and requirements, as well as responsibilities and conduct in college.

Higher education has long encouraged diversity in the student body (Rudenstine, 1996), including geographic, religious, cultural, language, economic, gender and racial diversity. Even so, it has only been during the last 30 years or so that the student bodies of our colleges and universities have begun truly to reflect the vast diversity of the nation and such recognition has manifested itself by nothing short of a remarkable increase in the numbers of women and racial and economic groups on campus. In fact, there has been a confluence of the racial and economic group contributions to diversity as the substantial numbers of minorities who have entered college have come from economic strata historically excluded from higher education. This enormous progress in providing access to higher education was no accident; rather, it was the result of political activism epitomized by the civil rights era, by a maturing of the American psyche and a recognition that national productivity requires that all segments of the population be well-educated, by broader recognition of the global community in which we live and the implication that we share ultimately but a single resource. Perhaps, most importantly, the change was brought about by a commitment from higher education communities to promote social welfare more actively rather than merely as a byproduct of the intellectual enlightenment deemed to result from college attendance. In promoting this commitment, Lyndon Johnson in speech concerning the "war on poverty" argued: You do not take a man who has been hobbled his entire life by ball and chain, and then suddenly remove the chain, and bring that man to the starting line of a race and say 'compete' and expect that you have been completely fair (Commencement Address, Howard University, 1965).

Thus, providing opportunity also meant providing support so that those hobbled by impoverishment, racial discrimination, and the expectation of failure could be helped to compete. The federal government initiated Upward Bound Programs in 1964 to encourage and assist promising disadvantaged and minority high school students to pursue higher education. Prior to such innovative expansion of educational opportunity, the higher education pipeline had functioned historically as if filters had been placed strategically to lessen the flow of certain types of students. The progress of the last thirty years has been analogous to fitting the pipeline with a pump, rather than a filter, to help move students through. This pump is represented in large part by the college level developmental programs offered around the country to assist students in the development of academic skills, effective study habits, and appropriate strategies for succeeding in college. Interestingly, the big push to offer developmental programs began after World War II with the GI Bill and services designed to assist returning veterans to adjust to the demands of college (Levine, 1993). Counseling and study skills services designed for veterans were expanded and modified as the next wave of "new students" entered college during the 1960s. By 1970, over 1,400 college "learning centers" were in existence with the general task of helping students to develop effective learning strategies and insights needed for success (Sullivan, 1978). These developmental programs shared a commitment to helping students learn and achieve, and did so through summer programs, supplemental instruction programs, tutorial programs, and other special courses targeted specifically to meet the developmental needs of students who might otherwise be denied access to college. The nature and focus of such programs, of course, vary and exemplary models are described in this chapter, of which the comprehensive model is but one.

The basic theory behind developmental programs at the college level is that students who are motivated can be helped to develop the kinds of skills necessary for academic success even though they are not as well-prepared for college success as many others. It means that such students have potential, but for a variety of reasons do not have the kind of competitive credentials that others may bring to college and so they are likely to have an initial uphill battle before they will actually go on to achieve success. Generally, it means they will need to be helped early on in their college careers to develop academically and personally so as to perform and to persist in the competitive college environment. It means that such students must learn of college professor's high standards and expectations even as they raise their own expectations of the caliber of work they must produce to fulfill course requirements. It means that developmental students must develop a realistic appreciation for the quality of work that is done by other students. It is easy, but misguided for developmental learners to dismiss capable students as "nerds" or "brainiacs;" nor should developmental students belittle their own abilities, rather they must develop a personal sense of self-efficacy that says they know what to do and how to do it in order to succeed. These are some of the ancillary notions promoted by the comprehensive model. Together with sound academic advising, intensive instruction, and peer support, this variety of approaches serves to promote effective socialization to the academic community. The outcomes of the comprehensive model speak for themselves. Standardized test scores do not predict success for developmental students. Indeed, although students in our comprehensive program enter a highly competitive university community with standardized test scores that are two hundred points below the norm, they nonetheless achieve impressive levels of academic success. In addition to grade-point averages as a measure of success, comprehensive program students have a graduation rate of about 76 percent while the national average for all students is about 50 percent (Adelman, 1995).

The Comprehensive Model provides a variety of specific services and activities that support the cognitive development of developmental learners, and, in addition, the comprehensive model supports students in the affective domain. The program provides a system in which faculty and advisors combine their efforts in a single office; the classes, in particular, provide a means for students to express viewpoints and strategies that are validated by faculty and peers even as these ideas may be refocused to promote student academic development and progress. The frequent communication between faculty and advisors allows quicker response to potential problems and more effective control of the advising functions. Finally, the comprehensive program, with its proven track record of success, provides students with the sense of belonging that helps them to feel a part of the larger institution.

Chapter 6

ഇൗരു

A Counseling Model for Developmental Learners: A Comprehensive Approach

Martha Maxwell

Counseling has been a service offered by programs for low achieving students ever since professional college counselors began to take over student counseling from faculty in the 1930s. That counseling benefits students is amply documented by Rayman and Garis (1989) who concluded "...freshmen who use counseling services are more likely to succeed in college than those who do not" (p. 129).

Counseling freshmen developmental students is very important because many enter college with a crippling load of emotional baggage. They bring with them problems from many different sources for they are not just underprepared in skills and coursework, but they are academically at-risk for many other reasons as well. They may be working full-time with family responsibilities, or have minimal support from key family members, or may expect to fail college courses no matter what they do or have other personal difficulties that limit their success. Some are recovering from alcoholism or drug use or mental illness. As Roueche and Roueche (1993) explained, "Today's (open-admission) students are at risk in a number of ways that complicate and make obsolete the old definition of college students" (p. 1).

Today's developmental students differ from those we considered underprepared in the 50s and 60s in that their difficulties are greater. Often, they don't know that they don't know and they don't understand what college professors expect. They need comprehensive services including effective counseling, advising, and mentoring as well as academic skills development and courses that will increase their background knowledge if they are to survive in college.

Students who were previously unsuccessful in school tend to reject the teaching methods, materials and strategies that were used to teach them in elementary and high school; they need to be treated like the adults they are and taught with different approaches and materials. Most need counseling to help undo the lingering effects of the negative attitudes, emotions, and fears they experienced in their earlier schooling. Returning adults often need counseling to help them readjust to playing the role of student again.

In this chapter I will discuss how counseling can help in developmental programs and the different roles counselors play as team members in a successful program for underprepared students, as well as the strategies that can be used to help at-risk students survive and succeed in college. In addition, typical kinds of student problems and the psychodynamics of failure will be described and examples of successful programs presented.

Counselors must be an integral part of the developmental program team. They can not remain 'stand-alone' professionals who work with students behind closed office doors. The role of the counselor in a developmental education program is different from that of the traditional college counselor who meets and talks with students in an office in a counseling center. To be sure, counselors in a developmental education program may still counsel individuals and groups but their main duty is to provide outreach activities with students and staff and reduce the perceived formality and distance of counseling by making it more accessible to students. In other words, their job is not restricted to crisis intervention, but rather they function to prevent crises from occurring. To this end they also have the responsibility of convincing both students and staff of the uses and benefits of counseling and how to create a supportive environment for students.

Counselors must be included in program planning, attend regular staff meetings with instructional staff and participate in the program evaluation. The counselor's position must be integrated with those of program faculty, and staff including tutors. The counselor should participate in training receptionists and paraprofessionals such as tutors who interact with students. They should select, train, and supervise mentors and provide assistance to the instructional staff in understanding and coping with students' learning difficulties.

Figure 1. A Comprehensive Model for Developmental Learners

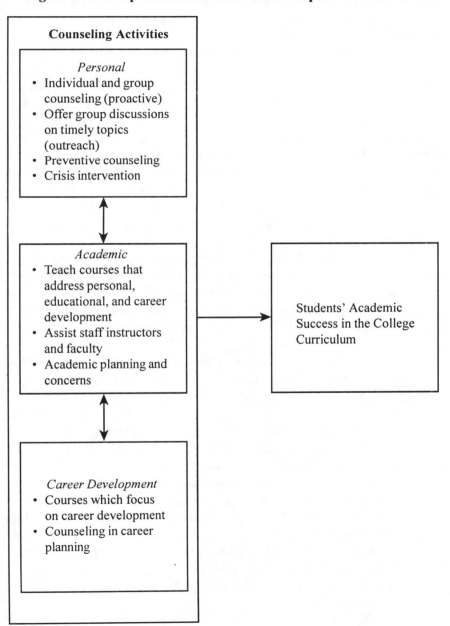

In other words, counseling services that enhance student success must proactively meet the needs of students in three areas: personal, academic and career development (Rayman & Garis, 1989). A comprehensive mode is shown in Figure 1. This means that the counselors must have as their primary goal planned programmatic counseling rather than waiting until problems occur to help students.

By a proactive counseling model emphasizing outreach programs, we mean that intervention programs can be initiated before problems become crises. In other words, counselors should not wait until students are desperate. As Rayman and Garis (1989) stated, " We know what the presenting problems (for freshmen) were in the past and what they are now, and what they are likely to be in the future" (p.139). It is also important that counselors stress short-term, approaches and address a wide array of outreach programs. They should offer groups on timely topics, teach courses with credit that address personal, educational, and career development concerns and serve staff, instructors and faculty. Although there may be times when counselors are called upon to provide crisis intervention service as well as individual help, their main function should be preventative.

In order to offer appropriate groups and services, it is assumed that counselors keep up with changing student problems through regular surveys, interview studies, etc. For example, they might offer groups on test taking skills and include information on how to overcome common difficulties in taking computer administered exams timed appropriately during the semester.

Counselors must be confident enough in their beliefs about counseling to deliver what they know students need in the way of assistance and deliver it before students ask. Also, counselors must be more directive in working with underprepared students than with students who have previously been successful in their pre-college schooling (Rayman & Garis , 1989).

Among the individual and group services that counselors should offer are academic planning and concerns, career planning, and social/personal issues. In addition to teaching credit courses, they can offer mini courses on time management, improving interpersonal relationships, study skills and personal issues like exam panic or homesickness. For example, counselors at a southern university located in the mountains that recruited many students from a large coastal city offered a popular counseling group for freshmen called "I hate this place." Counselors can offer computer assisted assessment and guidance to support freshmen development and provide handouts and other aids on these areas.

Outreach services should include on-line Internet information services. For example, Paul Treuer has developed a course called Introduction to College Learning at the University of Minnesota Duluth with an on-line textbook, *The Student Handbook* (http://www.d.umn.edu/student). Among other applications, students use the web-based assessment tools in the Student Handbook for self-diagnosis and, if necessary, referral to campus resources. *The Student Handbook* (an on-line program) has a wide range of modules grouped into three competency areas: academic, personal/social, and career. Within academic, for example, students can work on basic skills, academic planning, study skills, research, problem-solving, communication skills, computer literacy, leadership, and knowledge in major field of study. Likewise, the text has subheadings, with web text or links, to personal/social and career issues and describes the persons and their location on campus who provide assistance in these areas. On a large campus where services are dispersed, having a well designed Web page for new students can be a very important student service.

Also when necessary, counselors must make direct referrals to the psychiatric service, health services or other support services. They should cooperate with residential life and peer-counseling or peer-mentoring programs. The latter can be particularly effective with low achievers, particularly if those chosen to be peer mentors started college as developmental students and are now successful upperclassmen. Appointing students to these positions is also a good way to recognize and reward former developmental students. Personal and career development courses offered by counselors are particularly effective when offered during the second term of the freshman year (Rayman & Garis, 1989).

Helping Faculty Understand Student Motivational and Behavioral Problems

Counselors can serve another important role by helping faculty understand and deal with student motivational problems. For example, a developmental skills instructor wrote, "The hardest things for me to adjust to is students' passivity in class and resistance to homework. My students are for the most part wonderful, smart people. But they don't value knowledge intrinsically. They also seem to view reading as very boring. I guess it is when compared to video games and action movies." (L. Lane, personal communication, March 25, 1997).

Furthermore, faculty in other disciplines face the same problems and complain of "students who behave with passiveness and caginess and don't want to be engaged in learning; who are reluctant to pursue self-help strategies despite strong encouragement to do so and don't take their instructor's advice" (Petit & White, 1996, p. 2). Explaining that some students become abrasive, unruly, and disrupt the learning process if it threatens to reveal their deficiencies, Petit and White (1996) quoted a professor as saying "They don't come to class or they drop out or try to bribe the instructor. Guys want to become your closest friend and ally—young ladies think they can impress you with as much of their body as they can get away with" (Petit & White, 1996, p. 8).

A statistics instructor wrote, "With my community college students there is also a motivational problem: Increasingly, I cannot get students to do the homework, let alone a group project outside of class. They simply refuse, and seem willing to take the C rather than the A they could get if they really worked. Or they just do not believe that they will get only a C until it is too late. Many students act like they are still in high school. I think they get the message that reading is not important and that encourages them to do the minimum they can get away with" (Annette Georgey, personal communication, March 16, 1996).

Because developmental students direct more behavior at the teacher, teaching becomes more stressful. "Students are quick to blame and intimidate faculty which creates an adversarial student teacher relationship" (Petit & White, 1996, p. 9). Faculty members in open-admissions institutions face the dilemma of maintaining academic standards while, at the same time, challenging very underprepared students to meet them . As one faculty member stated, "They compare you with other teachers and give you poor evaluations," leading Petit and White (p. 8) to conclude that the mismatch between faculty and student expectations has left both parties unfulfilled. As a result of this clash in values, faculty tend to offer more depth and less breadth in their courses and add remedial content, inflate grades and struggle with the question of whether to pass students who don't know.

Since low achievers place a lot of stress on instructors and are more likely to blame their teachers for their failures and act out in class, faculty can profit from counselors' input and support on how to deal with classroom behavior problems. Counselors can also assist faculty in establishing clear policies on handling psychological crises including behavioral problems in the classroom, and how to communicate these policies to other faculty, instructional staff, and students.

Mentoring

In my opinion, mentoring is the most important part of a comprehensive program for low achieving students and counselors play a vital role in selecting, training, and supporting mentors. Mentoring can be defined as a "one to one relationship between an older person and a younger person that is based on modeling behavior and extended dialogue between them" (Lester & Johnson, 1981, p. 50). Although mentoring has both formal and informal aspects, it is the informal aspects that are the most powerful. Astin (1993) pointed out that interaction with faculty and staff is a crucial factor in getting students involved with college and Noel, Levitz and Saluri (1985) considered mentoring as an invaluable way of improving student retention.

Mentors play many roles—as an information source, or one who listens to problems, or as an academic advisor, social or activities advisor and problem solver. Studies have shown that mentoring is particularly helpful to students who have not decided on a major, minority students and freshmen women. Women are now the majority of students attending college and are more willing to seek counseling help than men. Women of color who often face isolation, exclusion and attitudinal barriers in higher education may gain in self-affirmation and remain on campus longer if they are mentored. Studies have also shown that students who are mentored increase their confidence in seeking goals, making decisions, solving problems and, in general, developing a more positive attitude toward the overall institutional environment (Johnson, 1989, p. 122). Fleming (1984) reported that mentoring was a critical factor in the success of Black students on both Black campuses and predominantly white campuses , that the importance of having "one caring person" to student success applied to Black students too, and that the race of the mentor was not an issue (Fleming as quoted in Johnson, 1989, p. 121).

Usually, faculty members, counselors, and academic advisors are recommended as mentors, but upper-classman, graduate students, even other campus staff like the head of the campus police can serve in a mentoring capacity and be accepted by students. Certainly, the pool of mentors should reflect the diversity of the student body—in gender, racial and ethnic diversity and should be comprised of persons willing to undertake training and spend the time necessary with individual students: persons who have the ability and the desire to establish rapport with students and are sensitive to student differences. Experts in student mentoring emphasize that mentors should undergo comprehensive training programs with periodic retraining as essential components of the program. The training should be structured and include skill development, program philosophy and knowledge of the campus support services (Johnson, 1989). Mentors also need training both in how to develop relationships as well as how to end them.

"The key to mentoring is caring. Many freshmen need someone who cares and can help them through the academic maze and the confusing process of becoming mature and achieving academic success. Mentoring is one important and caring solution to enhancing freshman success" (Johnson, 1989, p. 128). In successful programs for underprepared students, students see a mentor one hour a week at a minimum, and counselors are responsible for organizing and supervising the mentoring program. Mentors should follow students very closely and contact them if they fail to keep appointments. If your program has a large number of students, you will need many mentors and a very well organized and highly structured mentoring system. Mentors can encourage reluctant students who won't otherwise volunteer for help, to use the various support services you offer and ensure that they follow through. Remember, you may have excellent skills courses, tutoring support and other services, but if you do not have a mentoring system to support individual students and insure they use the services they need, many of your students will fall through the cracks.

Who Are the Developmental Students?

If you were to visit a typical developmental skills class, you would be surprised at the diversity you would encounter for developmental students range widely in age, ethnic background, physical ability and in many other ways. Some are adults returning to school after many years—insecure and with rusty skills. Others are high school dropouts, while some planned to enter technical fields after high school, but now want college. They may be certified as learning disabled or victims of poor schools that never challenged them or international students or refugees who acquired their previous schooling in a language other than English. Some are disadvantaged minorities from ghetto high schools; a few are graduates of expensive prep schools. Some were ignored by their teachers—those whom no one bothered to encourage to consider going to college (Hardin 1988). Many are convinced that they can't learn certain subjects like writing or math. Some have handicaps in vision, or hearing or emotional problems which interfere with learning and others have more subtle handicap such as learning disabilities or attention deficit disorders that limited their ability to learn in the past but were not detected before college.

Another group of developmental learners have been called *The Users*—students who lack clear cut academic goals and use the educational system for their own purposes (Hardin, 1988). Their main reason for being in college is to receive financial aid and other benefits and they aspire to get the minimum grades that will enable them to continue in school. So they apply little effort to studying. Obviously they need more than academic assistance: they need counseling and other support services, but are unlikely to seek them out. Interestingly, if these system-abusers can become excited about the prospect of learning, they can become excellent students, but they are among the most difficult to teach (Hardin, 1988).

Large Numbers of Developmental Students Increase the Need for Services

During the 1992-93 academic year, about 1.6 million students—13 percent of all undergraduates-reported taking at least one remedial (or developmental) course while a U. S. Office of Education (Black Mansfield & Farris, 1991) study showed that 29 percent of 1990 entering freshmen took developmental courses.

Although many people associate college developmental education with minority students, most developmental students are white (American Council on Education, 1996; Boylan, Bonham & Bliss, 1993). Nearly two-thirds (65 percent) of the individuals who took these courses were white; however, students of color enrolled in developmental classes at higher rates comprising more than one-third (35 percent) of those who took remedial courses in 1992-93, but less than one-quarter (23 percent) of those who did not. Data show that students in need of remediation were more likely to be from low-income families, were born outside of the United States, and speak a language other than English at home. Twenty-nine percent of today's freshmen take developmental courses and low socioeconomic status is a better predictor of who needs developmental courses than is race (American Council on Education, 1996).

First Generation College Students

Developmental students often are the first generation of their family to attend college. Having left behind families and friends who did not attend college and do not understand its customs, they face even greater problems than their peers in adjusting to college. Most parents worry about how the college experience will change their child, but they usually know and accept the value of a college education and are supportive. However, parents of first generation students have even stronger fears about what college will do to their sons and daughters. These new freshmen may not only lack support from their relatives but encounter family objections, contempt and ridicule. Single mothers hoping to prepare themselves for a better job may be bitterly attacked by their mothers for "abandoning their babies" for college; Latino women who want to attend college may be blocked from higher education by their fathers and husbands for going against their customs, and regardless of ethnic background, any 18 year old woman maybe criticized by her relatives for not being married . The families and friends of young men from some groups who go to college see them as traitors to their family and friends and urge them to grow up, quit school and get a real job.

Thus, first-generation college students may be accused of leaving their culture, abandoning family values and becoming a threat or a stranger to their families and friends. Steven Brookfield (1990) called this "culture suicide"—the situation where students lose their former support network as a result of the changes they undergo while attending college. Since they face conflicts between family values and college, counseling can aid them and may be necessary in resolving these difficulties.

Common Skills Problems

Despite their differences, these students has one thing in common— they are weak in the basic reading, writing, and/or mathematics skills that are so essential to succeeding in college, and are weak in background knowledge of most school subjects as well. Since they have poor skills, they may not be able to read college text books nor write the required essays and papers nor understand how to work the mathematics problems. And because they did not develop these skills in the past, they also lack the concepts and information that their peers, who have been reading and writing avidly for years, have mastered.

How do developmental students differ from regular students? Research suggests that the answer is that they differ in the intensity of their weaknesses in basic skills and often have debilitating attitudinal problems. Because they have been made painfully aware of their weaknesses, they may suffer from low esteem and other affective difficulties. Although they share many of the same difficulties that their better prepared peers have, they are behind and need to catch up and may need to develop motivation to improve.

Although most have been low achievers and had negative school experiences, which will make it very difficult to succeed in college, they may not be ready for nor see the need for change. They may insist on responding to college demands with the same unsuccessful techniques that exacerbated their failure in earlier years. In other words, they need to be reprogrammed for academic success.

Their responses to their difficulties differ too. Some are angry, aggressive, others are passive rote-learners, or acting out their frustrations or they may choose to reject help. If referred by an instructor, they somehow manage to get lost between the instructor's office and the counseling service. Most aren't intrinsically motivated toward school work, and some external motivators work, some don't. For example, grades mean little, but credit (by implication getting through college rapidly) is often a more effective motivator.

For many developmental students, but not all, being successful in school has eluded them. Thus, they share many traits with college students who find themselves on academic probation.

Dealing with the Effects of Failure

Students who are failing come in for counseling reluctantly, if at all, when sent by advisers, and if they come, they tend to be in a state of deep depression or denial. Therefore, poor achievers are not the college counselor's favorite clients, and the research on the efficacy of counseling in improving the academic achievement of failing students reveals a dismal picture. Barbara Kirk described the counselor's quandary in a book on underachievement written in 1965 as follows:

> Universally in these cases (students on academic probation), the counselor reports that it was a matter of extreme difficulty to obtain any direct discussion of the problem with the counselee, however obvious and apparent the problem, and however voluntarily the counselee had sought counseling. Moreover, the recurrent report is that it was extremely difficult to obtain a description or discussion of any of the counselee's feelings, or even, in many cases, situations or vicissitudes which might be expected to occasion strong counselee reactions. (Kirk, 1965 as quoted in Maxwell, 1997, p. 150)

She added that the clients show no surprise when they learn they have done extremely well on ability tests and that their excuses for their poor grades are "unrealistic, superficial, and largely implausible." The counselor must work very hard with these students, and the prognosis is poor (Kirk as quoted in Maxwell, 1997, p. 150).

If students on academic probation who voluntarily come in for counseling pose problems , what about the probationary students who don't follow through when help is recommended? Sharon Silverman and Anne M. Juhasz (1993) investigated this question that has baffled counselors for ages—why students who are on academic probation reject help. Asking what factors contribute to the lack of responsiveness to offers of help to students on probation, they interviewed students, who after being notified that they were placed on probation and offered help, failed to respond after three contacts. They found that help rejectors demonstrated unresolved conflict in the area of trust versus mistrust and were skeptical about offers of help, had strong feelings of autonomy and felt incapable of independent action.

The help rejector was characterized by lack of friends, companions, and family support, as having low self-confidence and feeling that they are unworthy they present a personality profile predominated by the need for safety, love/belonging, and esteem. None of the students studied had shared their academic probation status with their family or close friends—in other words, their failure was the best kept secret of all and probably the most devastating for the them since it interfered with their social and personal relationships and limited their opportunity for satisfactory experiences with those who might be supportive.

This study suggested that successful programs have to meet the help-rejectors unmet needs of love and belonging and unresolved conflicts and these students need to be informed in a very personalized way not just by having the dean send them letters. These characteristics of students who fail in college add impetus to the need for preventative counseling.

Returning adults who are enrolled in developmental courses usually are more highly motivated and more willing to follow professors' advice and instruction although they may be quite naive about effective study techniques and lack skills. On the darker side of the picture are the underprepared teenagers fresh out of high school whose teachers face a different set of problems—students who don't know that they don't know and refuse to take responsibility for their own learning. Typically, these are students who have graduated with good grades from academically weak high schools although many students who just barely passed express the same over-confidence and engage in similar behavior patterns. Some come from inner city high schools; others from rural schools that send few students to college, and some even come from undemanding private schools where they have not had to study.

These students who are unaware of their deficiencies are the most difficult to teach. Some are confident that they will do well in college and that it will be the same as high school where no matter how little effort they put in to studying, they were passed. They have unrealistic aspirations and rarely heed advice from faculty or anyone else—it's almost as if they have to fail before they are willing to listen.

As Sue Hashway, a developmental mathematics teacher at Grambling State University (LA), described them, "I teach at an open-admissions institution. I have many students who never had the appropriate high school background in math to prepare them for college. Some have never had Algebra while others completed their math requirements for graduation in the ninth grade and have a three or four year lapse in which they have taken no math. The poorer the student's attitude toward math, the greater the possibility of a long lapse.... With these teen-aged students, college seems to be high school with more opportunities to socialize. Others have extremely unrealistic views of their strength and weaknesses" (S. Hashway, personal communication, June 15, 1995). You may have to extend yourself further with high risk students until they learn the ropes and begin to understand the college culture.

If these students are admitted to an open—admissions college without a strong, well-coordinated program, it intensifies the problems for faculty. As Petit and White (1996) pointed out: "When an institution treats large numbers of underprepared students as if they require no special resources, it places a heavy burden on faculty and puts them in an uncomfortable, compromising position. So many of these kids require what amounts to academic reconstructive surgery....Overcrowded classes leave (faculty) with no choice but to water down the content of their courses" (Petit & White, 1996, pp. 9-10).

Misperceptions about College Success

Many are convinced that they can not learn in school. School success is just not part of their universe. So one of our hardest jobs is convincing our students that they can learn if they only put in the effort. Weak students often believe that school work comes easily to bright, successful students who never have to study. There's a trick to it, they think, and if they could only master it, they'd be brilliant—so they fall for advertisements about speed reading. I've known students who tried to speed read their calculus texts and when it did not work, they tried other equally inane quick tricks that also failed.

The excuses students give for their poor performance also give us clues about their problems. For example, some students have an external locus of control (i.e., students who do poorly blame the test, or the teacher or say they can't do this because they aren't bright enough—compared with successful students who blame themselves if they don't do well and say things like "I should have worked harder" (Rotter, 1966, p. 3). Today we are more concerned with what Bandura (1982) called "self-efficacy"—the degree to which a student is confident that s/he can learn.

Recent studies shed light on this phenomenon. In the 60s and 70s, college administrators assumed that if their colleges admitted high risk students, they should be given the best teachers in order to help them succeed. Research shows that is not so—even with outstanding instructors, high risk students still failed. What made the difference was whether the student felt that he or she was capable of learning the subject—not how skilled the lecturer was. In one study, high risk students in a psychology class were given "attributional retraining"—that is, an experimental attempt to change their "locus of control"—to convince them that they could learn the subject. Attributional retraining works like this. First, the class is shown a film in which the professor describes a situation when he faced failing in college and wanted to give up but a friend talked him out of quitting and encouraged him to keep trying. He succeeded and went on to graduate, etc. Next, students were given items from an intelligence test and instruction on how to work the problems—and shown that, with practice, they could succeed. They were given feedback on each item so that they quickly learned how to do it. As a result of the attributional retraining, the researchers found that high risk students scored better on quizzes after lectures (so they probably listened more), did more homework in the course, and made higher grades than they had previously (Perry & Penner, 1990).

What does this suggest about how to motivate high-risk students? Note, there are two principles here—first, describing a situation in which you had difficulty in learning and how you solved it. e.g., my taking an economics exam after being out of college for four years and spending the whole hour on one question. Second, breaking each task down into small parts and making sure that students learn bit by bit and giving them feedback as to whether they're right or wrong also helps change their attitudes from doubt to assurance. In other words, give them frequent feedback. The principle is that students need to know that learning takes time and work but that with effort you can get there. But telling them this isn't enough. You have to show them!

Some know they don't know (they're willing to try to learn); others don't know that they don't know—they have to be helped to discover what to learn and why. Others think they know and don't. (An example of the latter is the tragedy of U.S. students' math scores in international comparisons. Although U.S. students score lower than students in any other developed nation and even lower than some underdeveloped ones, studies show that U.S. students think they're good at math!)

Control Theory

One of the universal problems of the college freshman—that we emphasize with freshmen is time management—a major problem for college freshmen everywhere. Recent research on the effective use of time has turned up some interesting results. First, time management is a more complex task than we used to think and is probably comprised of several factors. The most important of which is whether students feel they're in control of their own time, not just whether they keep schedules, set priorities, and do the right things. For example, women score higher on time management scales,—i.e. they know the right things to do, but they are lower on the crucial factor of feeling that they're in control of their own time. It's as if women instinctively expect to be interrupted, or are waiting to be interrupted.

Another study that looked at freshmen time management attitudes and compared these with cumulative GPAs at the end of the senior year, found that students who were good long range planners don't do as well in completing college as those who were good at short-range planning. This is sort of counter-intuitive result since colleges are always pushing freshmen to decide on their majors, think about what they want to do with their lives, etc. What it seems to mean is that students who have rigid long range goals and have the steps they must take to meet them firmly in mind, may have trouble making the day to day adjustments that college often requires and the student who is a short-range planner is more flexible and can adjust to the many frustrations involved—professors who change their minds about tests, schedules, etc.

Studies of developmental students consistently show that programs where teachers are concerned with students' attitudes and emotions about their school work are more successful than those where the teacher concentrates only on teaching the subject. So developmental students may be different than the college students who can survive despite large lectures, indifferent instructors and impersonal settings. However, many of the strategies that work well with developmental students work equally well with average or high achieving students. For example, courses where they get instant feedback. But the reverse is not true. Developmental students, at least initially, don't do well in the traditional lecture/discussion courses that better prepared students can pass.

Some of the recent research results support our traditional study skills teaching strategies, others seems counter-intuitive to ideas we have long accepted. For example, the finding that students who are good at short-range planning are more successful than those who prefer long range planning suggests that we'd better examine our assumptions and perhaps conduct more research to examine this question so that we can plan more effective intervention strategies. Affective factors such as locus of control, self-esteem, and self-efficacy appear to be vital factors in how well students learn. Even in something as apparently simple as time management, the key seems to be whether the student feels able to control her own time, not her activities nor the logs nor the schedules she keeps nor the priorities she sets. Certainly these studies can give us clues about how to work with the students who manage to fail despite our best efforts. Whether we are teaching courses or counseling students on skills, it is clear that it's not what we teach, but the way that we teach it and even more the way students feel about their ability to learn it that determines whether and how much they will learn.

Test Anxiety

Students seem to have few qualms about discussing their test anxiety. If a program to alleviate test anxiety is advertised, students will volunteer, and they frequently come in to discuss their test fears with instructors, counselors, skills specialists, friends, or anyone who will listen. Instructors can identify exam-panic victims easily, even in large classes, for they turn in blank bluebooks on exams.

Psychologists now generally support the idea that there are at least two kinds of anxiety—facilitating anxiety and debilitating anxiety-based on the hypothesis that anxiety is debilitating only to students who have learned a habitual class of interfering responses. Without these interfering responses, the authors believe, test anxiety leads to task-relevant responses and good performance. For example, some students agree with the test item: "Anxiety helps me do a better job on an exam."

Exam anxiety can camouflage other problems, and academically weak students are just as susceptible to it as those with strong skills. In diagnosis, it is important to determine whether the student's anxiety is due to lack of study skills or basic reading inabilities or is a learned way of responding to evaluative situations or a condition precipitated by poor instruction. In my experience, the most pernicious cases of exam panic occur in students whose anxiety masks a deficiency in reading for inference, a deficiency in logical thinking, or a refusal to read material carefully. Controlled, intensive practice on the skills these students have avoided is necessary, for neither deep relaxation, desensitization, intensive therapy, nor tranquilizers will result in improved performance, though these treatments may reduce the anxiety felt about tests.

Ideally, testing should be a positive learning experience, one in which students recognize their goals, are assured of their knowledge, and feel competent. However, students rarely feel satisfied after taking final examinations or standardized tests. In fact, exams are dreaded and feared or, at best, tolerated as an inevitable part of a college education.

Many of us as students, however, have had the experience of suffering a bout of amnesia in the middle of an examination. This is a most frustrating experience indeed, especially when an hour or two after we turn in our bluebooks, the ideas we were struggling so hard to recall pop back into our heads.

Always endemic among college students, exam panic currently seems to be reaching epidemic proportions, judging from the number of programs offered by counseling and learning centers. It is therefore essential that anyone who works with college students be aware of its dynamics.

First, it is important to realize that many students are genuinely afraid of failing. In fact, they are paralyzed by anticipated failure. Not just underprepared college students who have failed in the past, but also those who have excelled in school fear failure. Of course, our school system encourages this fear from the first grade on by reinforcing the idea that to be a worthwhile person, one must succeed in school. Unconsciously or consciously accepting society's values, equating one's worth with being bright and getting A's sets the stage for continued frustrations as one ascends the educational ladder.

If students feel that grades reflect their self-worth and attach great significance to them—that is, equate failure with letting down family, friends, former teachers, or other significant persons—they will be susceptible to exam panic. Individuals handle this tendency in different ways. Some become superstrivers and fiercely compete, others suffer deepest despair, and some avoid situations in which they will be tested. Sometimes fear of failure is genuine, as in a student who has not prepared for the exam; sometimes it represents an overreaction, or what might be termed a neurotic anxiety. Students with this type of apprehensiveness will undoubtedly be anxious about reading, homework, exams-anything that they feel represents a threat. Treating severe cases of text anxiety can be very difficult and take a very long time.

Study Avoidance

Some college students refuse to put their full efforts into studying. Not studying gives them an excuse if they fail; if they had invested time and effort in studying, then failing would confirm that they were not really very bright. They protect themselves from this exigency by procrastinating, studying too little and too late, developing myriad excuses for failing, or, if despite all, they do pass, dismissing responsibility for their grade by saying that the test was easy.

The Test Anxious Student

Research findings on test anxiety suggests that highly anxious test takers divide their attention between themselves (their own internal cues) and the task; they spend time doing things that are not related to the test. For example, they worry about how well they are doing, reread the same questions, ruminate over choices, notice where others are on the test, and observe that their peers are finishing faster. These superfluous activities guarantee poor performance on tests that require one's full attention

Studies also suggest that test anxiety can be either facilitating or debilitating. It is facilitating when it results in students' paying close attention to the test, but debilitating when students engaged in responses that interfere with the task.

Treatment Methods. If your diagnostic attempts have eliminated inadequate study skills and poor reading as possible causes of exam panic, and you find that the student can perform adequately in the subject as long as tests are not involved, you may wish to consider using relaxation therapies.

In addition to providing a strong study skills and test-taking skills program, you can work with professors in improving examinations, and encourage them to experiment with anxiety-reducing ways of administering tests. For example, administering exams on the computer where the student responds by indicating the letter of his/her answer on the keyboard and also his/her degree of certainty. If the student misses the item, s/he receives additional information about the concept on a projector, and gets a chance to try another question on the same material. This enables students to take the test whenever they feel ready and saves the professor valuable class time that would otherwise be spent giving the exam. Besides, the students receive their test results immediately after the test. Another stress reducing technique is to train peer counselors to administer test-anxiety scales and help students use self-administered relaxation tapes.

Reversing the Expectation of Failing

On the other side of the exam panic coin is the student who expects to fail and apparently is unwilling to do anything to change that expectation. For a long time educators believed that if marginal, at-risk students were exposed to the best teaching a college has to offer, they would do well. But experiments on control theory shows that this does not happen, for unless students feel that they have some control and can influence their environment, their capacity to learn from good instruction is limited. Students feel they lack control if they believe they cannot learn the subject or if there are unannounced tests, poorly organized lectures, unclear assignments, and other situations that they find difficult. However, research suggests that giving students with low perceived control feedback on individual aptitude items before a lecture temporarily altered their perceptions of control and improved their performance (Perry & Penner, 1990; Whimbey & Whimbey, 1975).

Perry and Penner studied the effects of attributional retraining, a therapeutic method for reinstating psychological control, which involved showing the class an 8-minute videotape of the professor recounting an instance when he was in college and despite repeated failure persisted because a friend urged him to and went on to complete his studies through graduate school. He encouraged students to attribute poor performance to lack of effort and good performance to ability and proper effort. Also the students were given a chance to improve aptitude scores with feedback. As a result of these brief interventions, students with external locus of control (i.e., those who place the blame for their failures on outside factors such as bad teaching or a poor exam) improved their performance on the test following a lecture, a test a week later, and on their homework performance.

These studies give us clues about how to work with students who manage to fail despite our best efforts. Whether we are teaching courses or counseling students on skills, it is clear that it's not what we teach, but the way that we teach it and the way students feel about their ability to learn it that makes the difference in whether they learn.

Descriptions of Successful Programs

Most at-risk students have been previously identified by college entrance or placement tests and/or previous grades in high school, but many in open-admissions colleges have not. Some programs try to identify at-risk students as early as ninth grade; others wait until they walk in the college door. Whatever the case, new, at-risk students need a thorough orientation program at entrance and mentoring and/or an orientation course as well as counseling, advising and skills courses during their first term. It is also important that students be given credit and permitted to take one carefully selected regular academic course.

Although we've long known how to run successful programs for underprepared students—indeed, some Black Colleges have been doing it well for generations—it takes careful selection, counseling services that students will accept, intensive mentoring, as well as academic skills and content in a highly structured program

Donovan (1976) described his successful program in "Alternatives to the Revolving Door" as an intensive care unit where students are not given choices but are provided with an atmosphere best described as "tough love." Roueche and Snow (1977) encouraged developmental educators to use an interdisciplinary program curriculum managed by a team of instructors, counselors, and administrations. In this system, the students can progress step-by-step through a well planned program in which each member of the team contributes unique skills, creating a learning environment for professionals as well as students. Without exception, the one variable that separated the successful developmental program from those with moderate success (those with 80-90% persistence and high levels of achievement) was that instructors spent as much time on self-concept development as on teaching basic skills. The excellent developmental educator "understands that the content she is going to develop only makes sense if the students value themselves" (p. 39).

A recent example is the pre-professional program at Xavier College, a small Black college in New Orleans that has led the nation in placing Afro-Americans into medical school since 1993. Virtually all of their students who are admitted to medical schools go on to become doctors. Xavier also graduates a higher proportion of its students. What's their "secret"? They provide a supportive and nurturing environment to first-generation college students who are likely to be unaware of the support facilities and opportunities that their college offers. Finding that many entering students were unprepared for their rigorous science and math courses two decades ago, Xavier set about to change that with summer workshops for high school students, new strategies for teaching mathematics and science, small classes, custom-designed textbooks that contain daily homework assignments, sample problems, reviews of fundamental mathematical concepts and vocabulary. For example, "If doing a science problem requires advanced algebra, the workbook offers them a quick math review"(Fletcher, 1997, p. A-13).

Also, at Xavier students enroll in small classes that are taught by senior professors who give tests frequently. They participate in an extensive tutoring program, and are given writing classes linked with science courses. Students meet with an advisor once a week and are closely monitored on their attendance and course work. They also receive personal , intensive and continuous advisement and counseling about what it takes to get into and succeed in graduate and professional schools and they are tutored on test-taking skills . As one student said, "I was very impressionable in high school...but, from the day I got to Xavier, I was directed. I constantly had someone looking over my shoulder and that helped. To me the entire benefit was the structure of the programs." (Fletcher, 1997, p. A-13). Most of the pressure and structure is characteristic of the first two years, after that courses resemble science courses in other universities.

The underlying factor in Xavier's success may be the commitment and mind-set of the faculty and their belief that their students can succeed. Call it a "desk-side manner" if you will, but it is a rare exception in higher education today where the prevailing philosophy is to bring them in and let them sink or swim—it's their decision!

Summary

Successful programs for high risk students are labor-intensive, time consuming, and require committed staff who can provide a safe, nurturing yet highly structured environment for students to overcome their previous negative experiences with school. Counseling services must be closely integrated into the total program and be proactive, providing preventative services for students, staff and faculty. Counselors should offer a variety of formal and informal individual and group programs for both students and staff including, but not limited to, offering credit courses in personal/social, academic and career planning, informal groups to meet students' special needs, and setting up and supervising mentoring programs.

Developmental students, if left to their own devices rarely use the services provided for them nor will they search out sources of help. Rather, they need counselors and mentors to encourage them to use services and see to it that they use what they need. Successful programs must be coordinated with counseling and be comprehensive, highly structured, and conveniently located so they are accessible to students.

Chapter 7

℘Cℛ

Developmental Academic Advising Model

Thomas J. Grites

Never before in the history of American higher education has the diversity of students attending our institutions been so evident. Ethnic, cultural, racial, and age differences have always existed on our campuses, but the ranges within each of these differences have expanded considerably in the last few decades. International students, economic and educationally disadvantaged students, and older students who are changing careers, upgrading job skills, re-starting interrupted academic pursuits, or simply fulfilling lifelong learning desires now constitute a much larger percentage of our enrollment demographics.

This diversity of students has presented challenges in all aspects of the higher education milieu, including curriculum revision, instructional strategies, scheduling, and most student and academic support services. One of these services, however, stands out among all the aforementioned components as a comprehensive process that encompasses all of them in some way. Academic advising, when viewed in the broadest context and delivered appropriately, is the only process that interfaces with almost every other aspect of the higher education environment, including multi-level administrative units, the faculty, and other student support services (Glennen & Vowell, 1995). Further, it is the only process that engages all students in every term of their enrollment.

With such a pervasive and continuous nature, the academic advising process provides a natural vehicle to recognize the diversity noted above, to identify the characteristic needs of each group, to develop services that will meet these needs, and to facilitate plans of action that will maximize the learning opportunities and potential for each student.

The academic advising process is itself, however, a new one for college students. All students, including those in developmental education programs, are introduced to an academic advising program, and usually to a specific academic advisor, upon entry to the institution. This formal link to the institution, its programs, its resources, and its services is frequently underutilized, however. The model presented below provides a framework for maximum utilization of institutional assets that results in the fullest development of student potential.

Describing the Model

Because of the enormous growth potential for students, and because of the range of growth opportunities provided through this process, the concept of "developmental academic advising" (Winston et al., 1984) has been adopted by many advising programs around the country. The National Academic Advising Association (NACADA) has also endorsed this concept and has outlined a set of developmentally-focused goals for advising programs (Gordon, 1988). These are:

1. Assisting students in self-understanding and self-acceptance (values clarification, understanding abilities, interests, and limitations).

2. Assisting students in their consideration of life goals by relating interests, skills, abilities, and values to careers, the world of work, and the nature and purpose of higher education.

3. Assisting students in developing an educational plan consistent with life goals and objectives (alternative courses of action, alternate career considerations, and selection of courses).

4. Assisting students in developing decision-making skills.

5. Providing accurate information and institutional policies, procedures, resources, and programs.

6. Making referrals to other institutional or community support services.

7. Assisting students in evaluation or reevaluation of progress toward established goals and educational plans.

8. Providing information about students to the institution, colleges, and/ or academic departments (pp. 112-113).

With these goals as a general framework, it seems most appropriate to use the definition by Winston et al.'s (1984) as the operational one for this model. They defined the concept of developmental academic advising as:

> a systematic process based on a close student-advisor relationship intended to aid students in achieving educational, career, and personal goals through the utilization of the full range of institutional and community resources. It both stimulates and supports students in their quest for an enriched quality of life. Developmental advising relationships focus on identifying and accomplishing life goals, acquiring skills and attitudes that promote intellectual and personal growth, and sharing concerns for each other and for the academic community. Developmental academic advising reflects the institution's mission of total student development and is most likely to be realized when the academic affairs and student affairs divisions collaborate in its implementation. (p.19)

The definition parallels that of the National Association of Developmental Education's (NADE) definition and goals of developmental education. Specifically, NADE describes developmental education as "sensitive and responsive to the individual differences and special needs among learners," and articulates the goals of developing "the skills and attitudes necessary for the attainment of academic, career and life goals" (NADE, 1996).

Furthermore, Higbee (1996) described the relevance of Chickering's (1969) seven vectors of college student development for developmental learners. These same vectors served as part of the basis for the definition by Winston et al. (1984).

Another parallel between developmental education and developmental academic advising is evident in Payne and Lyman's (1996) description of the evolution of the former and of Crookston's (1972) introduction of the developmental academic advising term and concept. Payne and Lyman (1996) differentiate developmental education from remediation, while

Crookston (1972) contrasted the traditional, routine, "prescriptive" advising approach with his developmental approach. Both of these sources focus on individual student potential and growth, shared responsibility, mutual respect, and a careful evaluation of outcomes.

Clearly, this concept of developmental academic advising is in concert with the definition of developmental education described throughout this book. It is in concert mostly because it is, first and foremost, a teaching process (Crookston, 1972; Frost, 1991).

Winston et al. (1984) articulated seven essential conditions necessary to achieve the goal of developmental academic advising. A close examination of these principles reveals the similarities between those engaged in the developmental academic advising approach and the goals of developmental education professionals in general. The similarities are noted as follows:

1. Academic advising is *a continuous process*. As students (generally) progress through a self-assessment of their academic interests and abilities, choosing specific academic curricula, and fulfilling degree requirements, so too, do developmental education students (specifically) recognize their academic skill deficiencies, pursue a developmental curriculum, and proceed through the established curriculum to graduation. In rare cases do these processes culminate without interruption, reassessment, and change.

2. Academic advising is *concerned with quality-of-life issues*. Both developmental academic advisors and developmental educators seek to promote and integrate the educational, psychological (personal), and career growth of students in an optimal learning environment. Both seek to maximize their students' academic success in overcoming deficiencies in order to enhance personal and career successes in the future.

3. Academic advising is *goal-related*. Academic advisors assist students in establishing both short and long-term goals; developmental educators tend to focus on the more immediate goals of skill development in order to enhance the opportunity for longer range goals to be set and achieved.

4. Academic advising requires *a caring human relationship*. Of course we'd like to think that all our endeavors in higher education assume this

characteristic, but certainly the academic advising and developmental education roles should exemplify, if not personify, this relationship. It is often the caring component that determines the success achieved by marginal students.

5. Academic advisors should be *models for students to emulate*. Advisors who demonstrate self-direction, responsibility, and shared decision-making with their students mirror the exact kinds of behaviors that developmental students need to observe in their teachers. Only when developmental students begin to exhibit these productive behaviors themselves will they be able to overcome their deficiencies and master the balance of expectations for them in the college environment.

6. Academic advising must integrate the *expertise of both academic and student affairs professionals*. The development of college students occurs in several realms (educational, psychological/personal, and career). Rarely is there an individual who can assist students in reaching their fullest potential in all areas. Academic advisors employ the assistance of staff in admissions, financial aid, learning assistance, career planning, the faculty, and other personnel; developmental educators rely on tutors, counselors, mentors, and academic advisors for the success of their students. In all cases, the full complement of institutional resources needs to be known and utilized by all constituencies who have responsibility for student success.

7. Academic advisors should utilize as many *campus and community resources* as possible. In addition to the campus offices and personnel, many internship, volunteer, service learning, and job placement opportunities are readily available around most campuses. Specific learning programs, tutorial assistance, and counseling services are regularly made available to developmental education students, either on or off the campus. The range of opportunities currently made available through distance learning capabilities are especially conducive to this additional assistance.

The definition and principles of the developmental academic advising concept model described above provide a framework through which all students can benefit. Developmental education students can especially benefit from this approach, since they often require more frequent and more strategic interventions, as well as more support from professionals and role models.

Designing the Model

A successful model of developmental academic advising must recognize the uniqueness of developmental education students, and it must enhance the opportunities for their success. Such a model must be realistic, broad-based, flexible, and itself goal-directed. One of the goals of NADE is "to enhance the retention of students," which is certainly a concomitant goal of any developmental academic advising program.

Tinto (1987) presented a model of institutional departure upon which the developmental academic advising model presented here is based. Tinto's (1987) model portrays voluntary student withdrawal (as opposed to dismissal); it is longitudinal in nature (a process rather than an event); and it is social and interactive (not only academic or didactic). The model of developmental academic advising described here is also longitudinal, social, and interactive.

Tinto (1987) described this longitudinal process of voluntary withdrawal as dependent on the student's prior background (family, education, etc.), on his/her intentions and personal commitments toward further education, and how these characteristics interact with both the student's social and academic experiences in the institution. As these interactions occur, the student decides how positive (or negative) they are and ultimately decides whether to stay (or leave).

The developmental academic advising model (see Figure 1) exhibits a similar design, in that it based upon the student's background characteristics, and it is interactive with many institutional and community resources. It is, perhaps, the essence of the interactions described by Tinto (1987).

Pre-Admission Characteristics

All students apply to our institutions with certain characteristics and conditions that contribute to their success or failure. These characteristics include their academic skills and abilities, their individual goals and objectives, their academic and career interests, and the kinds of support they receive to pursue their degrees.

The student's *academic skills and abilities* have traditionally been judged by ACT/SAT test scores, high school grades, subjects, and class ranks, and sometimes by alternate measures for nontraditional aged students.

Each student brings his/her own *specific goals and objectives* to the higher education setting. These can range from simply trying to accommodate

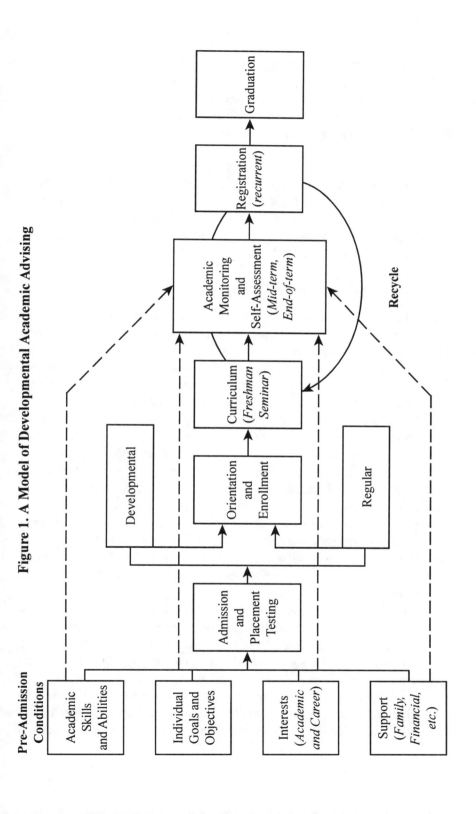

Figure 1. A Model of Developmental Academic Advising

their parents' wishes to achieving a 4.00 GPA and gaining admission to a prestigious graduate or professional school.

Many of these students have identified their *academic and/or career interests*, or at least have eliminated some of the options that are available to them.

The range of *support* these students receive can also vary widely, both financially and personally. Some students have fully financed their education through scholarships, grants, or family contributions, while others struggle with loans, multiple jobs, and credit cards. Most students enjoy the encouragement and motivation provided by friends and family members, but others continually confront resistance, criticism, and obfuscation.

Admission and Placement Testing

Although each student brings a unique combination of characteristics to our institutions, the institutions tend to respond to them in rather routine ways. Admissions offices tend to focus on the estimates for academic success, that is, the students' "academic skills and abilities." In most cases, students are also asked to indicate their "academic and/or career interests" by selecting a major program of study, even prior to their admission.

The student's "specific goals and objectives" and "support" received are frequently ignored at this stage of the process, although these could very well be the characteristics that most affect student retention. Consider the possibilities. If the student has well-developed goals, and the institution is able to facilitate the achievement of those goals, then a good match is made. However, if the institution cannot provide the necessary facilitation, support, etc., then a mismatch is evident, and attrition is likely. Or even worse, if the student's goals are ill-conceived, then whether the institution is facilitative or not will not matter, attrition is likely. In other words, there is perhaps only a 25% chance that students will remain in the institution, irrespective of their abilities or interests.

However, most institutions do use some form of placement testing in reading, mathematics, writing, foreign languages, and/or the sciences once the student has been admitted. Some use the same measures as those used in the admissions process; some use other commercial testing products; and some develop their own.

It is through this testing process that developmental students are identified and upon which the developmental education processes begin. However, these students encounter the same general campus processes as all other students, and this is why the developmental advising model is appropriate for all students. Each of the following campus processes presents a specific situation in which academic advising is a critical—and often required—component. These processes are most critical for developmental education students.

Orientation and Enrollment

The student's primary introduction to the institution normally occurs in an Orientation Program. The formats for such programs vary widely, ranging from multiple days over the summer to only a few hours just prior to the beginning of classes for the (Fall) term. Frequently, these programs have a specialized aspect for developmental education students. In all cases, however, some academic advising component is included.

This is the first real opportunity for the developmental academic advising *process* to function within the model. Students are introduced to the multiple options available to them, and they begin to make choices based upon their own unique pre-admission conditions. Here is where developmental students are often confronted, for the first time, with the reality that their abilities, goals, and interests might not be in concert with the demands of the institution. It is where the developmental academic advising process must begin by "providing assistance in the mediation of dissonance between student expectations and the actualities of the educational environment" (Habley, 1981, p. 46).

The Curriculum

All students complete the registration process in accordance with the institutional curricular demands, expectations, and requirements. These can range from specifically prescribed developmental courses for the developmental students to "block" schedules for most freshmen and to highly flexible options. All these students are attempting to fulfill some component of their general education. Some are attempting to confirm their interest and ability in an academic major. Others are exploring their options and opportunities without any pre-determined commitments.

A curricular feature that has grown in popularity, and in effectiveness among institutions is the freshman year experience concept. This concept has included well-integrated academic, co-curricular, and extra-curricular functions and activities, including common themes and readings, homogeneous groupings in residence halls, lecture series, and social gatherings.

One aspect of the freshman year experience efforts that best exemplifies this concept is a course that is explicitly targeted to new students, usually first-term freshmen. These courses are known as Freshman Seminars, College Success, Introduction to College, University 101, and the like. The content in such courses can include study skills, orientation, health and wellness, career development, and/or significant academic components. Descriptions of the characteristics of such courses are described in Gordon and Grites (1984) and in Fidler and Fidler (1991).

These courses are especially appropriate for developmental education students in order to provide them with any additional individualized instruction and assistance they might need. In fact, Simmons, Wallins, and George (1995) found that the retention rate of "low achievers" was the only significant difference in their study of at-risk students who took a Freshman Seminar course.

Probably the most important aspect for developmental education students is the relationship that is normally developed between the student and the instructor in these courses. This relationship often maximizes the academic and social integration described by Tinto (1987). It is in these courses that the developmental academic advising process establishes its strongest foothold.

Where such freshman year programs and courses do not exist, the challenge for institutions to structure a vehicle that will provide a developmental academic advising approach becomes more difficult. In all situations, however, some aspect of the institution's curriculum is attempted by every student each term.

Academic Monitoring and Self-Assessment

Once the academic term is underway, many institutions employ a variety of efforts to insure that students succeed, especially in their first term. Mandated advising appointments, mid-term grade reports, and voluntary workshops are some of the ways students are monitored for their academic integration. During this time, students also begin to assess their pre-admission conditions in a relative sense. This is the most critical point in the developmental academic advising model, that is, to increase student retention and success.

Each student's academic skills and abilities are routinely tested in classes, in study groups, and on papers and exams they submit. They begin to realize how they compare to other students and in what areas they need to develop. If developmental students are homogeneously grouped in certain courses, then they must be alerted to the reality that their skills and abilities will again be tested (in a relative sense) when they enroll in other courses. On one hand this could be a shock; on the other, these students might well have benefited from the longer transition into a successful academic integration.

Similarly, as students become more aware of their *relative* skills and abilities, many begin to reassess both their personal goals and objectives and their academic and career interests. Some students realize that their own expectations for themselves have been set too high or have been overestimated; others find that they have talents, abilities, or interests they didn't know they had.

Apart from their academic performance, the students' range of support for their efforts can also change during this time. Significant changes in their financial and/or personal support and resources would likely force a reassessment of their own expectations as well.

At the end of each academic term most institutions review each student's performance to determine whether any academic action (warning, probation, suspension, Dean's List, etc.) should be taken. These actions can also stimulate students' reassessment of their plans. If the action taken is a negative one, the potential for attrition is high, but even if no action is taken, each student's own decision to return or to leave the institution is made at this time.

In all these situations the developmental academic advisor plays a key role. The advisor assists students in reviewing their progress, in exploring their new options—whether they have become limited or have expanded—and in developing a new path toward success in these options. For developmental education students, this process is critical to their success, since they have likely already experienced some setback and/or delay in their degree progress and aspirations.

Registration (recurrent)

Once each term is completed students register for the courses they will attempt in the next term. The registration activity normally includes some kind of advising activity as well. Although these two activities often occur concurrently, they are not synonymous.

The developmental academic advising model suggests that the (developmental) academic advisor renews the processes of curriculum review, academic progress, and future planning with each student. This renewal is a natural part of each new registration period, but it also occurs between each of them. Developmental academic advising is an ongoing process, facilitated by the advisor, and it recurs throughout the student's career until graduation—the ultimate success criterion for this model.

Institutions that employ the developmental academic advising model will likely experience more satisfied and better educated students, who tend to remain at the institution to achieve their academic, personal, and career goals. An early example that included many of the components of the proposed model and that resulted in many of these achievements was reported by Patrick, Furlow, and Donovan (1988). As Tinto (1987) concluded,

> Research supports the notion argued here that the character of one's integrative experiences after entry are central to the process of voluntary withdrawal. Of particular importance are those experiences which arise from the daily interactions between students and faculty outside the classroom. Other things being equal, the more frequent those interactions are, and the warmer and more rewarding they are seen to be by the student, the more likely is persistence—indeed, the more likely is social and intellectual development generally. (p. 84)

For developmental education students, this model seems imperative.

Structuring the Model

One limitation that has consistently challenged this model, however, is the realization that not all academic advisors, particularly those from the ranks of the full-time teaching faculty, are willing to undertake this comprehensive role. Therefore, an examination of the structure of a developmental academic advising model is necessary.

In order for the developmental academic advising model to achieve its fullest potential, that is, in the same way that we strive to have our students achieve, there are four specific components of human resource management that must be considered. Although these components should be addressed in all aspects of higher education management systems, they seem to be minimized, and even ignored, in some academic advising programs. These key components are described below, as they relate to advising programs.

The first component is the *selection* of academic advisors. It is normally assumed that teaching faculty members will be expected to teach courses, conduct research, publish journal articles, obtain grants, serve their communities, serve their institutions on committees, and advise students;

and it is further assumed that each of these functions will be performed relatively well.

The personnel required to implement the kind of developmental academic advising model described above are extraordinary, whether they come from the ranks of the teaching faculty or are hired explicitly to provide advising services. These individuals must, first of all, be committed to the developmental educational processes of all students, and in each of their contexts; they must be tolerant of indecision and of incremental progress in their students; and they must continuously be supportive and challenging at the same time.

These advisors must also be knowledgeable of the resources of the institution and the community around it; they must know how and when to use these resources and to facilitate appropriate referrals when necessary. Finally, they must willing to learn new strategies, techniques, methods, and materials for insuring student success through this role, which leads to the next component—training.

The *training* of academic advisors to implement a developmental academic advising program is essential. Routine tasks of selecting courses, verifying graduation requirements, and signing class schedules are minimized under this model, while the teaching of responsibility, decision-making, self-assessment, and career and life planning are constantly promoted.

Developmental academic advisors use a plethora of information; therefore, they must receive adequate and timely materials, such as handbooks, computerized data, calendars of deadlines and events, curriculum changes, and new sources of assistance. In addition, they might need to enhance their own skills of communication and understanding to work successfully with the diversity of students recognized above. Only a well-organized, well-supported, and well-delivered training program will equip traditional academic advisors with these skills and resources necessary to function as developmental academic advisors.

The next component of a successful developmental academic advising program is that of *evaluation*. An overall programmatic evaluation is rightfully expected of an advising program, but individual advisors should also be evaluated periodically. Both evaluations (program and individual) must be done in concert with the goals, objectives, and expectations of the program, and both should include formative and summative elements.

The obvious asset to evaluation is the improvement of services. Only from an assessment framework can developmental efforts be truly judged. Some of the criteria used to assess successful advising programs in this model—and especially appropriate for developmental students—include retention rates, progress toward degree completion, course completion rates, GPAs, incidence of academic probation and dismissal, extent to which support services are used, and other factors reflecting specific institutional goals and objectives.

The fourth component of this model is the one that is probably most often ignored—*compensation, recognition, or reward* for providing this essential academic support service. This is especially true for programs that use teaching faculty as the primary providers of this service.

The concern is not so much with specific compensations or rewards per se, but rather in the relative weighting or priority that is given for performance in this role. Teaching faculty are generally rewarded with salary increments, tenure, and promotion for their performance as classroom teachers, researchers, publishers, grantwriters, committee chairs, community leaders, officeholders in professional associations, and sometimes as academic advisors. It is in this larger scheme of faculty performance that academic advising is often recognized only minimally, if at all.

Unfortunately, the four components described above have not been adequately addressed in most academic advising programs around the country. For example, Habley (1993) reported that, while between 75—90% of all academic advising in the United States is conducted by faculty members, only 9% of the 404 institutions in a national survey reported that all their departmental faculty are expected to meet certain selection criteria to become advisors; 54% of the institutions reported that "some" departments use selection criteria. In other words, the message is "Anyone can do it."

With respect to the training of departmental faculty advisors, Habley (1993) reported that only 38% of the institutions require advisor training in all their departments and another 37% require training in some. Where it does exist, however, the training effort typically involves a single workshop of one day or less, and the content of that workshop is heavily dominated with "informational" skills (academic policies, registration procedures, test score and transcript evaluations, etc.). Little effort is expended to assist faculty advisors in the concept and role of the developmental model.

Given these limited efforts in the selection and training of faculty advisors in academic departments, it is not surprising that an evaluation scheme is also lacking. Habley (1993) reported that 54% of the institutions used student evaluations in all or some of their departments, 51% used some method of advisor self-evaluation, and 50% used a performance review by a supervisor. However, there is *no* evaluation component in nearly 50% of the institutions. Here the message given is "Who cares?"

Finally, Habley (1993) reported similarly disheartening results regarding the recognition and reward for the faculty member's role as an academic advisor. He reported that no released time was provided, nor were salary increments granted, in more than 75% of the institutions; that only 54% of the institutions recognized some "minor consideration in promotion and tenure;" and that only 13% granted any type of award for excellence in advising. It becomes very obvious, very quickly that faculty members will likely expend their efforts in areas where recognition is greatest, and this is clearly not in the advising role.

These results graphically illustrate the minimal effort, attention, and resources that are dedicated to academic advising programs in general. To establish and deliver the kind of program described above in the developmental academic advising model, significant changes need to occur. To target such a model for developmental learners is even more critical.

Clearly, only certain individuals should be selected to advise developmental students; these selected individuals must receive a reasonably comprehensive orientation and training program; they must be evaluated for their performance; and they must be recognized by the institution for their efforts. Only under these expectations and conditions for our academic advisors can we expect our developmental students to succeed.

Implementing the Model

Regardless of the institution's commitment to the above components, that is, the fiscal and human resources allocated directly to them, the developmental academic advising model can still be achieved, albeit with some difficulty. Some specific strategies that would facilitate this achievement, particularly for developmental students, are described below.

Advisor Assignment

All new college students, but especially those identified as developmental learners, need a strong human link to the institution—someone to whom they can speak with comfort and confidence; someone for whom they have respect; someone in whom they can confide; someone who can assist them. This person is often thought to be the academic advisor. Frost (1991) described the importance of informal, out-of-class contacts with faculty, made especially fruitful through the academic advising relationship. The potential for success is evident. However, academic advisors might have a group of 25 or more advisees, along with many other students from their classes, those from previous classes, graduate advisees, etc. that also seek their assistance. The time demands on the conscientious advisor can be inordinate.

One way to capitalize on both the learner's needs and the advisor's economy of time is to assign these students to one of their initial instructors as their academic advisor. Of course, the instructor must agree to this dual role and must use the opportunity to facilitate a complete developmental education.

The dual instructor-advisor role and relationship enables significantly more individualized contact with the students in the classroom. This contact provides a wealth of opportunities to foster student growth, not only in areas of academic skill development, but also in the areas of personal and career development. Institutions that have implemented freshmen year programs, especially those that include designated freshman seminar courses, have a natural vehicle to provide these opportunities in a systematic way.

This single strategy in the model can serve to achieve success in developmental learners more efficiently and more effectively than any other. What other vehicle provides personal contact with one's academic advisor at least two to three times per week?

Student Support Groups

Corollary to the instructor-advisor assignment is the notion that the students assigned as such will usually quickly identify themselves as peers in several different ways. The natural outgrowth of being in a class together will likely be the informal support group that evolves. As these students begin to learn more about each other and about themselves, they will also recognize the cohesion they have built collectively. Such peer support will readily be recognized and utilized by the developmental instructor-advisor.

Intrusive Advising

Glennen (1976) introduced this term and concept through his programs to increase the retention rates of freshman students. His approach has been employed in a variety of institutions, and all have met with successful retention efforts. Developmental academic advisors who also use the intrusive approach can significantly influence the retention rates of their students. Spann, Spann, and Confer (1995) provided a thorough description of seven strategies to be considered in this approach, along with the description of two campus programs that have used it successfully. Brown and Rivas (1995) also outlined a similar strategy specifically targeted for students of color.

The fundamental strategy used in the intrusive approach is simple: don't sit back and wait for students to come for advice (innately, they probably won't, at least voluntarily), but rather "intrude" upon them by initiating the contact. This can be accomplished through letters, phone calls, visits to residence halls and cafeterias, notes to their instructors, e-mail messages, attendance at events and activities, setting up tables in public areas, or in the classroom. Whatever the specific techniques employed, however, the intent is to demonstrate knowledge, awareness, and most of all, caring and concern for one's advisees.

For developmental learners this can be a critical effort. Too often these students have allowed their deficiencies to exacerbate their potential for failure, simply because of their own inertia or lack of confidence. The intrusive techniques keep these students alerted to their learning situations, focused on their own improvement strategies, and ultimately made the recipients of their own success.

Referrals

No matter how dedicated or well-trained an intrusive developmental academic advisor might be, there are always other sources of necessary assistance. What the advisor must achieve, however, is the knowledge of all the kinds of referral sources and services available to students, and how to access them most productively.

Learning centers, tutoring assistance, study groups, career services, technology labs, and the library are ready resources on most campuses for our developmental learners to use to enhance their success. The academic advisor must insure that these students take advantage of every available resource and opportunity to achieve that success.

Positive Attitude

Developmental learners are frequently stigmatized by others (and by themselves) as inadequate, inferior, less than capable, and/or out of place. But in the real essence of developmental education, the academic advisor recognizes each student's levels of skill and ability and works to improve upon them. The developmental advisor, as educator, seeks incremental progress in these students and reinforces each of their successes. In effect, the developmental academic advisor attempts to reverse the stigma of these students by helping them understand and accept where they are developmentally so that they can even more fully appreciate their successes.

These few strategies can truly serve to achieve the goals of the developmental academic advising model, even when all the structural components are not in place. These strategies can be achieved individually and are so achieved by the academic advisor who personally adopts the model.

Summary and Comment

The developmental academic advising model presented above provides a vehicle for an ongoing effort that fosters student development in each of the educational, career, and personal lives of college students. The characteristics and conditions under which this model is most effective reflect those that should be expected of all the educational processes within the higher education environment. Finding ways to introduce, implement, and maintain such a model will likely result in students' persistence toward their goal of graduation, their overall satisfaction with their institutions, and their own increased skills and abilities that will enable them to become better citizens and more productive members of the workplace. It is a model based on student success.

One observation needs to be made, however. This model has been presented in the context of the needs of the developmental learner. The model is just as appropriate and effective for all students.

Gordon (1992) predicted that advisors will become increasingly specialized because of the diversity described initially herein, and because of the increasing complexity of our institutions. To categorize students under any rubric, and to attempt to construct a model to fit each unique group, however, is not likely the most productive use of the human, fiscal, or physical resources of our institutions. Furthermore, to pigeonhole students contradicts the overall goals of student development and of higher education itself. It is incumbent upon our academic leaders and student affairs professionals to continue to identify and utilize appropriate models, such as this one, that promote and facilitate the total growth and development of all students. "Developmental advising will need to become the rule rather than the exception" (Gordon, 1991, p. 194).

Chapter 8

ഉ൭ൟ

An Alternative Assessment Model for College Admission and Matriculation

Augusta A. Clark, Andolyn B. Harrison, and A. Phillip Butler

Introduction

The sample entry below is one that has been written in college journals. It is the story of Gigi as told by underprepared students who each year see themselves as not having the knowledge, competency and motivation—beyond what is measured by standardized tests—to enter college and obtain a degree. Such students run the risk of being overlooked as prospective successful students because decision-makers are unwilling to gamble first on admitting them, and second on believing that they have the abilities to succeed.

Gigi's Story:

I chose to attend college and was filled with anticipation on becoming the first generation college graduate in my family. My happiness turned to woe on the first day that I reported to the campus to meet with my advisor.

I have never been an outstanding test taker; however, I always gave standardized exams what I considered to be my best shot. Before graduating from high school, I took the ACT and earned a composite score of thirteen. I was not admitted as a regular student, but got into college on a conditional status. When I reported to the college, I informed my advisor that I was a poor test taker, but if afforded the opportunity, I would do well in my course work. My advisor refused to hear my pleas, so I inwardly said, 'I have not unpacked my trunk yet. I will send it back home.' My advisor was appalled to hear I would return home because I was being required to enroll in remedial classes. He conceded and blurted out, 'You will be given a grace period of one semester in regular classes. But you will not do well because your test scores are low. However, because of your insistence you have the one semester.' I enrolled in regular classes and, to the surprise of many, I made the honor roll at the end of the first semester. My advisor simply greeted me with a staunch demeanor at the beginning of the next semester. No congratulatory comments were offered, but I was just so happy to be in college.

There is evidence to suggest that developmental education students have problems getting admitted to postsecondary institutions. During the initiation of developmental education programs, Tomlinson (1989) recognized that the implementation of admission standards would be one of eight problem areas facing successful developmental education programs in colleges and universities. Seven other problematic areas cited for developmental education programs included: 1) problems of funding; 2) staff recruitment and retention; 3) placement standards; 4) minority student enrollment; 5) quality of tests; 6) relevancy of curriculum; and 7) perceptions of the programs. Admissions difficulties do exist and they may be due to the fact that traditional admissions methods based on the familiar admissions models do not work for all students. The criteria generally used in the traditional models are counterproductive for developmental students. A major quantitative factor used in admissions decisions is a standardized test score. The extant models rely heavily on standardized test information and exclude multiple sources of academic evidence enabling developmental students to be given the highest opportunity to be admitted.

The thesis of this chapter stated boldly and with conviction is this: developmental students can be successful in obtaining admissions to and advancing through programs when those who make admissions decisions use models that take into consideration both qualitative and quantitative factors when scrutinizing individual applications. The primary two issues supporting this conviction center on these statements:

• There are skills, other than academic test taking skills, that students should possess in order to prepare them for college.

• There are pieces of obtainable evidence which will paint a clearer picture of students' achievements and potential .

An Historical Perspective: The Admissions Beginnings

The history of general higher education admissions and programs for remedial education specifically have interesting beginnings. Research tells us that preparatory programs were established as early as 1841 at Brown, Harvard, and the University of California (Rose, 1989) and as late as 1849 at the University of Wisconsin. There is consolation for current developmental educators. Underprepared students have been admitted to and served by institutions of higher learning in America for over 150 years (Elifson, Pounds & Stone, 1995). Previously, colleges and universities established their own entrance examinations. During this period of time in the late 1800s, students were admitted to colleges with certificates. This practice started in 1870 at the University of Michigan. Wechsler (1977) identified the Ivy League colleges such as Brown, Cornell, and Pennsylvania who admitted some students by certificates. What has just been described is what the authors coined the First Wave Admissions Policies. The procedure for admissions was to submit certificates. A commonly held philosophy was that students who came from wealthy families and had the resources to finance an education should be the ones allowed to attend college. Cross (1974) alleged that not only did students from aristocratic families have the finances for an education, but they also did not have the prerequisite skills to do well in school. This documents the rigorous standards for admissions during this time period. Wealthy students had the money and they also needed to have the education to go along with the dollars in order to maintain their positions in life. During this First Wave, an additional factor was the exclusion of women, ethnic minorities, and the poor. These groups were excluded because they did not have the financial means and because of the existing racial and gender bias of the time. None of the "excluders" were even included in the pool of applicants.

In 1920, Columbia University was one of the first colleges to require intelligence testing as part of admissions procedures. Intelligence tests (IQ) were used because the American demographics had changed. Immigrants began seeking postsecondary educational opportunities. Academicians felt that immigrants were underprepared so intelligence tests were used as barriers that screened out groups of students. The use of IQ testing signaled the Second Wave Admissions Policies. Intelligence tests were used for admissions even though they did not always have validity and were not aligned with what was being taught in the schools.

In the mid-1960s, there was a drastic change in the admissions scenario. Here we had the initiation of the Third Wave Admissions perspective with the enactment of the Higher Education Act of 1965. There was a shift in the advocacy of who should have the opportunity to turn the dream of entering college into a reality (Boylan, 1988). Through this legislation, funds were made available to individuals who previously were unable to fund a postsecondary education. Additionally, the Civil Rights Act of 1964 made entry into historically black postsecondary institutions possible for a large number of minorities.

> Institutions began opening doors to what Cross (1974) would appropriately term "new students". In her classical work, *Beyond the Open Door,* Cross defined these students as "those scoring in the lowest third on traditional tests of academic ability" (p. 13). The belief behind the open door concept was that anyone who wanted to—regardless of prior academic performance—should have a chance to go to college. Reasonably, it could be argued that the "new students" needed "new accommodation" which included "new ways" of providing academic and support services. Literally and figuratively, postsecondary doors opened. Baby boomers, as well as others, clamored for access into institutions of higher education. However, Havighurst (1960) expressed concern during this period of time. He felt an attempt to use intelligence test scores in greater selectivity and the availability of financial aid would present a problem. He stated: "Those most likely to lose opportunity are youth of working class backgrounds who do not do especially well on scholastic aptitude tests or in ordinary academic work, but who have a potential for college work that can be developed...." (p. 5)

With President Lyndon B. Johnson's push to give anyone who wanted to a chance to go to college, the country moved into an era known as The Great Society. Students went through the late 60s and early 70s on Basic Educational Opportunity Grants (BEOGs). They were able to enter colleges without any problems in admissions; however, there was the recognition that some students needed intense academic support.

The Fourth Wave Admissions began at a time when there were more students applying for admissions than colleges and universities had spaces to accommodate. Consequently, the selection process became more stringent. Havighurst (1960) was prophetically correct. Students who did not do well on standardized tests, or in regular academic work, were the losers. Unfortunately, as the enrollment grew, the losers included more than just the students from the working class. With this Fourth Wave there was a reduction in space and a need to create the community college. Concomitantly to the Fourth Wave, there was tremendous growth in community colleges. Community colleges were designed and had as their mission a desire to serve students who attended higher education schools locally—and perhaps developmental students—as well as other students. Because of the need to help local students determine if they wanted to go on to higher education, community colleges expanded during this time.

The literature abounds with studies and research on admissions practices and requirements conducted during the late 1960s and on through the 1980s. The voluminous accounts attest to the fact that debates on standards for college entrance were heated. These discussions ranged from legal, moral ethical issues to the biases based on gender, race, and economics. At the eye of the storm of the Fourth Wave Admissions was the issue surrounding standardized testing. Considerable discussion was given to this topic for several reasons. Standardized tests were perceived by many students and their parents as being their greatest barrier to access. The tests were viewed with disdain by various groups because of the perceived unfairness.

Educational Testing Service (ETS), developers of the SAT, and the American College Testing, the developers of the ACT, are still giants in the admissions process. They still have clout. The force of ETS or ACT is not being challenged here. However, an examination should be made of the controversy surrounding the issue since the alternative model being proposed makes optional the submission of standardized scores as a criterion for admission. The traditional admissions models place heavy weights on standardized scores. It should be noted that both the ACT and SAT have come under close scrutiny and criticism. Much more has been written about the SAT than the ACT. The majority of references may be made to the SAT, but they both are viewed in the same light by the authors.

Originally called the Scholastic Aptitude Test, and recently re-named the Scholastic Assessment Test, the SAT was introduced in 1941 as an alternative to written tests in subjects such as mathematics, science, history, and literature. Constructed as a multiple choice test, it had promise for determining college readiness because it was objective, efficient and inexpensive (Ratitch, 1996). Standardized testings have dominated admissions procedures from the Second Wave Admissions at Columbia University up to the Fourth Wave.

Certain authors have claimed that what the test was initially designed to do is not what it is now being used to determine. Jencks and Crouse (1982) asserted that the SAT was originally supposed to help colleges with finding capable students in attendance at high schools rated low to moderate in academic quality. Able students graduating from exclusive private and prestigious public schools were easily identified by colleges and universities. The College Board, the governing arm for the SAT, wanted to "standardize" college admissions to overcome problems caused by colleges having different entrance requirements and examinations. Although the College Board said they did not want to control testing, they did.

Cases have been argued vociferously for and against the use of standardized tests as one of the criteria for admission to college. Certain authors have claimed that it is difficult to rely on high school grades as predictors of success in college because there are too many factors to consider or too many variables that cannot be controlled. Perhaps the signal for the Fifth Wave Admissions procedures came with those who argue in favor of using standardized tests to select candidates for admission. The movement was towards what the authors term "the common standards approach." For instance, Unger (1995) believed that SAT "set a common standard for students throughout the country regardless of race, creed, color or religion; regardless of the schools they attend; and, regardless of whether, as in some cases, teachers give favored students higher grades than they deserve and thus improve their chances of getting into college" (p. 42).

Early in the debate for the Fifth Wave was Henry Chauncey (1961) former president of ETS. In a report to the Board of Trustees, he echoed a similar thought of "standards with a common approach." Chauncey observed that:

> Unlike the personal interview, the classroom test, or the teacher's subjective evaluation, the objective test is a common touchstone. It gives all students who take it the same chance, asks them to run the same race—even though they have had different economic backgrounds, different educational, cultural, and social opportunities. (Educational Testing Service, Annual Report, 1960-61 pp. 25-26)

Still another argument on the importance of SAT as a means to gauge the universal "same standards" of applicants from various schools throughout the country was proposed by Chauncey and Dobbins (1963):

To the college admissions officer, the transcript of grades from one high school looks very much like the transcript from any other. An "A" average earned in a highly academic high school where most graduates go on to college may mean something quite different from an "A" average earned in a high school where academic learning is secondary to vocational training. With candidates' transcripts coming from as many as a thousand different high schools each year, however, the college admissions officer has no infallible way of knowing what the reported grade means. Lacking a method for interpreting the information sent to him about the candidates for admission, he needs some means for deciding which ones are the ones most likely to succeed in the studies offered by his college. (p. 110)

As increasing standards were dealt with, one would think that there were no arguments against the "same yard stick measurement" belief. That is, the same questions given to all students under the same conditions. However, Gregory Anrig (1995) a former ETS president, argued in a unique way to maintain the SAT rather than dropping it: "Do we really want to go back to the 'good old days' in American higher education? Those were the days when admission to many colleges and universities depended on the prestige of your private or public high school, who your parents were, whether a relative was an alumnus/a (and a donating one at that) and whether you would 'fit in' with a student body much like its predecessors over the years" (Anrig as quoted in Crouse & Trusheim, 1988, p.147).

The results of a study by Larose and Roy (1991) support the finding of others that affective, social, and cognitive skills play a more significant part than academic potential for achievement during the first semester. This is especially true with students considered at risk of failing (Abrams & Jernigan, 1984; Maxwell, 1981; Nisbet et. al, 1982; Scott & Robbins, 1985; White & Sedlacek, 1986). In the study by Nisbet, Ruble, and Schurr (1982), the researchers used the unconventional criteria such as study skills inventory, and reading skills survey to see if other data provided insights into the success of developmental students. The study showed that unconventional predictor variables did result in an improvement in the predictability of students who were likely to have academic difficulty in college.

Hess, Grafton, and Michael (1983) reported from the study they conducted that one of eleven affective variables had promise in predicting grade point average of freshmen. That variable was a self report by students on what they perceived to be their level of preparedness in mathematics and natural sciences.

Portfolio Assessment Model (PAM)

Prior to describing/discussing the PAM, the authors believe it necessary to state assumptions upon which the model was based.

1. That the college which chooses to implement this model is operating beyond the Fifth Wave Admissions. The higher education institution views students not as statistics but human beings who can do more than compute and recall facts.

2. That the college no longer believes a student can be represented with a single score. The student, in other words, is greater than the sum of his/her parts or SAT scores.

3. That the general admissions policy is such that the college has moved away from the traditional approach to a non-traditional approach.

4. That the model is not just for developmental education students. The model can be also used with students in the regular education program.

5. That the model can be utilized as an admissions and a progression model.

A Portfolio Defined

One generally thinks of a portfolio as being a portable case which contains a collection of drawings, pictures, writings, and the like. Simply defined in this context, a portfolio tells a story or paints a picture of a student's work across all domains. It is a powerful source of information about a student. In a discussion with educators in the Northwest Evaluation Association, Paulson and others (1991) reported a working definition of portfolio as "a purposeful collection of student work that exhibits the students' efforts, progress, and achievement in one or more areas" (p. 60). Paulson (1991) suggested guidelines which should be included in portfolios. In addition to containing the selection and judging criteria, portfolios should include input from students as to the contents as well as evidences of student reflection. Typical portfolios include a variety of information in the form of scripts, research reports, narratives, musical scores, sculpture, models, and photographs.

One approach to portfolio organization is to allow students to determine the content. The contents represent students' attempt to structure and present in a meaningful way what was taught. Another method of organizing is to have someone else determine before hand what to include. These may include specific projects or products. While the general focus may be determined by the assessor, in this case the admissions officer, the exact nature or specific selected choices may be determined by the student. The PAM incorporated both methods.

General Uses of Portfolios

The idea of using portfolios in various ways to make judgments about student progress, achievement, and potential has found its way here; for it has been determined that this is a means by which alternative assessments can be used for expression of self and evaluation rather than with a single examination. Fittingly, a college in Oregon makes use of a portfolio pathway for admissions. This will be further discussed in the section where other models are examined.

Schools in one state piloted the portfolio approach. As reported by Stemmer (1992) and his colleagues, Michigan attempted to prepare students for the world of work. Students discovered, developed, and documented their skills in the Employability Skills Portfolio (ESP). Several pieces of information were included in the ESP among which was the Academic Skill, Personal Management Skill, and Teamwork Skill folder. Figure 1 shows the sample criteria used to assess these skills.

Portfolios, in and of themselves, have the potential of having many uses. They are powerful and they empower. Portfolios can be used as assessments for student learning. They can also empower students to become self-directed and reflective learners. Portfolios can provide a way of assessing students who normally do not fare well with traditional methods of assessment. Hasit and DiObilda (1996) used portfolio assessment at the college level in a developmental education reading class. Their study of this method was, in part, a response for critics who say that standardized tests do not assess literacy needs accurately.

Other Admissions Models

Mention is made here of four colleges with unique and innovative approaches to admissions. Two selective colleges in Maine may be classified as being progressive enough to operate differently than other higher education institutions.

Figure 1. Michigan's Employability
Skills Portfolio (ESP)

Academic Skills:

◆   read and understand written material
◆   understand charts and graphs
◆   understand basic math
◆   speak and write in the language business is conducted

Personal Management Skills:

◆   attend school/work daily and on time
◆   know personal strengths and weaknesses
◆   demonstrate self-control
◆   follow written/oral instruction

Teamwork Skills:

◆   actively participate in a group
◆   listen to other group members
◆   express ideas to other group members
◆   be sensitive to the group members' ideas and views

SOURCE: Stemmer, P. Brown, B. & Smith, C. (1992) The Employability Skills Portfolio. *Educational Leadership, 49*, p. 33

Bowdoin College and Bates College examined their admissions policies which formerly used standardized scores. They analyzed the value of test scores and experimented on their own to find another way to view the admissions procedures. From the experiments they conducted, the results were encouraging enough to warrant them changing the way tests were used in their admissions process. Bowdoin College in 1969 was one of the first colleges that no longer required the SAT for admissions. Schaffner (1985) described the rationale for the paradigm shift. When the policy was announced, four arguments were presented:

1.   'Personalization' of the admissions process allowed the admissions staff

to form detailed impressions of each applicant so that the reliance on unidimensional test scores was less necessary.

2. The policy gave evidence that test scores were less important factors that the public thought them to be.

3. Standardized tests were claimed to reflect socioeconomic opportunity and therefore to stand as barriers to college for qualified minority and disadvantaged applicants; public concern over this issue remains strong today.

4. An 'evidence gap' was asserted that SAT scores had not been shown to be good predictors of academic performance in the college (p. 55).

The experience at Bowdoin was encouraging because students for whom standardized scores were not submitted did survive. Bates College followed Bowdoin's lead. The faculty made a bold move and voted in 1984 to make SATs optional for admissions. According to Hiss (1990, pp. 15-16), there were four issues related to the decision:

1. Research suggested "the value of testing was reasonably modest whether alone or in tandem with other credentials."

2. "The SATs were producing in hundreds of thousands of teenagers a kind of mass hysteria, an unholy amalgam of passive surrender and frantic coaching...and if (coaching) does work, it is simply one more advantage in the process for the rich, and means the tests are hardly standardized...if (coaching) does not work, the students are wasting their time, their money, and (most importantly) their self-confidence."

3. School officials "sensed that SATs were sometimes unhelpful, misleading, and unpredictive for students whom the school has always been interested: minority students, rural, and Maine students."

4. The school wanted to send out a message, "Bates cares about intellectual integrity, hard work, and real achievement."

Hiss, the former Dean of Admissions at Bates and now a Vice President for Administrative Services, confirmed for the authors that making the decision to have optional SATs was one of the best things Bates ever did. Hiss has been quoted as saying, "We have looked back at average GPAs and academic survival rate. Every time we've looked, the academic survival rate of students (whose standardized scores were not known prior to admissions) has been over 99 percent." Bates gambled and took a chance to admit students differently. The risk paid off for the students as well as for the school.

In addition to concentrating on traditional variables such as high school records, academic pursuits and honors, extra curricular activities, and teacher and school recommendations, reviewers of applications to Bates also took into consideration community involvement, personal interest, and use of free time. This action complemented the philosophy and the mission of Bates College as espoused in the school's brochure. The literature from Bates supports the school's beliefs because it seeks to admit students who have promise; students who are representative of multi-cultural, multi-ethnic groups; and students who bring with them various educational, socioeconomic, and geographical backgrounds.

Two other colleges, Sarah Lawrence College in New York and Lewis and Clark College in Oregon, have demonstrated uniqueness in their admissions policies. Both colleges make use of student portfolios in the admissions process. The Lewis and Clark College catalogue provided a rationale and an explanation for using this approach:

> In response to increasing questions across the country about the validity of standardized test scores as predictors of college success, the College began using the innovative Portfolio Path to Admission in 1991. Students electing the Portfolio Path must submit three academic teacher recommendations and an academic portfolio and may choose not to submit standardized test scores. (p. 211)

Sarah Lawrence College initially had two concerns with the use of portfolios: one with who would prepare them and another with how would large numbers of applications be managed. They came to the conclusion that they would work with school officials to make sure that the portfolios were actually representative of students.

Description of Portfolio Admissions Model (PAM)

We are proposing that admissions officers go beyond the Fifth Wave admissions policies alluded to earlier in this chapter and make use of an unconventional means of assessing students for admissions. One component of this model makes provisions for use as a matriculation model in developmental education programs.

The Portfolio Admissions Model, which is used in this chapter, does not eliminate all of the negative factors found in traditional models. Instead, it creates additional factors that need to be integrated in a broader admissions perspective. PAM takes into consideration what many developmental educators advocate. One major definition for developmental education embraces the notion of "cognitive and affective growth of students of all levels of the learning continuum."

In this model, unlike traditional models, there is not an over reliance on cognitive factors used in the admissions equation. No doubt, there are cognitive skills which students need to possess in order to succeed in college. The model incorporated research findings on both cognitive and non-cognitive factors. Meaningful affective skills often help students overcome deficits in cognitive skills areas. Utilization of this model would empower students with the ability to present to admissions officers materials representative of their potential. Artists and photographers present their drawings and pictures in portfolios. Similarly, the Portfolio Admissions Model paints a picture of what students have achieved; thus, indicators of potential. Figure 2 graphically depicts the model.

A visual glance of the model in Figure 2 indicates a comprehensive approach to seeing the applicant in totality. The various squares are comparable to windows of a student's academic, social, and personal self; his or her world which has developed over years. Bits and pieces allow the observer to see several dimensions of the student's work, performance, beliefs, abilities, attitudes, accomplishments, affiliations, aspirations, service, and much more. If one were to open the Johari's window to the soul for admissions purposes, a complete view of the student's potential to succeed in college is exposed.

The large center square is at the heart of the model. A brief explanation is given of the selected academic and cognitive factors included in the model.

Academic Abilities

The square at the top of the model lists the essential academic abilities needed for successful progression in college: Read, Speak, Write, Compute. When developmental learners enter college, they enter with varying levels of knowledge, skills and abilities. They typically have deficiencies in the Basic Skills Areas: English, (verbal and written), Reading and Mathematics.

Figure 2. Portfolio Assessment Model (PAM)*

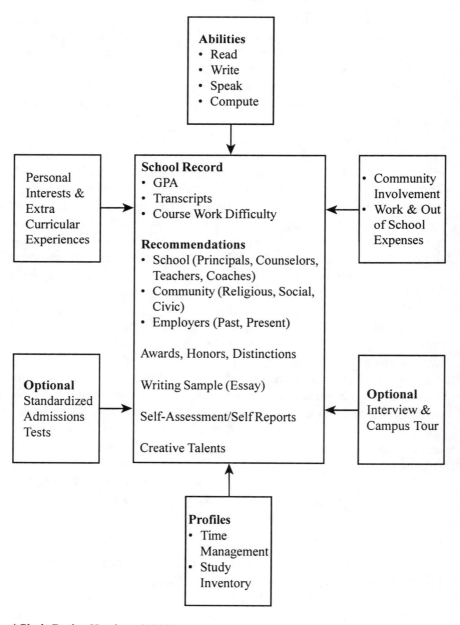

*Clark-Butler-Harrison (1997)

And, more often than not, they have had little—if any—exposure to computer technology. One important role of Developmental Education is to accept these students where they are and assist them with the necessary tools to correct their weaknesses and enhance their strengths (Cross, 1976).

Recommendations

Within the largest square, the validation by persons who have known the applicant is requested: School (Principals, Counselors, Teachers, Coaches); Community (Religious, Social, Civic); and Employers (Past, Present). It is of extreme importance to recognize the essential nature of those entities that affect the lives of developmental learners; these entities have the greatest degree of influence on such learners. What better way to learn about the learner's capabilities than through letters written by various and significant individuals close to the student?

There is a need for the establishment of a collaborative relationship between the college/university and the public school system, community organizations and employers. Having this kind of relationship, and a better understanding of who the students are can be an important factor in determining their capabilities for collegiate success.

School Record

Three of the traditional academic criteria are requested: GPA, Transcripts, Course Work Difficulty. In order to assess the academic needs of developmental learners and prepare them to move from developmental courses to the regular college curriculum, there must be access to their school record. This access ensures the ability to ascertain special needs and prescribe the appropriate educational plan.

Other Assessment Areas

The final set of affective and cognitive factors brings a balance to the other central components: Awards, Honors, Distinctions; Writing Sample (Essay); Self-Assessment/ Self Reports; and Creative Talents. Coupled with the academic assessment is the acquisition of information pertinent to any awards, honors and/or distinctions that developmental learners might have. Being underprepared does not preclude the ability to have participated in events or activities which allowed for the enhancement of strengths as well as the display of creative talents.

Also included is a self-assessment/self-report. Developmental learners must be made comfortable enough in a non-threatening environment to disclose their strengths and weaknesses. One way to do this and personalize the information is to have them write an essay on a topic of interest to them.

Profiles: Time Management and Study Inventory

In order to determine what developmental learners are doing and are not doing, an informal type of survey should be administered. This survey should include questions pertinent to all activities they do during the course of a day (i.e., personal, social, cultural, spiritual, academic, etc.). The provision of this information, then, can assist with the development of a time management schedule. Such a schedule will help these students to "correct their weaknesses."

Factors that Impact Success

Community Involvement and Work and Out of School Experiences. Although there are many factors that have an impact on success, community involvement, along with work and out of school experiences, tend to have a high degree of influence on developmental learners. Low self-esteem tends to drive them in situations that may or may not be conducive to wholesome development. It is for this reason that structured community activities and out of school experiences are crucial in the development of an educational plan for these students.

Personal Interests and Extra Curricular Experiences. At the cornerstone of the cognitive domain is that of the affective. Personal attitudes, beliefs, and values define who a person is. This definition assists with the personalization of the best means possible for developing the total person. An effective educational plan can only be developed when as many characteristics as possible are brought to the forefront. Then and only then can needs be met.

Standardized Tests. It is a tradition in higher education to require certain scores on various tests for either admission or placement. Since there is evidence that there is no real correlation between the score on an admission test, for example, and the ability to successfully complete course work, there is a movement in this country to have the SAT and ACT used as optional admissions criteria. By doing so, a student's total profile (i.e., high school record, extra-curricular activities, honors, awards, distinctions, etc.) can determine their admission to college.

On the other hand, placement testing is still necessary after being admitted in order to determine the level of knowledge held by developmental learners. Whether they are able to negotiate the test or not does not matter; while they might be placed at a level based on the test score, opportunities are provided for them to demonstrate mastery of the information via course work and exit testing.

Interview and Campus Tour. Of significant importance is the ability of developmental learners to visit the prospective campus and be interviewed by appropriate campus personnel. By doing so, these learners will become more knowledgeable about not only the college/university environment, but also programmatic thrusts and expectations. Moreover, the intent is to ensure somewhat of a "comfort zone" for these students once they begin their matriculation.

Utilization of the Model

As in the case with most models, a clear delineation of usage and degrees of importance must be determined. PAM, as described earlier, encompasses a myriad of "cognaffective" factors (Young, 1997) which allow for a 360 degree student assessment. Therefore, sequential steps follow:

1. University announces the decision to try a different approach in determining the admission of students.

2. University establishes an Agreement of Articulation for collaboration and cooperation between university officials and school district personnel .

3. University shares the portfolio concept, structure or design, and the procedures for collection of information to be included with the articulated schools. Students are educated on what is being done, why it is being done, and how they can begin to design the portfolio. A combination of required information and self-selected items will be evident in the portfolios.

4. University staff does follow up visits to Agreement Schools to verify that the students are actually doing this and to note the progress. Those that will be interested in applying for admissions the PAM way will be asked how they are doing: If you want to attend this college, it is

suggested that you use this approach and keep documentation of what you have been doing.

5. University personnel begins training of staff to practice the methods or procedures for scoring and rating the portfolio contents and determining the criteria for each entry overall and a rating against the criteria given. In other words, these are the standards or benchmarks. How close does the students' work match this?

6. Portfolio Evaluation Team assesses students' portfolios for admissions.

Matriculation Component: An Explanation

Once the student is admitted, he/she is required to take a placement test. The results of this test, along with other pertinent data from the portfolio packet, determine whether or not the student takes path one (developmental) or follows path two (regular).

Students who do not do well on the assessment part after being admitted and whose skills are not up to par will take the path leading to developmental education. Other students whose skills meet the criteria will move into the regular college path.

This is where the matriculation piece of the model comes into focus. While the PAM gets students admitted, a piece of the model (The Academic Ability—read, write, compute, speak) assesses strengths and weaknesses. Once these skills are identified, this piece of the model guides and monitors the students as they progress: first, through the developmental program, if they are developmental students; next, through the regular program, if they are determined eligible; then through the major program of study they selected; and finally, out the college doors as they exit at graduation. This matriculation component of the model operates much like an Individual Education Plan (IEP). It is tailored to the individual needs of the students; the needs are matched with the standards and criteria that should be mastered (those set forth by the institution, developmental education unit) and linked to the support services the entire institution can provide. Together with the pieces of information from the portfolio and with the confirmation or validation from the placement test such as the Nelson Denny Reading Test, developmental educators say to students: "You were right about your weakness in reading. The traditional reading test and other data we analyzed confirmed it. We will work with you to improve these skills. For

Figure 3 shows the matriculation component of the model.

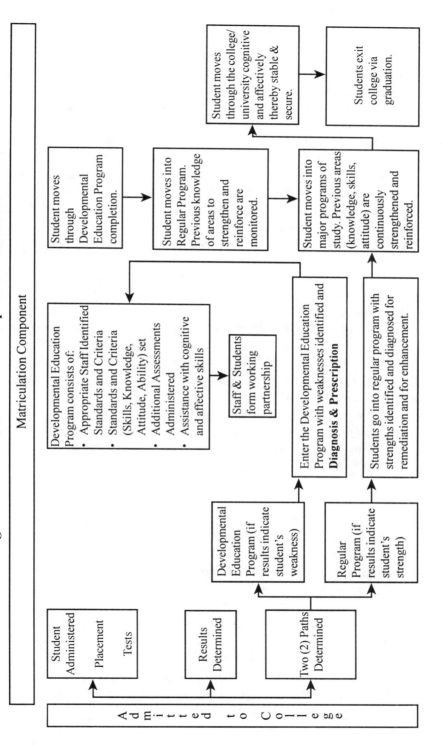

developmental educators care about you, and we know what skills, knowledge, attitudes students need to master in order to be successful in reading. You will be successful not only in this developmental program, but also in the regular education program, and then graduate. If you are willing to work with us, we (developmental educators) are willing to work with you, too, on the skills and processes. Together, we can succeed. You will be able to see where you are and how you can get to where you need to be. We even know affective skills such as interpersonal relations, self-concept, and motivational and other success related strategies such as time management, and critical thinking skills that will assist you along the way". While a component is useful for the initial assessment, no single method—not even this innovative portfolio method—can be used alone or solely to effectively assess and then place the students.

As shown earlier, PAM illustrates the degree of progression through which a student should go in order to successfully exit any Developmental Education Program. More specifically, however, is the list of components that constitute a Developmental Education Program that will allow for program exit. Therefore, the steps in this progression and their explanations follow:

- **Appropriate Staff**
  Due to the necessity of being sensitive to the needs of this clientele only, Developmental Educators should be the ones with direct contact, for they are professionally prepared and well aware of those characteristics which require special and unique attention.

- **Standards and Criteria**
  In addition to the appropriate staff, students' skills, knowledge, and abilities levels must be determined with a prescribed set of activities for enhancement. Additionally, attitudinal instruments should be administered as a means of determining where these students are in terms of values, beliefs, and self-esteem.

- **Additional Assessment and Additional Assistance with Cognitive Skills**
  Other assessment instruments/activities are required in order to ascertain as much information as possible about the students to be served. The more Developmental Educators have, the more they will be able to structure appropriate learning activities.

These steps, then, allow for staff to work efficiently and effectively with students as they move through the Developmental Education Program.

Rationale for Portfolio Design

The American Council on Education (ACE) in *Minorities on Campus: A Handbook for Enhancing Diversity*, recommended that secondary institutions include nontraditional measures in the admissions evaluation. ACE's rationale for this recommendation was based on the national data which revealed that minorities tend to have lower SAT scores and socioeconomic standings than white students. Therefore, just limiting admissions based on SAT scores is insufficient. It was suggested that multiple criteria for admissions purposes be used. When colleges rely too much on standardized tests, many Black and Hispanic students will be eliminated simply because they do not perform well on tests. If college and universities can make use of additional criteria such as musical or athletic abilities or the factor of an applicant being the son or daughter of an alumnus or alumnae, then institutions can consider other factors.

Another impetus for the development of such a model was derived from the literature concerned with success for high risk (developmental) students. Abrams and Jernigan (1984) wrote:

Colleges must develop a new system for selecting high risk applicants. The failure of the traditional scales, coupled with the lack of any other prematriculation variable correlating with academic success in college, demands new approaches. (p. 272)

PAM is one example of that new approach.

An article in *Black Issues in Higher Education* (Shabazz, 1995) signaled a change in times in which it may be necessary to move Beyond the Fifth Wave policies. Listed were more than 150 colleges and universities who no longer required SATs as one of the criteria for admissions. The National Center for Fair and Open Testing, an organization which advocates doing away with standardized tests for admissions, was mentioned in the article. More than 240 schools, where such scores are options for admissions to programs offering postsecondary education, are listed with this advocacy group. A more recent update on the question of standardized tests being "a measurement of what" was the focus in *Black Issues in Higher Education* (September, 1997). The number of colleges and universities where scores are optional has increased to 280. The authors, like Howard Gardner, argued that students show intellectual abilities in ways far beyond which standardized testing measures. Gardner (1983) has written much about the seven kinds of intelligence (linguistic, logical, spatial, bodily, musical, interpersonal, intrapersonal). Students possess intellectual capabilities for more than two of the seven that are commonly assessed through standardized testing: linguistic and logical. The challenge the authors give to admissions personnel is to look beyond the straight, narrow traditional approach to admitting students. There are so many students with talents that are untapped; talents that may be overlooked when determining who does and does not appear desirable for admittance to college.

As for Gigi, the student in the beginning of the chapter, she graduated with the degree in Social Welfare, received a master's degree in counseling, and is currently enrolled in the doctoral program in Developmental Education. Gigi now sits on the other side of the desk where her advisor once sat. She can identify with developmental students who need to be motivated in order to achieve. Her parting statement to all—especially the advisor who told her to go home—is "Through adversity, I have emerged."

Part III:
Models of Curriculum and Instruction

Chapter 9

ഔ∞

A Supplemental Learning Assistance Model for Developmental Learners

Wilton A. Barham

Introduction

As early as 1636, when Harvard became the first college in the United States of America, educators were faced with the need to establish some form of remediation for students enrolled in Latin (Boylan, 1988). Along with the expansion of American higher education came an increase in underprepared college students. By 1915, according to Maxwell (1979), over 350 colleges offered programs to prepare students so that they could meet the admissions requirements. Boylan, Bingham, and Cookman (1988) informed us that these programs expanded to over 2500 in 1988. Today, as in the past, higher education institutions across the country have been seriously engaged with trying to provide learning assistance programs for students from diverse backgrounds representing many socioeconomic, ethnic, age, and cognitive levels (Van, 1992).

A consequence of underpreparedness is the very high attrition rates reported by many colleges and universities for decades. High attrition among first year college students continues to be a trend (American College Testing Program, 1996). In 1986, Tinto (1987, p.1) predicted that of the nearly 2.8

million students who entered higher education for the first time, over 1.8 million would leave without receiving a degree (cited in National Center for Supplemental Instruction, 1996). Subsequently, pressures from politicians and education advocacy groups for an improvement in this situation have resulted in the implementation of many supplemental learning assistance programs. These programs are expected to eliminate students' deficiencies in the basic skills of reading, writing and mathematics or improve their study and learning skills. Students' poor self-esteem, high anxiety associated with learning or testing, and attainment of low standardized test scores are also the concern of the developers of these programs (Hardin, 1988; Van, 1992).

Some examples of supplemental learning assistance programs include *Learning to Learn Thinking Improvement System* (Heiman & Slomianko, 1986), *Special Mathematics Workshops* (Watkins, 1989), *Power Course Modules* (Yates, Barham, Shure, & Story, 1984), *Higher Education Learning Package* (Luvaas-Briggs, 1984), *Learning Strategies Course* (McKeachie, Pintrich & Lin, 1985), and the *Learning Strategies Program* (Denton, Seybert & Franklin, 1988). Other forms of supplemental assistance are *Adjunct Courses* (Dimon, 1994), *Review Groups, Peer Tutoring* (Clayton, 1995), *Peer/Faculty Collaborative Learning* (Davis, 1995). While many of these programs have been reported as being successful or effective, the focus of this chapter is on the very popular and effective supplemental learning assistance program, *Supplemental Instruction Model (SI)*. The historical and educational setting which provided the impetus for the development of SI is first discussed. This is followed by a discussion of the theoretical framework on which SI is based, an overview of the Supplemental Instruction model, and culminates with a selective review of research on SI.

Historical and Educational Setting

The Civil Rights Act of 1964 fueled the demands for access, educational equity and equal opportunity to a more diverse population in the American higher education system. It was the high point in the movement to democratize the system of higher education as we know it then. This brave decision led Cross (1971) to state in her book, *Beyond the Open Door: New Students in Higher Education*, that

America has made a commitment to open the door to educational opportunity to all of her citizens. The opening of that door—even three quarters the way—is a significant accomplishment, but it is not enough. For some students who have been underrepresented in colleges, the door to traditional postsecondary education opens only on more of the same kind of education that has failed to serve them in the past. (p. xi)

Nineteen ninety marked the twentieth anniversary of the Black Action Movement (BAM) strike at the University of Michigan-Ann Arbor. The year before Cross' observation, students were experiencing more of the same kind of education that had failed to serve them in the past. So these "new" students (as Cross referred to them) demanded and won, among other things, the university's commitment to equal access as a top priority along with the increase funding for Black student recruitment and retention programs. This is only one example of the kind of agitation that covered the American higher educational landscape during this period.

While the pressures were strong for an egalitarian philosophy of access to postsecondary education, Cross also informed us that egalitarians maintained that anyone who wanted to pursue further education should be helped to do so, regardless of economic resources and past academic achievement. The Higher Education Act of 1965 provided the legal authority for the establishment of the TRIO programs which channeled Federal dollars to colleges and universities to help make access a reality. There were other financial assistance programs that were established as part of the Economic Opportunity Act and the Elementary and Secondary Act.

But who were and are these "new" students? What were their interests? What sets of challenges did they bring to the classrooms and halls of our higher education institutions? In her book, Cross indicated further that the "new" students were Caucasian and Ethnic Minority males and females with the distinguishing characteristic of having a low level of academic achievement on traditional measures in the traditional curricula. We were informed that they were not as interested in academic pursuits as the traditional students. That is, they generally expressed their greatest interest in activities not stressed in schools. Cross presented some recommendations that would help us to meet the challenge of educating a non-traditional student body and not just providing "the simple extension of traditional education to broader segments of the population..." (p. 155).

Maxwell (1979) focused "on the problems students have in adjusting to the demands of college, the nature of these problems, their causes, strategies for their prevention and treatment, and the programs that have been developed to ameliorate them" (p. 1). We further learned that the "new" students were underprepared and underachieving, and often defined as "high-risk" or "at-risk". But this is not new; we have always had academically weak and poorly prepared college students. For example, in 1852, Henry P. Tappan in his inaugural address as President of The University of Michigan asked: "Of what avail could the learned professors and preparations of a University be to juvenile students? ... To turn raw, undisciplined youth into the University to study the Professions, to study the Learned Languages and the Higher Sciences is a palpable absurdity" (Maxwell, 1979, p. 7). Ten years later, the subject of underpreparedness was a topic of debate in the May 17 and June 14, 1989 issues of the Chronicle of Higher Education (Beckett, 1989; Kearney, 1990; Kelly, 1989).

As students and community activists, such as those of the Black Action Movement, demanded effective academic skills support programs, colleges and universities responded by establishing and developing basic skills courses (required or voluntary; credit or non-credit), summer bridge programs, tutorial services (individualized instruction), and learning centers. The earlier failures or ineffectiveness of these programs led to the development of more effective diagnostic methods of identifying the external/institutional and internal reasons for students' problems. Some examples of the external/institutional reasons are less sensitivity to the institution's standards and requirements, large class sizes, and not understanding professors' criteria for grading. The internal reasons include physical and learning disabilities, weak learning skills, social adjustment difficulties or emotional and attitudinal problems (Kearney, 1990; Maxwell, 1979). Clinical psychological counseling centers or components gradually became an important addition to the broad range of services available for a more diversified student body.

It was reported that by 1987, 82 percent of all institutions and 94 percent of public institutions offered at least one course considered to be remedial or developmental in nature (Abraham, 1987 as cited in Hardin, 1988). By then, too, all the various learning assistance programs were referred to as developmental education programs; their users were known as developmental education students, a more acceptable euphemism for "underprepared students," "underachieving students," "disadvantaged students," "nontraditional students," "high-risk students," "at-risk students," "new students," etc. Despite this demonstration of commitment on the part of many institutions, there are many who think colleges and universities should not be providing these services [e.g. "anti-diversity advocates, some state and federal legislators (Kelly, 1989); and some faculty and administrators.] In addressing the question of "Who belongs in college?", the designations of "developmental education" and "developmental education students" are appropriately describing the programs and the students for whom these programs were developed. Hardin (1988) proposed a distinction between the underprepared and incapable student by defining the developmental education student as a "poor chooser," the "adult learner," the "ignored student," the "foreign student," the "handicapped student," or "the user." These are all capable students. She suggested that "with good teaching and good support systems, there will be many who do make it" (p. 6).

Many researchers have informed us that many of our developmental education programs are successful or have been somewhat effective (Boylan, 1985; Greenburg, 1983; Heiman & Slomianko, 1986; Kulik, Kulik & Schwalb,1983; Martin, Blanc, & DeBuhr, 1982; Maxwell, 1990; Morante, 1986; Noel, 1978; Noel & Beal, 1980; Noel, Levitz, Saluri, & Associates, 1985; Upcraft, Gardner, & Associates, 1989; Watkins, 1989). However, we still lose many developmental education students; they become part of our drop-out statistics. Is the Supplemental Instruction (SI) model the answer to the problem of poor student performance and attrition? Before I attempt to provide an answer to this question, it is important to discuss the theoretical bases for the proposed model.

Theoretical Framework for Supplemental Instruction

The techniques utilized by many SI leaders are adapted from theories of intellectual development proposed by several well-known scientists/ educators, including Piaget (1964), Bloom et al. (1956), Dale (1969), Arons and Karplus (1976), Keimig (1983) and Perry (1970). In addition, research in college student development and retention by Astin (1987), Light (1990), Noel (1978), Pascarella and Terenzini (1991), and Tinto (1987) offered tremendous insights for the development and refinement of this model. The following summaries of three of these theories are useful for better understanding of the components and goals of SI.

Piaget's Learning Theory

Piaget's (1964) explanation of learning is summarized as follows: 1) Learning is not spontaneous; rather, it is provoked by situations and experiences; 2) "Development is the essential process and each element of learning occurs as a function of total development rather than being an element which explains development" (p. 176). In other words, development determines learning; learning does not determine development; 3) Piaget contended that "Knowledge is not a copy of reality" and that " To know an object is to act on it" (p. 178). Knowing something means you can transform it, modify it, interact with it, and manipulate the variables associated with it. In addition, knowing something is not limited to memorizing, reciting, and copying; 4) Knowledge comes from operational structures (mental structures) that allow for mental operations. Operations are interiorized, reversible, and always linked to other mental operations; and 5) The central problem of understanding development (and hence learning) is to understand the formulation, elaboration, and functioning of these structures.

He indicated that there are three steps of development: (1) Sensory-motor stage. Intellectual development begins with the development of a series of structures necessary for later thought processes. Until these structures develop, later learning must wait; (2) Pre-operational stage. This stage is a bridge between the sensory-motor and the operational stages. Piaget sees this stage as a time for restructuring and refinement of the mental structures acquired during the sensory-motor stage; and (3) Operational stage. This stage consists of two sub-stages: (a) a concrete operational; and (b) formal operational. During the concrete operational stage, individuals have the ability to reason about objects or concrete experiences. They can gather data from the object or experience, can organize the data, and can carry out mental manipulations on the data. At the operational stage, individuals can perform mental operations using not only objects and experiences but also hypotheses.

Bloom's Taxonomy of Educational Objectives

Our understanding of Benjamin Bloom's contribution to teaching and learning is through the modeling of his conceptual framework known as Bloom's Taxonomy. It was designed to assist teachers in their determination of the range of curriculum objectives and a hierarchy of learning skills. This hierarchy is referred to as levels of understanding. Students are expected to make the transition from functioning at the knowledge (lowest level) through comprehension, application, analysis, synthesis, and evaluation (highest level) (Bloom et al., 1956).

In the classification of educational goals, teachers are empowered with verbs for use in stating cognitive outcomes. For example, representative verbs in the hierarchy are: Knowledge (define, repeat, record); comprehension (translate, restate, discuss); application (interpret, apply, employ); analysis (distinguish, analyze, differentiate); synthesis (compose, plan, propose); and evaluation (judge, appraise, evaluate).

Dale's Cone of Experience

Dale's "Cone of Experience" (see Martin, Blanc, et al., 1983) presents the theory that learning progresses from concrete (hands-on) experiences to abstract thought and that the base of concrete actions is necessarily large in relationship to abstract thought that relies on verbal and visual symbols to stimulate learning. Dale's theory asserts also that intellectual life functions primarily on very high level of abstraction of symbolization and that students need experience at concrete levels before they can solve abstract questions and problems with good comprehension.

In moving from concrete to abstract thought, students are engaged in activities of action, activities of observation, and abstract representations. Activities of action, for example, include hands-on, experiences involving the five senses, and directed experience with a purpose. Activities of observation include radio, records, trips and demonstrations. The third level, abstract representations, include verbal and visual symbols. The following is a discussion of this exemplary learning assistance and retention program for developmental education students.

Overview of the Supplemental Instruction Model

Reports and studies have indicated that, traditionally, providing learning assistance has meant relating process-oriented information such as study skills, speed reading, mnemonic devices, time management, and test-taking strategies, in the hope that these aids will promote academic achievement (Denton et al., 1988; Hines, 1989). However, none of these strategies teach students how to learn. This fact has been recognized during the 1970's and early 1980's, and some examples of the responses to this problem were the development of programs/models and courses such as the Supplemental Instruction (SI) Model (Blanc et al., 1983; Martin, Arendale, & Associates, 1992; Martin, Blanc, DeBuhr, & Associates,1983; Martin, Blanc, DeBuhr, Alderman, Garland, & Lewis,1983); Learning to Learn Thinking Improvement System (Heiman & Slomianko, 1986); Special Mathematics Workshops (Watkins, 1989); Power Course Modules (Yates et al.,1984); Higher Education Learning Package (Luvaas-Briggs, 1984); Learning Strategies Course (McKeachie et al.,1985); and the Learning Strategies Program (Denton et al.,1988).

While the problems related to instruction for developmental students were being addressed, the problem of retention was also prominent on the minds of program instructors and administrators. Among the numerous factors that appear to influence retention rates are student perception of progress toward an academic career goal, a high level of faculty-student interaction, and personal counseling and academic advising programs (Blanc et al.,1983).

The Supplemental Instruction Model/Program is a learning enhancement and retention program which was developed at the University of Missouri-Kansas City (UMKC) by the university's Student Learning Center staff in cooperation with Arts and Science faculty (Martin, Blanc, DeBuhr, & Associates,1983; Martin, Blanc, DeBuhr, Alderman, Garland, & Lewis,1983). The developers of the model/program (See Figure 1) recognized that as students go from high school to college, they move from being a memorizer to that of an independent thinker-reasoner; critical thinking and problem-solving skills are necessary for learning (Fuller, 1984; Hines, 1989; Rumelhart, 1980; Sternberg, 1984, 1985a, 1985b; Weinstein, 1984; Whimbey, 1984; Whimbey & Lockhead, 1982). These skills are evident in the learning/understanding of content areas such as science and mathematics. SI focuses on the cognitive as well as the process skills necessary to promote critical thinking and independent learning in the college/university setting.

It differs from the typical learning center programs which offer services primarily designed to address the needs of high-risk students in two major respects. First, the emphasis has been shifted from the identification of high-risk students to high-risk courses. High-risk courses are defined as those traditionally difficult entry-level courses that deal with unfamiliar or abstract concepts in which students often are reluctant to ask questions or become more active participants in class. Students' D and F rates and withdrawals usually exceed 30 percent of course registrants. Second, the services are attached directly to each course. That is, the SI program sets up a regular schedule of out-of-class review sessions in which groups of students work together to master course content; it has organized services on an outreach rather than a drop-in basis. These sessions provide an informal, non-threatening setting for students to review the material, use the language of the discipline and organize their notes in a way most helpful to them. Other criteria for high-risk course designation may be: (a) large class sizes, (b) students' perception of a course as one that is very difficult and is likely to affect their decision to pursue a particular career, and (c) a course that has several instructors (Blanc et al.,1983; Lewis,1983; National Center for Supplemental Instruction, 1996).

**Figure 1. Supplemental Instruction:
Content, Procedures, and Outcomes**

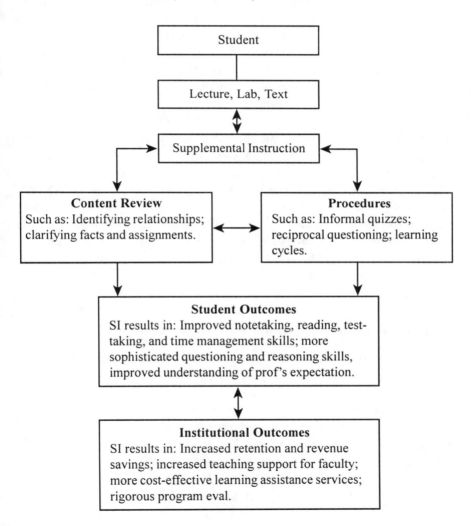

Martin, Blanc, DeBuhr & Associates (1983) presented four arguments that weigh heavily against the traditional organization of learning centers which focus on the needs of high-risk students: 1) there is an assumption that standardized testing is sufficient to identify those who are likely to leave the university. Experience and the statistics show that those who drop out do not fit a high-risk profile, while others with such a profile (Martin, Blanc, DeBuhr & Associates,1983; Martin, Blanc, DeBuhr, Alderman, Garland & Lewis, 1983) often succeed; 2) there is another assumption that the support staff have time to remediate skill deficits of high-risk students before they develop a pattern of failure. Data collected at UMKC demonstrated that the rate of student attrition is highest within the first six weeks of any semester while most remedial efforts begin much later; 3) high-risk students who encounter difficulty are among those least likely to admit their weakness, to ask for assistance, or to be committed to participating in a regular schedule of academic support sessions; and 4) learning centers earn a remedial image when they advertise to encourage high-risk students to seek assistance. This image, they argued, mitigates against participation of other students who could benefit from the services but who do not consider themselves "remedial" or "high-risk." The authors further observed that attrition could not be addressed effectively by treating only those who show either symptoms or predisposing weaknesses. "The treatment must be generalized; the problem must be addressed at or near its source: the mismatch between the level of instruction and the level of student participation" (p. 3).

Method of Operating Supplemental Instruction

The SI is attached to specific high-risk or historically difficult courses and the campus SI program is supervised by an on-site professional staff or faculty member. This individual, SI supervisor, is responsible for identifying the targeted courses, gaining faculty support, selecting and training SI leaders, and monitoring and evaluating the program (LoCascio, 1991; Martin, Blanc, DeBuhr & Associates,1983; Martin, Blanc, DeBuhr, Alderman, Garland & Lewis,1983; National Center for Supplemental Instruction, 1996).

Maxwell (1979) mentioned that "directors and staff members of academic support services, whether large, comprehensive learning centers or small, departmental skill components, continually face problems in defining their roles in the campus community, in relating to faculty members and administrators, in clarifying and communicating their functions to students, and in forming their perceptions of themselves" (p. 151). The SI program addresses the issue of the relationship with the faculty member/ professor. Certain informal agreements and understanding between the SI supervisor and the professor are prerequisite to attaching SI to a course. They are the following: (1) the professor should allow SI to be initiated in his or her course; (2) the professor should help in the selection of an SI leader and allow the SI leader to sit in the class and assist students with content needs in the review sessions; (3) the professor should assist SI leader in preparing handouts; (4) the professor should allow the SI leader to make appropriate announcements and distribute questionnaires in the class; and (5) the professor should give each test and final course grade to the SI supervisor.

As mentioned, SI is designed to assist students in mastering course concepts while it simultaneously increases student competency in reading, reasoning, and study skills. Learning center specialists or supplemental instruction leaders, whose content competency has been approved by the course instructors, attend the course lectures where they take notes and complete reading assignments. The leaders also schedule three or four fifty-minute SI sessions (e.g. as implemented at the University of Missouri-Kansas City) or longer (e.g. as implemented at the University of Illinois at Chicago College of Pharmacy's pilot SI program) each week at times convenient to the majority of the students; their attendance is voluntary.

SI leaders are trained by SI supervisors to provide quality instruction in reading, writing, and thinking skills necessary for content mastery. The individual selected as an SI leader may be an upper-class undergraduate or a graduate student who has taken the course from the service instructor (preferably) and received a grade in the range of B to A. The leader is presented as a "student of the subject" who "presents an appropriate model of thinking and languaging behavior in the field" (Blanc et al., 1983, p. 81). The role of the SI leader can vary "according to the nature of the discipline and the instructor's teaching style and priorities" (Blanc et al., 1983, p. 82). Each instructor assists in defining the SI leader's role.

In suggesting that we may be fostering dependence in "at-risk" minority students when we only provide process-oriented information, Hines (1989) was sharing her and other's experience with us, which is that students' "most common need is for the prerequisite learning and thinking skills that are basic to content mastery" (Blanc et al.,1983, p. 82). Furthermore, Blanc et al. reported that evidence provided by Arons and Karplus (1976) suggested that fifty percent of entering freshmen have not attained reasoning skills at the formal (abstract) operational level (Piaget & Inhelder, 1958). They indicated that "students who appear to operate at the concrete (non-abstract) level consistently have difficulty processing unfamiliar information when it is presented through the abstract media of lecture and text...Rarely do they ask or answer questions that require inference, synthesis, or application" (p. 82).

Martin, Blanc et al. (1983) reminded us that "seldom do college students have direct experiences with the course content. SI leaders can provide some concrete experiences and exposure to many more examples to help bridge the gap between representational teaching and concrete learning" (p. 38). Martin, Blanc, DeBuhr & Associates (1983) have also pointed out that students in college will have difficulty understanding concepts that involve control of variables and proportional relationships because they don't know how to think in these ways. In other words, they are not functioning well at Piaget's formal operational stage. One of the tasks as an SI leader is to help them develop these kinds of thinking skills. The authors went on to advise SI leaders:

> That is best done by relating the new concepts to things they already know and demonstrating how the variables are being manipulated or how proportions are being used. It is also very important to help students figure out what they do and do not understand about a concept, and to assist them in framing the kinds of questions they need answers to so that they will understand. (p. 37)

It is, therefore, extremely important that the SI leader becomes very aware of the quality of the students' questions and responses and provide appropriate assistance in enhancing the learning of those students whose levels of thinking interferes with the mastery of new concepts. Students are also given assistance in identifying important relationships; clarifying fact; understanding charts, diagrams, and formulas; establishing a meaningful frame of reference; clarifying assignments; engaging in self-testing; and predicting test questions. The SI leader uses procedures such as informal quizzes, reciprocal questioning, "learning cycle" (e.g. Fuller, 1984; Karplus et al.,1976), processing notes, task management, and information mapping. For example, the SI leader reviews students' lecture and text notes and models appropriate note-taking techniques, introduces effective reading styles and procedures, provides test-taking assistance, helps students to design effective study schedules, and provides backup tutoring. A more comprehensive treatment of the integration of skills and course content is given in Blanc et al. (1983), Martin and Blanc (1981), Martin, Blanc, DeBuhr & Associates (1983) and Martin, Blanc, DeBuhr, Alderman, Garland & Lewis (1983).

How do institutions pay for SI? While external grants are possible as part of a more comprehensive institutional grant proposal [e.g. Health Career Opportunity Program (HCOP), Fund for the Improvement of Postsecondary Education (FIPSE), and the TRIO federal programs or a foundation grant], most SI support comes from internal institutional resources which include: (a) payment of SI leaders through the Work Study Program; (b) departmental contingency funds for equipment, supplies, and salary of SI leaders; (c) joint department/college and Counseling Center/Learning Center support where the Counseling Center/Learning Center contributes staff time for training and supervision; (d) tuition waivers for SI leaders (for those with 0.25 or more appointment); and (e) university-wide support through Student or Academic Affairs units. For example, at the University of Illinois at Chicago where I was an SI leader and supervisor, in addition to financial support from the College of Pharmacy, $16,000 was received from the Student Activity Funding Committee (SAFC) for academic years 1989-1991. Another example is as follows (National Center for Supplemental Instruction, 1996, p.8):

> During the 1980-81 academic year, UMKC provided SI services to 566 students in 10 courses at a cost of $34,500; an average of $60.96 per student. The total program costs increased in FY 1995-96 since SI was offered in 41 courses, additional supervisory personnel were required and wages had increased since 1980.

Colleges and universities must seek more external funding for the establishment and maintenance of SI programs as traditional funding sources disappear or decrease.

As was indicated, this discussion of the SI program was not meant to be exhaustive. A more detailed presentation can be seen in Martin, Blanc, DeBuhr & Associates (1983), Martin, Blanc, DeBuhr, Alderman, Garland & Lewis (1983), as well as information that can be supplied by the National Center for Supplemental Instruction at the University of Missouri-Kansas City (UMKC); this includes advice for the training of SI leaders, the conduct of SI, and the evaluation of the effectiveness of the program or model. In the early 1980's the SI model was certified as an Exemplary Educational Program by the U. S. Department of Education. UMKC has received grants through the National Diffusion Network (NDN), to help over 160 colleges implement this model (LoCascio, 1991). At this point, it is appropriate to ask: "How successful is the SI program/model?"

Selective Review of Research
on Supplemental Instruction

Between January 1982 and September 1995, over 614 sites throughout the United States have adopted SI; more than 1,100 individuals have been trained since 1982; and the number of students impacted by the SI program nationally each semester has been approximately 300, 000 (National Center for Supplemental Instruction, 1996). It becomes relevant to ask, "How effective has this model been for the participants?"

Evidence for supporting claims of effectiveness of SI have been reported by researchers from UMKC and other institutions that have implemented SI. These studies use a basic quasi-experimental design which compares performance of the voluntary treatment group (SI Participants) with the control group (Non-SI Participants). The population studied includes students enrolled in courses in which SI was offered including those who participated in SI and those who did not. The data usually consist of course rosters and background data such as ethnicity, standardized entrance test scores, and high school rank. A student survey was administered on the first and last day of the course to find out students' motivational level as well as their evaluation of SI and their reasons for not participating in SI. Data analysis included the use of independent T-tests and Chi-square tests (National Center for Supplemental Instruction, 1996).

Several claims of effectiveness have been reported. They are as follows:

Claim 1: Students participating in SI within the targeted high risk courses earn higher mean final course grades than students who do not participate.

Claim 2: Despite ethnicity and prior academic achievement, students participating in SI within targeted high risk courses succeed at a higher rate (withdraw at a lower rate and receive a lower percentage of D or F final course grades) than those who do not participate in SI.

Claim 3: Students participating in SI persist at the institution (reenrolling and graduating) at higher rates than students who do not participate in SI. (National Center for Supplemental Instruction, 1996, p. 9)

The National Center for Supplemental Instruction (1996) reported results from six studies at UMKC from 1980-81 to 1995-96 (N=375 SI courses;

14, 667 SI participants): SI participants earned significantly higher percentage of A and B final course grades ; significantly lower percentage of D and F final course grades and withdrawals; and significantly higher mean final course grades than Non-SI participants (p < .05 [Chi-square] and p <.01 [Independent T-tests]). For example, in 1995-96, 40 percent of students in SI classes participated in SI ; SI participants had a higher percentage of A and B final course grades (71% vs. 49%), lower percentage of D and F final course grades and withdrawals (29% vs. 51%) and a higher mean final course grade (2.75 vs. 2.47) than non-SI participants. National SI field data for 146 institutions, 2,875 courses, and 298,629 students for years 1982-83 to 1992-93 showed similar results. In other words, they support the claims of effectiveness. Research has shown that the SI and Non-SI groups are generally similar in terms of previous levels of academic achievement, standardized test scores, high school rank, ethnicity, and motivational level. This certainly gives much credibility to the reported results (claims). Evidence for the claims have been reported in Martin, Arendale, and Associates, (1992) and Martin and Arendale (Eds.) (Winter, 1994).

Hawthorne and Hawthorne (1987) examined the effectiveness of SI using structural equation modeling and path analytic techniques to answer the following question: "After controlling for the confounding effects of marital status, age, high school rank, and ACT scores, what is the actual effect of attending the SI study sessions on course grade, semester grade point average, and reenrollment?" (p. 2). The authors reported that after analyzing data (N=461) for students enrolled in three courses (sociology; introduction to psychology; and math for general education, general zoology, and introduction to chemistry), it was determined that participation in SI had significant direct effects on course grade (β = .14, equation R^2 = .426, p < .05), semester GPA (β = .10, equation R^2 = .745, p < .05), and reenrollment (β = .14, equation R^2 = .182, p < .05). The three effects were all independent of the other factors in the model. Also, SI participation was indirectly related to semester GPA and reenrollment due to its relationship to course grade. Although this model is a variant of the UMKC model, it proved to be effective on the small undergraduate college where it was implemented.

Grimes (1989) reported that preliminary data from an SI model-testing program in the College of Pharmacy, The University of Illinois at Chicago (UIC), indicated that 103 out of 131 students attended SI review sessions throughout the Fall, 1989 semester. SI review sessions were conducted in medicinal chemistry and it was observed that voluntary SI attendance in the first five weeks appealed to 73 to 83 percent of students who received final grades from A to E. About 50 percent of every letter grade group attended SI at a frequency of 46 to 100 percent of the sessions offered. This related directly with the fact that 101 students indicated on a pre-SI questionnaire that the course needed review sessions. A post-SI questionnaire sought students' perceptions of the helpfulness of the SI sessions, competency of the SI leader, effectiveness of the combination of study strategies presented, and likely impact of SI on students' academic performance, among others. Ninety two point seven percent found the sessions somewhat to very helpful (N=96), 100 percent said that the SI leader was somewhat to very competent (N=99), 93.7 percent reported that the combination of study strategies was somewhat to very helpful (N=94),and 89.3 percent said that it was likely that the SI program had a positive impact on their academic performance in the course. The author indicated the need for further multivariate statistical analyses involving SI attendance, demographic variables, selected qualitative variables from the questionnaire and final course grades.

In an evaluation study of the same medicinal chemistry course at the UIC College of Pharmacy in Fall 1990, Fjortoft, Bentley, Crawford and Russell (1991) reported that regular SI attendance (11-20 sessions) was found to be a significant predictor of final course grade for non-white students (N=136; $p < .05$). Also, one hundred percent of the students responding to an end-of-term survey reported that the SI sessions were somewhat to very helpful (N=94). The authors used the statistical method of multiple regression to describe the relationship between sex, ethnicity, age, predictive index (measure of ability), SI attendance, and final grade obtained in the course. Another observation was that SI attendance did not have an effect on final grade for white students or for non-white students whose SI attendance was moderate (3-10 sessions). Reasons for group differences may be determined after further research.

It is now more common to participate in presentations at developmental education conferences and read reports that focus on results of preliminary and follow-up studies of SI programs on small and large colleges and universities. They are very positive and promising. While the impact of the SI program has been quantified by differences in student performance and retention rates, what combination of factors operate to influence higher levels of academic performance? Blanc et al. (1983) and the National Center for Supplemental Instruction (1996) reported that the program staff at UMKC, as well as participating faculty and students, assert that the following factors make substantial contributions: (a) the service is proactive rather than reactive. Students receive assistance before they encounter serious academic difficulty; (b) the service is attached directly to specific courses; thus, instruction in reading, learning, and study skills has immediate application; (c) SI is viewed by faculty and students as a program of enhancement, not remediation. Academically proficient students as well as less able students participate; and (d) SI sessions promote a high degree of student interaction and mutual support. This interaction leads to the formation of peer study groups and facilitates the mainstreaming of minority and disadvantaged students.

Conclusion

It is very apparent that there are efforts underway to support students in our community colleges, four-year colleges and universities. "Developmental education is helping people who have the motivation and interest to reach toward further education" (Thompson, 1988, p. 18). However, the challenge to educate the many thousands of deserving students remain great. Those of us who provide these services must remain truly committed to the goals we set for ourselves. SI and other programs, represent the dedication and creativity that will make these services truly successful.

SI results in improved note-taking, reading, test-taking and time management skills; more sophisticated questioning and reasoning skills; improved understanding of professors' expectations and frame of reference; and increased levels of success in high-risk courses: these are student outcomes. It also results in increased retention and revenue savings; increased teaching support for faculty; more cost-effective learning assistance services; and opportunities for more rigorous program evaluation: these are institutional outcomes (Blanc et al.,1983; Martin, Blanc, DeBuhr & Associates,1983; National Center for Supplemental Instruction, 1996).

Chapter 10

ඊාႠ

A Systems Model for Designing Curriculum for Developmental Studies

Olatunde A. Ogunyemi

The National Association for Developmental Education (1996) defined developmental education as "a field of practice and research within higher education with a theoretical foundation in developmental psychology and learning theory. It promotes the cognitive and affective growth of all post-secondary learners, at all levels of the learning continuum. Developmental education is sensitive to the individual differences and special needs among learners. Developmental education programs and services commonly address academic preparedness, diagnostic assessment and placement, affective barriers to learning, and development of general and discipline-specific learning strategies." This chapter concentrates mostly on the cognitive aspect of the definition above. The university and instructors cannot just put together a series of courses that they think will serve the purpose, they must systematically analyze the situation to develop instruction and services that will adequately meet the needs of their learners. Before presenting any curriculum design models, it is necessary to adequately define curriculum and to review the various models that are proposed. There are various definitions of curriculum. Haas and Parkay (1993) said "the curriculum is all of the experiences that individual learners have in a program of education whose purpose is to achieve broad goals and related specific objectives, which is planned in terms of a framework of theory and research or past and present professional practice" (p. 3). Walker (1990) defined curriculum as "the content and purpose of an educational program together with their organization." (p. 5). The definition that I am espousing for this chapter is by Ornstein and Hunkins (1993). They defined curriculum as "a plan for action or a written document that includes strategies for achieving desired goals or ends" (p. 9). The way an institution defines a curriculum will dictate the type of model that it uses to design its curriculum. A model allows the designer to answer the questions: "Where are we going?," "How will we get there?," and "How will we know when we get there?" There are several models or approaches to curriculum design. They are, subject-centered, student-centered, problem-centered, and systems approach.

Subject-centered model, as the name implies, incorporates those designs that concentrate on the subject matter to be presented. They are more prevalent in secondary schools and universities (Ornstein & Hunkins, 1993). In the model, content could be organized according to how essential thoughts have been developed in the various subject areas (subject design), students could be encouraged to see the basic logic of each discipline (discipline design), content that appear to fit logically together could be integrated (broad fields design), or students could be encouraged to learn general procedures and processes that are not specific to a particular discipline but are applicable to all.

The learner-centered model focuses mostly on the learner and is used mostly at the elementary school level. In this model, learning should be based on the learners' lives, needs and interests (child-centered design), the designer could analyze the students natural experiences to link them with formalized knowledge (experienced-centered design), learning should be geared towards educating and emancipating students from the current corrupt and repressive society that cannot cure itself (romantic design), or we could stress the development of positive self-concept and inter-personal skills (humanistic design).

The problem-centered model focuses on cultural traditions and addresses societal and community needs that are currently unmet. In this model, the designer could focus on life situations and social challenges (life situation designs), or on problems arising out of common human activities (core design), or on contemporary social problems (social problems, reconstructionist design).

The last model is the systems approach. While all the other models emphasize particular areas, the systems approach takes a more global approach to the design of curriculum. This model looks at curriculum from a systems standpoint. A system is a set of interacting components arranged to perform some warranted operations (Gentry, 1994). Hence, the model is a procedure for creating instruction where each step requires input from previous steps (Dick & Carey, 1996). It is a process to identify need, select alternative methods for meeting needs, develop methods, implement, and evaluate the new system. I am presenting this model for developing curriculum for developmental learners because it combines all the good points of all the other models. It is a process that combines people, materials, facilities, equipment and procedure to achieve a desired goal. These various entities interact with each other (Figure 1).

In order for the curriculum to be effective, we must consider the following in our planning and development:

- Goals should be based on an analysis of the environment of the system.

- The design of the program must be sensitive to the entering competencies of the students and also, of their long- and short-term academic goals.

- We must pay attention to planning instructional strategies and selecting media.

- Evaluation must be an integral part of the design, development, and implementation phases.

- Students must be measured and graded by their ability to achieve desired standard and criteria rather than by comparing one student with another.

This chapter is divided into the following: needs' analysis, choosing the type of intervention needed, task and instructional analysis, developing instructional strategy, media selection, and evaluation.

Needs Analysis

Before starting on the project, I propose that you appoint a team first. The ideal team should include faculty, an instructional designer, a production person, and an evaluator. The faculty should have expertise in the content

Figure 1. A Model for Curriculum Development
for Developmental Learners

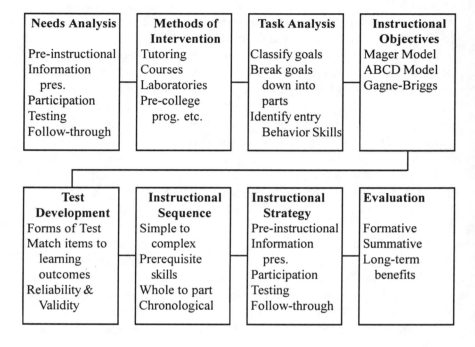

area and must be willing to devote time and energy required to complete the project. The instructional designer should have expertise and experience in the principles of designing instruction. The person should be outside of the content area. This will allow the person to be objective in the type of recommendations espoused. The person should have the ability, respect, and expertise to coordinate the group. The instructional designer will collect, interpret, and report instructional data. The major role of the production person is to provide technical expertise on the various methods that the team will investigate. The person should have expertise in media production. The evaluator will be responsible for developing evaluation instruments for the project. This person will also be responsible for collecting evaluation data and reporting results.

Before continuing with the discussion of needs analysis, let us dispel some misconceptions. Some people equate developmental education with remediation. While I agree that developmental education may include remediation, it cannot just be remediation because one cannot remediate what is not there. To people who assume that developmental education is remediation, they will contend that this step is not necessary. To them, if students score below a certain level on the American College Testing (ACT) examination, they should take remedial reading, writing, or mathematics. For example, if the cut off score on the ACT is 16 and a student makes less than that, he or she is placed in a remedial class. The problem with this is that not all the students need to be in such class. There may be other extenuating reasons that contributed to the student's low performance. Students who do not really need the class may see college as extension of high school. Thereby, they may not apply themselves to the rigors of college work. On the other hand, the situation may contribute to the low self-esteem that they bring to college with them.

Second, a person may need the services of developmental education in one subject area but not in others. Third, a developmental student in one institution may not be one at another college. For example, a student who is classified developmental at a selective admission institution may not be classified as such in an open enrollment institution. Therefore, each institution should do thorough needs assessment before developing services for developmental learners. In this section, I will present the various aspects of needs analysis for the institution.

Doing a needs assessment will allow program planners to focus attention on salient problems. We can use its results to decide whether to modify existing programs or to develop new ones. Needs assessment allows us to justify focusing attention on some needs and not others. Lastly, it provides baseline information against which to assess subsequent changes in student performance.

Dick and Carey (1996) defined needs assessment as "the formal process of identifying discrepancies between current outcomes and desired outcomes for an organization" (p. 347). The first step in a needs analysis is data collection. According to Seels and Glasgow (1990), when collecting data, we must provide answers to the following questions: What do I need to know? How will I collect the information? And whom or what will I use as source of information? (p. 60). In answering "What do I need to know?" we can collect information from various categories. Am I going to base the needs on facts and knowledge information? In this case, we are concerned with the knowledge base for the field. For example, if we are analyzing college algebra, what are the specific requirements for students entering such course? In other words, what basic competencies should the learners completing college algebra have, and what should they know before entering the course? In addition, we may want to know what the future requirements for the course will be. This will be based on trends in the field and the society.

Another type of data one may collect in the "What do I need to know?" category relates to the skills and competencies of the learners. Using the example above, what mathematical skills do our students tend to have? If they do not have the basic skills required to complete a course in college algebra then, we can say that they need some type of developmental instruction. However, if they already have the pre-requisite skills, we need to continue our analysis to determine the cause(s) of the problem. In this case, we can seek the opinion of the present and former students. They will provide insight into the causes (for example, lack of proper study skill, poor note-taking strategies, low self-esteem, etc.) of their problem.

In the "How will I collect information category?," we are interested in the method for collecting data. There are various methods for collecting data. We can collect data through surveys, group brainstorming sessions, Delphi approach, or existing goals. We can send survey instruments to experts in the field to find what kind of skills our students should have before and after taking the regular college level courses or we can gather them together in brainstorming sessions. The Delphi technique is the process of seeking consensus from experts without the face-to-face pressure to change or to conform. We can also collect data from documents such as student records and tests. Because of data collection, we will have information on "what ought to be." Then we can find out the kind of knowledge and skills that our students generally bring to us ("What is"). We can then identify the discrepancies between "what is" and "what ought to be" and the nature of the discrepancies.

After we have collected data on the discrepancies, we will generate our goals. These will be statements of "what ought to be." We should then prioritize the goals. The reason for this is that we know that it is impossible to eradicate all needs. By prioritizing, we are able to select the most important needs. The criteria for prioritizing will include constraints and resources (Seels & Glasgow, 1990). The constraints are costs, length of time need has persisted, the number of learners exhibiting needs, the time required to meet need, philosophy of the institution, organization, and the utility of remediation. Resources include facilities, space, personnel, and material. Before proceeding to the next section, we need to discuss learner characteristics. Information about the types of learners we cater to is very critical to the curriculum development effort. Kemp, Morrison, and Ross

(1996) collected data on academic information, personal and social characteristics, characteristics of non-conventional learners, and learning styles. Academic information should include high school grade point average (GPA), grades in specific courses, performance on standardized achievement tests (for example, ACT and SAT), and performance on diagnostic instruments (may be developed locally). Personal and social characteristics include age, socioeconomic status, intended major and motivational and attitude toward various subjects. Other data will include information on whether students are first generation college students.

Characteristics of non-conventional learners will include groups such as culturally diverse learners, learners with disabilities, and adult learners. Culturally diverse learners are those students whose "backgrounds and behaviors differ markedly from those of the majority of learners" (Kemp, et al., p. 45) at your institution. Disabled learners will include those students with physical and learning disabilities. The adult learners are those students who are returning to higher education after a break in their academic career. The break may have been because of employment, raising families, incarceration, or other things that may have prevented them from attending college immediately after high school graduation. Their reasons for returning to college range from retraining to skills upgrade. According to Kemp et al., learning styles involve learning condition and the students' cognitive learning styles. Learning conditions include environmental factors that affect learning. Kemp, et al. suggested that we collect data on immediate physical environment, student's emotionality, individual sociological and physical needs. Students' cognitive learning styles involve how they perceive the information, process the information received, and organize the information received. Next, I will discuss alternative methods of intervention.

Methods of Intervention

After developing the goals, the design team should select the method(s) of intervention. In other words, the team must answer the question, "What can we do to meet the need(s) we identified?" These include tutoring, courses, laboratories, pre-college programs, and summer only programs. This list above is not exhaustive however, because of time constraints, I will only discuss the ones listed. Select tutoring when you are sure that all the students' needs are helped in specific areas that do not have to be courses. In addition, when you think that the needs are too divergent to be served by any course you should use tutoring. Other situation where this may be more appropriate is when you think that the students will perform better in small groups or one-to-one settings. You can design your tutoring program to help students with classroom assignments or with enrichment activities. The major advantage for having tutorial programs is that the student will have human interaction in a non-threatening environment.

Courses will be necessary if you determine that there are clusters of information relating to a particular course that the students have not mastered. I will discuss this in more detail later. Laboratories are centers that you can develop to support content areas. They can be writing laboratories that are designed to improve student's writing abilities. You can also have mathematics and reading laboratories. To set up laboratories, you must have a system for identification and referrals to ensure their adequate use.

To deal with the problem of under-preparedness, several institutions are starting pre-college programs. The purpose of such programs is to assist the students before they finish high school. Activities such as career counseling, tutoring, college day, and mentoring could be part of the pre-college programs. Some programs even attempt to identify and provide help for at-risk students from junior high school and beyond. To have such a program, your needs assessment should focus on anticipated or future needs. I suggest this because at the middle school or high school levels, it is difficult to identify specific academic problems that the students will have in college. Summer only programs can be designed as bridge to students who do not have the pre-requisite skills that they need to succeed in college. To design pre-college and summer only programs, you should follow the guidelines for developing courses.

The goal of this section is to help you to select the method(s) that will help you to meet the needs you identified during the needs assessment phase. You should not haphazardly select a method but, you should base your selection on the goals that you set as a result of your needs' assessment. If you decide to develop courses, you need to write instructional objectives based on the goals that you wrote.

Task and Instructional Analyses

Before you can write instructional objectives, you should first break your goals down into manageable and measurable chunks. This break down is called task or instructional analysis. Dick and Carey (1996) defined instructional analysis as "the procedures applied to an instructional goal in order to identify the relevant skills and their subordinate skills and information required for a student to achieve the goal." (p. 346). According to Seels and Glasgow (1990), "Task analysis asks, What are the performance requirements for this job or function? Instructional analysis asks, What must be learned in order for someone to perform this task? What are the requirements for learning?" (p. 109). There are various types of analyses and you should use the one that is more appropriate for the goal(s) you identified. Procedural analysis is best suited for goals that fit into the psychomotor domain. Cluster analysis is best suited for verbal information goals. Hierarchical analysis is best for goals that can be classified as intellectual skills.

In psychomotor goals, you are interested in what the learner will be doing at a particular step. Hence, we call it procedural analysis. You are interested in the procedures the learner will go through to accomplish goals. For example, if the goal is to be able to access a mainframe computer, we will then break that goal into the steps it will take for one to do the task. However, as you break down the goal into the various steps, some of them may fall into intellectual skills or verbal information domain. In this case, you should use the right type of analysis to break down that particular step.

When your goal is in the verbal information domain, the order of learning the material is not important. For example, if the goal is to learn all the 50 states, it does not matter if one learns Alabama before Nebraska. In this case, our goal is to break the various components into manageable chunks, for example, geographical clusters. This is why we call this cluster analysis.

In the intellectual skills domain, the order that one learns the information is very crucial. For example, in order for a student to be able to solve complex algebraic problems, that student must know applicable rules. The same applies to the rules, the student must always know applicable subordinate skills. Therefore, at each step of the analysis, you are asking the question "What must the student know in order to perform the skill?" This is why we call it hierarchical analysis. What if the goal is to improve the student's study habits? We realize that this goal is dependent on the students' attitudes. How can we make sure that they will choose to do what we taught them? This goal is in the affective domain. You should break it down using any of the other analyses. For example, for the goal above, we will use both the hierarchical and procedural analyses. The students will need to know good study skills and the steps for developing those skills. Once the students demonstrate competence in the other areas of the domain, we will assume that they will choose effective study habits. Next, I will present the steps in goal or instructional analysis.

The first step is to classify the goal into the appropriate domain. The next step is to break the goals down into its subordinate skills. In the third step, you should identify the entry behavior skills. These are skills we expect the students to have before they enter the course. There are three benefits for doing these analyses. The first is that the result serves as an instructional blueprint that can guide in the design of the sequence of instruction. Second, it provides a guide for teachers in planning instructional assignments. It provides the teacher with a list of tasks the students should accomplish and the sequence in which they should accomplish them. Lastly, it aids evaluators in studying the learning process and in evaluating the project. Now you are ready to write your instructional objectives.

Instructional Objectives

The first step is for the team to write objectives for the course(s). The objectives should specify the action the learner will exhibit after instruction, the conditions under which actions will take place, and the standard or criterion for assessing performance. There are various methods of writing objectives—Mager model (Mager, 1962), ABCD model (Stamas, 1973), and Gagne-Briggs model (Gagne & Briggs, 1979). The Mager model has three components. The first one is you have to identify the performance expected after instruction. Second, you have to identify the condition under which the student will perform. Lastly, you have to specify the criteria of acceptable performance. The ABCD model has four components—audience, behavior, condition, and degree. Behavior is the same as performance in the Mager model and degree is the same as criterion. The only difference is that the ABCD model calls for a specific description of the target audience.

The Gagne-Briggs model has five components—situation, learned capability, object, action, and tools and constraints. Situation is the same as condition in the Mager model. Learned capability, object, and action are from performance in the Mager model. Action refers to the what the learner will be doing that will be readily observable by another person after the instruction. Object refers to what the learner will produce as a result of the action performed. Learned capability is the evidence of the capability that the student acquired. Tools and constraint are substitutes for criterion in the Mager model, and refers to how the action must be carried out. This will include tools needed, what students can use and what they cannot use. Next, you should develop tests to match the objectives that you have developed.

Test Development

There have been debates on where tests belong in the instructional design paradigm. Some argue that since the goal of instruction is to measure student achievement, tests should be part of evaluation. While this argument is right, it does not explain when the design team should develop the test. This chapter focuses more on the development of the test than when it should occur in the process. In this section, I will discuss test development. The first thing the design team should do is to decide which form of test they plan to use. The three major forms of tests are pretest, embedded, and posttest. Pretests are tests administered before instruction takes place. There are various purposes for pre-testing. One is for diagnostic purposes. You can use this test to identify the specific problems that the student has. When your purpose is to use pretest as a diagnostic tool, you must have a set of competencies to measure, then develop the test items to measure them. One can also use it as baseline data. In this situation, we can collect data on where the students were before instruction and compare that to where they are after instruction. When this is the purpose for your pre-test, it must either be the same as the posttest or must be a parallel form of it. In this case, our test should measure the objectives that we developed for instruction.

A third purpose for pre-testing is to measure prerequisite skills. This kind of test measures whether the students have appropriate preparation for the instruction. This can also be used as a tool for needs assessment because we can determine which students are ready for the topic and which ones need remediation. When developing a prerequisite skills test, one should first write the objectives for the skills.

The second form of test is embedded. Embedded tests are those that you administer during instruction. This is like the "pop quiz" only; it is well planned in this case. Embedded tests are used to measure if the students have mastered the enabling objectives. Posttests are generally administered after the instruction. Their major purpose is to measure if the students have mastered the skills presented in the instruction. Regardless of the type of test, your design team must do several things. First, you must write the test items immediately after completing the objectives. This will allow your team to develop only items that measure the skills called for in that objective.

Secondly, you should carefully match your test items to the learning outcome. For example, the test items for the objective—"at the end of this course, you will be able to identify the steps of instructional design" will be different from the ones for the objective that states "at the end of this course, you will write a detailed description of needs assessment." In the first objective, we can measure effectively by asking for a list, matching, or multiple-choice items. In the second objective, the best method to use is essay. Your team must also deal with the reliability and validity of the test items. This has to do with the questions "Is the test measuring what it is supposed to measure?" (Validity) and "How well is it measuring it?" (Reliability). The first question can be answered by carefully matching the tests with the objectives. The second question is harder to answer because it has to do with the number of items that the students must answer to demonstrate mastery. For example, if we have only one item and a student passes that item, can we safely conclude that the student has mastered the objective? You must remember that the student may have guessed the correct answer. You must have enough items to differentiate between students who have mastered the objective and those who have not.

Other things that you should consider are the amount of test taking time, guessing parameter, grading time, test conditions, and test format. When developing the test, we must be aware of the amount of testing time we will have. The number of items must not be too much for the time available for the test. The major reason for developing test items is to differentiate between those who have mastered the material presented and those who have not. Therefore, when writing the items (especially multiple choice), you should make sure that your distracters are plausible answers. After developing the test items, the next step is to develop the instructional sequence.

Instructional Sequence

Instructional sequence is "the efficient ordering of content to help the learner achieve the objectives" (Kemp, Morrison, & Ross, 1996, p. 109). The way you sequence the instruction will depend on the type of skill that the objective calls for. For example, the sequence of an objective that calls for psychomotor skills is pretty much suggested by the procedure. There are four major sequencing schemes: simple to complex learning, prerequisite learning (logical dependency), whole to part learning, and chronological learning (McNeil, 1996; Ornstein & Hunkins, 1993).

In simple to complex sequencing, you organize the content such that easy, concrete content is presented before presenting complex content. In prerequisite learning, you sequence the content in such a way that the students are taught prerequisite information and tested for mastery before moving to the next logical more complex content. In whole to part sequencing, you present the whole task to be learned first. This will allow the student to have a general idea of the information or situation to be learned. In chronological learning, you sequence the instruction in the order of its development.

Other sequencing schemes are world-related and concept related. In content that represents objects, people, and event, it is sequenced in a way that is consistent with the real world (Kemp et. al., 1996). "The concept-related method draws heavily from the structure of knowledge. It focuses on the interrelationships of concepts rather than on knowledge of the concrete" (Ornstein & Hunkins, 1993, p. 239). The first thing you need to do is to select the scheme that best fits the skills you want to present. Then arrange the content in an orderly fashion according to that scheme. Now that you have written the objectives of instruction, developed test items to match those objectives, sequenced your content, it is time to develop your instructional strategy.

Instructional Strategy

Now that you have identified where you are going (goals and objectives) and how you will know when you get there (test), it is now time to device a method for getting there. Instructional strategy is "an overall plan of activities to achieve an instructional goal" (Dick & Carey, 1996, p. 347). The first step is to decide which delivery system you will use to instruct. You should decide whether instruction should be self-paced, instructor-led, or whether to deliver through the growing electronic media. Although there is an overlap between instructional strategies and media selection, I will discuss media selection later in this chapter.

The decision on which delivery system to use should not be haphazard. It should be based on factors such as the nature of the skill that the objective(s) calls for and the skill level of the students. For example, if our objective require hands-on presentation, a self-paced delivery system will not be appropriate. After deciding on the delivery system, you should then focus on how to organize the content to be presented. There are five components to organizing the lesson. They are: pre-instructional activities (Dick & Carey, 1996) or introduction (Seels & Glasgow, 1993), information presentation (Dick & Carey) or body (Seels & Glasgow), learner participation (Dick & Carey) or body (Seels & Glasgow), testing (Dick & Carey) or assessment (Seels & Glasgow), and follow-through (Dick & Carey) or conclusion (Seels & Glasgow).

Pre-instructional Activities

These activities occur before formal instruction. Gagne (1972) suggested the first step is to gain the students' attention. The purpose of this is to focus their attention on the task to be learned. It is also to motivate them to learn. Keller (1987) developed the ARCS model to help achieve this. The model consists of four components—attention, relevance, confidence, and satisfaction. According to Keller, there are six attention strategies—incongruity and conflict, concreteness, variability, humor, inquiry, and participation. In incongruity and conflict, you may introduce a fact that appears to contradict the student's prior knowledge or learning. In concreteness, you present concrete information such as visuals or models that will help keep their interest. In variability, we catch and hold the students' attention by varying voice tones, movement, presentation style and so on. Humor can also help you to gain and keep attention. However, one must be careful not to allow the humor to distract from the instructional activities. In inquiry strategies, you consistently involve the students in problem solving activities that will capitalize on their interests.

The second component of the ARCS model is relevance. Its intention is to allow the students to attach value to the learning task. Instruction should show the learners how the new knowledge matches what they already know. Secondly, it should show the current value of the material to be learned. You could also show the connection between the learning experience and the student's future goals. Fourth, you can use exemplars or people who have been through the process as models or as guest lecturers.

The third component is confidence. You should clearly inform the students what they are going to learn. You should also sequence the material in such a way that students can proceed in order of increasing difficulty.

The last component of the ARCS model is satisfaction. One strategy is to allow students who have mastered a particular task to help others who have not finished. Another strategy is to provide unexpected rewards during tasks that are not too exciting. Another strategy is the use of reinforcements.

The second component of pre-instructional activities is to inform the learners of the objectives. This will help them to focus their attention on the expected outcomes. The next step is to stimulate recall of prerequisite skills. We can achieve this by either administering a test covering the prerequisite skills or briefly discussing them.

Information Presentation

The purpose of this step is to present information necessary for students to master the objective. Smith and Ragan (1983) suggested using expository or discovery approach. In expository approach, you present the students with generalities such as concept definitions or statements of rules before giving them examples. In discovery strategy, you present the example first and encourage the students to deduce the concept (p. 143). Dick and Carey (1996) explained that a primary error of this step is to present too much information or information that are not related to the concept to be learned. Some strategies are specific to particular skills. For example, if the objective call for learning facts (verbal information), you should present them with the objects of the fact. If the fact is abstract, the first task will be to make it abstract. Then you could employ rehearsal-practice tactics for them to memorize the fact.

If the skill required is a concept, you should first present the distinguishing characteristics of the concept. You should also present examples and non-examples and explain why they are such. You may also help the students to develop mnemonic devices. You should also provide adequate practice.

For skills relating to rule, Markle (1969) suggested rule-eg and eg-rule approaches. In the rule-eg approach, you proceed with instruction and then provide several examples. In the eg-rule approach, you present several examples first and then ask the learner to device a rule for the examples. To teach motor skills, you should present step by step directions to complete task. You should also provide opportunities for practice. To teach skills relating to attitudes, you should first present an acceptable model to the learners. The model could be in the form of demonstrations or role-plays. The next step is to ask the learners to develop verbal or imaginal models of behavior. The last step is to provide opportunities for both mental and actual rehearsal of the acceptable behavior (Bandura, 1977).

Learner Participation

According to Dick and Carey (1996), learner participation is one of the most powerful components of the learning process. The learners should be given opportunities to practice learned skills and receive feedback. Seels and Glasgow (1990) suggested that practice opportunities must allow students to perform the task actively. Practice is most effective when it occurs immediately after presentation of new material, while information is still fresh in students' minds. There must be multiple opportunities for practice. Learning seldom occurs after only one try at a task (p. 166).

Testing

The purpose for testing at this point is to measure whether the students have mastered the task before proceeding to the next one. This will allow you to decide whether the learners need remediation or reteaching.

Follow Through Activities

This is the step that Gagne (1972) called enhancing retention and transfer. The purpose of this section is to present opportunities for the learners to review and elaborate on the new tasks they learned so that they can use them in the future. The first thing to do is to summarize and review. This is when the essential concepts or ideas are reviewed and the students are given opportunities for extended practice. Secondly, you should help students transfer new learning by providing opportunities to apply their learning to real life situations and future learning tasks.

Media Selection

Media selection is sometimes dealt with the same time you are deciding on your instructional strategy. It has to do with the best media to present the content. According to Romiszowski (1988), several factors affect the choice of media for a particular instruction. The first one is the method that you selected during the instructional strategy phase. A second factor is the learning task itself. A third factor is the learner characteristics. The fourth factor is practical constraints such as finance, time, and what is available. The last factor is the teacher who will be disseminating the instruction. You have to be sure of the likes and ability of the instructor to use the prescribed media.

The first step to select media is an analysis of the learning context. For example, the type of actions your objective calls for will dictate the type of media. You need to answer questions such as "Can students effectively learn information from printed text?," "Will visuals stimulate recall of presented information?," and "Does the skill require precise timing and muscular movement?" In addition, the type of presentation stimuli will affect media selection. A second step is a thorough knowledge of the learner characteristics. For example, if your learners do not have the maturity for self-direction, a self-instructional system may not be appropriate. Their ability to work in a group may determine your choice of group instruction. The size of your group will dictate the type of media. Other learner characteristics such as reading level, ability, and learning style may affect the type of media you select.

Evaluation

The last step in your curriculum design model is evaluation. The purpose of evaluation is to gather and analyze data that allows people to measure the effectiveness of the curriculum. It allows them to decide whether to revise, maintain, or eliminate a curriculum. There are two types of evaluation—formative and summative. Formative evaluation is the process of collecting data and information that one can use to improve the curriculum (Dick & Carey, 1996). We usually do formative evaluation while developing the curriculum. To plan an effective formative evaluation, you need to consider purpose, audience, issues, resources, evidence, data-gathering techniques, analysis, and reporting (Gooler, 1980). You need to determine the purpose of evaluation. You should determine the purpose by consulting with the stakeholders (administrators, faculty, etc.) in the curriculum. The next step is to determine who will receive the results of the evaluation. The type of information you collect will depend on who will receive the report. For example, teachers will be more interested in information such as readability, flow of information and other issues relating to content. Whereas, administrators may be interested in cost and how the curriculum fit into regular curriculum.

The next step is to determine the major objectives of the evaluation. You need to determine the specific questions (for example, the match between the content and objectives) that evaluation will answer. A fourth step is to determine the resources that you need for the evaluation. Resources may include faculty, instructional designers, equipment, and data-gathering instruments. Next, you need to determine what type of information you will need to answer evaluation questions. Then you need to decide the method you will use to collect data. The method could include tests (written or oral), observations, surveys, interviews, exhibitions, etc. The next step is to decide how you will analyze the data collected. For formative evaluation, this should be confined to basic descriptive analyses of the data collected. Lastly, you need to decide how and when to produce the report of evaluation.

At each step of your curriculum development, you should complete a formative evaluation to determine if the materials are doing what you purport them to be doing. The premise for this is that it is easier to modify smaller documents that endeavoring to modify a fully developed curriculum.

The purpose of summative evaluation is to determine the effectiveness of the developed curriculum. By its purpose, you can surmise that we usually do summative evaluation after delivering instruction. Some of the issues that you should address are:

Effectiveness of learning
Efficiency of learning
Cost of development and delivery, and the
Attitudes and reactions of learners, faculty, and staff to the curriculum.

Long-term Benefits of the Curriculum

We have been discussing a model for designing effective curriculum for developmental learners. One thing we should have in mind is that a developmental learner is someone who needs the extra help to succeed in college. We should not only be interested in the instructional material, we should also be interested in the affective growth of the students. If you follow the model prescribed here, you will be developing a top-notch curriculum for your developmental students.

Chapter 11

ഇരു

A Collaborative Writing Model for College Students with Emphasis on Cultural Diversity

*Evelyn Shepherd-Wynn, Lorraine Page Cadet
and Ernesta Parker Pendleton*

Introduction

Through our experiences as writing instructors, we recognize that a framework is needed to synergize desirable collaborative writing approaches with effective cultural teaching methods that we consider to be necessary and applicable to developmental education programs in postsecondary institutions. The research indicates that a number of collaborative learning models have been designed with culturally diverse students in mind (Davidman & Davidman, 1994; Nieto, 1992). These models support the premise that collaborative learning is a viable approach congruent with the teaching of culturally diverse students, especially the Group Investigation Model (Sharan, 1980) and the Cooperative Integrated Reading and Composition Model (O'Connor & Jenkins, 1993). Research reveals that when these models are utilized, students tend to have higher achievement scores, higher critical and creative thinking skills, as well as accelerated reading comprehension, writing performance and socialization skills. Although these models were designed for the elementary and secondary levels, they have implications for culturally diverse students at the postsecondary level, particularly since there has been a renewed interest in collaborative writing as postsecondary institutions seek alternative ways of improving students' writing skills.

This renewed interest can be attributed to the demand for educational assessment and accountability as a result of the increasing number of culturally diverse students in postsecondary education, many of whom are developmental students. Locke (1992) reported that by the year 2075, African Americans, Alaskan Natives, Native Americans, Hispanic Americans, Asian Americans, as well as other minorities, will constitute the majority of the United States population. Meanwhile, Morganthu (1997) estimates that by the year 2050, the population of the United States could increase by more than 500 million, more than twice the increase reflected in the 1990 census. With the emerging demographic changes in society, there is a critical need for innovative and interactive instructional approaches to enhance the cognitive and affective skills of culturally diverse students. Educators must seek new instructional alternatives to respond to the nature and needs of students with culturally diverse backgrounds. As they search for instructional alternatives, collaborative writing is emerging as one of the preferred instructional approaches. In view of these facts, this chapter's purpose is to present a model utilizing collaborative writing (See Figure 1) and to identify and examine appropriate approaches of collaborative writing that can be conducive to teaching writing to culturally diverse college students.

Design and Orientation of the Model

Teacher and Student Self-Disclosure

In order for collaborative writing to achieve its maximum potential with culturally diverse students, the collaborative writing model should be socially designed and consensus oriented which is achieved through disclosure, the first aspect of the collaborative process. Disclosure is a term borrowed from the field of counseling. Counselors tend to place a great deal of emphasis on one's ability to self-disclose intimate details of one's life. They consider it to be a major attribute of the healthy personality. Jourard (1964) argues that one's ability to be open during the disclosing process is an indication of one's mental health. Consequently, the more open students are during the

**Figure 1. Shepherd-Wynn's Collaborative Writing Model
for College Students with Emphasis on Cultural Diversity**

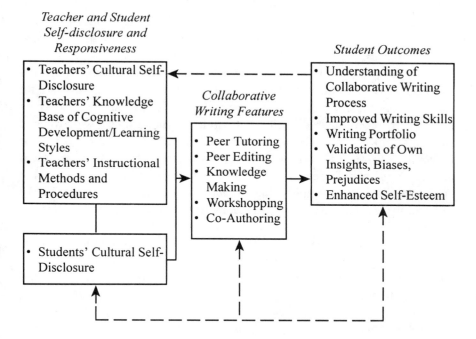

collaborative process, the more likely the writing task will be a success. Disclosure enhances all other approaches of collaborative writing by encouraging students to share their inner selves with others to improve their communication skills. It also enables students to engage in deep levels of communication that can have positive effects on their cognitive skills. When using disclosure in the classroom, however, instructors should plan carefully and set specific guidelines to create a "protected" environment. This view is supported by Bleich (1995) and Bruffee (1993) who acknowledged that disclosure is not merely "opening up" or "expressing oneself" in the academic environment, but rather an initiative with personal, political, and sociological implications. If students do not openly express themselves, communication will remain on the surface, making it less likely that collaborative writing will be effective.

In order for instructors to effectively facilitate collaborative writing, they should first begin by examining their values, beliefs, prejudices, and attitudes concerning culturally diverse students. Instructors should recognize their prejudices through disclosure which can provide an opportunity for them to become knowledgeable of their views regarding these students. According to Henry (1986), a teacher's self-awareness [self disclosure] enables him or her to look at his/her own beliefs, attitudes and behaviors towards culturally diverse students which will help them to develop and implement specific methods that can best assist students with their own self-awareness.

Banks (1981) supports the premise that instructors typically perceive culturally diverse students as not being as academically inclined as Anglo students. As a result, a number of instruments have been designed to assist teachers in examining their cultural theoretical orientations toward diverse students. For example, Banks' "Self-Awareness" and Henry's "Cultural Diversity Awareness Inventory" are two instruments which may be utilized by teachers to help reeducate themselves in order that they too may understand and respect individuals regardless of their differences. Banks further argues that instructors' attitudes help to create an atmosphere in which students can learn.

Postsecondary institutions must train teachers to be culturally responsive by providing them educational opportunities so they will become knowledgeable of the culture of minority students. Therefore, we recommend that prior to employing disclosure, instructors should be provided training to help them become culturally sensitive toward and acquire an understanding of students from various cultural backgrounds. At the beginning of the academic school year, instructors should participate in workshops where they can employ practical disclosure exercises and examine their cultural orientations along with reviewing the literature. Instructor attitudes and perceptions of culturally diverse students determine the level of expectations they set for these students and the kind of treatment students receive in the classrooms (Hernandez, 1989; Sleeter & Grant, 1988).

Consequently, understanding the importance of disclosure is perhaps one of the most crucial skills instructors can possess when teaching collaborative writing. Instructors who are willing to express their thoughts and feelings may be better received by culturally diverse students, thereby encouraging these students to develop more positive self-images and attitudes. After instructors have disclosed and examined their own belief systems concerning culturally diverse students, they must then begin to guide students in examining their own belief systems utilizing disclosure. They must encourage students to participate in various experiences to increase their knowledge about the beliefs and values of other groups. During class orientation, instructors should administer a disclosure survey. Disclosure will help students learn how to be comfortable with members of other cultural groups by accepting, respecting and appreciating the other group. In turn, students will learn to acknowledge the existence of other cultures by understanding the nature of other groups and by recognizing the complex process of culture.

Although the research on disclosure is limited, the findings have been varied. For example, Mead (1994) has demonstrated a high degree of interest in disclosure through her research. She studied students ($n = 16$) enrolled in a professional writing class in order to reorganize course objectives. In order to prepare students to write collaboratively, Mead divided the students into four groups with each group consisting of four students who were assigned to design a brochure for real clients during the course of three weeks. During the first week, Groups One, Two and Four accomplished the collaborative task successfully because all members brainstormed, analyzed, revised and shared equally in the writing. However, in the second week Group Three experienced dissensus because they did not assign or share tasks and they did not attend meetings. Because of the dissensus, Group Three evaluated the dynamics of their group and discussed the problems that prohibited them from successfully completing the collaborative writing project. Mead then decided to reorganize the course based on the following objectives: (a) to provide opportunities for students to collaborate with the instructor as mediator, (b) to provide options for students in selecting projects and group members, and (c) to provide opportunities for students to become familiar and comfortable with dissensus.

Although Mead's focus was on self-disclosure and writing, other studies have focused on self-disclosure and the student's ethnicity. For example, several studies on self-disclosure among college students indicated that culturally diverse students have a preference for disclosing to individuals of their own ethnic group (Durrani,1981; Noel, & Smith, 1996). Other findings indicated that students produced greater self-disclosure because of similarities in attitudes (DeWine et al., 1977). The degree to which a comfort level is established, therefore, affects the extent and ease of disclosure among student groups. Once instructors and students have completed the disclosure aspect of the collaborative writing process, students should receive an orientation that establishes the philosophical approach on which collaborative writing is based. This part of the orientation prepares students to engage in the collaborative activities. During the orientation students are involved in preparation activities and experiences that give them the proper mindset and attitudes they need to successfully negotiate the writing process.

Collaborative Writing Approaches

Collaborative writing advocates argue that this approach has synergistic benefits which are advantageous to teachers and students across disciplines (Bruffee, 1984; Connors & Lunsford, 1993). This observation tends to be true since collaborative writing is a multifaceted enterprise with many approaches. The suggested collaborative writing approaches for inclusion in a collaborative writing model at the postsecondary level include peer tutoring, peer editing, co-authoring, workshopping, and knowledge making. Although there are a number of other approaches of collaborative writing, these tend to be the most appropriate for culturally diverse college students. The activities in this collaborative writing model are not designed to be structured in a sequential or linear manner. They are designed to be recursive in nature; therefore, the model is spiral as is the writing process. These collaborative writing approaches are discussed in isolation with no specific preference for order; however, it is important to note that they can be interrelated. In order to facilitate this model, a description of these approaches and their implications/utilization for culturally diverse college students are provided below.

Peer Tutoring

Using peer tutoring to teach culturally diverse students involves and demonstrates an appreciation of their unique views and approaches to the writing assignment and fosters the notion of collegiality. Since writing is such a personal enterprise, both peer assisted writing and peer tutoring recognize and exploit the element of values similarity among the student cohort. Often culturally diverse students are less defensive with each other than with a teacher or authority figure. In some Asian cultures, for example, it is impolite to look directly at adults. Ideally, therefore, the peer tutor is available not so much to correct mistakes as to offer comments and discussion of the assignment in a non-threatening atmosphere. As culturally diverse students engage in the writing process among a supportive peer environment, they often are able to grasp concepts more clearly, ask questions more freely, and understand the weaknesses in their writing more fully.

Peer tutoring also can be helpful in stressing the discipline of writing which involves not just cognitive and intellectual concerns, but emotional expression as well. As students examine the purpose for their writing and the intended audience, they tend to approach writing more personally and benefit from the feedback of the objective reader/tutor. In this sense, for the culturally diverse student, the peer tutor may be preferable to computer-assisted instruction which may yield linear, competency based improvement of grammar skills, but not the personal growth that comes from higher order thinking requiring value judgments and greater interpretive skill.

A number of studies have been conducted by college instructors who employed collaborative writing as an instructional approach to examine the effects of peer tutoring in the classroom. For example, Scott (1995) conducted a study to assess students' attitudes towards two kinds of collaboration: peer assisted writing and peer tutoring. The sample (N = 237) consisted of students in ten different courses with nine different teachers from seven universities in five states. Scott administered a questionnaire to determine students' attitudes toward collaboration consisting of two types of items: statements about which students ranked their responses on a scale of 1 to 5, and open-ended statements which they completed. Scott's questionnaire also included a Group Writing about the experience of fully collaborative design and development of written documents. He utilized the SAS statistical package. The response on the survey as a whole was overwhelmingly positive. The means of the five items on peer-assisted writing were generally higher than those of the group writing section, but overall, Scott's findings indicated that students are aware of the value of both kinds of collaboration.

Peer Editing

Peer editing, like peer tutoring, assumes varying levels of writing proficiency. In the culturally diverse classroom students may be grouped or paired in such a way that stronger students are able to point out flaws in the written essays of other students. Students comment on the grammar, development, word choice, and overall clarity of expression in the work. For example, in the English Component of the Student Support Services/ Intensive Educational Development Program at the University of Maryland at College Park, peer editing is used as a means of allowing stronger students to assist their weaker peers. In a Program where one-third of the participants are African-American, one-third are white, and one-third are Asian, Hispanic and other ethnicities, students work collaboratively to bring out the best in each other.

The value of peer editing among such a population is that it allows some students to assume greater responsibility by acting in the teacher's role. Mutually beneficial, peer editing causes the editors to seek a better understanding themselves if they have to explain their comments in criticizing the work of others. Students receiving the editing will feel more confident in submitting work that has been proofread and assessed prior to submission for a grade. They all gain a greater appreciation for the value of the teacher's comments.

Peer editing is an instructional approach that has been given considerable attention (Clifford, 1977; Dobie, 1992; Lewes, 1981). Dobie (1992) implemented a study to explore the needs and goals of adult students ($N = 22$) enrolled in freshman English courses at a large but not a highly selective university. These students were selected to serve as a cross-section of older students enrolled in these classes. Data was gathered from four questionnaires, a self-analysis, teacher observations, and student interviews. The researcher's findings revealed that the first stage of adult students entering college is perhaps the most cumbersome and that their reasons for returning to college were indeed serious ones. In addition, adult students were reported as very confident about their returning to college. Moreover, the findings revealed that adult students did not rate writing highly although they felt positive about what writing courses had to offer. Overall, Dobie concluded that adult students are unrealistic about what college can offer them and about what a writing class would require of them.

Lewes (1981) conducted a study to examine the effectiveness of peer editing in a college composition seminar. Students ($N = 13$) met once a week for four hours utilizing the workshop approach. They were required to write short essays consisting of three to five typed pages each week following an assigned mode of discourse; however, students were allowed to select their own topic. For the first assignment, both the students and the instructor edited the essays line by line. Then primary trait scoring was used. Other evaluations used included the non-judgmental description of the essay suggested by Peter Elbow. During the weekly meetings, students discussed audience expectations, genre, and levels of style. Lewes reported that at the end of the semester, the writing of the students had improved and that editing became more critical and reliable. Students also began to grade their peers on the quality of both their editing skills and their writing performance. It is important to note that the students' evaluations did not differ from those of the instructor.

Clifford (1977) implemented an investigation to test the effectiveness of two methods of teaching writing to college freshmen ($N = 92$) in a remedial composition class. Students were randomly selected from each third name from entering freshmen who received a raw score between 40 and 50 on the Cooperative English Test, Form 1A at Queens College of the City University of New York. Both students and instructors were then randomly assigned to classes. The students were randomly assigned to six classes: two classes each were taught by three instructors of comparable training and skill; each taught one class in the traditional manner and one class with a collaborative composing approach. For example, instructor one taught a collaborative class ($n = 15$) and an experimental class ($n = 16$) as well as instructor two ($n = 13$) and ($n = 16$); and instructor three ($n = 15$) and ($n = 17$), respectively. Students were administered pre-posttests. A writing sample was used to determine the students' experiential writing performance scores and the Cooperative English Tests, Form 1A and 1B, were used to determine the students' mechanical knowledge and vocabulary knowledge scores. After the pretests, the experimental group followed an eight-stage sequence. First, students brainstormed about a particular topic and then wrote freely for fifteen minutes on assigned autobiographical, expressive and expository topics and then they were required to sit in small groups reading and evaluating their first drafts. Students then revised their drafts based upon their peers' comments and brought five copies to class for more detailed discussion using feedback checklists. Students then gave their essays to another group to be evaluated. Finally, students with similar problems and concerns were grouped for instructor discussion.

Students in the control groups followed a five-stage sequence. First, they sat together as a class with strictly teacher-led discussions on various grammatical concepts, punctuation conventions, usage questions and sentence patterns. Then, students discussed various rhetorical conventions led by the instructor which was followed by a lecture on rules, patterns, strategies and conventions of traditional rhetoric. Next, students' writing samples were used to pinpoint various errors common to students' essays. Finally, the instructor explained correction symbols and comments made in students' essays at the end of each class.

As Clifford's study indicated, peer editing involves the added responsibility of assessing not just the performance of the writer, but the editor as well. Usually peer editors will attend to the earlier drafts of a paper with the teacher assessing the final product and assigning the final grade. Professional oversight assures that the process demonstrates fairness (an important concept among culturally diverse students), accuracy, and real writing improvement.

Co-authoring

Co-authoring involves cooperation at the highest level as well as respect for the opinions and abilities of others. Co-authoring is an opportunity for culturally diverse students to write jointly and learn from each other in a collegial environment. For culturally diverse students, co-authoring may provide the confidence and focus required to solicit their best effort, since effective co-authoring demonstrates personal growth, interpersonal competence, and an opportunity for achievement motivation.

Co-authoring, however, is not without its problems. Usually the same grade is received by each writer. Assessment is especially difficult, therefore, in instances where one writer has assumed greater responsibility than another even though the assignment is submitted under joint names. In such a case, the teacher must clearly spell out the criteria for grading as well as exercise clear supervision of the writing process.

One advantage of co-authoring for the culturally diverse student is that it requires the development of consensus, concession, bridging, and other rhetorical strategies in ways that create greater understanding. Another advantage of this strategy is that it enables students to self-plan the writing activity thereby drawing on the strengths each brings to the process. And finally, co-authoring gives each participant an effective helper offering concrete suggestions, feedback, and additional resources.

The writing skills of students can be enhanced by co-authoring (Saunders, 1986). Saunders reported results similar to Coleman (1987) in a collaborative descriptive writing project. She found collaborative writing to be an effective tool for helping students overcome the fear of making suggestions to peers about a piece of writing. As used in a developmental writing class, the project involved only a one paragraph paper, assigned early in the semester. After a class discussion of the importance of using concrete details in writing, students were paired with other members of the class for a collaborative assignment. Each pair of students picked a location on campus to describe. The finished paragraph did not specifically name the location. Instructions included the two students reaching a consensus on their dominant expressions about the location. Through this process of coming to an agreement, the students discovered that suggestions and evaluation can be positive instead of merely negative. The pairs elected a leader to read the paper to the rest of the class, and the class guessed the location described. The assignment encompassed the various learning styles students bring to class and taught the importance of concrete specific detail and audience awareness.

Peer Tutoring, Peer Editing, and Co-Authoring Combined

As indicated earlier, these collaborative writing approaches may be combined into one instructional approach in the model. These three paired approaches can be used to teach culturally diverse students because they tend to include all elements that enable students to improve their writing skills while simultaneously enhancing their interpersonal skills. Although most research tends to use only one of the approaches, Shepherd-Wynn (1999) implemented a study that has clearly demonstrated that peer editing, peer tutoring and co-authoring combined can be beneficial to students. Shepherd-Wynn conducted a study on 440 English composition students enrolled in fifteen sections of Freshman Composition 101 ($n = 267$) and 102 ($n = 173$) courses at Grambling State University to investigate the effects of collaborative learning (peer tutoring, peer editing, co-authoring) on the students' writing anxiety, apprehension, attitude and writing quality. The Daly-Miller Writing Apprehension Test, Thompson's Writing Attitude Survey, and Emig-King Writing Attitude Scale were administered as pre-posttests. The students wrote five essays: first and fifth were pre-posttests; second, third and fourth employed peer editing, peer tutoring, and co-authoring techniques. Holistic scoring was used to measure the students' writing quality on the pre- and posttest essays (writing samples) as well as the three essay assignments that utilized the collaborative writing approaches.

During the first week of the study, English composition students wrote a 50 minute in-class narrative essay as a pretest in response to a prompt. During the second week of the study, students were asked to write a descriptive essay in response to prompts. The English composition students wrote their essays outside of class individually and turned in two typed copies of their essay at the next class meeting. Prior to the next class meeting, each English instructor preassigned English composition students whose writing ability levels ranged from low, middle, to high to peer editing groups of two. Each peer editor was responsible for marking the errors using a peer editing checklist and adding any comments which he or she believed to be constructive and beneficial to the author of the paper. After each essay had been edited and returned to the original author, recommended corrections were discussed between the author and the peer editor. Meanwhile, each English instructor monitored the peer editing activities but was not involved in the actual editing of the essays. They were, however, involved in explaining materials and/or advising about procedures in a facilitative role. For each collaborative writing assignment, each author made revisions outside of class and submitted the edited copy (rough drat) and two typed copies of the revised essay (final draft) to the English instructor for evaluation. After each English instructor had evaluated the essays using holistic grading, he or she returned the essays to the writers and conferred with them prior to assigning the next collaborative essay. Each essay was read by two English instructors, serving as raters, while a third rater was used when two raters assigned a score that had a difference of more than one point. Then the two closest scores were used to determine the essay grade (A, B, C, D, F).

During the fourth week of the study, the students wrote a definition essay. Again, they wrote the essays individually outside of class in response to a prompt and submitted three typed copies of their essay at the next class meeting. Prior to the next class meeting, each English instructor preassigned English composition students whose writing ability levels ranged from low, middle, to high to peer tutoring groups of three making sure not to group the same students as in the peer editing activity. Each English composition student brought three typed copies of his or her essay to class so that each member of the triad could be able to discuss the essay orally and complete the peer tutoring checklist. They spent a minimum of fifty minutes of the peer tutoring session reading aloud and discussing the strengths of weaknesses of each essay following the prescribed checklist until all members of the triad received feedback. The revising and grading procedures were the same as applied for the peer editing essay.

During the sixth week of the study, each English instructor preassigned four students per group and asked them to co-author an exemplification essay in response to a prompt. The English composition student wrote the essay jointly both in and outside of class. Students were informed that they could meet as many times as they desired outside of class. This element of collaborative writing, co-authoring, also required the students to implement strategies they learned in the peer editing and peer tutoring activities. The English composition students completed the essay as a group for which one grade was assigned to each member. To conclude the study, English composition students wrote a 50 minute in class persuasive essay as a posttest in response to a prompt.

The three collaborative writing assignments coupled with the pre- and posttest writing samples were used to determine the writing quality of English composition students. The differences in the scores assigned to Essays I and V depicted the amount of gain experienced by the English composition students in regards to their writing quality. Shepherd-Wynn's (1999) study employed a comprehensive research design (pre-posttest, predictive, comparative and ex post facto). Because the design was sufficiently complex, inferential statistics were employed, including univariate analytical techniques within the context of paired-sample t-tests and independent sample t-tests, correlation analyses (Spearman Brown's Intercorrelation Coefficient and Pearson's Product Moment), ANOVA.ANCOVA, and multivariate procedures with emphasis on discriminant analyses (MANOVA/ MANCOVA, multiple regression/stepwise regression diagnostic procedure) and path analysis to determine the differential effects of the independent variable, collaborative learning (peer editing, peer tutoring, peer authoring), and the dependent variables (writing anxiety, writing apprehension, writing attitude, writing quality) as well as the effects of the fixed factors (gender, course enrollment status, instructor).

Pearson's correlation coefficient showed a significant relationship between combined collaborative writing scores with anxiety ($r = -0.191$, p < 0.01), apprehension ($r = -0.196$, p < 0.01), and quality ($r = 0.869$, p $<$ 0.01) with marginal effects on attitude ($r = -0.099$, p < 0.05). Spearman Brown coefficient revealed no correlation between gender and enrollment status ($r = -0.066$, p > 0.20). Enrollment status, gender, and instructor showed significant correlations with combined ($r = 0.182$, p < 0.001; $r = -0.244$, p < 0.001; $r = 0.263$; p < 0.001, respectively) and writing quality ($r = 0.129$, p < 0.001; $r = -0.161$, p < 0.001; $r = 0.360$, p < 0.001, respectively).

Discriminant analyses showed students preferred peer tutoring, authoring and peer editing, respectively. Independent-sample t-test showed no gender difference on pre-anxiety and pre- posttests apprehension. Paired-sample-t-tests mean scores for pre- posttest writing samples increased (67.34 to 77.89); anxiety decreased (79.03 to 77.25); apprehension decreased (66.76 to 62.77). Paired-sample-t-tests showed attitude moved downward (63.26 to 59.58). Finally, path analyses showed peer editing had a significant relationship with and direct path to anxiety ($r = -0.20$, p < 0.001, Y $= -$ .0113, p < 0.001) and apprehension ($r = -0215$, p < 0.001, Y $= -0.168$, p $<$ 0.001); it also revealed a significant relationship between peer editing and writing quality ($r = 0.601$, p < 0.001 with $\beta = 0.347$, p < 0.001); and an indirect effect between peer tutoring and attitude ($r = -0.085$, p < 0.05). Path analyses also showed a significant relationship and direct path between peer tutoring and apprehension ($r = -0.178$, p < 0.01, Y $= -.0115$, p < 0.01); and a significant relationship between peer tutoring and writing quality ($r = $ 0.737, p < 0.001 with $\beta = 0.644$, p < 0.001). Path analyses revealed a relationship between peer authoring and attitude ($r = -0.064$, p > 0.05), apprehension ($r = -0.062$, p > 0.05) and anxiety (r $= -0.061$, Y $= -0.061$, Y

= -0.095, p > 0.05). There was a significant relationship between peer authoring and writing quality (r = 0.595, p < 0.001 with β = 0.373, p < 0.001).

As a result of these findings, Shepherd-Wynn (1999) concluded that collaborative learning is a viable instructional approach for improving English composition students' writing quality. She further concluded that the combined collaborative writing approaches (peer editing, peer tutoring, co-authoring) were as effective as the individual collaborative writing approaches in reducing English composition students' writing anxiety and writing apprehension, with both having marginal effect on writing attitude. Other conclusions drawn were that peer authoring is significantly correlated with English Composition students' writing quality, peer editing strengthens the critical skills of the peer editor and provides immediate feedback for peers being evaluated, and students who are highly apprehensive have weaker skills than students with low apprehension. Based upon these findings, Shepherd-Wynn's (1999) study is particularly significant because it employed three of the most commonly used collaborative writing approaches individually as well as synergized the three collaborative writing approaches for the treatment. Moreover, the study is significant because of its implications for the teaching of writing to culturally diverse students.

Workshopping

Workshopping and the peer group learning experience can be beneficial, particularly in large culturally diverse classes of varying skill levels. It allows participants to focus on the purpose of writing for particular audiences. Critiquing each other's writing enables culturally diverse students to strengthen lines of communication and forces interaction among students who might otherwise be content as passive learners. It develops leadership skills as well as writing skills by simulating the type of group roles and tasks likely to be encountered in the workplace and throughout life.

In the workshop setting students may present mini lessons, critique papers and engage in holistic grading, activities traditionally reserved for the teacher. So-called "writer's workshops" help to gauge audience reaction and response to works in progress. This type of cooperative interaction in a laboratory setting improves the quality of the learning experience for culturally diverse students by reinforcing what has been taught and focusing on improving effort, not crushing it. Workshop resources, moreover, tend to be chosen more creatively than those used in traditional classrooms. The term "workshop" seems to invite experimentation and creative thought. Experienced writers may be brought in along with audiovisuals and other instruments thereby appealing to the learning styles of more diverse students.

Freeman (1997) explained that mathematics students who work in small groups using the workshop approach tend to achieve higher grades than students who receive traditional instruction. This is perhaps due to the fact that a great deal of mathematical research stems from discussions between mathematicians. Because mathematicians collaborate when conceptualizing procedures, a number of studies have examined the influence of collaborative learning on students' mathematical skills. For example, Wood (1992) studied math students ($N = 52$) at Central Florida Community College in Ocala to determine the impact of computer lab tutorials and cooperative learning on mathematics achievement, retention rate, mathematics anxiety, mathematical confidence, and success in future mathematics courses. The participants were enrolled in two sections of intermediate algebra; one section was taught using cooperative learning approach/experimental ($n = 29$) while the other section was taught using the traditional lecture approach ($n = 23$) with the same instructor teaching both classes.

The experimental group was divided into groups of two to four students based upon their placement tests. Participants who had equivalent achievement scores were placed in the same group. All group members received specific rules regarding homework assignments, computer laboratory assignments, tests, and attendance and responsibilities to observe during the study. Groups also had the responsibility of deciding how these rules and responsibilities should be achieved. For example, some groups met in various locations on campus while others conferred via the telephone. In addition, the participants were given 15 minutes of class time to discuss homework. Once a week, the participants were given computer laboratory assignments. Although no grades were assigned for the computer laboratory assignments, the participants self-reported the completion of the assignments. The participants completed the tests as a group for which one grade was assigned with each member receiving the same grade. The only individual grade the experimental group received was the final examination grade.

Both the experimental group and control group received the same assignments and tests. In addition, they were administered the Fennema-Sherman Mathematics Anxiety and Confidence Scales test as a pre- and posttest. The study's results indicated that a total of 38 participants completed the study: 23 in the experimental and 15 in the control group. Sixty-nine percent of the participants in the experimental group received a course grade of A, B, or C while only 52% of the participants in the control group received a course grade of A, B, or C. Yet further findings revealed that 80% of the participants in the experimental group were successful in their subsequent math course while 87.5% of the participants in the control group were successful in their subsequent mathematics course. The control group also showed greater increases in post-course confidence and greater reductions in anxiety than the experimental group. Although the participants in the traditional lecture group performed slightly better than the participants in the cooperative learning groups, the researcher concluded that workshopping can be a very effective teaching tool.

After participating in a workshop on peer critiquing, Flynn, McCulley, and Gratz (1982) conducted a study to determine the influence of peer critiquing and the use of writing models in the preparation of scientific reports. The sample consisted of 60 to 70 biology sophomores who were divided into four groups: one reference and three treatments. During the first two quarters, a reference group wrote their scientific reports following the traditional format using an outline without additional directions. The first treatment group constructed their scientific reports using both peer critiquing and model analysis. The second treatment group wrote their reports using only model analysis while the fourth treatment group composed their reports using only peer critiquing. All groups attended the same lab session and received the same instruction.

Two teaching assistants evaluated the papers using primary trait assessment. The findings revealed that the treatment groups scored higher than did the reference group. The results of ANOVA revealed that there was a significant difference in mean scores but did not indicate where the differences existed. In addition, the results of the Duncan multiple-range test indicated that the three treatment groups increased the overall quality of their scientific reports significantly while the group that used only modeling composed better reports than other groups. The researchers concluded that the scientific reports written by treatment groups were better organized and provided better discussions of the data collected during the lab sessions. They further concluded that writing model analysis, peer review and revision will increase the quality of written scientific reports.

Knowledge Making

Knowledge making is a relatively new feature of collaborative writing. Knowledge making is a conscious attempt to develop the higher order thinking skills as identified traditionally in Bloom's taxonomy of learning (1956). As such, it rests on the student's ability to associate from his own culturally diverse experience and transfer those connections to create new knowledge. Through activities such as free discussion and brainstorming culturally diverse students are encouraged to draw upon personal experiences, make direct and logical analogies, elaborate and extend, and use various other techniques of knowledge making.

Once culturally diverse students develop to the point of being able to uncover or create knowledge, they can assume greater responsibility for learning. Self-directed learning, which is the goal of most developmental programs, is crucial for empowering culturally diverse learners as they move through Perry's (1971) stages of personal development from dualism to relativism and onward toward commitment.

Since knowledge making focuses on cognitive development, it involves metacognitive processes as well by which students examine the very development of thought. Students get to explore cognitive styles and gain more understanding of their own approaches to learning, studying and, ultimately, writing. The cyclical nature of writing-thought-writing becomes internalized and the student assumes ownership of the processes.

Implications for Further Research

The idea of improving writing mastery through the use of cooperative learning strategies has gained popularity in high schools and colleges across the nation both in response to limited English proficient students as well as employers who have criticized the writing skills of graduates at both levels. A *Washington Post* article (Matthews, 1997) discusses how system-wide schools in the greater Washington, D. C. metropolitan area are becoming involved in these new approaches to teaching writing in the 1990s. The same is happening on the college level, especially as it relates to culturally diverse populations. In general, these strategies have proven to result in greater engagement in the writing process than traditional methodologies, higher cognitive skill involvement, and more social interaction. For culturally diverse populations, especially where some are speakers of other languages, cooperative/collaborative learning also serves to increase multicultural interaction and understanding.

Educating for leadership in the new millennium requires self-direction. The cooperative/collaborative learning strategies discussed encourage both peer and student/faculty interaction in ways not afforded by traditional pedagogy. These suggested changes in educational practice seem to more clearly address the nature and needs of developmental students today; research is needed to determine their value in improving retention and graduation rates among these students. In addition, it would be interesting to determine whether these approaches work as well with other disciplines as with writing.

More studies need to be done on the effect of peer editing on the writing of the higher ability student. To assume that the writer is the only beneficiary of the editing assistance is highly questionable, yet little research exists which examines the effect of this process on the peer editor.

An investigation is also needed to better assess the impact of cooperative/collaborative learning strategies on teaching protocols. While it appears at first glance that such strategies would lessen the demands on teachers' time and effort, more preliminary development, extra assessment tools, training, and other qualitative investment may place a heavier burden on the teacher than is immediately observable.

The model presented in this chapter provides a framework for conceptualizing the process of writing development using cooperative/collaborative learning strategies. We have suggested that this model is particularly suited for culturally diverse student populations. More research is needed to determine if these particular methodologies are more effective among some students than others, for example, returning women, older students in general, Hispanic students, and the like.

At present, cooperative/collaborative learning appears to offer useful strategies for engaging culturally diverse students in the writing process. These strategies seem to respond more comprehensively to the developmental needs of students as they seek to navigate the college community. The choice of instructional method, moreover, should always be a reflection of the desired student outcome, and if we seek to empower students maximally to render quality service to others, the cooperative/collaborative strategies discussed above seem to respond effectively to both the cognitive and affective development of culturally diverse students. The challenge for us as educators is to bring the various aspects of these peer interactions into harmony with program or institutional goals and mission.

Conclusion

In response to changes in learner profiles (i.e., limited English proficient, culturally diverse, learning disabled, and so forth) educators have sought to adapt instructional methodologies to better respond to student needs. The various peer response groups mentioned are being used increasingly on the college level following their success among non-traditional groups at the lower levels.

For the teaching of writing/composition, this methodology has grown in popularity in recent years because of its success in engaging the culturally diverse student more fully in the writing process as various studies have shown (Applebee, Langer & Mullis, 1986; Dyson & Freedman, 1991). Moreover, Prather and Bermu'dez (1993) found that Limited English Proficient writers ($n = 46$) improved their writing skills after exposure to small group conditions, and Ziv (1983) noticed that peer response group comments became more critical with greater familiarity with the process. However, Berkenkotter (1983, 1984) found that among freshmen, students' writing did not directly improve as a result of peer comments. Consequently, while studies have produced mixed results concerning the benefits of peer response groups, they have definitely influenced the move away from traditional pedagogical methods in today's classrooms at all levels.

What peer response groups have lent to the teaching of writing for culturally diverse students is the opportunity for face-to face discussion of works-in-progress, collaborative revision, and dialogic attention to language skills in a "safe" environment. For culturally diverse students, language skills will be enhanced greatly as peer response groups gain even greater use in the college writing classroom.

Chapter 12

ℰᏆᏅᏜ

A Whole Language Model Employing Collaborative Activities to Teach Developmental College Readers

*Evelyn Shepherd-Wynn, Ada Harrington Belton,
Peggy R. Porter, and Loretta Walton-Jaggers*

Introduction

The 21st century is ushering in a period of neo-egalitarianism in postsecondary education. Access to higher education has broadened as colleges and universities welcome increasingly larger numbers of nontraditional students. These students find themselves seeking their education in the midst of a pedagogical paradigm shift. The familiar classroom lecture format their predecessors encountered is giving way to classrooms organized around collaborative activities. Collaborative/ cooperative learning brings together small groups of students with diverse cultural and academic backgrounds and learning styles (Smith & MacGregor, 1992). These groups enhance learning by creating a cohesiveness rather than an individualistic or competitive classroom spirit.

Slavin (1987) defines cooperative learning as a "set of instructional methods in which students are encouraged or required to work together on academic tasks" (p. 31). Johnson, Johnson, and Holubec (1990) define cooperative or collaborative learning as an instructional method that uses small groups in order that students may increase their learning. Smith and MacGregor (1992) define collaborative learning as an umbrella term to a variety of educational approaches involving joint intellectual effort by students' exploration or application of the course material. Everyone in the class is participating, experiencing learning in public, rather than in a private manner.

Interest in collaborative learning has increased over the years as educators have become aware of its effectiveness. As early as the 1920s and 1930s, researchers began studying how students learn effectively through social communication in a non-competitive environment (Dewey, 1936; Maller, 1929; Meiklejohn, 1932; Rosenblatt, 1938). During the 1980s, the American Association of Community and Junior Colleges reported that collaborative learning was the preferred teaching/learning strategy for all college classrooms (Tyrel & Parnell, 1988). During the 1990s, Newman (1991) and Smith, Johnson, and Johnson (1992) focused on the application of cooperative/collaborative learning. Newman noted that collaborative instructors de-center teaching; they coach students and become learners with their students. Smith, Johnson, and Johnson cited the following trends for the use of cooperative/collaborative learning in higher education: (a) Cooperative/collaborative learning is experiencing a rapidly growing interest; (b) it equals or surpasses the effectiveness of lecturing in helping students conceptualize material and in helping them develop cooperative skills; (c) it is being implemented in a wide range of courses and programs, including health sciences, law, engineering, math and science, writing, communication, study skills, professional development, and teacher preparation; and (d) it can be applied in a variety of ways, including cooperative lectures, base groups, formal task groups, structured controversy discussion groups, jigsaw groups, and computer enhanced classes.

Collaborative learning groups are very important to the developmental learner who needs the psycho-social benefits of participating and interacting with other students. Critical elements of these groups have been identified in the literature.

First, there is positive interdependence, which means that all members of the group are committed to helping each other learn successfully. Second, individual and group accountability allows the individual group member's strengths and weaknesses to be evaluated. According to Belenky, Clinchy, Goldberger, and Tarule (1986), the individual learner within the group is able to surpass shallow understandings of the content by sorting out his or her own ideas and syntheses of the content and formulating his or her own opinion. The third critical element is face-to-face promotive interaction, which occurs through verbal problem solving, discussions, and peer support and encouragement. The fourth critical element, group processing, occurs when members of the group evaluate through discussion the effectiveness of their team efforts and the successful completion of their academic tasks. Finally, the fifth critical element focuses on the role of the instructor, that of a facilitator who organizes and plans strategically to meet the needs of the individual members of the group. The instructor assigns and explains what specific interpersonal skills are mandatory for a successful group (Cooper & Mueck, 1990; Johnson, Johnson & Holubec, 1994; Thompson & Tayman, 1997).

Need for Collaborative Learning

As students and instructors gain computer expertise in order to compete in the global workplace, instructors must not overlook the social aspects of learning. With the increasing use of technology in colleges and universities, educators must carefully plan to engage students in face-to-face classroom activities because of the often impersonal nature of technology. Furthermore, computer assisted learning can easily encourage educators to revert to individualistic and/or competitive learning structure. Boyer (1990) recommends that students work together on group assignments in which there is verbal interaction because "cooperation in the classroom is as essential as competition" (p. 13). Mergendoller (1997) states that when instructors use technology such as computer assisted instruction for teaching basic skills, success will depend on the social dynamics of the classroom and the personal characteristics of the students.

Some educators such as Baines (1997) assert that there is no conclusive evidence that student achievement is gained with the use of technology. Nevertheless, many educators are aware of the social dynamics that are essential for learning, and they are developing group activities to use with computer assisted programs. The students collaborate on projects using problem solving or by creating and designing projects with the computer. The end result is the satisfaction derived from a finished project that has been a combination of the groups' talents and ideas (Dillon, 1996; Scholten & Whitmer, 1996).

Corporate leaders are requiring that their workers not only be computer literate but that they also possess competency in thinking skills. A survey of Fortune 500 CEO's revealed that students should be adequately prepared for the 21st century with rational, higher order thinking and problem solving skills which will be just as important as writing, reading and interpersonal communication proficiency. Collaborative learning as a strategy encompasses all of the skills a student needs to succeed in the global marketplace.

Need for Collaborative Learning in College Reading Instruction

Traditionally, college reading instructors have designed courses for the developmental learner to include skills and objects that have focused primarily on knowledge and application of basic skills in vocabulary development, comprehension, and study skills. The students usually study or practice these skills independently with some degree of implementation/ application. However, collaborative learning offers many advantages for developing and enhancing the reading skills through social interaction and self-esteem development. Oftentimes, many developmental learners have difficulty comprehending content-area texts due to the technical vocabulary. Additionally, there is a need for the developmental reading program to use diverse strategies that focus on the application of literacy skills. As a result, a whole language approach, which involves a variety of collaborative learning opportunities, offers many advantages for developing reading, language arts, study skills, interaction in small groups, and application of skills presented in isolation. This chapter describes how a whole language model using metacognition and psycholinguistics in collaborative activities helps to increase reading and study skills for developmental learners.

Figure 1. The Whole Language Model Using Collaborative Activities

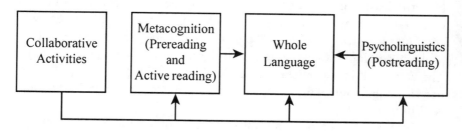

The Whole Language Model
Using Collaborative Activities

The whole language model incorporates whole language as an instructional approach that is undergirded by the dual theories of metacognition and psycholinguistics (See Figure 1). The purpose of the model is to describe how whole language helps to improve reading comprehension and study skills for developmental learners to more effectively gain meaning from college reading assignments. The social interaction of students with diverse cultural backgrounds of learning styles, academic background, and other factors such as personality traits and gender differences, provides the structure within which developmental learners can enhance their critical thinking skills.

Group Selection Guidelines

In order to implement the whole language model, the faculty should select group members to participate in the collaborative activities. First, students should not be placed arbitrarily in groups (Johnson, Johnson & Holubec, 1994). To insure the organizational and structural effectiveness of collaborative groups, faculty should assign students to groups based on the results of such assessment instruments as the Nelson-Denny Reading Test and the Myers-Briggs Test. These tests determine students' reading levels and personality types. In addition, informal inventories and surveys may be used to determine the students' attitudes, apprehensions or interests regarding reading. To provide for diversity, faculty should select students based on their race, ethnicity, gender, age, and their level of academic preparation. Following these group selection guidelines when implementing the whole language model, faculty insures that the small collaborative groups will be comprised of at least four members no more than five with diverse backgrounds to interact interdependently.

Next, instructors should provide for the smooth operation of the groups. First, the instructor should establish a clear purpose for each group and make certain that all group members understand that purpose. Second, the group members must realize that they will be dependent upon each other to fulfill an assigned task, and that they will be monitored independently in their various roles, as well as a group. Although the instructor initially assigns roles to members of the group and explains the responsibilities of the roles, it is important that members of the group realize that the roles and responsibilities will rotate within the group. The leader directs the discussion; the recorder writes the results of the discussion and reports to the entire class; the monitor observes the dynamics of the group and keeps the group focused; and the evaluator critiques the results of the discussion or assigned task.

Whole Language

As stated earlier, whole language is derived from the dual theories of metacognition and psycholinguistics. Therefore, this section of the chapter provides a brief discussion on whole language, metacognition and psycholinguistics, including selected studies which demonstrate the effectiveness of whole language. As we approach the 21st century, whole language as an instructional approach is emerging as the major thrust for teaching reading and study skills at the college level (Caverly, Mandeville, & Nicholson, 1995; Nist & Mealey, 1991). Whole language can be defined as a philosophy, a theory, or a set of beliefs (Moorman, Blanton & McLaughlin 1994). For example, in 1987, Altwerger, Edelsky, and Flores asserted that whole language is an intrinsic social act where students participate in small reading groups. Goodman (1989), on the other hand, viewed whole language as a philosophy that synergizes oral and written language development with a focus on developing thinking and increasing knowledge. Later, Wise (1993) argued that whole language is reading, speaking, writing, and/or listening. She further explained that it is the study of words, sentences, paragraphs, selections, subject areas, and sometimes the entire curricula. According to Goodman and Goodman (1990), whole language involves focused and significant use of language, orally and written. They further pointed out that "There is no artificial breaking down of language learning into sequences of abstract skills and no synthetic language designed to control the form of written language out of the context of its functional use" (p. 247).

Although the definitive aspect of whole language may be controversial, many of its chief proponents argue that it is one of the best approaches for helping students to learn (Goodman, 1986; Wise, 1993). In line with this view, Hornstein, Heine, and Heine (1992) outlined five principles for teaching college students using the whole language instructional approach. They contend that college students learn best when context is in wholes rather than fragments, when they perceive and participate in authentic uses of what is being learned, when they appreciate and participate in collaborative learning settings, when they are able to decide upon what they learn and when and how they learn it and when they are provided opportunities to reflect on their learning.

Most advocates tend to agree that the philosophical orientation of whole language combines the views of Piaget, Dewey, Vygotsky, and Halliday (Goodman, 1989; Monson & Pahl, 1991). Piaget, for example, influenced the whole language movement by showing how students develop their own conceptualizations. They do not depend upon someone to transfer knowledge to them; rather they construct their own knowledge. Vygotsky, a Russian psychologist, contributed to the whole language movement by exploring the relationship between the student's learning and the impact of his or her social interaction. Although the student is primarily responsible for his or her own conceptual development, the teacher plays the role of facilitator. He further believes that because the social interaction of a student during the learning process is important, collaborative learning activities are highly recommended (Dixon-Krauss, 1996).

M.A.K. Halliday, another whole language advocate, supported the movement by synergizing language arts and other subjects. He developed a system that examined students' behavior during the social context while learning language. Halliday contends that when students use language, they are simultaneously learning language, as well as learning through and about language (Kress, 1976). While language and thinking are developing concurrently, knowledge is constructed and concepts and schemas are developed. Finally, the research of Goodman and Goodman (1981) has provided a framework for understanding the reading process and how it develops. These whole language advocates support the notion that whole language can occur in collaborative learning activities.

Whole Language Studies

The literature search revealed a large number of studies that investigated the effectiveness of whole language as an instructional approach to teaching reading at the elementary and secondary levels. However, the literature revealed that college teachers have begun to utilize whole language as an instructional method to teach reading (Caverly, Mandeville, & Nicholson, 1995; Nist & Mealey, 1991). The effectiveness of the whole language approach depends not only upon the commitment of the student but also upon the commitment and perception of the teacher. Therefore, it becomes necessary to first review several studies that deal with faculty perception on whole language prior to reviewing the literature regarding the effectiveness of whole language to teaching reading to developmental readers.

Although there are numerous studies at the elementary and secondary level, only a few studies were found that investigated whole language instruction at the higher education level. Christensen (1990), Ransom and Weisenbach (1994), and Roos (1993) conducted studies to examine faculty perceptions concerning the use of this approach within the college reading classroom. Ransom and Weisenbach (1994) investigated student teachers' ($N = 100$) perception of whole language as an instructional method after completing a whole language reading course and their student teaching experience. Participants at Ball State University ($n = 90$) and the University of Indianapolis ($n = 10$) answered three questions: 1) What happens in your mind when you read? 2) As a teacher how do you think you will teach reading? and 3) Why are you planning to teach? The researcher used the means of proportion method to compare the responses to the questions. The responses to question one revealed that metacognition ($p < .01$) and use of context ($p < .05$) were significant after the reading class, but not after student teaching. Phonics was the only area of significance ($p < .01$) after student teaching. The responses to question two showed that after the reading class, the whole language approach was significant ($p < .01$). After student teaching, the students' responses to teaching phonics and teaching comprehension were also significant ($p < .05$) and ($p < .01$), respectively. The responses to question three indicated that student teachers wanted to work with children ($p < .01$) after completing the reading class.

Roos (1993) measured changes in student teachers' ($n = 42$) theoretical orientation toward reading after a reading course on whole language, skills and phonics. Student teachers were placed in an experimental group ($n = 27$) receiving whole language instruction and a control group ($n = 15$) receiving skills and phonics instruction. The participants took the Theoretical Orientation to the Reading Profile (TORP) as a pre- and posttest. The results of a t-test showed a significant difference between the groups (t (40) = 3.68, $p < .001$). In analyzing the total test mean scores, an increase in the posttest scores indicated that there was a movement toward a skills/whole language orientation, which suggests a major shift from a subskills or phonics perspective to either a skills or whole language theoretical perspective.

Christensen (1990) examined inexperienced and experienced teachers ($N = 60$) in a reading course to determine their perception regarding whole language instruction. Before the reading course, the teachers took a survey to measure the their degree of interest (low, moderate, high) in whole language activities to determine whether there was a difference between their ratings. These findings suggested that the teachers preferred whole language instruction to skills based instruction.

The research on faculty perception led to a number of studies that have been conducted to examine the effectiveness of whole language instruction on developmental students' reading performance (Sammon, 1988; Stallworth-Clark, Scott, and Nist, 1996). Stallworth-Clark, Scott, and Nist (1996) examined student characteristics and instructional techniques on the academic performance of developmental college readers. Multiple regression and commonality analyses were used to analyze the data. Students (n = 523) were divided into four groups of instructional approaches, including whole language, basic skills, strategy training-plus, and strategy training. The students' reading course grades were as follows: whole language (M = 83.58), basic skills (M = 83.08), strategy training-plus (M = 78.82), and strategy training (M = 74.43). Students who received whole language instruction earned the highest reading course grades. The results for the students' reading exam-post scores were as follows: strategy training-plus (M = 77.23), whole-language (M = 76.11), strategy training (M = 75.88), and basic skills (M = 75.48). The instructional approaches had marginal effects on the students' reading exam-post scores. In the reading-intensive core-curriculum courses, the students' grade point averages were as follows: strategy training-plus (M = 1.90), whole language (M = 1.75), strategy training (M = 1.61), and basic skills (M = 1.58). Similar to the reading exam-post scores, the reading-intensive core-curriculum courses did not make a significant difference in students' grade point averages in either of the four instructional approaches. Meanwhile, after student teaching, their responses were significant ($p < .05$) showing that they originally had a desire to teach. These findings supports the assumption that student teachers' perceptions influence the utilization of one instructional approach over another. However, since developmental students have various learning styles, it would be futile for student teachers to prescribe whole language instruction for everyone.

Sammon (1988) investigated freshmen developmental readers ($N = 217$) to determine whether there was a positive correlation between their scores on the Degrees of Reading Power Test and the Reading Comprehension Subtest of the New Jersey College Basic Skills Placement Test. The students were placed into a lower division course (RLA-107) and (n = 91) into a higher division course (RLA-109). Sammon performed a two-way analysis of variance (ANOVA) to analyze pre- and post- test data. Pre- to post- test gains for both levels of reading were significant (107: $F = 286$, $p < .0001$; 109: $F = 73.18$, $p < .0001$). These findings further revealed that students receiving whole language instruction made the most significant gains. The theoretical support and empirical studies discussed above build a strong case for using whole language as an instructional approach. This instructional approach which utilizes metacognitive strategies has proven successful in teaching developmental readers.

Whole Language and Metacognition

The theory of metacognition focuses on strategies students employ when reading. Some of the metacognitive skills involved in reading include (a) Clarifying the purposes of reading so that it can be understood explicitly and implicitly; (b) identifying the message; (c) stressing the major content; (d) observing activities to determine whether understanding is taking place; (e) probing to determine whether comprehension has been achieved; and (f) providing curative measures when comprehension is not achieved (Brown, 1980).

Metacognition primarily emphasizes self-regulatory strategies. It is based on the premise that learning is self-directed and requires social interaction which stresses cooperative learning. Researchers such as Dewey (1910) and Huey (1968) support the notion that reading involves metacognitive skills which comprise comprehending and studying. Students should be capable of self-monitoring their comprehension and should be capable of organizing study schedules and designing study strategies. Although Whimbey et al. (1980) argue that a student's metacognitive skills normally begin around the age of eleven, many students do not develop these skills until later. Students who tend to utilize metacognitive strategies know how to solve problems, think critically, and apply their intellectual skills are those who possess well-developed metacognitive abilities (Piper, 1992).

In the model, the developmental reader is initially independently involved in the reading process metacognitively. The instructor guides the reader through this process of pre-reading and actively reading for meaning. The student is developing an awareness or self monitoring of what is known from past experiences or what is unknown, and combining this new information with what is already processed in the long term memory. While the instructor prepares each student to work independently, there are several steps in the pre-reading process: The instructor provides the frame of reference by asking the student to pre-read the text by skimming to gain an idea of what is about to be read. After skimming by reading the title, introduction, bold-face headings, first sentences of the paragraphs, and the conclusion, the student will do the following (a) Make a prediction of what the reading selection or chapter is about; (b) write or state what information is already known about the topic; (c) establish a purpose by asking what information will be sought while reading; and (d) write three or four questions that the reading selection or chapter may answer (See Illustration 1A).

Next, the student begins to actively engage in processing the information while reading. The student reads with questions in mind that he or she has established. While reading actively and using metacognitive strategies, the student can comprehend the information by visualizing, making associations, or by establishing what is known or unknown (See Illustration 1B). Finally, the student will be involved in postreading activities to determine how much is remembered literally about the reading selection or chapter. Summarizing and mapping are two ways for the student to organize and internalize the main ideas or significant details in his or her own words (Wong, Wong, Perry & Sawatsky, 1986).

Illustration 1A. Metacognitive Strategies: Pre-Reading Activities

I. Preread the article by skimming: look at the title, introduction, bold face heading, first sentences of paragraphs and the conclusion.
    A. Prediction (What will the article be about?)
    B. Prior Knowledge (What information do I already know about the topic?)
    C. Purpose (What information will I seek to find as I read?)
    D. List three questions you think the article may answer.

Illustration 1B. Metacognitive Strategies: Active Reading Strategies

II. Read the article for comprehension with your questions in mind.
    A. Underline the main idea for each paragraph, and write the main ideas in your own words in the margin.
    B. Circle unknown words and use word part meanings or context clues to define them.

    Summary:
    A. Identify Main Idea _____
    B. List the Details _____

Metacognitive Studies

To provide further evidence concerning the efficacy of metacognition and reading, a number of studies have examined the effectiveness of metacognition and reading behaviors among college students. Many researchers have claimed that college students who employ metacognitive strategies tend to be better readers (Aweiss, 1993; Kaufman & Randlett 1993; Mikulecky & Adams, 1986; Schorr, 1982). Kaufman and Randlett (1983) conducted a study using the comprehension of the Nelson-Denny Reading Test to determine whether the use of metacognitive strategies could distinguish between good freshman readers, those scoring above the 80th percentile, and poor freshman readers, those scoring in the lower 20th percentile. Examiners, relying on observable non-verbal reading behaviors and taped interview sessions, rated students' use of one of the following metacognitive strategies: environmental, observable or unobservable. Kaufman and Randlett's findings indicate that good comprehenders use more metacognitive strategies than poor comprehenders to help lessen their misunderstandings, suggesting there is a difference between strategy types used by both comprehenders.

Aweiss (1993) conducted a study concerning the kinds of knowledge and strategies beginning second-language readers used to build their own consistent patterns of meaning and experience. The participants were five Arabic college students, (2 males and 3 females). The reading behavior and cognitive processes of foreign language learners were investigated. These students were trained to use the think-aloud procedure. Four short informative texts of 150-175 words written with various text structures, styles, about different subjects were used.

In a 1986, Mikulecky and Adams administered the Attributional Styles Questionnaire (ASQ) and the Metacognitive Behavior Scale (MBS) as homework assignments to students on academic probation. Based upon the results of the ASQ scores, students were grouped as internal (scored at the bottom 10%), external (scored at top 10%) or neutral (middle score 80%). Based upon the results of the MBS, students were grouped as high (12-28), middle (7-11), or low (0-6) on metacognitive behavior. Mikulecky and Adams' findings revealed that there is no significantly demonstrated relationship between reading behaviors applied to college textbook reading and the attributional styles of college students on probation. The findings further indicated that there is no evidence for a significant relationship between attributional styles and metacognitive reading abilities among reinstated college students with average reading abilities.

Schorr (1982) conducted a study to examine college students' ($N = 26$) comprehension monitoring strategies as they assembled a model according to directions. The students were divided into three groups: group one ($N=8$) consisted of illustrations without text; group two ($N=9$) consisted of text without illustrations and group three ($N = 9$) consisted of both text and illustrations. The study resulted in four primary categories—planning, following directions, evaluating mistakes and reacting to mistakes and several other subcategories. Of the four categories, the only category to positively influence student performance was following instructions.

An evaluation of students' mistakes, the third category, revealed a significant relationship between evaluation and time $r = .46$ ($p < .009$) and between evaluation and errors and $r = .532$ ($p < .003$) while the fourth category, reactions to mistakes, failed to reveal a significant relationship when compared to the variable to time. Schorr concluded students' speed and accuracy increased when mistakes were identified and corrected quickly. Further, Schorr found that students took longer to complete a task when a great deal of remedial strategies were used. The studies show that metacognition focuses on self-regulatory strategies. Since metacognition is based on the assumption that learning is self-directed, developmental learners are able to discuss, and question information while working in collaborative group activities which in turn enables students to become more aware of their organized learning.

Whole Language and Psycholinguistics

Psycholinguistics is the study of the relationship between linguistic and psychological behavior. Psycholinguists study first and second language acquisition; the relationship between language and cognition, or thought; and how humans store and retrieve linguistic information, or verbal processing. The language acquisition component of psycholinguistics begins with the study of child language acquisition, which helps to determine how humans acquire language, and has helped to contribute significantly to the area of psycholinguistics. There are two hypoteses of language acquisition. The first hypothesis is derived from the structuralist school of linguistics, which is the behaviorist approach. This approach maintains that children learn language through imitation and positive-negative reinforcement. The second hypothesis is the innateness theory, which indicates that the acquisition of human language is a biologically in-born characteristic. This innate language-learning ability is linked to physiological maturation and begins to decay around the time of puberty. The generative/transformational school of the linguistics is the derivative of the innateness hypothesis, which was pioneered by Chomsky (1965).

These theories of language acquisition that involve the study of child language acquisition also aid in the exploration of how adults acquire language. Adults learn language largely through memorization and positive-negative reinforcement. The psycholinguist studies adult language acquisition to determine whether the decay of the innate ability during puberty or psychological and cultural factors are possible causes of how adults acquire language.

The verbal processing component of psycholinguistics is next, involving four skills: speaking, listening, reading and writing. Frank Smith (1965, 1973) and Smith and Goodman (1971) have been the most prolific theorists regarding how humans acquire and use language. They indicated that students have a natural ability for language. They also hypothesize that children need a supportive environment in which language can develop. According to Smith and Goodman there are two levels of language functioning; a surface level (sounds and representations) and a deep structure level (meaning of the printed word). These two levels require different skills. Language is processed at a deep structure level, developing into how language acquisition has implications for how a student learns to read. Smith (1976) further contends that children acquire spoken language skills by making conjectures concerning what they think are the important differences in the physical representations of speech. They do this by setting up their own grammatical and semantic rules, by testing conjectures on a trial and error basis, and by learning via feedback whether a rule applies or not. Smith indicates that this learning proficiency is crucial in learning how to read. We have learned from Smith that in spoken language, the child or adult must relate print and meaning. In speech, meaning is related to the orthographic system. According to Smith (1976) children come with prior knowledge and cognitive skills to the learning process in order to learn how to read. Adults or college students use this same process in interacting with the printed page to gain understanding. Goodman (1968) asserts that reading is an interactive process between the reader and the printed page, and a meaning constructing, not a meaning extracting process.

In implementing the psycholinguistic aspect of the model, the postreading activities are continued as the student uses his or her background of experiences (schema) and new information to discuss the reading selection or chapter. Then the student pairs with another student to share and listen to each others' interpretation of the reading. This peer interaction helps the student to think critically about the reading and to listen to a different perspective. The peers can analyze, interpret, and draw conclusions based on the meaning and extent of their comprehension of the reading selection or chapter. The instructor assigns comprehension questions about the reading for homework. The student must independently justify the selection of his or her answer to each comprehension question and be prepared to participate with his or her group members in discussing the answers.

Next, the discussion is expanded to the total group, in which students begin working together to complete a specific task such as answering comprehension questions to establish a consensus about the answers. The leader guides the discussion of the comprehension questions with each member of the group responding and contributing. The group members depend on each others' answers in order to reach a consensus. Each student is graded independently for completion of the comprehension questions. The leader of the group directs the discussion of the comprehension questions and makes sure that each member understands the answers. The recorder writes the results of the group's answers. The monitor keeps the group focused and the evaluator shares his or her observations regarding how well each member participated toward completing the assignment. After the students have reached a consensus about the answers to the comprehension questions, the instructor guides the students with pre-writing, writing, and post-writing activities of an essay in response to a reading selection.

Illustration 2. Psycholinguistic Strategies:
Post-Reading Activities and Pre-Writing Activities

After you have read the article, and without looking back, think of a precise statement of the author's main idea and think through the key points supporting this idea. Write this statement and key supporting points which will summarize this article.

SUMMARY:

Main Idea: _____

_____

Details: _____

_____

DISCUSSION:

With your partner, take turns listening to each other and take notes which can be used for your essay.

    A. Explain the main point and details of the article.

    B. Discuss whether your pre-reading questions were answered.

    C. What new information did you gain?

    D. How has your perception or point of view changed or remained constant about the subject?

    E. What points do the two of you agree or disagree concerning the article?

    F. What conclusions can you draw from the article?

Illustration 3. Peer Review Guide for Reading Selection

Name of Writer: _____

Date: _____

Name of Receiver: _____

Title of Essay: _____

I.   INTRODUCTION

    1. Does the writer identify the author, reading selection and source correctly?

    2. Does the writer summarize the reading by clearly stating the main idea(s) and significant details?

    3. Does the writer use the *Time* magazine reference effectively?

    4. Are there quotes from the article and reactions to the article?

III. CONCLUSION

    1. Does the writer answer the three questions to fulfill the conclusion?

    2. Does the writer leave the reader with a definite impression and conclusion about his or her viewpoint?

The students then read each others' essays aloud to the group. The group members select the best essay to be read aloud to the entire class. These essays can be produced in a college publication and used as models for future students. This publication enhances the self-esteem of the developmental reader. Developmental readers participating in collaborative groups, employing the activities above, become more actively involved in the postreading process because they gain meaning when reading passages. Since psycholinguistics helps developmental readers gain meaning during the postreading process, studies have been conducted to examine the effectiveness of psycholinguistics.

Psycholinguistic Studies

An examination of several psycholinguistic studies with college students indicates the importance of gaining meaning of reading passages through the productive language process of speaking or verbal interaction and writing (whole language), in other words whole language; and the receptive language processes of reading and listening (Bernitz, 1997; Chai, 1967; Daiute, 1981; Ehri, 1981; Malik, 1990; Palij, 1989). These language processes involve thinking skills which enable the college reader to gain meaning or to meaningfully comprehend reading passages. Much of the research on psycholinguistics began in the 1950's and 1960's, and most recently, many psycholinguistic studies are based on English as a Second Language (ESL) college students.

Goodman and Burke's (1972) classical studies on miscue analysis and Goodman's (1965) analysis of dialect or language differences in learning to read influenced Bernitz (1997) to take a different look at earlier hypotheses regarding language differences and reading comprehension, using the miscue analysis. Bernitz contends that teachers must change their negative attitudes about speakers with low-status dialects. The "rejection of students' dialects and the educators confusion of linguistic difference with linguistic deficiency interferes with the natural process by which reading is acquired and undermines the linguistic self-confidence of divergent speakers." Divergent speakers, whether Black or White, are handicapped because of linguistic discrimination which is imposed on them by uninformed teachers. Bernitz conducted a study of second, fourth, sixth, eighth, and tenth graders with low average and high proficiency levels. The study consisted of observing the oral miscues of subjects reading and retelling of a complete selection. A miscue is defined as any observed response (OR) which is different from the expected response (ER) to the text. Most of the subjects were Black because of the inner city locale of Detroit. Only seven of the 94 subjects revealed more than 20% dialect-involved miscues. The groups in which the dialect-involved miscues were found are as follows with Black subjects with 10L indicating low; 2HA, high; and 4A, average.

2HA: 1-31%   6L: 2-30%
4A: 1-28%8   L: 1-25%
6A: 1-23%   10L: 1-28%

It was found that there is no consistency on the dialect-involved miscues in oral reading. Dialect variations occurred quite frequently between and within racial groups. There were only a few subjects that revealed any significant number of dialect-involved miscues. In fact, some did not reveal any dialect miscues, which was evident in each grade-proficiency group, except four. Some readers with no dialect-involved miscues show frequent divergent dialect instances in retelling. The study revealed that Black speakers of low-status dialects can be proficient readers.

Malik (1990) studied the oral reading behavior of English as a Foreign Language (EFL) students. It was hypothesized that EFL students may transfer psycholinguistically, in reading comprehension, use of comprehension strategies, and reading speed in oral reading, when the expository text that is used is culturally familiar and culturally unfamiliar for the subjects. There were 15 EFL students who were the subjects used in this study. The procedure included 15 Iranian proficient readers who scored 80 or above on the Michigan Test of English Language Proficiency (MTELP) at the university of New Mexico. The materials used were based on Iranian culture which was culturally familiar. And the other protocol was based on Japanese culture which is non-familiar for the subjects. Three aspects of the subjects' oral reading behavior were compared: (a) reading comprehension, (b) reading process and strategies, and (c) reading speed.

The expository texts used were based on the belief system of the two cultures. These selections were taken from the *Encyclopedia Britannica* (1982) with 550-600 words. Each subject read the two texts with a week between each reading, so that overlapping of the information read would not occur. A control factor was implemented for the administering of the texts. The subjects were directed to orally read the text and then to retell immediately after what was understood from the text. The reading and retelling were recorded by the researcher to code the miscue data and retelling comprehension score.

In analyzing the data, a modification of Goodman and Burke's (1972) Reading Miscue Inventory was developed. This instrument was developed by Altwerger and Resta (1985) called Miscue Analysis Profile (MAPro). The subjects' retelling were used to indicate the subjects' comprehension scores. The miscue data was computed, with percentages of each column of the MAPro, to show the subjects' reading comprehension strategies, predicting, confirming/correcting, and integration scores. The *t* test (correlated samples) was used to determine the significant differences between the dependent variables in the familiar and non-familiar texts. Pearson product moment correlations additionally were calculated in studying the interrelationships of the reading comprehension score, integration score, and reading speed of the two texts. The .05 level was the rejection level.

Malik's (1990) findings revealed that when students read familiar text reading comprehension is significantly higher because of the retelling of the immediately after the oral reading. The schemata plays an important role for comprehending written information. In predicting, the subjects use of syntactic and semantic information is more effective for familiar texts than for non-familiar texts. Integrating strategies is more effective for the familiar text. Oral reading was unaffected.

Palij (1989) conducted a study which assessed the language background differences of college students. The purpose of the study was to identify the language background factors related to language processing with an instrument for the assessment of the experiment, and to utilize the instrument to show the results with a psychology subject pool. The researcher developed a language background questionnaire to survey Introductory Psychology students at New York University in 1987. Fifty to sixty subjects were administered the language background questionnaire. An hour was allowed for completion of the forms which were distributed in numbered packets.

The groups were designated according to the following criteria (a) General background characteristics of the subjects, (b) general background and analysis of differences among the group as in terms of background measures, reading measures, and English and Non-English language abilities, (c) age acquisition of English and analysis of differences among these groups in terms of background measures, reading measures, and English and Non-English language abilities, and (d) whether English was ranked as the subjects best known language or second best known language and differences between these groups in terms of background measures, and English and Non-English language abilities. Palij (1989) results showed that the most significant factor with the bilingual grouping was that bilinguals who acquired English at the age of six differed from the English speaking and bilingual speaking subjects who acquired English as a first language or as a second language before the age of six. This difference was manifested in the cognitive performance of the subjects.

Ehri (1981) conducted a study to determine the developmental differences between children (5th graders), and adults (college students) in recalling sentences which were prompted (or contained "mnemonic devices) by nouns within the sentence to help with their retrieval of the sentence. The subjects memorized two- noun sentences so that each time one of the nouns was shown in the sentence. They were able to recall the rest of the sentence. There were 32 fifth graders and 32 college students who were given payment as an incentive for their voluntary efforts. Six independent variables on recall were manipulated, using an analysis of variance for assessment of the effect of these variables. The variables were age (fifth graders vs adults), lists (four different sets of 32 sentences), trials (five test trials each following a study trial), grammatical relations among the pairs; verb voice (active and passive), and noun (prompt position, first and final position in the sentence).

A tape recorder was used for each subject to hear the sentences with the noun prompts. The oral responses of the subjects were recorded. Immediately after each subject interpreted the sentence, he or she was directed to press a buzzer. It was found that the position of the noun prompt (the depth of its embedding gin the surface structure of a sentence) indicated no significant difference between fifth graders and adults recalling and producing sentences.

Daiute (1981) studied the psycholinguistic aspects of the writing process and the relationship to a psycholinguistic model of talking. The model shows how a significant number of syntactical errors are made in writing, based on how students talk. An analytical study of 450 syntax errors was categorized and explained by the psycholinguistic model of the writing process. The purpose of the study was to determine whether sequences that had been independently shown to stimulate semantic recoding occur before the beginning of a syntax error. There were 215 New York area college freshmen whose placement examination essays were analyzed for sentences with syntax errors. The errors were classified within the framework of the writing model and analyzed to identify the characteristics resulting from the limitations of the short term memory. There were 11.3% errors in the sample's sentences. Daiute classified seven types of error sentences: fragments, overlapping sentence, distant modifier sentence, non-parallel sentence, gapped sentence, repetitious sequence sentence, and multi-error sentence. The fragment was the most frequently-occurring error type (30%) of the sample. Overlapping sentences was the second largest error type (26.2%) of the sample. The distant modifiers appeared frequently (11.5%). The distant modifier appeared infrequently (1.8%). The study found that in examining written error sentences, that the psycholinguistic model of talking helps to explain written errors, and as a result, helps teachers to more effectively guide their students through the writing process.

Chai (1967) investigated the differences between children and adults through psycholinguistic experimentation. The purpose of the study was to determine how ambiguous sentences can be resolved. The subject consisted of four age groups: fifth, seventh, and eighth grade children and college sophomores. There was a set of 176 sentences which had pronouns embedded with ambiguous antecedents. The subjects' task was to select the most appropriate referent in each sentence. The experiment consisted of three controlling variables, sentence types, four grammatical forms, and four verb-pair clauses. There were responses to the data from the four age groups. The selection of the age groups showed the differentiation between children's inability to resolve the pronominal referent (resembling a pronoun, while functioning as another part of speech), to the uniformity of choosing the pronominal referent suggesting that children have difficulty with the task.

The written instructions were in a test booklet, divided into two parts, one with 48 nonsense syllables in the sentences as verb-pairs, and the other half did the opposite. The results of the sophomore group indicated they could more easily resolve the ambiguity within the sentence by reducing the meaning of a key word from two to one. Eighth graders were able to resolve the ambiguous sentences when real-verbs were used instead of nonsense verbs. Seventh graders were not successful, and fifth graders were unable to resolve the pronominal ambiguities. The empirical research on psycholinguistics helps faculty to understand how developmental readers process information. Consequently, psycholinguistics has been proven an effective strategy for helping faculty determine how developmental readers acquire language.

Conclusion

Although a number of developmental college learners have a strong desire to enhance their reading skills, many obstacles may hinder their success. Consequently, faculty are exploring ways to provide appropriate strategies and opportunities for developmental readers to improve their reading skills. In this chapter we show how using whole language as an instructional approach along with metacognitive and psycholinguistic strategies in collaborative group activities can be used to help enhance developmental readers' reading and study skills (See Figure 1). Reading is an active rather than a passive activity; working in collaborative groups provides opportunities for developmental readers to learn in a social context. Collaborative group activities allow developmental readers who are unable to critically decipher information due to inexperience and inadequate reading strategies *to* improve their information processing skills while working with peers in a noncompetitive environment.

The research that examined metacognition and reading clearly pointed out that when developmental readers apply their prior knowledge and experiences to a particular text when studying in collaborative groups, they are more likely to better self-appraise and manage their own learning. Thus, metacognitive strategies help developmental readers become more aware of how they read, thereby encouraging organized learning. Helping developmental readers use metacognitive strategies during the prereading and active reading processes helps them to improve their reading skills.

Moreover, the research literature provided evidence that when faculty employ whole language as an instructional approach in a collaborative environment, developmental readers have more time to write, greater opportunities for feedback, and more time to gain meaning from the text. Whole language as an instructional approach may involve numerous and on-going experiences for students to improve their reading. These experiences provide opportunities for students to develop and expand language skills, enhance self-esteem and promote an awareness, understanding and acceptance of others (See Appendix A). Finally, whole language plays a vital role in helping developmental learners improve their reading skills.

The research concerned with psycholinquistics and reading showed that using psycholinguistic strategies to teach reading is an effective approach during the postreading process. The research further revealed that when students are provided opportunities to share their information with each other, their reading skills are enhanced. Developmental readers working in collaborative groups learn to summarize and explain information as well as teach each other in their groups.

As we approach the new millennium, the typical college population will be more diverse in age, race, ethnicity, and gender with a wide range of reading skills. In order to meet the needs of all developmental learners, it is critical that faculty continue to *seek* innovative strategies to help them improve their reading skills. Since faculty are beginning to combine techniques, it is recommended that faculty use the Whole Language Model Using Collaborative Activities to improve the overall reading skills of developmental readers.

Appendix A

A Creative Collaborative Activity
for Promoting Whole Language

As long as faculty are aware of the theoretical base and the basic elements involved in implementing whole language as an instructional approach, they can use their own creativity to design and implement instructional strategies across the curriculum. The planning process must also involve the needs of the learner, their background experiences, the objectives and skills of the lesson, as well as materials and resources that will be used to implement the lesson to achieve the objectives.

One activity that was successfully developed and implemented at Grambling State University (GSU) with sophomores, juniors and seniors in a Teacher Education Children's Literature class was "The Talking Box" exercise. This particular exercise was used to demonstrate a technique/ strategy for using the whole language approach in the classroom. After participating in the collaborative group activity, students shared their written products with elementary students at Alma J. Brown Elementary , one of the GSU Lab schools. This activity provided opportunities for whole language experiences to be utilized at two levels. First, Teacher Education majors were directly involved in whole language experiences through "collaborative writing" exercises in the classroom. Secondly, those same students then used their written products to present creative activities to the elementary school students using creative whole language strategies.

As a follow-up to a literature review discussion on Whole Language, the GSU Teacher Education students participated in a hands-on activity which was used as an example of implementing Whole Language in the classroom. The following procedure was used in the exercise which was labeled, "The Talking Box Activity".

1) The teacher placed a large brown box on a table, filled with various objects. The students were not allowed to see the objects initially.

2) The class was randomly divided into four groups for a collaborative learning experience. Each group had to identify a group leader and a group recorder.

3) The teacher took the box to each group and asked a group member to pull out two items from the box without looking inside of the box.

4) The task of each group was to develop a "written product" in story form based on the two items pulled from the box. Their written product must have a title, and creatively express the inclusion of the two items pulled from the box.

5) The "written product" must be the result of a collaborative effort. The facilitator must insure that everyone has an opportunity to provide input as he/she builds and expands on each other's points. The recorder writes the story as the ideas are jointly agreed upon by the group.

6) Each group had an opportunity to share orally the "written product" with the entire class making the "talking box."

The following "Written Products" were presented by each of the four groups. The names of the group members and the two items that were selected from the box are included.

Written Products

Group I
Items Selected: Curly gift ribbon and Styrofoam plate

"A Lady Named Curly"
By Tammy Harris, Parrish Hartley, Crescent Campbell-McGlone,
and Adaryll Moore

There once was a lady named Curly,
    Who lived in a styrofoam house.
At first she had no friends at all,
    Because she was such a grouch.
One day while she was shopping in the store,
    She found a friend indeed.
This tall, slender man with green
    Spotted hair said, "Hi, I'm Mr. Reed."
They laughed, and talked,
    And had a grand time, both enjoyed the afternoon.
Little did she know, to her surprise,
    Mr. Reed would become her groom.
Soon he took her to a Sweetheart Dance,
    Where they truly "stole the show."

Then she saw a man staring at her;
> Someone she didn't know.

Then, to her surprise, this tall, dark, stranger suddenly made Miss Curly
> quiver.

When he smiled at her and quickly said, "Hi, I am Mr. Silver."
In the deepest voice that you've ever heard, he said with a smile on his face,
> "Curly, I would like to dance with you, in this very large place."

She was scared to move,
> But, she couldn't refuse, so Curly gave him a chance.

And Mr. Silver danced with her,
> Again, and again, and again.

But suddenly, Mr. Reed stepped right in and said,
> "Curly, it's time to go. We have had great fun, you've danced and danced,
> and I truly love you so."

From that day on they both were a pair,
> They lived happily ever after without a care.

Group II

Items Selected: Small Brown Envelope with Four Markers Inside, Scissors

"It's Not Smart to Mark"
By Veleka Gray, Cassandra Johnson, Lonea Sherrard, and Clifton Theus

Once upon a time there was a Daddy Marker, a Mother Marker, a Sister
Marker, and a Brother Marker. They were called the Mark-A-Lott Family.
They lived in a golden house with a silver doorbell. Every morning the
Mark-A-Lott Family would go to the bus stop and mark the buses that went
by. There was someone in their town that did not like this. His name was
Officer Big Blue Sharp. He did not like this activity because it was vandalism.
He warned the family many times to stop the marking. He would say to
them, "It's not smart to mark." The Mark-A-Lott Family would always
respond by saying, "You can't stop the Mark-A-Lotts, you can't stop the
Mark-A-Lotts, and you know this man!" So one day while Officer Big Blue
patrolled the neighborhood, he came across the Mark-A-Lott Family
preparing to mark on one of the school buses. Officer Big Blue Sharp became
very angry because they were marking the school bus while the children
were inside. He jumped out of his police car and started to snip at them. He
was trying to snip off their tips so they couldn't mark anymore. The Mark-
A-Lott Family started to run while Officer Big Blue Sharp tailed closely

behind. Unable to get away, Officer Big Blue Sharp snipped away every marker's tip. Starting with the daddy, then the mother, the sister and the brother. This caused all of the ink to dry out in all of the Mark-A-Lott family's markers. They were never able to mark a bus again.

Group III

Items Selected: Small Tape Recorder

"*Taco Cabana Restaurant Cup*"
By Richae Jackson, Victoria Ross, Ernest Sterling, and Anita Warren

One scorching day in Pepperville, there lived the greatest detective in all of Texas, Peppie Pierre. Peppie was head spy for the local paper, the *Pepperville Press*. While relaxing in his office waiting on a story, Peppie received a call from his friend Peno, who worked at the Taco Cabana Restaurant in Taco, Texas. Peno was upset about what was happening at his restaurant. Peno shouted, "The good peppers are disappearing!" "Calm down Peno, Hector the Recorder and I are on our way", Peppie stated. Peppie and Hector arrived at the restaurant disguised as tourists on vacation.

One night Peno overheard the Cabana Mob Boss sending out orders to the Cabana boys to capture more good peppers from old Mr. Hernandez's garden. So Peno called Peppie and Hector to collect evidence and bring the police to the "hide-out" in the back of the restaurant where they sliced and diced the jalapeno peppers that they had captured. Incidentally, these good peppers were to be placed in the cooking cup. Peppie said, "Yes, of course, I will call the police". So Peppie and Hector gathered their supplies and went right over.

Back at the Taco Cabana, the Cabana boys were hard at work unpacking the peppers they had collected. Of course, they did not know that Peppie Pierre and Hector the Recorder were hard at work collecting the evidence needed to give to the police as soon as they arrived. The police arrived and Peppie directed them inside where the action was taking place. The police entered and yelled, "Freeze, Cabana Mob, come out with your hands up, you are caught red-handed"! Peppie Pierre and Hector the Recorder received praise for solving the crime.

Peppie Pierre and Hector returned home as heroes. They printed the article in the *Pepperville Press*. Subsequently, they received an award for the article and the sting operation. Most of all, everyone was happy knowing that the good peppers were safe once again.

Group IV

Items Selected: Small Christmas Ornaments, Angels (12) and Small Black Clip

"Clip and The Nation of Angels"
By Rhonda Bell, Elizabeth W. Corney, Sicura Lemora, and Amy Davis

Once upon a time there were twelve angels in a magical land. This land was called the Nation of Angels. These angels were unique because there were six sets of twins. Identical twin angels were very rare. The rare angels went around to all parts of the world giving sweet dreams to all children. At night when the children went to sleep, the angels would sneak under the pillows of the sleeping boys and girls to give sweet thoughts to their dreams. The secret was that each twin had to work cooperatively with the other twin in order to make the children dream good thoughts. Each set of twins would go into a different neighborhood to give sweet thoughts to the children. By doing this, the angels would make sure all the children of the world could have sweet thoughts for their dreams every night. They had to make sure that not a single child was left out.

On the neighboring side of the Nation of Angels was Clipland. Clipland is place where the evil Clip lived. He decided to plot against the Angels of Dreams. One day, the evil Clip went to the Nation of Angels and stole one twin of each pair. He kept them captive in Clipland. Clip worked at the school and his job was to clip all of the children's work together. All day long, the children wrote stories about their dreams. Because the dreams of the children were so detailed and long, the children wrote pages and pages of their dreams. Clip had to arrange, organize, and clip their work together. This job took up most of his day, and by lunch he was really tired. Most of the time, he barely had time to eat lunch before the children would write more. He was tired of having to work so hard. Finally, Clip decided that if he captured one of the twins, from each set, then the children wouldn't dream good thoughts and the children wouldn't have anything to write about. Therefore, he would not have so much work to do.

Well, the day after he kidnapped one twin for each set, the children didn't have anything to write about because they didn't dream the night before. They just sat there staring out of the window trying to think of something to write about. By the end of the day, the children had only come up with one paragraph. So Clip was very happy, because he could rest. All day long he would take naps. He ate several snacks throughout the day.

He soon got bored with eating and resting all day. By the time he returned to Clipland he had nothing to do because he had eaten and rested at work. Eating and resting all day got boring. When he got home to Clipland, he had nothing to do. After a week of not having anything to do, Clip decided to let each twin go. After he let the twins go, the children started having wonderful dreams again. Though Clip was now overwhelmed with work, he was happy to be busy clipping and organizing all the children's work again.

Chapter 13

ℰᴖℭ℞

Disentangling the Message from the Medium: Using Appropriate Educational Technology in the Classroom

B. Runi Mukerji and Kathleen G. Velsor

Only by being true to the full growth of all the individuals who make it up can society by any chance be true to itself.

—John Dewey

The demographics of today's first year college student classes are clear indicators of the challenges we face as university professors. As we approach the 21st century, the United States and the world will change at an increasing rate; this cultural pluralism is inescapable (Greene, 1993). As we begin to prepare for an even more demanding profile of students, we must begin to understand that college can be a center for culture and a place for creating a community of learners who are culturally responsive to each other.

As educators involved in the curriculum planning, instruction, and assessment of learners in postsecondary institutions, we are keenly aware that our responsibility in the classroom is not limited to the delivery of curricular content, but that we must facilitate students' learning experiences by building upon the learning styles that they bring with them. The issues that we face with developmental learners are in the main, not unique to any single population, but cut across the boundaries to encompass the issues with all the learners today. That is, we must take into account the new mode of learning that has developed as a function of the unprecedented exposure that this generation of learners have had to technology, media and computer game playing. This is a fundamentally different information processing style that they bring with them into the classroom. A paradigmatic shift must take place in our perspective as educators to take this new mode of information processing into account for all learners. The issues unique to developmental learners are super-imposed upon this broader general base, and represent specific modifications.

The business of education has been impacted little by the technological revolution even though its customers have been. In the context of education, the new forms of communication technology that have become available must be recognized not just as tools or aids to instruction, but as a powerful set of forces that already has dramatically reshaped the landscape of human activity.

Trends of New Technology in the Schools

Just in the past 12 years, the number of students per computer in US Public schools has dropped from 125 students per computer in 1983-84 to 9 in 1995-96. Other forms of information technology (IT) have also seen dramatic changes during an even shorter span of time: the presence of Cable TV has increased from 57 percent of all schools in the US in 1992-93 to 74 percent in 1994-95; CD-ROMs from 7 percent in 1991-92 to 37 percent in 1994-95; modems from 16 percent in 1991-92 to 34 percent in 1994-95; satellite hook-ups from 1 percent in 1991-92 to 17 percent in 1994-95 (Quality Education Data National Database, 1997).

We, as educators, have yet to truly acknowledge the impact of the technological revolution that has changed the way in which information exchange takes place, and that has made the computer into a household appliance. In a recent study of the computer use, it was noted that teenagers log onto the Internet considerably more than their parents do. They regard it as a new kind of phone and use it to e-mail their friends, as well as to seek out information for structured activity such as doing their homework (Kraut & Kiesler, 1996, as reported in Murray and Graham, 1996).

No other medium has heretofore enabled the learner to have such an active role in the process of what is learned. The fact that the computer can serve as the repository of data has shifted emphasis in the learning situation from fact acquisition to the processes of organization, application, and transfer of knowledge to the discovery of more complex rules and relationships.

Traditionally, the key player in the dissemination of information was the teacher. The advent of new technological systems, such as the Internet, enables the learner to access information independently. Some have argued that this independent access renders the teacher obsolete. We believe this to be a superficial misreading of the issue. Far from obsolescence, we believe that this change in context powerfully redefines the teacher. It is the teacher who becomes the architect of the learning context within which the learner can construct knowledge in meaningful ways. And nowhere is the role of the teacher more crucial than for the developmental learner. The new technology systems support the autonomy of the independent learner with appropriate skills and strategies to access and organize information. It is the teacher-architect who must design the systems with the developmental learner to enable them to acquire the cognitive strategies that will make them more autonomous.

Arguments about medium versus method cannot be made in the absence of the learner. We believe that the characteristics of the learner is a key issue that needs to be brought more clearly into focus. Seifert and her colleagues (Seifert, McKoon, Abelson, & Ratcliff, 1986; Seifert, Robertson, & Black, 1985) indicated that the ability of people to process new information more efficiently depends upon their ability to perceive the similarities in theme and content of the new information to their prior knowledge. Given that we have a generation of learners in the classroom who have been weaned on information provided through non-textual sources such as TV, video, and computers outside the classroom, it is not a far stretch to believe that they would benefit from exposure to content through such sources within the classroom. Furthermore, since interaction with and through computer and video games has been a significant part of their socialization from a very early age, the interpersonal aspects of the learning environment would be facilitated when using this type of educational technology within the learning situation.

On the surface, it would not seem that persuading educators to incorporate educational technology is a problem. Certainly, it is not, and the impetus to get bigger and better toys in the classroom is ubiquitous throughout the educational hierarchy. There is however, little dialogue about the impact of technology on the nature and content of instruction, on the role of the teacher within such an environment, or the basis of assessment.

As Ross (1994) has pointed out, the lack of analysis of the effects of media on method can lead to sloppy design of materials that are accepted by users simply because they utilize "high status" delivery media such as interactive video, computer based instruction, etc.

The needs of the developmental learner are more specific than these products suggest. We need to design high impact learning experiences which capitalize on these elements while enhancing needed content. It is important for us as educators to recognize that what we teach, and even more importantly, what we choose to assess, is an explicit representation of what we value as an outcome of learning. Similarly, an educational computer program is not just ancillary teaching aid, but is a rhetorical (meaning, persuasive) statement of the valued learning outcomes on the part of the teacher-architect. If these two sets of values are not consonant with one another, it will lead to ineffective instruction, inefficient learning, and ultimately, to unfair assessment.

In this chapter we will identify a number of factors that have been identified as key to the learning process, and indicate ways in which these factors need to be addressed for the developmental learner, and the ways in which Information Technologies readily accommodates these learning needs.

While there are many variables that affect learning processes, contemporary cognitive theory appears to emphasize small but consistent group of variables that are critical to effective learning. Below, we will present a brief discussion of a number of key theories that are representative of this approach.

Theorists such as Rogers (1974), Rogers and Freiberg (1994), Carroll (1990), Van der Meij and Carroll (1995), and Knowles (1984a, 1984b) have pointed to the personal involvement, experience, self-direction and discovery learning as key to the process of effective learning, particularly for the adult learner. Rogers differentiates between two types of learning: cognitive learning which corresponds to academic knowledge such as vocabulary or the rules of grammar; and experiential learning, which refers to applied knowledge that meets the need and wants of the learner, such as learning the theories of special education because they have a learning disabled sibling. Rogers sees experiential learning as equivalent to personal change and growth.

Experiential learning is characterized by personal involvement, is self-initiated, is marked by self-reflection, and is a process that has pervasive effects on the learner. According to Rogers, every human being has a *propensity* and *motivation* to learn, and significant learning takes place when the subject matter is personally relevant to the learner, and the classroom climate is such that the threat posed by learning is minimized. Within this framework, we conceptualize the principles laid out by Rogers as indicating the role of the teacher as the facilitator or architect of the learning situation by: (1) constructing a positive climate for learning; (2) providing clear goals and objectives for the learner; (3) providing appropriate resources; (4) managing the affective and intellectual components of the learning process; and (5) staging a reflective component to learning.

Knowles (1984 a, 1984b) and Carroll (1995) have applied and amplified these principles in their application to the adult learner. Both of these theorists underscore that for the adult learner, the learning situation must make explicit the purpose of the learning, that the learning activity be meaningful, purposeful and problem-centered rather than content-centered. Both theorists point out that most learning paradigms give short shrift to the prior knowledge of the learner in the learning process and importantly, and in a point of departure from most current educational theories, both theorists see errors and mistakes not as a failure to learn, but as a process that intrinsic is to discovery learning, and a basis for the learning of the self-regulation of the learning activity.

Consistent with these principles, Sticht's (1988) functional context approach to learning was specifically developed for adult technical and literacy training, but it has major implications for learning of basic skills in general. This functional theory approach, which has been successfully used in Navy programs to teach reading and mathematical skills, emphasizes the importance of the learners prior knowledge in the learning environment, the use of materials and equipment that allow the learner to apply newly learned concepts to real-life situations, and incorporates procedures to facilitate the transfer of knowledge learned in a class-room setting to the Areal world."

Lave (1988) and others (Brown, Collins, Duguid, 1991; McLellan, 1994) emphasized that all learning occurs within a context. In the most simplistic analysis, this context is usually assumed to be the classroom within which the learning occurs. But in fact, the context of learning is far wider, and must include the context within which the learned information is to be used and the activities that call for the use or application of that knowledge. While abstract knowledge can be acquired in an isolated or solitary context, the use of knowledge never is. Therefore, if the task is to provide knowledge that can be translated into skills, the learning environment must acknowledge that social interaction is a critical component of learning. In situated learning models, learners are perceived as people who through the process become increasingly integrated members of a "community of practice" which embodies beliefs and behaviors to be acquired. The process of acquiring expertise must occur within a context that validates that knowledge. Therefore, knowledge must be needs to be presented in an authentic context, that is, settings and applications that would require that knowledge in the real world, and also in a setting that facilitates social interaction and collaboration.

The Relevance of Education Technology

Happily, we as educators live in a in a time where educational tools are available that fulfill these needs of self-direction, authenticity, self-regulation, and problem-centeredness very neatly. A simple example is a good computer game such as "Oregon Trail" or "Sim City." Using this type of software, the learner can become an active participant in his own learning. Games require the learner to use the basic knowledge of the game and the computer as they construct the necessary information to play the game. To win the game the learner must analyze basic strategies and apply his knowledge, and learn from his mistakes. Setting the criteria for learner success becomes a natural outcome of the performance. The student performances became part of the continuous assessment process. High interest and goal-directed learning experiences empowers the developmental learner to integrate many higher-order skills. The challenge is, therefore, to design classroom lessons that do engage the developmental learner to play, in ways that parallel these kinds of game playing activities, and incorporate the same kinds of constructive learning strategies and skills.

Bridging this gap can be an invitation to educators to look beyond the obvious and to develop a more universal approach to learning. The demand is to facilitate learning by creating a structure that begins using each student's personal intelligence and encourages students to interact with each other as they solve a task. Integrating newly acquired skills with content can ease active learning: "Active learning lies at the heart of effective, lasting education" (Chaffee, 1992, p.8). There is little doubt that we learn a great deal from experience and even more when a teacher asks students to reflect on learning. This allows students to act responsibly because of our newly assimilated experiences.

Technology, computers, multimedia, or smart classrooms, as we have already discussed, stimulates the passive intelligences of the developmental learner. For our purposes we will focus on computer-mediated communication as a theme for our case study. Business once confined computer communication to technical users but with the presence of the Internet on most college campuses it has become a natural medium for first-year students to explore. In networks, students can exchange stories, edit, or broadcast any written document. They can send data and messages instantaneously, easily, at low cost, and over long distances (Kiesler, Seigel, & McGuire, 1984). Heeding McLuhan's warning that the instantaneous communication of today leads to fragmentation and isolation, creating learning experiences that allows for a continuity of a theme and idea becomes ever more important, especially for the developmental learner. The guiding question is: "How do we as college professors manage the most relevant and appropriate learning experiences for our first year college developmental learners?"

In the article, *Constructing a language of action: The literacy experience*, (O'Neill, Perez, & Velsor 1993), the authors use a three-step model that allows for students to construct meaning from literature. Using this as a basis, we can begin to develop a model to enhance learning for all classroom experiences. The *constructing a language of action* (CLA) model is a three-step process. For our purposes, we have incorporated the first three steps with the addition of another to complete the learning experience.

CLA Case Study

In response to the needs of our incoming first year student, we have designed a course of study that addresses the many faceted components of what we believe are important for their success. The thrust of this academic experience is to "Provide an intensive orientation to college that will enable the students to take charge of their learning and to achieve their educational goals." Our class size averages about twenty-five students. The students receive a credit for the course with a grade of pass or fail. The affective goal is to have our first year student from many diverse backgrounds and academically disparate experiences to work together, to build a sense of a first-year community and to respect each other for their way of knowing.

Step I

Students are required to introduce themselves to the class, their cultural background and to explain where they would like to be ten years from the first day of class. Students hesitate at first but they soon share their heritage and their dreams for the future. The introduction helps students to validate themselves and allows for all students to know who have common interests among them, share a common major, and or course of study. It should be noted that many students are not clear about their future professional goals, and will often say that they are interested in "Making a lot of money and having a family." They are encouraged to consider a possible or feasible field of interest, and as a first task, are asked to find information about that field or profession using the Internet. The students are given instruction to enable them to access the Internet, search for information, and are given some strategies to guide their searches. Before the students begin the project, they are asked to collectively format a guiding question to help the class to focus on the theme. One class selected: " How will a college degree from SUNY Old Westbury help me to be what I want to be?." The students typically enjoy their "ride" and return to share the stories of their search, the **retelling.**

There are four requirements for a retelling:

1) They must relate their research to their background and to what they hoped to obtain in the future.

2) They must present the retelling to the class on a particular date in any way they choose.

3) They must keep their retelling a secret from their classmates.

The following is a list of suggested ways that they are able to use to retell their experience:

- Oral mode — Retelling your research in conversation to a partner; to tape record; and video taped conversation to your mother, friend, significant other or your "imaginary friend."

- Visual mode — Retelling your story through drawings, collage, puppetry, clay sculpture, or a computer graphic.

- Written mode — Retelling your research using a memo, script writing, poetry, journal entries, or short story.

- Movement mode — Retelling the research through pantomime, drama, shadow play, or dance.

- Music mode — Retelling the research through song, rhythms, or instruments (O'Neill, Perez, Velsor, 1993).

4) They must "dress the part" of the professional that they are retelling.

The retelling may be as elaborate as wearing a lab coat and stethoscope, in order for them to visualize themselves in the role they will play in the future, or be quite simple, in that they are required to dress in clothes that are more formal than jeans and t-shirts. This process may be very difficult for developmental learners. In part, this may be due to their lack of self-esteem and lack of confidence in themselves as students. However, participating in this process is a vital part of building the "community of practice" alluded to earlier, and their resultant performance goes a long way in validating their comfort in this role.

Each student is required to become an "active learner." The computer functions as the medium to reach information; the structured process allows for students to incorporate the content into their intelligences and to validate the experience with their peers. The retelling lessons are marvelous: they allow students to think about themselves. They have to reach inside themselves, they have to organize their time, and develop a medium for expression that authentically represents their experience. The social context of the assignment motivates the students to present themselves and their experience at their best.

Step II

The retelling sets the stage for the next phase, the collective phase where groups of students work together to develop an interview for a professional in their chosen field. The collective step assists students in the decision-making process concerning their career goals. This also allows groups of students with similar interest to work together toward a common aspiration. In addition, this process allows students to understand the requirements, responsibilities, and demands of professional life in the real world, in a way that is not threatening or intimidating. The process of developing questions for the purposes of interviewing a person other than themselves, requires them to concretize their assumptions about the real meaning of the workplace, career activities and the function of specific professional skills. They are also learning to recognize the dimensions along which evaluations are made in the real world, in a context where they are personally safe from the threat of evaluation. This activity also promotes complex skill-building (sequencing of questions, manner of eliciting information, structuring responses) in a context that is "real world" generated, problem-oriented, and through a process of social and collective interaction.

The groups are based on similarity of professional domains. Most of our incoming first year students will identify a degree in business, accounting or management as their primary goal. The second largest group is interested in computers, psychology, the sciences and teacher education. No group can be larger than five or smaller than three.

After the students brainstorm a list of questions, they are asked to share these questions with the class. These examples help the instructor to refine and direct a lesson on questioning techniques and inquiry skills.

The students are then asked to use the Internet to find a professional who they can "chat with." When the students identify themselves and begin the exchange, they become more committed to the project. They are excited about talking to professionals in their fields.

After the students have compiled the responses to the questions that they had developed, they return to retell this collective experience. This second retelling helps them to document the experience. Students begin by using their data to draft their ideas in a collaborative manner with their peers and the community (O'Neill, Perez, Velsor, 1993). In the process they develop, charts, script talks and the experience become real. Suddenly, "chat rooms" leave the category of "Junk Learning" (Kay, 1991, p.141) and becomes a purposeful learning activity for our students. The second retelling is more exciting then the first. The students begin with the guiding question they had started their search initially, and must integrate that context into their second retelling presentation.

Step III

The students are then asked to write a short reflective essay explaining what they have learned through this experience. Emphasis is placed on the decision process and the students are told to use the data that they have discovered to support their responses. This allows the instructors to assess the impact of the learning experience on the individual student's decision processes. Each student is also required to use the college advising staff and the College catalogue to set up a plan of action: What are the requirements for graduation? What courses should they take? When should these courses be taken? Are there other deadlines or requirements to be met, such as general education requirements, placement exams, and graduate school preparation? When students block in their schedules as first year students, the registration process from term to term is less stressful and helps our students to stay on track academically.

Step IV

The last phase of the Invitation to Learning courses is to "take action" concerning their career goals. Students should work together to develop an "Advisement Brochure" for the career tracks that are represented in their particular class, incorporating information about some or all of the areas described below:

I.   Majors that are particularly suited for particular career paths.

II. Courses required for these majors.

III. Prerequisites and sequence in which these courses need to be taken. This may be developed as a model of general education requirements and major course. registrations across the semesters at the institution.

IV. Information about professional societies, clubs, etc.

V.   Information about certification exams or licensing exams, etc.

VI. Graduate schools requirements.

These "Advisement Brochures" may be made both informative and attractive by incorporating photographs and other materials. There are a number of widely available software packages such as *Adobe Photoshop* and *Aldus PageMaker* that can be used to create such materials.

Students would recognize that these brochures would become part of the materials that would be used by the institution for recruitment, advisement, and career planning for both the current student body as well as future and prospective students. The specific skills that this course of study would provide would be :

1. Expository writing skills.

2. Using technology for data gathering, analysis, and presentation.

3. Planning and sequencing skills.

4. Elements of research skills in terms of finding specific information from the Internet.

5. Learning to use Word processing, desktop publishing, visual display skills for developing the brochure; and

6. Developing new modes of behavior: at the verbal and nonverbal level. Also, knowing the ways that professionals comport themselves, in dress, speech and body language.

Summary and Conclusion

Our intention in creating this model was to provide a structure for classroom learning that would translate psychological and educational theory about developmental learners (specifically those who are first year college students) into a plan of action. We have placed a great deal of emphasis on technology as a learning style because of the unprecedented exposure that these learners have had to technology. This *computer learning culture* as Papert (1987) has pointed out, has provided the impetus for utilizing technology effectively in the classroom. Furthermore, these students need a chance to develop their learning skills with an authentic task. We believe that structuring a learning experience which allows students to explore real life career goals, while completing a plan of action, will facilitate their self management skills, and allow them to become more independent thinkers and problem solvers.

Computers can provide a positive effect on cooperative learning strategies. Staging a positive experience for the students helps them to break down some of the barriers that have had a negative effect on their desire to learn. Further, since using the computer to play games is a well-learned and comfortable activity, this process allows students a safe context within which to learn new skills and problem-solving strategies.

The computer context also build upon the way in which most of the students have learned to process information: not in a linear and text-based manner, but in a 'hyper-text' or branching and interactive manner which is closer to the way in which they have quickly processed game-based, non-threatening material. By using this model for "Invitation to Learning," the first-year-to-college students will learn in a far more engaging and interactive process, helping them to respond to the next phase of their lives by examining their professional career choices. "We have the theories, practical wisdom and interactive technologies. It is up to us to put it all together" (Sagor, 1988, p. 33). It is up to educators to design and implement models of instruction that build upon the needs of today's college students, while providing them with the skills they need to succeed.

Chapter 14

ഇഗ

Learner Characteristics and Computer Feedback Strategies: A Model for Developmental Students

Gabriel O. Fagbeyiro

Learning is a permanent change in behavior as a result of reinforced practice. The task of learning involves several complex information processing functions including encoding, storage, and retrieval (Schmeck, Ribich, & Ramanaiah, 1977). Feedback is one form of instructional support that aids the learning process. It can be generated internally during the learning process or derived from an external origin (Tobias, 1982). For example, an amateur driver learning to drive a car knows immediately when he veers off course and can adjust the steering accordingly. Feedback may also be derived from an external medium. A teacher telling a student whether a given response is correct or not is an example of feedback from an external origin. Feedback is extremely useful in providing additional information about a certain task or in motivating the learner (Bardwell, 1981; Cohen, 1985). Consequently, most feedback encountered during the learning process are either informational or motivational. Informational feedback is provided in the form of corrective statements and a detailed explanation of the problem when a learner gives an incorrect response. Motivational feedback is often provided as a reward for a correct response.

Developmental students exhibit different types of learning characteristics and individual capabilities. Consequently, they require different levels of instructional support. While some students need little assistance, others rely on much extra help, practice and feedback. However, most instructions equally provide the same type and amount of feedback to the learners.

Differences in student learning preferences and individual locus of control further suggest that adapting instructions to the needs of the learner is necessary. Locus of control is a personality attribute which refers to the perception of causal relationship. An individual's locus of control can be measured on a continuum with the two poles defined as internal or external. A person with an external locus of control perceives outcomes to tasks as being a result of luck, chance, fate, or under the control of some powerful others (Rotter, 1966). By contrast, individuals with internal locus of control perceive the outcome of an event to be contingent upon their own behavior or their own relatively permanent characteristics. These individuals have strong beliefs that they control their own destiny. They are typically more alert to those aspects of the environment which provide useful information for future behavior (Reid, 1977; Seeman & Evans, 1962). And they are more likely to take steps to improve their own environment (Gore & Rotter, 1963; Phares, 1965). Thus, while some learners rely on others for analytical information, some learners are more comfortable with their own analytical ability.

Stewart (1983) stressed that instruction is most effective when different learning styles and preferences of learners are accommodated. One such type of assistance that incorporates instructional tasks and learner attributes is computer-based instruction (CBI). The adaptation of problem frequencies and other functions of CBI may be under the control of the student (learner control) or the computer (program control). When controlled by the program, the number of examples attempted and the types of feedback used are dictated by a learner's aptitude in solving the problems. When the learner has control, the number of problems attempted will be a function of the student's motivation, aptitude, and awareness of any learning deficiency.

Feedback is extremely valuable in CBI because it prevents the reinforcement of misconceptions, thus disallowing learners from proceeding with faulty information or incorrect assumptions (Finnegan & Sinatra, 1991; Sloanne, Gunn, Gordon & Mickelson, 1989). The effectiveness of feedback depends largely on the type of control strategy used in a CBI lesson. When feedback presentation is under the control of the student, a learner has the capability to request feedback without first responding to an instructional query. While this may facilitate lesson walkthrough, it may not necessarily assist in encoding of new information (Gagne, Briggs & Wager, 1988). In order for feedback to be effective, a good CBI should ensure that students cannot not view feedback without first generating their own answers (Kulik, Schwalb & Kulik, 1982). However, this can sometimes result in too frequent practice which may fragment the continuity of instruction and affect learner's motivation (Bangert-Drowns & Kozma, 1989). Moreover, when the learner control option is available in CBI, a student has the freedom to determine the type of feedback desired. While elaborative feedback has been associated with higher performance scores in instructional tasks, unfortunately, learners most in need of the extra help offered in elaborative feedback are the least likely to select the option when it is available (Carrier, 1984; Tobias, 1976).

Although accommodating learners' differences has been suggested as a means for increasing the effectiveness of instructions, the mere use of learner control strategy for adapting feedback presentations may not be appropriate in every situation. Students individually interact with the CBI differentially depending upon their executive control and expectancies. Gagne, Briggs and Wager (1988) stated that executive control and expectancy are two processes that activate and modulate the flow of information during learning. Gagne (1980) defined executive control as strategies to select (cognitive) strategies. Students use executive strategies when they exercise executive control. Executive strategies enable learners to review the cognitive strategies they have, to discriminate among them appropriately, and to persist in searching for the best strategies that would work in a particular situation. Possession of executive strategies is highly correlated with prior achievement.

Expectancy, according to Gagne, Briggs and Wager (1988), is related to learners' perceptions of what they will be able to do once they have learned a particular task. This, in turn, may affect how an external situation is perceived, encoded in memory, and transformed into performance. Aspects of expectancy include learners' attitude toward school and motivation to learn specific subject matter. Consequently, expectancy plays a large role in students' diligence, self-discipline, and willingness to work hard.

When using the learner control technique in CBI, differences in executive control and expectancy between students could lead to differential achievement. Belland, Taylor, Canoles, Dwyer, and Baker (1985) conducted a study to examine the relationship between learner control and feedback selection. Surprisingly, they found that the learners who understood the concepts presented in the lesson continually selected the elaborative feedback option. Those who were not performing well on the lesson did not select the elaborative feedback option in spite of their apparent need for additional information.

Learner ability is another viable contributor to performance in CBI. Even though some developmental students exhibit high ability, most are lower ability learners. Steinberg (1984) emphasized that students with low ability do not form effective learning strategies or make effective use of learner control options. Tobias (1976) and Carrier (1984) also stressed that low ability students are likely to select fewer than adequate amounts of instruction and terminate instructional lesson prematurely. In contrast, high ability students tend to manage instructional sequence better, but habitually select more than adequate amount of instruction.

These findings suggest that learner control of feedback may not be an effective approach for adapting instruction to individuals. The realization of allowing learners the freedom to chart their own course through an instructional task is enormous and compelling. Since students do not always make optimal instructional decisions, it is obvious there is a need for further research to make feedback in CBI more effective for the learners. As a result, the degree of flexibility and type of options allowed in CBI must be carefully based on the knowledge of the target audience.

Learner Characteristics and Computer Feedback Strategies

The primary purpose of a study that was undertaken by Fagbeyiro (1995) was to investigate the possible interactions between different types of computer feedback strategies and learning achievement of students with varying abilities and individual characteristics. A secondary purpose was to determine the effectiveness of adaptive feedback presentation strategy in familiar and unfamiliar computer-based instructions (CBI).

This study was guided by certain premises relating to learner characteristics, feedback, and computer-based instruction. First, computer-based instruction provides a unique means for individualizing instruction by accommodating individual differences and specific characteristics of the learner. Individuals with different ability levels and personal characteristics usually require varying amounts of instructional support and help. Support and assistance may be in the form of feedback that students receive when undertaking an instructional task. Different types of feedback may be provided to enhance learning. Elaborative feedback generally contains extensive explanation and additional information useful to the learner. During instruction, the presentation of feedback may be under the sole control of the student (learner control), the computer (program control), or adapted on the basis of pretask or on-task performance (adaptive control). Adaptively controlled feedback could be used to present either corrective statements or elaborative feedback when learner performance indicates such needs.

Research Questions

It was anticipated that the findings of this study would contribute significantly to the development of better feedback strategies, management of learner freedom, and effective computer-based instructions for the developmental learner audience. To provide focus for the research experiment, data relevant to the following research questions were gathered:

1. How do control strategies in CBI affect learners' achievement?

2. How do control strategies in computer-based lessons affect study time?

3. How does individual locus of control affect learning achievement?

4. How does self-testing ability affect learners' achievement?

5. What effect does lesson familiarity have on learning achievement of students?

6. What type of feedback is likely to be the most effective in CBI lessons?

7. Can the adaptive feedback strategy result in increased learning achievement?

Fagbeyiro's Computer Feedback and Learning Achievement Model

I designed the model in Figure 1 to aid the investigation of the problem and research questions outlined in the previous sections. This model depicted the relationships between main lesson variables. There were two CBIs: Familiar lesson and Unfamiliar lesson. Each CBI had three feedback treatments: Learner, Adaptive, and Program control. The model also showed

		CBI Lesson Contents					
Learner Characteristics		*Familiar Lesson*			*Unfamiliar Lesson*		
Locus of Control	Ability	Learner Control	Adaptive Control	Program Control	Learner Control	Adaptive Control	Program Control
Internal (Origins)	High						
	Low						
External (Pawns)	High						
	Low						

Figure 1. Fagbeyiro's Computer Feedback and Learning Achievement Model depicting a 2x3x2x2x2 interrelationships matrix between familiar and unfamiliar CBI lessons, CBI feedback treatments, learner characteristics, and related 24 cell design.

two learner characteristics variables: Locus of Control and Ability. Locus of Control had two levels: Internal (Origins) and External (Pawns). Ability also had two levels: High Ability and Low Ability. The interrelationships between the lesson variables produced a 2x3x2x2x2 matrix, which resulted in a 24-cell design.

Research Hypotheses

In order to accomplish the goals of this study and to test for interactions between the variables depicted in the research model, the following hypotheses were proposed:

1. There will be a significant interaction between students' locus of control and feedback treatments in familiar and unfamiliar CBI lessons, such that internal students will reflect higher posttest scores and learning achievement when receiving the learner control treatment; whereas, external students will perform significantly better with the program control treatment.

2. There will be a significant interaction between learners' ability and feedback treatments in familiar and unfamiliar CBI lessons, such that high-ability students will reflect higher posttest scores and learning

achievement when receiving the learner control treatment; whereas, low-ability students will perform significantly better with the program control treatment.

3. An adaptively controlled feedback strategy in which elaborated feedback is presented to students whose performance indicate a need for additional instruction will result in better learning achievement and efficient learning time than learner control and program control feedback strategies, in familiar and unfamiliar CBI lessons.

4. Interactions between learner characteristics, CBI lesson contents, and feedback treatments will have a significant effect on feedback selection, learning time, posttest scores, and learning achievement.

Scope of Study

I developed, wrote, and programmed two computer-based instructions (CBI) for the study. Lesson materials in the two CBIs were from the area of mathematics. The first instructional lesson was on the familiar topic of operations on real numbers. The second lesson presented a less familiar instruction on the topic of binary number systems conversion. The CBI lessons had three feedback treatments: Learner control, Adaptive control, and Program control (see Figure 1). The CBI kept records of learner interactions including response pattern, feedback preferences, scores on practice items, and learning time.

The learner control treatment allowed students to choose any of the feedback options available. The adaptive control differed from the learner control by taking over the function of feedback presentation when learner performance dropped below some predetermined criteria. The most elaborative form of feedback were presented to learners until performance improved. This enabled learners to focus more on instruction without having to monitor their own performance or making other instructional decisions. Learners could regain control of feedback when performance improved. In the program control treatment, the function of feedback presentation was the sole responsibility of the computer at all times. Elaborated feedback was given to incorrect responses. The details of the study are discussed below.

Methodology

Sample

A total of 439 students participated in the study. Two hundred sixty-seven (267) subjects completed all of the required components. The subjects were developmental education students at Grambling State University (GSU). They enrolled in Basic Mathematics courses in the fall semester 1994. GSU is a predominantly historical black institution with an enrollment of about six thousand students. The University is located in the township of Grambling in north central Louisiana. More than half of Grambling State students come from various parts of the nation. Thus, GSU has a good representation of students from around the nation.

Students who are enrolled in basic skills courses at GSU exhibit various characteristics of developmental learners. The students are largely made up of minorities who have come from poor, middle income, and wealthy homes alike. The majority of the students are college freshmen recently graduated from high school. Most are traditional college students within the ages of 17 and 20. Besides their various demographics, the students also have very diverse prior knowledge in mathematics and most are underprepared for college work. All of the subjects in this study have computer laboratory assignments as part of their course requirements. Thus, the students are knowledgeable in using the laboratory computers and are experienced in other preparatory CBI lessons in mathematics.

Research Design

A 2x3x2x2x2 factorial design was proposed for the purpose of the study (see Figure 1). The two levels of CBI lesson contents were classified as (1) Familiar and (2) Unfamiliar. The three levels of CBI feedback treatments were (1) Learner control, (2) Adaptive control, and (3) Program control. The CBI lesson contents and feedback treatment variables collectively represented the different instructional treatments that were used in the study. The third independent variable, learner characteristics, has two levels which were classified as (1) Locus of Control and (2) Ability. The Locus of Control variable, in turn, has two levels: (1) Internal and (2) External. The two categories reflected individual locus of causal relationship which was established through the administration of Rotter's Internal-External Scale. The Ability variable also had two levels; (1) High and (2) Low. The categories represented individual self-testing ability which was determined through the administration of Weinstein's Learning and Study Skills Inventory.

Apparatus

Each subject completed one of two computer-based lessons which were administered in the computer laboratory. Two CBI lessons and a master program were developed for the study. The computer programs were designed for use on IBM personal systems, or compatible computers based on the Intel 80x86 processor architecture. Each CBI software disseminated tutorial and practice sessions on a different mathematics topic. One CBI software provided an interactive tutorial lesson on the topic of real number operations. Specific operations included the addition, subtraction, multiplication, and division of real numbers. The subjects used in the study have had prior knowledge of the concept. The second CBI lesson provided instructions on the process of converting binary numbers to decimal numbers. Generally, the subject matter is taught in the area of computer science. Hence, the subject pool was not familiar with the concept. Each CBI software had three versions of the same lesson. The versions differed only in the degree of learner control over feedback presentation. The master program was developed to validate passwords and assign the subjects to CBI lesson treatments. Besides providing accesses to the CBI lessons, the master program was also used in administering the study. The administration menu is illustrated in Figure 2. The program enabled me to enter subjects' data into the master file, refresh subjects' accounts, view performance data, and generate statistical data file. In addition, the master program ensured that learners who have successfully completed the instructional tasks could not retake the CBI lessons. The program also prevented incomplete or garbled data from being written into the master performance data. In addition to running on IBM computers, the CBI programs were coded to execute over computer networks as well as on stand-alone systems.

Instrumentation

Personality data were collected through the administration of Rotter's Internal-External (IE) Scale and Weinstein's Learning and Study Strategies Inventory (LASSI). The IE scale provided data on individual locus of control, and the LASSI yielded pertinent data on self-testing ability of subjects. In addition, prior knowledge of lesson contents and performance data relevant to the study were gathered using the scores from the adapted pretest and

Figure 2. CBI Administration Menu. Screen display showing various administrative routines available in the master interface program.

```
                    CBI AMINISTRATION MENU
    _____

                C  =  Create User Account
                R  =  Refresh User Account
                D  =  Delete User Account
                M  =  Build Master DataFile
                S  =  Construct Statistics File
                T  =  Construct Text File
                V  =  View Cross Tabulations
                Q  =  Query DataBase
                X  =  Exit

                Enter Transaction Code:

    _____
```

posttest, respectively. Each subject also completed an informed consent agreement form prior to participating in the study.

Internal-External Scale. The construct of individuals' locus of control, one of the two personality data used in this study, was established through the administration of Rotter's Internal-External (IE) Scale. The instrument is useful in measuring aptitudes relating to the degree in which causality of behavior is attributed to oneself or to sources external to self. The scale was instrumental in identifying and placing students alongside a continuum with two ends categorized as internal and external. Hannafin (1984) suggested that internally governed students typically assume personal responsibility for their performance and behavior. Consequently, these students perform best under learner control situation. In contrast, those who perceived themselves as externally governed respond to imposed instructional demands, thus performing best under program control conditions.

The reliability and content validity of the IE scale is well documented. Rotter (1966) reported several studies of internal consistency which yielded correlation in the range of 0.65 to 0.79. Test and retest reliability, with the retesting done after one or two months, were in the range of 0.49 to 0.83.

Learning and Study Strategies Inventory. Weinstein's (1987) Learning and Study Strategies Inventory (LASSI) was used to measure aptitudes relating to self-testing ability of learners, the second personality data used in the study. A good self-testing skill is essential when using the learner control option in a computer-based instruction. The LASSI instrument is made up of 77 multiple choice items which could be used to measure attitude, motivation, and self-testing ability of learners. Learners' scores on the self-testing scale measure their awareness of the importance of self-testing and reviewing, and the degree to which they use these methods. Students who ranked above the 72 percentile were classified as high-ability subjects. Those scoring below were categorized as low-ability subjects. The self-testing items of LASSI have a coefficient alpha of 0.75 and a test-retest reliability of 0.78.

Pretest and Posttest. The pretest used in the study contained ten (10) multiple choice questions. Five questions related to operations on real numbers. The questions were adapted from the printed test bank which accompanied the subjects' mathematics textbook (Keedy & Bittinger, 1991). The questions tested the students' knowledge on order of operations involving addition, subtraction, multiplication, and division of real numbers. The questions were designed such that students must strictly observe the rules governing the order of operations when solving each problem. The remaining five questions on the pretest related to conversion of binary numbers to decimal numbers. These set of questions were adapted from a widely used computer textbook (Parker, 1990). The questions dealt with calculating multiplier values, calculating the product values, and computing the decimal equivalence of binary numbers.

A posttest was administered to the subjects at the conclusion of the instructional tasks. The posttest comprised of 10 multiple-choice problems covering various operations on real numbers and binary number conversion. Similar to the pretest, the items were adapted from the printed test bank which accompanied the subjects' mathematics textbook (Keedy & Bittinger, 1991), and a renowned computer textbook (Parker, 1990). The questions paralleled those encountered in the pretest and within the respective CBI lessons. Five questions were based on solving real number operations, and the remaining questions were based on binary number conversion. The questions on real numbers tested for competency on operations involving real numbers. The questions on binary numbers tested for competency on determining multipliers and product values, and calculating decimal equivalence of binary numbers. The pretest and posttest were paper and pencil examinations.

Materials

I programmed two CBI lessons which focused on two unrelated topics in mathematics. One of the lessons disseminated information and offered practice items on the topic of real number operations. The CBI was referred to as familiar lesson. The second lesson taught the procedures necessary to convert binary numbers to the decimal number system, as well as offered practice items. The CBI was referred to as unfamiliar lesson. Three different versions of each lesson were developed to operationalize the three different feedback presentation strategies. The treatments were referenced as learner control, adaptive control, and program control. Figures 3 and 4 are examples of the screen display for the familiar lesson. Screen display for the unfamiliar CBI lesson is depicted in Figure 5.

Three types of feedback were available for each practice items in both CBI lessons. The feedback included (1) Knowledge of Response which informed learner whether the response given was correct or incorrect; (2) Knowledge of Result which informed learner whether the response given was correct or not, and provided learner with the correct answer; and (3) Elaborated Feedback which informed learner whether the response given was correct or incorrect, provided learner with the correct answer and a detail explanation or simulation of the problem.

Under the learner control treatment, students were given full control over feedback presentation. They were able to select the type of feedback desired. By contrast, learners in the program control treatment were not given the opportunity to make feedback selection. The CBI programs automatically presented the most elaborative form of feedback to incorrect responses. The adaptive strategy functioned similarly to the learner control treatment at the onset. However, the opportunity to select feedback is replaced by the program control strategy if performance drops below a pre-established criterion. The most elaborative form of feedback is then presented until learner's performance meets or exceeds the criterion level, at which point, the learner regains control over feedback presentation.

Figure 3. Order of Operations. Screen display for Objective 1 in the familiar CBI lesson. This portion of the CBI familiarizes learners with the algorithmic process required to solve real number problems.

ORDER OF OPERATIONS - OBJ. 1

Rules for Order of Operations

1. Do all calculations within grouping symbols first.
2. Evaluate all exponential expressions.
3. Do all multiplications and divisions in order from left to right.
4. Do all additions and subtractions in order from left to right.

Previous ⟵   Next ⟶

Figure 4. Solving Real Number Problems. Screen display for Objective 2 in the familiar CBI lesson. This portion of the CBI provides seven examples to illustrate the rules for order of operations that were introduced in objective 1.

SOLVING REAL NUMBER PROBLEMS - OBJ. 2

Example 1:   **Operations**

Simplify: 15-2 * 5+3

        15-2 * 5+3   multiplying
        15-10+3   subtracting and adding from left to right
        5+3   adding
        8

Previous ⟵   *Next* ⟶

Figure 5. Calculating the Decimal Equivalent. Screen display for Objective 3 in the unfamiliar CBI lesson. This portion of the CBI simulates the binary to decimal number conversion process. Seven binary number examples were provided prior to presenting the practice items.

DETERMINING THE DECIMAL EQUIVALENT - OBJ. 3

Once the product values have been determined for the digits in a binary number, the **DECIMAL** equivalence can be calculated by:

1. Adding the product values together. Here is an example:

Binary number	$\longrightarrow$	1 1 0 1
		* * * *
Multipliers	$\longrightarrow$	8 4 2 1
Products (add)	$\longrightarrow$	8 + 4 + 0 + 1
Decimal Equivalent	$\longrightarrow$	13

Previous $\longleftarrow$ *Next* $\longrightarrow$

Statistical Analysis

The null hypotheses in the study were tested and analyzed using the Statistical Package for the Social Sciences (SPSS) (Hull & Nie, 1981). An alpha of .05 was used in all tests of significance.

A sample of developmental students was selected from an undergraduate population. Each subject was randomly assigned to feedback treatments (learner control, adaptive control, and program control) in one of two mathematics CBI lessons. Pertinent data were gathered before, during, and after the lessons, and the data were analyzed for aptitude-treatment interactions. The variables involved and their associated meanings are presented in Table 1. The independent variables were CBI lesson contents, CBI feedback treatments, and learner characteristics which include locus of control and ability. The dependent variables were CBI feedback selection, learning time, posttest scores, and learning achievement. The learning achievement scores were computed as the difference between the posttest scores and the pretest scores. If pretest score is higher than posttest, learning behavior of high and low-ability students. Both high and low-ability subjects in the learner-control treatment selected more elaborated forms of feedback than those in other groups. The program-control group re-attempted practice

Table 1. CBI Lesson Variables

Variable	Description
Response	Knowledge of response. Feedback which informs learner whether the response given is correct or not.
Result	Knowledge of result. Feedback which informs learner whether the response given is correct or not, and provides learner with the correct answer.
Elaborated	Elaborated feedback which informs learner whether the response given is correct or not, and provides the correct result and detail explanation or simulation of the problem.
Attempt	Number of times learner retried practice items prior to responding correctly or requesting feedback.
Revoke	Number of times learner lost control of feedback in the Adaptive treatment.
Reinstate	Number of times learner regained control of feedback in the Adaptive treatment.
Time	Learning time or time on task. Amount of time required to complete the CBI lessons.
Practice	Scores on practice items in the CBI lessons.
Pretest	Pretest scores.
Posttest	Posttest scores.
Achievement	Learning Achievement. The difference between posttest score and pretest score.

achievement is zero. Learning time was recorded and calculated by the computer. The computer also recorded on-task performance data including feedback selection pattern, number of practice items attempted, and number of correct and incorrect responses.

A large number of individual analyses were conducted on the data collected in both lessons. Means, standard deviations, and cell sizes were computed for the locus of control, ability, lesson time, and other performance data. Numerous frequency distributions and tabulations of responses and feedback selections were made. In order to determine the existence of group differences simultaneously across all dependent variables, multivariate analysis of variance (MANOVA) was conducted to verify the null hypotheses. The MANOVA was used to analyze lesson data and test for possible interactions among the variables identified in each of the four hypotheses.

In addition to the multi-factorial analysis, univariate F-tests, correlation analysis, and discriminant function analysis were conducted in follow-up tests. The follow-up tests were conducted to examine the specific nature and extent of group differences. The univariate statistics were used to examine the effects of canonical variables on each dependent variable. The correlation analysis were required in order to establish the relationship of the dependent variables to the main effects. The discriminant function analysis was conducted to determine the contributions of dependent variables to the predictability of the main effects. The discriminant analysis was better than separate univariate F-tests because of its capability to provide simultaneous examination of variables. Its use, in this study, helped alleviate some of the experimental errors that may occur when repeated univariate tests are utilized. A detailed analysis of results of the study is presented in the following section.

Results of Data Analyses

Frequency Distributions

A total of 439 students participated in the study. Those who did not complete the experiment were eliminated from the analysis. The actual sample distribution for the CBI lessons is depicted in Table 2. The sample size was made up of 113 males and 154 females. There were 69 internal-high ability, 68 internal-low ability, 66 external-high ability, and 64 external-low ability students. Eighty eight (88) subjects received the learner-control treatment, 98 received the adaptive treatment, and 81 received the program-control treatment.

Table 2. Actual Sample Distribution in both Lessons

Characteristics	Familiar Lesson			Unfamiliar Lesson		
	Learner	Adaptive	Program	Learner	Adaptive	Program
Internal						
High Ability	10	11	10	12	15	11
Low Ability	12	12	9	10	15	10
External						
High Ability	12	11	10	10	12	11
Low Ability	10	12	10	12	10	10
n	44	46	39	44	52	42

Note: Familiar $n = 129$, Unfamiliar $n = 138$, $N = 267$

Performance in Familiar CBI Lesson

Each subject responded to 7 items during the practice portion of the CBI lessons, and 5 items each on the pretest and the posttest. The observed means of internal subjects who participated in the familiar lesson are presented in Table 3. An inspection of the table revealed some interesting contrast between the high-ability and the low-ability subjects. In the learner-control treatment, the high-ability students selected more elaborated forms of feedback (mean = .900) to incorrect responses. Under the same treatment, the low-ability students preferred the results only feedback, mean = 1.417. This confirmed Carrier's (1984) and Tobias' (1976) contentions that low-ability learners most in need of additional instruction are the least likely to select the option when it is available in CBI. The highest posttest scores for high-ability subjects were recorded in the adaptive treatment. High-ability students also reflected higher learning achievement. In contrast, low-ability subjects in the learner-control group had the highest posttest scores. Those who received the adaptive treatment showed increased learning achievement.

The observed means of external subjects are presented in Table 4. An observation of the table also revealed some apparent patterns in the learning

Table 3. Observed Mean of Internally-governed Subjects in the Familiar CBI Lessons

Variables	High Ability			Low Ability		
	Learner	Adaptive	Program	Learner	Adaptive	Program
Response	.100	.818		.667	.250	
Result	.700	.273		1.417	.333	
Elaborated	.900	.909	1.200	.750	1.833	2.000
Attempt	1.200	1.909	1.300	1.333	1.250	2.000
Revoke		.546			.583	
Reinstate		.273			.250	
Time	11.700	12.455	16.200	17.000	19.917	18.333
Practice	5.300	5.000	5.800	4.167	4.583	5.000
Pretest	2.400	3.455	1.600	3.083	2.667	2.889
Posttest	2.700	2.909	2.100	3.000	2.833	1.667
Achievement	1.000	.455	.900	.500	.667	.111

questions more times prior to viewing feedback. Similar to the internal subjects, external-low ability students lost feedback control more times than their high-ability peers in the adaptive treatment. They also did not regain control of feedback throughout the lesson. High-ability subjects had higher scores on posttest and demonstrated increased learning achievement under program control. In contrast, low-ability subjects had higher posttest scores under learner control, but reflected better learning achievement under the adaptive treatment.

Performance in Unfamiliar CBI Lesson

Observed means of internal subjects who participated in the unfamiliar lesson are depicted in Table 5. An inspection of the table revealed that subjects in the learner-control treatment selected elaborated feedback more

Table 4. Observed Mean of Externally-governed Subjects in the Familiar CBI Lessons

Variables	High Ability			Low Ability		
	Learner	Adaptive	Program	Learner	Adaptive	Program
Response	.750	.546			.250	
Result	.500	1.182			.417	
Elaborated	1.000	.727	2.000	.200	2.167	2.100
Attempt	2.750	.636	3.400	1.200	.583	1.700
Revoke		.546			.583	
Reinstate		.182				
Time	25.250	15.455	13.800	19.400	18.833	15.300
Practice	4.750	4.546	5.000	6.800	4.167	4.900
Pretest	3.000	2.091	1.800	3.800	2.500	3.500
Posttest	1.750	1.909	2.000	3.400	3.000	3.000
Achievement	.500	.727	.800	.200	.917	.100

than other forms of feedback, regardless of ability. High-ability learners in the adaptive treatment and low-ability students in the program-control group had the highest mean on number of attempts prior to feedback. High-ability subjects in the program-control treatment performed better on posttest and demonstrated better learning achievement (mean = 3.455). Low-ability students in the learner-control and program-control treatments had similar performance on the posttest (mean = 4.0), but Low-ability learners in the learner-control treatment reflected better learning achievement.

Observed means for external subjects in the unfamiliar lesson are presented in Table 6. Results in the table revealed that high-ability students in the learner-control treatment used the response feedback more frequently than other forms of feedback. This is an indication that the subjects proceeded through the lesson without the knowledge of results or elaborated explanation to practice items that were missed. In contrast, low-ability subjects in the

Table 5. Observed Mean of Internal Subject
in the Unfamiliar CBI Lessons

Variables	High Ability			Low Ability		
	Learner	Adaptive	Program	Learner	Adaptive	Program
Response	.750	.133		.200	.400	
Result	1.417	.533		1.000	.533	
Elaborated	2.000	2.933	3.364	2.400	2.800	2.900
Attempt	1.250	3.533	2.455	1.000	1.867	4.600
Revoke		.600			.867	
Reinstate					.200	
Time	17.500	15.467	17.727	10.600	15.000	16.900
Practice	2.917	3.400	3.636	3.400	3.267	4.100
Pretest	.667	.467	.636	.600	.533	1.200
Posttest	2.917	3.333	3.909	4.000	3.067	4.000
Achievement	2.583	2.933	3.455	3.800	2.667	2.900

learner-control group selected elaborated feedback more than other forms of feedback. Both high and low-ability students in the learner-control treatment had more attempts on practice items prior to receiving feedback. Low-ability students in the adaptive treatment group lost control of feedback more often than their high-ability peers. They also did not regain control of feedback during the lesson. High-ability students in the adaptive treatment performed better on posttest (mean = 4.667) and recorded better learning achievement. Similarly, Low-ability subjects in the learner-control group had higher scores on the posttest, and showed better learning achievement.

Mean and Standard Deviation in the CBI Lessons

Mean and standard deviation for the CBI lesson variables are presented in Table 7. The table shows computations for each lesson as well as the CBI lessons combined. An inspection of the table revealed that subjects in each lesson used the elaborated feedback more often than other forms of feedback.

Table 6. Observed Mean of External Subjects
in the Unfamiliar CBI Lessons

Variables	High Ability			Low Ability		
	Learner	Adaptive	Program	Learner	Adaptive	Program
Response	1.700	.167		.667	.800	
Result	1.000	.500		.667	.200	
Elaborated	1.300	1.000	4.091	1.000	2.900	5.000
Attempt	1.600	.250	1.182	1.667	.600	1.500
Revoke		.417			.500	
Reinstate		.250				
Time	11.900	15.500	16.455	19.000	11.700	10.500
Practice	3.000	5.333	2.909	4.667	3.100	2.000
Pretest	1.900	.167	.636	.667	.300	
Posttest	3.100	4.667	2.636	5.000	3.300	1.000
Achievement	1.700	4.500	2.364	4.333	3.000	1.000

The use of elaborated feedback in the unfamiliar lesson was twice that of familiar lesson. The use of elaborated feedback in the unfamiliar lesson was twice that of familiar lesson. The mean was 2.616 with a standard deviation of 2.433. In addition, subjects in the unfamiliar lesson had more attempts on practice questions (Attempt mean = 1.826), lost feedback control more times (Revoke mean = 0.232), regained feedback control less often (Reinstate mean = 0.043), and completed instruction in fewer minutes (Time mean = 15.022). Although, subjects in the familiar lesson performed better on practice items, they scored lower on the posttest compared to the pretest. The means were 2.736 for pretest and 2.535 for the posttest. This explains why learning achievement was considerably lower in the familiar lesson (mean = 0.581). In contrast, the subjects in the unfamiliar lesson scored very high on the posttest (mean = 3.428) compared to the pretest (mean = .630). This result reflected better learning achievement in the unfamiliar CBI lesson.

Table 7. Mean and Standard Deviation for CBI Lesson Variables

Variables	Familiar Lesson		Unfamiliar Lesson		Both Lessons	
	M	SD	M	SD	M	SD
Response	.302	.669	.391	.977	.348	.842
Result	.426	1.014	.500	1.055	.464	1.034
Elaborated	1.310	1.667	2.616	2.433	1.985	2.194
Attempt	1.589	1.943	1.826	3.020	1.712	2.555
Revoke	.202	.490	.232	.457	.217	.473
Reinstate	.062	.242	.043	.205	.052	.223
Time	17.116	8.317	15.022	6.866	16.034	7.659
Practice	4.961	1.881	3.500	2.623	4.206	2.404
Pretest	2.736	1.598	.630	.975	1.648	1.682
Posttest	2.535	1.199	3.428	1.940	2.996	1.683
Achievement	.581	.958	2.964	1.968	1.813	1.965

Overall, elaborated feedback were used more frequently in both lessons than other forms of feedback (mean = 1.985). Mean lesson time was 16.034 minutes, posttest was 2.996, and learning achievement was 1.813.

Tests of Null Hypotheses

Four hypotheses were analyzed for possible interactions between the variables depicted in the Fagbeyiro's Computer Feedback and Learner Achievement Model. Analysis of variance and relevant follow-up tests were utilized in the assessment. Alpha of .05 or better were used in all tests of significance to minimize the probability of committing Type I error.

Hypothesis One and Results. This hypothesis stated there will be no significant interaction between students' locus of control and feedback treatments in familiar and unfamiliar CBI lessons, such that internal students will not reflect higher posttest scores and learning achievement when

Table 8. Locus, Lesson, and Treatment
Interactions in CBI Lessons

Test	Locus (L)	Lesson (LE)***	Treatment (T)*	L x LE x T***
			F	
Pillais	.365	118.305	2.892	6.405
Hotellings	.365	118.305	2.896	6.691
Wilks	.365	118.305	2.894	6.548

Note: Wilks' Lambda is exact. Others are approximations.
*ps < .05.**ps < .01.***ps < .001.

receiving the learner control treatment; whereas, external students will not perform significantly better with the program control treatment. The main effects in the analysis were (1) Locus of control, (2) CBI lessons, and (3) Feedback treatments. The dependent variables were posttest scores and learning achievement.

Performance data relevant to the hypothesis were analyzed for aptitude-treatment interactions. Multivariate analysis of variance was conducted jointly and individually on the main effects. The results of the multivariate test are presented in Table 8. An examination of the interactions between locus, CBI lessons, and feedback treatments revealed significant results in all tests of significance (Pillais, Hotellings, and Wilks). The result of Wilk's lambda was $F(2) = 6.548$, p < .001. This indicated that interactions between the main effects were significant on posttest scores and learning achievement. Although, locus of control showed dismal effect on post-instructional performance, interactions between the CBI lessons and feedback treatments yielded significant individual results. The results for the lesson effect and feedback treatment were $F = 118.305$, p < .001 and $F = 2.894$, p < .05, respectively (see Table 8).

Univariate test of significance, discriminant function coefficient, and correlation analysis were conducted to re-affirm the results of the multivariate test. The main effects were analyzed individually and collectively for aptitude-treatment interactions. The results of these follow-up analyses upheld the multivariate test result. Since there were significant interaction effects between the canonical variables the results of the various analyses did not support the null hypothesis. Consequently, the formal hypothesis was accepted.

Hypothesis Two and Results. The hypothesis predicted that there will be no significant interaction between learners' ability and feedback treatments in familiar and unfamiliar CBI lessons, such that high-ability students will not reflect higher posttest scores and learning achievement when receiving the learner control treatment; whereas low-ability students will not perform significantly better with the program control treatment. The main effects in the analysis were (1) Ability, (2) CBI lessons, and (3) Feedback treatments. The dependent variables were posttest scores and learning achievement.

The results of the multivariate test are presented in Table 9. An examination of the interactions between ability, CBI lessons, and feedback treatments revealed significant results in all tests of significance (Pillais, Hotellings, and Wilks). The result, Wilks' lambda, was $F(2) = 4.560$, p < .01. This indicated that interactions between the main effects were significant on posttest scores and learning achievement. The main effects also showed individual significant results on the dependent variables. Although, the treatment effect was the least significant ($F = 2.862$, p < .05) on post instructional measures, interactions between ability and CBI lessons yielded better results. The results for ability and lesson effects were $F = 7.039$, p < .01, and $F = 130.003$, p < .001, respectively (see Table 9).

Univariate test of significance, discriminant function coefficient, and correlation analysis were conducted in follow-up tests. The results of these

Table 9. Ability, Lesson, and Treatment Interactions in CBI Lessons

Test	F			
	Ability (A)**	Lesson (LE)***	Treatment (T)*	A x LE x T**
Pillais	7.039	130.003	2.863	4.497
Hotellings	7.039	130.003	2.862	4.624
Wilks	7.039	130.003	2.862	4.560

Note: Wilks' Lambda is exact. Others are approximations.
*ps < .05.   **ps < .01.   ***ps < .001.

analyses largely re-ascertain the validity of the multivariate test which showed significant interactions between the main effects. Consequently, the formal hypothesis was accepted in lieu of the null hypothesis.

Hypothesis Three and Results. An adaptively controlled feedback strategy in which elaborated feedback is presented to students whose performance indicate a need for additional instruction will not result in better learning achievement and efficient learning time than learner control and program control feedback strategies, in familiar and unfamiliar CBI lessons. The main effects in the analysis were (1) CBI lessons, and (2) Feedback treatments. The dependent variables were learning achievement and time on task.

Performance data in both CBI lessons were analyzed for aptitude-treatment interactions. The multivariate test of significance was conducted jointly and individually on the main effects. The test results merely approached significant level, thus confirming the null hypothesis. Hence, there was no need for follow-up assessment and the formal hypothesis was rejected.

Hypothesis Four and Results. The hypothesis stated that interactions between learner characteristics, CBI lesson contents, and feedback treatments will have no significant effect on feedback selection, learning time, posttest scores, and learning achievement. The main effects in the analysis were (1) Locus of control, (2) Ability, (3) CBI lessons, and (4) Feedback treatments.

The results of the multivariate test are presented in Table 10. An examination of the interactions between locus, ability, CBI lessons, and

Table 10. Locus, Ability, Lesson, and Treatment Interactions in CBI Lessons

Test	F				
	Locus (L)	Ability (A)**	Lesson (LE)***	Treatment (T)***	LxAxLExT*
Pillais	.758	3.844	62.114	7.040	1.913
Hotellings	.759	3.844	62.114	8.145	1.967
Wilks	.759	3.844	62.114	7.591	1.940

Note: Wilks' Lambda is exact. Others are approximations.
*$ps < .05$.   **$ps < .01$.   ***$ps < .001$

feedback treatments revealed significant results in all tests of significance (Pillais, Hotellings, and Wilks). The result of Wilk's lambda was F (2) = 1.940, p < .05. This indicated that interactions between the main effects were significant on feedback selection, time, posttest scores, and learning achievement. Except for locus of control, the main effects also showed individual significant results on the dependent variables. The result of lesson effect ($F = 62.114$, p < .001) suggested that performance and achievement were also contingent upon CBI lesson contents. Similar observations were evident from the results in Table 7 which indicated higher posttest scores and learning achievement in the unfamiliar lesson.

Follow-up results of univariate, discriminant, and correlation analyses re-affirmed the multivariate test. The results showed that interactions between the main effects were significant for feedback selection, learning time, and post instructional performances. Thus, the stated null hypothesis was false, and the formal hypothesis was accepted.

Summary of Findings

CBI Lesson Contents

The type of CBI lesson received was found to have substantial effects on feedback selection, learning time, practice scores, posttest scores, and learning achievement. The mean for the three feedback options were higher in the unfamiliar lesson compared to the familiar lesson (see Figure 6). The use of elaborated feedback in the unfamiliar lesson was four times higher than the familiar lesson, an indication that instructional support is desired in conditions where the content is unfamiliar. Although, the sameamount of instruction and practice items were offered in both lessons, mean learning time in the unfamiliar lesson was about two minutes less than the familiar lesson. One possible reason was that learners who were unsuccessful at the onset might have rushed through the instruction. Perhaps this explains the lower mean score on the practice items in the unfamiliar CBI. The subjects in the unfamiliar lesson had higher posttest and learning achievement scores. Their mean achievement scores were more than five times higher than the subjects who participated in the familiar lesson. This result, however, could have been influenced by expectancy of learning something perceived to be beneficial. Although the subjects in the familiar lesson had higher pretest scores, their mean posttest scores were surprisingly low compared to the pretest average. The subjects had complained that they would have benefited from the study by learning new materials like their peers in the unfamiliar

**Figure 6. Feedback selection pattern
in familiar and unfamiliar CBI lessons.**

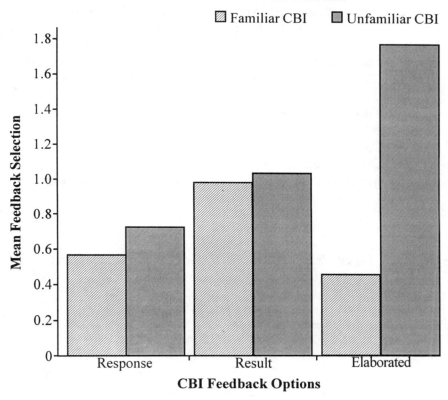

lesson. Thus, they felt like re-learning a subject matter in which they were competent put them at a disadvantage.

CBI Feedback Treatments

Feedback treatments were found to have resulted in differences in feedback selection pattern, learning time, practice scores, posttest scores, and learning achievement. The learner control and the adaptive control strategies were the only treatments which offered the option to select feedback. The subjects in the learner control treatment in the familiar lesson selected the result feedback more than any other form of feedback. Those in the adaptive treatment used the elaborated feedback more often. The subjects in the unfamiliar lesson preferred the elaborated feedback under both treatments. This is an indication that additional instructional support is needed in unfamiliar learning situations.

The subjects in the program control treatments in both lessons had the least amount of time on task. The program control groups also recorded the least performance scores on the practice items and the posttest. Mean learning time in the adaptive treatment was almost the same as the program control treatment. The difference in time of completion between the two treatments was less than two seconds. The subjects in the learner control treatment had the highest learning time. Perhaps this explains why they performed better on the practice items and the posttest. Although the learner control group had better posttest scores (see Figure 7), the adaptive control groups, however, reflected the best learning achievement in both lessons (see Figure 8). Unfortunately, this result merely approached statistically significant level.

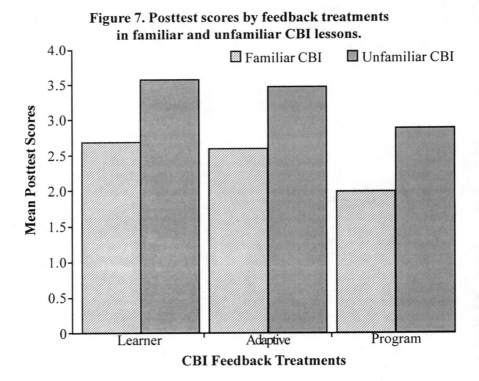

Figure 7. Posttest scores by feedback treatments in familiar and unfamiliar CBI lessons.

**Figure 8. Learning achievement by feedback treatments
in familiar and unfamiliar CBI lessons**

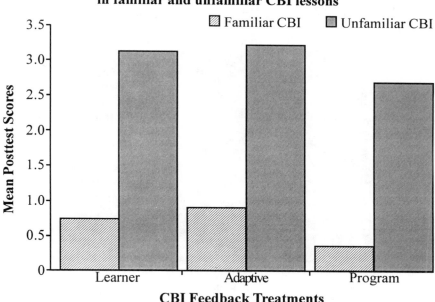

Locus of Control

Individual locus of control affected performance scores and learning time in the CBI lessons. The external subjects performed better on the practice items; whereas the internal subjects had higher mean posttest and learning achievement scores in both lessons. The internal subjects also completed the instructional tasks in less time. There were no noteworthy pattern found on selection of feedback. It appeared that the subjects selected and used feedback options according to task difficulty. Figure 9 depicts learning achievement scores according to locus of control in the familiar and unfamiliar CBI lessons.

Ability

Ability was found to have substantial effects on feedback selection, learning time, practice scores, posttest scores, and learning achievement. High ability learners selected the response and the result feedback options frequently than elaborated feedback. The lower ability students opted for

**Figure 9. Learning Achievement by Locus of Control
in familiar and unfamiliar CBI lessons.**

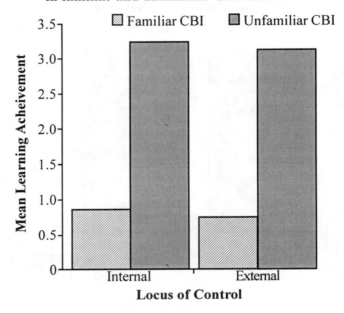

**Figure 10. Learning Achievement by Ability
in familiar and unfamiliar CBI lessons.**

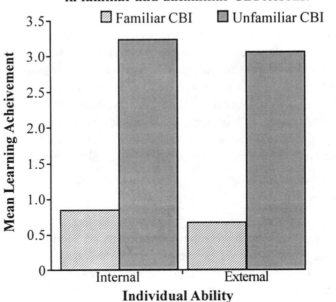

the elaborated feedback. It appeared that the low performance on practice items might have encouraged the low ability subjects to opt for the most elaborate form of feedback, the use of which seemed to have resulted in higher mean posttest scores. However, the results on learning achievement favored the high ability subjects (see Figure 10). They reflected better learning achievement and completed the instructions in fewer minutes compared to the low ability subjects.

Conclusions

The following conclusions are based on the results of the data analyses. The conclusions address the research questions presented earlier in the chapter, as they relate to this study.

Question One: How do control strategies in CBI affect learners' achievement?

The result of the data analysis in this study revealed that high and low ability students had higher mean practice score and posttest score under learner control. Although the results only approached statistical significance, learning achievement was superior in the adaptive control strategy. The least performance in the study occurred under program control.

Question Two: How do control strategies in computer-based lessons affect study time?

A review of the data analyses in this study revealed a significant increase in learning time under the learner control treatment. This finding confirmed that learners do not always make optimal instructional decisions in learner control situations. The minimum time on task was observed in the program control and the adaptive control treatments.

Question Three: How does individual locus of control affect learning achievement?

The results of this study revealed that internal subjects performed better than external subjects on the posttest and learning achievement scores. However, the results were not significant.

Question Four: How does self-testing ability affect learners' achievement?

Individual ability was found to have substantial affect on learning achievement of subjects who participated in this study. Overall results indicated that high ability learners achieved better than low ability subjects across the treatments.

Question Five: What effect does lesson familiarity have on learning achievement of students?

Contrary to prior research, the results in this study did not reveal significant increases in performance when learners have prior experience of the lesson content. The subjects in the unfamiliar lesson had higher posttest scores and learning achievement scores. The mean achievement score in the unfamiliar lesson was more than five times higher than the familiar lesson. The low performance in the familiar lesson appeared to have resulted from low interest in the subject matter.

Question Six: What type of feedback is likely to be the most effective in CBI lessons?

The results of this study confirmed that elaborated feedback was necessary in lessons which required learning complex concepts, or those that contain difficult or unfamiliar contents. The results showed that the use of elaborated feedback in the unfamiliar lesson was twice that of the familiar CBI. This indicated that additional instructional support was needed in unfamiliar or complex learning situations.

Question Seven: Can the adaptive feedback strategy result in increased learning achievement?

Performance data indicated that the strategy was successful in both lessons, even though the result was not statistically significant. The adaptive strategy resulted in increased learning achievement among the subjects, regardless of individual characteristics. Mean achievement scores in the adaptive treatments were higher than the learner and program control treatments. The high ability students reflected better learning achievement than the low ability learners. Similarly, the internal subjects had higher achievement scores than those who were externally governed.

Implications of the Study

This study provided valuable information relevant to design of Computer-Based Instructions for the developmental learner audience. The study also offered pertinent insight into developmental learner characteristics and the role of feedback in CBI. The results of the study led to the following implications:

1. Locus of Control had effects on performance and learning time in CBI lessons.

2. Ability had an effect on the use of feedback options, performance, and learning time in CBI lessons.

3. Lesson contents had an effect on feedback selection, performance, and learning time in computer-based instructions.

4. Content familiarity had no effect on feedback selection, performance, and learning time in CBI lessons.

5. Students make efficient use of feedback options in unfamiliar learning situations.

5. Elaborative feedback, in which additional information and assistance are offered, is desired in unfamiliar learning situations.

6. Developmental students desire adequate instructions and practice items in CBI lessons.

7. Expectancy plays a major role in developmental learners diligence, self-discipline, and willingness to work hard in learning situations.

Based on these implications, I have proposed the following stipulations in designing instructions for the developmental audience:

1. Introduce elements of expectancies very early in the lesson. The usual SWBAT (Students Will Be Able To) statement alone is not adequate. Inform students not only what they will be able to learn but what they can benefit from learning a particular concept.

2. Provide clear and concise directions to lesson contents.

3. Provide adequate instructions and practice items during the lesson.

4. Make available the option to view directions or algorithms relevant to problems during the practice portion.

5. Provide the option to retry problems with incorrect responses.

6. Make available the option to select different forms of feedback rather than coerce learners into viewing the same feedback.

7. Emphasize the use of elaborated feedback in complex lessons or in unfamiliar learning situations.

8. Adapt feedback presentation on the basis of on-task performance when learner characteristics is unknown.

9. Encourage learner to complete instruction rather than provide exit options, especially when teaching critical concepts or when participation in an instructional task is of essence.

10. Delay presentation of performance result until the lesson has been completed.

Suggestions for Future Research

This study was a preliminary investigation into the possible interactions between learner characteristics and different types of feedback strategies in CBI. Additional research might provide further knowledge on the needs of learners in different learning situations.

The sample size was one of the factors limiting the generalization of this study. As a result, similar studies might be conducted using larger sample sizes. The same lessons could be administered to a group of regular college students, or to groups of students from two or more universities. Their response, feedback selection patterns, lesson performance, and learning achievement scores might yield an interesting contrast.

Moreover, researchers with a limited sample size might want to rerun the study using the same subjects under familiar and unfamiliar lesson situations. This type of investigation could provide valuable insight into the needs of learners under different learning situations.

A revised version of the study could also provide better results. Researchers might modify the study to include more test items on the pretest, practice test, and posttest. The learning achievement formula may also be revised. The pretest and practice scores could be used in conjunction with the posttest scores to establish individual learning achievement. These revisions might produce a different result.

In addition, researchers might consider an investigation into possible interaction of feedback strategies and learner characteristics over a longer period of time. An entire course or series of lessons might be incorporated and taught using a CBI. It is possible that learners with different learning attributes might be affected differently over a period of time. A study conducted over a period of time might also influence a learner's awareness of the usefulness of certain forms of feedback in CBI.

Part IV:
Models of Assessment and Evaluation

Chapter 15

ℰⷦℭℛ

A Comprehensive Assessment Learning Model: The CAL Approach

Dorothy Bray

Introduction

Assessment Models are important in assisting colleges and universities to be more successful with large numbers of underprepared students. An important body of historical information contributes to a methodology for developing the models. This chapter addresses key issues which are blended into a new comprehensive model of assessment.

1. This model is designed specifically to help colleges with improving the success of large numbers of underprepared (*remedial*) students. A continuing trend—to assign a social value to remediation or programs for students underprepared for college level work—has led to a devaluing of this important educational function by some educators and social critics. Such arguments erode this viable educational process at the same time as renewed concepts add to the strong historical data to offer new and better model structures. This model proposes to adopt another terminology: *learning skills-preparation,* a less value laden term for instructional quality purists, which can replace the term *remediation.*

2. This chapter describes a Comprehensive Assessment-Learning Model, called CAL, which builds on previous fundamental assumptions about assessment processes.

   - For designers, discussions of past models will provide an understanding of the multiple purposes for assessment models. However, today's model looks different.

   - Several decades of design and implementation have expanded the functions and the detail of models.

   - We know so much more today, than before, about assessment and remediation of learning skills deficiencies and their appropriate roles in the college structure. Therefore, today's model methodology is less conceptual and more detailed.

   - Ongoing re-definitions of assessment have broadened its scope and contribute to more cross-functional systems in models.

3. Today's Assessment Models must bridge the rhetoric of reform and old issues of inflexibility of long established institutional and educational practices. The CAL Model reflects the capabilities of assessment driven reform of institutional processes and products:

   - New, required joint participatory structures have the capacity to effect substantive change in educational practice.

   - Competing and contrasting ideas about student learning, teaching, curriculum and assessment are reduced in this model.

   - Since the model requires a coherent institutional plan of student flow through the institution, both students and the institution are facilitated.

The Environment of Today's Assessment Models

Several powerful factors currently are exerting influence over the design and use of assessment models in postsecondary education.

1. The continuing trend for policymakers to view assessment as exerting a powerful leverage over educational practice continues to be attractive for those who frequently think of assessment as a barometer of educational quality.

2. The continuing trend that fewer and fewer high school graduates have the requisite skills competencies to succeed in college level instruction so that the "underprepared" students entering college have become a majority who are found throughout collegiate programs.

3. The growing trend that today's jobs and professions require even stronger, and ever-increasing competencies in reading, writing, mathematics, critical thinking and working in teams. Newer skill demands for college graduates extend the skills acquisition problems to all college students.

4. The new, most critical skill for all participants in today's jobs is the ability to learn and keep learning.

5. There is a new expectation by companies and industries of today's economy that their new jobs, primarily information driven, require a workforce skilled in communication, computation and capable of continual learning.

As a result, the considerable tension in academic institutions between the goals of educational quality and equality of opportunity for underprepared college students are out of step with newer challenges to improve the learning skills of all students on a continual basis. In the present colleges and universities, all students will require additional skill development—at entrance to college courses, during college courses and as preparation for graduation.

Colleges and universities now must provide a structural framework based on three guiding principles:

1. The guiding principle for all educational institutions, but especially colleges and universities is that they must utilize new models of learning and teaching while adopting systems that provide facts of student learning and skills acquisition on a continual basis.

2. Postsecondary institutions and their resident educators must develop a competence with assessment.

3. Assessment is now a necessary context to this mandate: Postsecondary institutions must ensure that students develop increasing levels of skills competence-required—not only for survival in college, but also in the jobs of today's new information-based economy.

Assessment models are now primarily for institutional frameworks to manage these key goals:

1. To direct students through collegiate experiences, processes and instruction.

2. To drive instruction geared to student success in learning.

3. To create college-wide reform of practices and procedures reflective of emerging local, state and national educational standards on institutional and student achievement.

A 1995 definition of assessment expresses five core themes which have contributed to more comprehensive Institutional Assessment Models (Angelo, 1995). The five core themes include: 1) Assessment should focus primarily on improving student learning, but not be limited to the classroom, 2) assessment of student learning must also include assessing the wide range of processes that influence learning, 3) a systems approach is values— understanding assessment as a process, 4) assessment should be used more effectively "to focus our collective attention" at departmental and institutional levels, using assessment as a vehicle to create linkages and enhance coherence within and across curriculum, and 5) managing the inherent tensions between assessment for improvement and assessment for accountability is a key issue.

Part I—Background: Two Decades of Development of Assessment Models

Role 1: Assessment Models and the Underprepared Student in Higher Education

During the 1970's colleges and universities began to be impacted by the open enrollment policies derived from the social ethic of The Great

Society—*that a college education was to be the entitlement of any individual of college age who desired to go* and who *could succeed in college.* At the same time, new definitions of academic standards required for graduation from high schools created a more egalitarian approach to grades, graduation standards, and admission to college. Student diversity became a predominant ethic for college admission as students poured into higher education institutions from different backgrounds—social, ethnic, economic, and academic.

The great accomplishments in expanding student access to postsecondary education since the 1970's created another set of problems for the 1980's and now 1990's: How can colleges and universities be effective and efficient with large numbers of underprepared students?

By the late 1970's all segments of higher education were impacted by three major trends in student demographics:

1. A majority of entering college students were deficient in the basic skills. For example, many students could not read at college level, high schools graduated many students reading below the eighth grade level, a large majority of students (up to 90 percent in some studies) could not demonstrate college level skills in mathematics, and most students (up to 70 percent in some national studies) could not write at college level.

2. The remediation of basic skills became the fastest growing area of the curriculum according to most of the literature of the early 1980's.

3. There was universal agreement on the need to develop basic skills but there was little information on how to achieve this effectively and efficiently.

A debate still centers on this question, "What is the impact of admitting to higher education institutions large numbers of students who are deficient in basic academic skills?" Three themes continue to be at the center of the controversy.

Access and Success. Are they contradictory goals if a majority of students are underprepared for college work?

Quality of Instruction. How can quality of instruction be maintained if a majority of students are not college?

Retention. How can colleges retain students if they are not prepared for college level courses?

Role 2: Assessment Systems—Key to Institutional Efforts for Student Success

In the early 1980's assessment systems began to play a critical role in many college plans to improve student success. Assessment and placement activities became increasingly valued as strategies that would help colleges with the wide range of learning and teaching problems of a diverse student clientele.

Assessment/Placement Systems were used by colleges to accomplish these explicit goals for dealing with large numbers of underprepared students: 1) Be effective and efficient in *guiding* large numbers of underprepared students through collegiate institutions, 2) help *diagnose and place* a wide diversity of students in appropriate classes and services, 3) *prevent the loss* of valuable human resources by increasing the success of the students admitted to colleges, 4) *bolster the academic performance* of all students, 5) be concerned for the *outcomes of learning* as well as the access criteria, and 6) be sure that *open access* to college is accompanied by instructional merit and quality.

During the 1970's and early 1980's, assessment in most colleges was a tool for describing student demographic and basic skills proficiencies at the time of enrollment.

Colleges gathered such information largely to create and justify special programs and services for serving an increasingly large and diverse student population. Assessment activities centered on basic skills testing for placement into college courses, giving rise to the premise that "assessment at entrance was what mattered the most, not post-testing" (Bray, Kanter in Banta, 1993).

Role 3: Models Inform State Policies

Ideally, models should inform policies. In California, a college-led collaborative effort used an Assessment-Placement Model to bring about wide-spread institutional change and to leverage a state policy reform to support the remediation of a large number of underprepared college students. This model performed multiple roles in guiding curriculum revision, student services changes and policies adjustments. In many states the educational issues of admitting large numbers of students to college who were lacking in the basic academic skills were joined with political issues of funding for postsecondary education. Assessment models, as the primary structural tool for colleges to deal with underprepared students, assumed wider roles, beyond their academic goals and objectives.

Many of the developers of Assessment models became advocates for local, state, and even national policy and their models became significant in emerging political agendas. As assessment models became instrumental for policy formation, new premises evolved, delineating a broader use of primarily academic models of assessment.

A California Model of Assessment/Placement. In most states, the tension between quality and access issues center around the topic of remediation programs and policies for students lacking requisite academic skills for college courses. In the late 1970's the topic of remediation became a key issue in state politics in California. The California Community College System, the largest in the world with 1.2 million students at that time, struggled with how to provide remediation to large numbers of academically deficient students entering its colleges under an open enrollment state policy. In that state, a college-led consortium developed an Assessment-Placement Model, which, eventually, became the impetus for new funding policies in California.

Historically, in California, the colleges themselves led reform movements regarding the issues of remediation linked to the implementation of assessment/placement models. In 1981 fourteen colleges in northern California joined together to develop concrete practices in assessment, to enable the colleges to increase the retention of its diverse student bodies. This cooperative venture, known as the LARC Consortium (Learning, Assessment, Retention Consortium), included 80 colleges by 1991.

In 1981, The LARC Consortium of the California Community Colleges developed a working model for a four step process linking the pre-assessment of students to an advising and placement activity which utilized the assessment information and guided student enrollment into classes. A fourth activity was a feedback-research system to provide data for evaluation and revision.

A draft document entitled *Providing for Academic Skills and Remediation in the California Colleges* (Bray et. al. 1986) described a number of recommendations, then under consideration, and subsequently adopted as state policy. After extensive policy review, the state adopted a series of policies as an *attempt to organize institutional responses to student underpreparation—must assess the students within a diverse and comprehensive context and framework—such as the LARC Assessment-Placement Model.*

In California's Master Plan for Higher Education (1988), state policy indicated that "Standards and access are not mutually exclusive, when assessment/placement processes are used to direct student flow." A holistic Assessment/Placement Model was to be the key element for admitting and placing students in classes in the Community Colleges. These recommendations also recognize the magnitude of the responsibilities of colleges for implementing a holistic model of Assessment in the complexities of an ever changing educational environment.

Figure 1. The LARC Assessment-Placement Model

This comprehensive model emphasized key concepts, now found in most new institutional models which define a relationship between assessment and instruction:

1. A comprehensive model includes *mutual goals* with counseling, instruction, and research.
2. *Student flow* through the institutions is a key factor in planning for the model.
3. A *critical path* of model activities provides a framework for providing continuous student information to the institution and to the students.
4. Data from this student critical path will be translated into research which can provide a basis for decision making.

Student Flow of LARC A/P Model

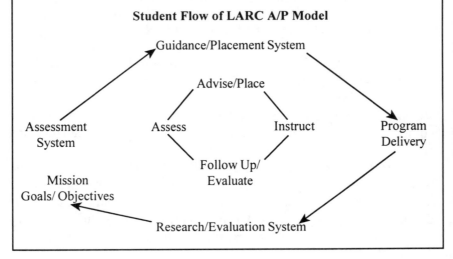

The Role of the California Community Colleges in Providing Remediation

1. Students needing academic assistance and additional preparation will be provided access through remedial programs to enable them to enter college classes in a reasonable period of time.

2. Basic to this policy was the delineation that the responsibility for student success was the joint responsibilities of the state (to provide for the goal), of the institutions (to deliver the goal), and of the students (to achieve the goal in a reasonable period of time).

3. The Board of Governors combined open access with clearly defined academic standards—directing that minimum academic skills levels be developed, appropriate for the different types of courses and programs offered. In addition, these standards would guide student exit processes from the college.

4. There was an emerging need was for a methodology for assessing the effectiveness of the student and the remedial programs since remediation was established as proper in principle and thus subject to quality, tests, evaluation, and review.

5. A mandatory assessment, counseling, placement and follow-up program was adopted as policy, along with funding processes to support the model on college campuses.

6. In the mission statement for post-secondary education, remediation was affirmed as an important function of the colleges and essential to helping inadequately prepared students to succeed at the college level.

7. A limit to the number of remediation course units was established as a reasonable limit for students to progress to college level courses.

Based on research conducted by the LARC Consortium, the state of California adopted a series of policies clarifying the linkage of the roles of remediation and assessment in the state's Community College System. These policies still remain a strong and forceful re-affirmation of the appropriateness of remediation in higher education.

Conclusion

Assessment models have been used in multiple roles: (1) in the 1970's and early 1980's, they provided information to colleges and universities at entrance about student skills preparation or lack of skills competencies (2) also, they assumed a broader role to provide critical information so that colleges could develop more support structures to enhance student learning and eventually, (3) they provided key information to state decision makers to inform policies on student enrollment and institutional.

Part II: Assessment Models and State Policies—The Accountability Role

In California the LARC Consortium connected the efforts of the state and of the practitioners to develop policy and assessment model guidelines for proposed solutions to assist the underprepared students in higher education. From these efforts, the linkage of assessment, remediation and quality instruction with the success of students in the institution was strongly validated. While some colleges were adapting Assessment-Placement Models with the goals of the LARC Model, others were adapting models to fulfill other state mandates. To provide outcomes assessment information to state decision-makers became a primary goal of other models. The funding policies for higher education helped determine each state's model development.

Connecting Assessment/Placement with Institutional Accountability

In the 1990's colleges in California began to develop another assessment model—an accountability or outcomes model based on evaluating institutional effectiveness, measured in large part by student achievement and outcomes. The state required the colleges to expand the Assessment-Placement Models. The goal, through Assessment Models, was to link student access and success into a unified and manageable accountability system with all of the state's colleges' data being unified into one state data base. The merging of these models was problematic because of the size and complexity of the state's student data (Bray, Kanter, in Banta, 1993, p. 323). Other states were exploring the accountability focus for assessment with more success.

Policies Inform Models

Assessment Models—Outcomes Assessment—Key to Institutional Accountability

Peter Ewell (in Banta and Associates, 1993) provides much of the information for this section from his comprehensive analysis of this topic in his Chapter, "The Role of States and Accreditors in Shaping Assessment Practices." By the late 1980's, most states had developed policies requiring assessment models for higher education institutions. The majority of public institutions undertook assessment to meet the terms of state mandates requiring information about student success to inform policy and budgetary considerations. By 1989 some two-thirds of the states required colleges and universities to develop assessment models generally based on the following characteristics.

Characteristics of Mandated Models of Late 1980's

The basic features of the characteristics, though details varied, including:

1. A requirement that each higher education institution develop an explicit plan for assessment, including statements of intended outcomes, proposed methods for gathering evidence and a proposed organization structure to accommodate the plan.

2. Substantial institutional latitude in developing goals statements in selecting appropriate methods for gathering evidence.

3. Mandatory reporting of results to state authorities on a regular basis.

4. The expectation that institutions themselves would pay the costs of assessment.

5. The general expectation that information resulting from local assessment programs would simultaneously induce campus level change and fulfill growing state-level demands for accountability.

6. The expectation that the results would eventually be helpful in developing state-level policies and in determining key areas of need for selective state funding.

The impact of these state mandates resulted in a mass movement by higher education institutions to implement these models. "A 1992 *Campus Trends Survey* reported the astonishing fact that 92% of the nation's colleges and universities by then engaged in assessment" (Ewell, p. 33).

Externally Mandated Models Result in Little Institutional Change for Teaching and Learning

If the activities of assessment have been so pervasive in higher education, why do we still need new models of assessment? *It is important to understand that most real campus efforts have been in the areas of planning for assessment—in particular in developing the requisite policies and organizational structures to make it happen and in choosing initial instruments and approaches.*

Most assessment models have made only a modest impact on the institution's practices of education. According to Ewell, the results of adding new assessment requirements on higher education are mixed. The results of new, extensive, assessment processes have been useful but expensive to attain. Another significant impact of the addition of assessment models to colleges has been the cost and expense of such processes and products. In the US in the past ten years most colleges and universities have invested heavily in organizational structures, technology, and staff to produce new and varied assessment information. Today, these models are proving hard to maintain.

Most college practitioners agree that one model of assessment has proved the most useful—that of mandatory assessment of basic skills at entrance to college—along with required, directed placement into remediation instruction prior to entering college level courses. This model of assessment, which arose primarily in the mid and late 1980's is generally found on each college campus.

Conclusion

To conclude, a two decade long pattern of development of assessment models has permanently shifted college philosophy and operations in favor of the realistic understanding. Many, if not most, students in today's higher education system are not academically skilled, less educated for college and job expectations and more diverse, culturally, and socially. Assessment systems are a necessary condition of the learning skills context in today's colleges and universities. Yet some leaders in the higher education systems still exhibit little understanding of the possibilities of Assessment Models in improving student success in their institutions, developing systems only in response to state mandates for accountability information. As a result, most of the campus commitments to using assessment models to improve learning have not resulted in a comprehensive campus approach which links assessment to improved student success. Postsecondary institutions now need to consider other actions which new models of assessment must specify.

Part III: Redefining Remedial as Learning Skills Development

The emergence of Assessment/Placement models as a predominant strategy to assist colleges with the learning skills development of large majorities of their students, occurred as new knowledge from other sciences and systems became available. These models were based on a combination of learning theories from educational psychology, cognitive and affective strategies from developmental psychology, and systems models from organizational theory. Many students lacked the basic academic skills in the areas of reading, writing, and mathematics needed to succeed in college classes. To be successful in college, these students required different experiences from previous students.

New Terminology Redefines Remediation

A new terminology developed to describe students with academic skills deficiencies. Depending on the college, these underprepared students were known as remedial, developmental, high-risk, low achieving, or disadvantaged. Identification of these students was generally based on their composite scores in mathematics, reading, or English tests coupled with information on study habits, attitudes, and goals (Bray, 1987).

For the 1990's, the concept of student readiness has been expanded to include collegiate academic skills development as well as basic learning skills development. In the 1990's the gap widened between the acquired academic skills in high schools and the required academic skills for colleges. In addition, another skills gap emerged-most jobs in the new economy demanded increasing higher levels of skills, particularly, problem solving skills. All postsecondary institutions were challenged to provide more structures for the mandate to be successful with students with basic learning skills deficiencies at entrance to college as well as to insure the ongoing development of their collegiate academic skills.

Twin issues are central to today's definition of "the underprepared student": (1) whether or not, students are ready for college work at entrance (2) and whether, by the time the students have graduated from college, they have the higher level skills expected of college graduates in today's society. In addition, improved definitions of abilities and ability levels have provided a broader view of what *underprepared* means. For example, Alverno College's pioneering work in assessment found that "skills abilities are recognizable in varied forms, in different disciplines and professional environments."

Past models reflected the tendency to address remediation as a two stage process. First, those educational efforts which attempted to correct deficiencies which should have been achieved before entering college referred to skills as deficiencies in *fundamental learning skills* and the programs as *remedial*. Second, those efforts which attempted to build *supplementary learning skills* necessary to succeed in college courses were referred to as *developmental*. Today's models reflect the emphasis on a learning skills continuum rather than separating skills instruction into remedial and developmental categories of instruction.

Underpreparation of College Students—
Prevalent Across College Programs

The continuing controversies of what to call college activities which assist students to gain academic skills has fragmented the dialogue on student skills proficiencies. New knowledge about learning skills development or deficiencies suggest that arguments on whether to call these students remedial or developmental are not reflective of the nature of the problem, as we know it today. For numerous reasons, underpreparation of college students is a universal phenomenon:

1. Remediation of underprepared students for academic course work is nearly universal in American education.

2. Many students will enroll in collegiate course work while simultaneously taking course to improve their learning skills.

3. Preparatory course work cannot be limited to "remedial instruction in

segregated programs or departments since these underprepared students will be enrolled throughout the institution.

4. The conditions of academic success are relevant for all students.

5. The processes established to assist remedial efforts are those which enhance all of the learning and teaching processes.

6. There is and always will be a continued need for remediation at all levels of higher education since the required levels of skills continue to increase.

Underprepared students are those who need to improve their academic skills in reading, writing, math, and critical thinking. They are not necessarily high risk, marginal, educationally disadvantaged or academically unsuccessful in high school or college. They are *diverse* in backgrounds. They are alike in that they need support to enter and succeed in college level courses. Today we view most students as not proficient in basic academic skills in the sense that they need more development and practice of communication skills, mathematical skills, critical thinking skills and even some core knowledge.

Need for Assistance with Learning Skills Requires Institutional Wide Models

The issue of increasing student performance is now part of the national agenda. Goals 2000 (National Education Goals) calls on every school and community to develop its own comprehensive plan to move all students toward high standards. There is and always will be a continued need for assistance with learning skills since the required level of skills both for success in college and on the job continues to increase. However, it is not a static process, but a continuum of readiness that institutions need to address with structure, coherence, clarity, and explicit outcomes. The institution's responsibility is to ensure maximum quality, responsiveness to student need, lowest cost, and least duplication of efforts (Providers of Remediation, Larc Consortium,1985). In addition, these institutional models must be dictated both by the needs of incoming students and by the needs of the employers who are responsible for their transition from school to work.

A New Operational Term to Replace Remediation. This model assumes that remediation is a *process* of providing for the learning skills development of students admitted to colleges. This process includes classroom instruction as well as other support activities to assist students in pursuit of their educational goals and objectives.

Since the unifying feature of this process is ***to equip*** students to succeed in college courses, we can refer to all assistance programs and activities as *"learning skills development."* This model makes the umbrella term *learning skills* operational for all college activities otherwise called *remediation*.

Preparatory Courses to Improve Learning Skills. The institutional course responses, which assist students to improve their inadequate college skills, are referred to as *preparatory courses which:* 1) Intend to prepare students to do college level work whatever their level of deficiency, 2) typically are organized as a sequence of courses and programs, and 3) are organized based on the assumption that there is a hierarchy of learning preparation skills which can be developed in a series of courses.

Figure 2 describes processes which manage student flow into Learning Skills Programs. One path for students is through the *Preparatory Sequence of Courses*, for developing skills required to enter college courses. The second path into learning skills is through an *Academic Skills Sequence* for developing skills to succeed while in college level instruction. Since in this

Figure 2. Learning Skills Placement: Sample One Semester Framework

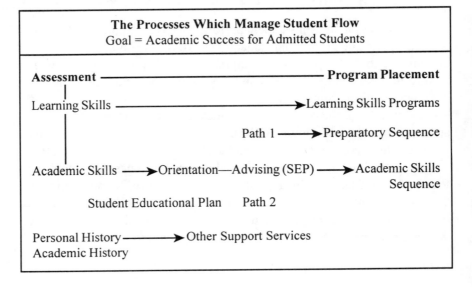

The Processes Which Manage Student Flow
Goal = Academic Success for Admitted Students

Assessment ────────────────────── **Program Placement**

Learning Skills ──────────────────────►Learning Skills Programs

Path 1 ──────►Preparatory Sequence

Academic Skills ──►Orientation—Advising (SEP) ──►Academic Skills Sequence

Student Educational Plan   Path 2

Personal History ──────► Other Support Services
Academic History

model, successful student performance in college is the core issue, the model prompts institutions to respond to this central curriculum issue: how to connect students to appropriate instructional programs. The model also prompts institutions to respond to a key student services issue: how to connect less competent students to college resources and resource assistance. Other key ingredients of student flow to learning skills programs require decisions. Other ingredients of managing student flow to learning skills programs require many institutional decisions, including the placement criteria, for placing students into learning skills or academic skills classes, a review of the curriculum content of skills courses which must be matched by student profiles, and to determine what standards will define a student's successful exit from the skills courses. Instituting these ingredients will prompt new faculty decision making, in concert with counselors and support staff.

Conclusion

The most critical factor of higher education in the last two decades is that most students in community colleges and many students in four year colleges are not ready for college work. A significant political factor is that decision makers view assessment as a successful tool for dealing with massive student lack of readiness.

The debate on student readiness problems has centered and continues to center around three themes: 1) Access and success—complementary or contradictory goals? 2) quality of instruction—complementary to or contradictory with large numbers of underprepared students? and 3) demonstrable student improvement—complementary to or contradictory of underpreparation?

Since deficiencies in learning skills is nearly universal in higher education, institutional models to address this issue can not be limited to "remedial instruction in segregated programs or departments." When viewed as *underprepared*, these students are found throughout the institution. Thus a total institutional effort is required. The conditions of remedial instruction, when juxtaposed with the conditions for *academic success* suggest that most college students will benefit from models organized to assist students to improve academic skills, at whatever level. Today, we view most students as underprepared in the sense that most need practice and development of academic skills. The reality of students "going on to college" is to gain more competencies in these skills. The reality of the total college environment being involved in developing academic skills is that " this is their business."

Higher education institutions now are at risk unless they can be successful with large numbers of underprepared students.

Part IV: The Promise of Modeling

Designing Assessment—Learning Models

As with other broad topics, there is no one best way to organize for assessment-learning models. The variety and scope of details required in establishing a comprehensive system, in turn, require an organized framework to guide development and implementation. Since assessment-learning models are based on the premise that individual student success is closely related to an institution's capabilities to organize for directing this process, a model-framework is essential. Indeed, John Roueche, one of the most prominent spokespersons for remedial education models and assessment, indicated in 1984 that *processes employed to manage students* are as important as, if not more important than instructional processes.

Emphasis on Student Flow Through Institutions

The models which are presented in this chapter are based on the premise that defining and delineating *student flow* through the institution is the key factor in planning for this model. The emphasis on student flow requires a *description of the logical order* in which the student will move through the **stages of the model**. This impacts on the institution's basic philosophy that the student is the center and reason for institutional organization and behavior, the reversal of a historical emphasis that the institution comes first, and that the student adapts to its elements.

Utilizing the language of modeling, a **critical path** of model activities provides a **framework** to specify **a continuum** of student, program, and institutional activities which must act in concert. This requirement, difficult enough to achieve philosophically for institutions, might be impossible to implement without a clear, coherent plan of organizational steps and decisions which can be delineated in a model. An Assessment-Placement Model, grown into an Assessment-Learning Model, not only facilitates a student's movement through colleges, but, as well, facilitates the change from school to work (Bray, 1987). Figure 3 describes a critical path of activities which direct the student flow. In the student flow process, the student is the customer. The student flow model organizes complex processes which involve multiple service areas or functions that are used by the student in his journey through the institution. Belcher and Strickland (1995) refer to a similar cross functional analysis as "service mapping." Service mapping provides an opportunity for students to bring new insights into their journey through institutions of higher learning. It also ensures that students receive complete service from their departments.

Figure 3. Student Flow in the CAL Model

Critical Path of Model Activities—Guides Student Flow	
Student Flow Through 10 Steps of Assessment	Processes/Products Employed to Inform, Advise and Guide Student
1. Prepare student profile condition	specify key traits of underprepared
2. Assess proficiency levels	using multiple measures of assessment
3. Prepare advisement plan	delineate student goals and objectives
4. Advise student	delineate individual student proficiencies/deficiencies
5. Place student in courses	bases on an array of courses and course
6. Advise student	match student to appropriate courses
7. Advise student	complete SEP (Student Enrollment Plan)
8. Instruct student	utilize formative and summative assessment
9. Collect data	student and course outcomes information
10. Follow-up	make recommendations based on student performance

Conclusion

Finally, the key to dealing effectively with a diverse student clientele coming to college is to develop an emphasis on the role of the student as primary. The central goal here is to be able to manage student movement through the college to enhance their success. Student flow builds a path and can be the integrating element of many disparate elements in collegiate environments. Assessment models which emphasize student flow are empowering systems. They can guide the institution's quest to improve quality while dealing with large numbers of academically deficient students.

Part V: The CAL Model

To ensure institutional vitality for continually improving the learning and teaching environment, today's assessment models can signal a new era of higher quality of learning and teaching. As well, they can maintain the previous institutional needs for defining student groups by skills proficiencies, providing adequate skills development instruction and describing required outcomes data for decision makers. Today's models have a dual role: (1) to be highly structured (2) while simultaneously, being highly supportive to learners and teachers.

The CAL Model—A Student and Institutional Support Model

The activities of the CAL model are built on three expanded actions and systems:

1. The Assessment System consists of two integrated activities: Assessment and Advising.

2. The Placement System with faculty and counseling staff sharing roles as *co-providers* of these services. Integral to this system also are the instructional components and its processes.

3. The Outcomes System integrates Outcomes Assessment and Follow-Up actions (see Figure 4).

Figure 4. Systems of CAL Model

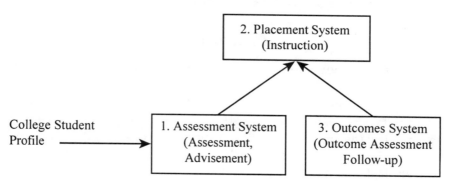

Since the assessment practices and plan flow from the institutional goals and mission statement of the college, the institution's goals should emphasize student achievement, degree completion, and transfer or job placement.

Today's Assessment Models need to provide information along several dimensions including the following: (a) Second language assessment; (b) utilization of computerized assessment instruments and technologies; (c) general education assessment; (d) outcomes information, both formative and summative, balanced between quantitative and qualitative data; (e) sensitivity to diverse learning styles and proficiencies. The assessment practices of the past decade have yielded improved definitions of the processes, practices and organizational results of the Assessment- Placement Model. Other assessment elements are added to the CAL Model as additional types of information are required now for college assessment. These elements include: 1) A new role for faculty as a team of assessors; 2) time efficient feedback in class and for tracking Individualized Student Educational Plan throughout college; 3) emphasis on feedback as a methodology, classroom based assessment techniques. There is a need for new terminology for working in a process environment. Grade doesn't fit but growth or progress descriptions do; 4) competency based assessment requires identification of critical milestone points which must be identified as benchmarks of student growth and success; 5) the assessment system must assume that we can attempt to determine higher levels skills of learning which are taking place— while the assessment system is gathering data a more basic levels; 6) a two-fold emphasis for the research system, on individual data, as well as aggregate data; 7) an emphasis for curriculum and teaching to interface to specify learning outcomes and activities; 8) new measures and methods for assessing student growth in the curriculum of general education; and 9) final examinations are to assess skills as well as context and content.

Conclusion

The CAL Model integrates the details from the earlier Assessment-Placement models. The model also adds elements emanating from a strong resurgence on continual improvement of the learning - teaching environment. The result is an enlarged model of assessment which is capable of responding to individual student needs as well as institutional system needs. Additional emerging issues which will need to be considered in Assessment-Learning Models depict recent practice and research in to (1) teacher competencies in "test" development, (2) "authentic" assessments which utilize student practice instead of multiple choice type tests, (3) test taker rights and (4) computerized assessments.

The CAL Model: Sequence of Activities and Systems Developing a Student Profile

The model focuses on the learner as central to the institutional assessment plan.

Step One: Develop a Sample Student Profile

The first step in the CAL Model is to develop a sample student profile of the underprepared student likely to enroll. The goals of the sample student profile are:

1. Outline the steps which will assist the students to be successful in college.

2. Address those elements in the college environment which are high risk obstacles to student success.

3. Define the characteristics of high risk students which contribute to their being successful.

4. Diagnose the levels of learning skills competencies.

In order to describe the student as a learner, use responses to the following learner centered questions for a sample profile to determine the students' fit or lack of fit with the institution: 1) What are the characteristics of the learner and 2) what are key obstacles to student learning based on these characteristics? From the responses to these two questions, the next key questions ask: 3) What methodologies will be most useful for successful learning and 4) What new skills will be assessed? In addition to assessing the basic levels of reading, writing, and math, the Model adds other core academic skills to be assessed such as fluency, the ability to ask questions, and listening skills.

In order to provide a model, which is capable of responding to individual student needs as well as institutional needs, colleges need to know, **Who is the underprepared student?** While colleges should develop a profile of their students who will need learning assistance, this model describes a hypothetical profile derived from a variety of descriptions of the underprepared students.

The major characteristics of the students may derive from their diversity, as well as their skill deficiencies The following are characteristics common to the underprepared student in higher education:

1. The students represent a wide range of reading levels on a diagnostic test, but, in common, they have difficulty reading prescribed classroom materials, and, often cannot read these materials in a timely manner.

2. Most will not be able to demonstrate college level mathematical skills.

3. Most will not be able to demonstrate college level writing skills, particularly those required by expository writing, the most dominant writing mode required in college.

4. Their social and classroom behavior is highly reflective of the cultural gaps their social and cultural backgrounds may bring to a college classroom.

5. The context of the college environment will be problematic to them: (a) Often they are not ready for the independence and pace of learning which is required in college, (b) attendance patterns are weak, and (c) typically have no declared major at entrance.

6. They often postpone taking core general education or major's courses, thus lengthening their time in college.

7. Low motivation may be combined with other "required college behaviors" to produce a wide range of at risk behaviors in classes such as: (a) Unable to deal with conceptual conflict in logic; (b) lack of creative insight, or curiosity about learning; (c) low individual accountability; (d) low interpersonal and cognitive skills of listening, communications both as an individual and in group interactions.

8. May be limited or unable to demonstrate required common criteria of core classes: (a) Wide range of communication skills, (b) problem solving skills (c) critical thinking skills, (d) appreciation of the arts, (e) ethical implications, (f) cultural pluralism and awareness of diversity, (g) modes of inquiry, (h) interdisciplinary methods, and (i) creativity.

9. Typically, attempts a load of 13 units per semester, completes 2-3 units less than taken.

10. Most will drop out during the freshman year. (*Core Curriculum: Report of The Task Group For the Commission of Instruction* California Association of Community Colleges, March 31, 1987).

System 1—Assessment. The Assessment System consists of two systems integrated into one: (1) Assessment, and (2) Advising. The Assessment Plan is depicted in Figures 5 and 6.

Step Two: Develop the Assessment Plan

In this system, assessment is not just tests, but a broad information gathering system. In order to integrate assessment into instruction, a variety of assessment activities are incorporated into college practice to provide on-going qualitative and quantitative information before instruction, during instruction, and after the course completion. A successful marriage of assessment and instruction will require new definitions and practices for both activities. Practitioners of both activities will have to let go of older attitudes and behaviors and understand the new purposes of educational assessment.

Step Three: Develop the Advising Plan

The portion of the model requires a significant link between the activities of Assessment, Advising, and Instruction. In the decades of developing

Figure 5. Developing a Perspective for an Assessment Plan

Delineation of:

1. Institutional specific objectives.
2. Multiple measures of assessment.
3. Processes and a timeline for analysis/review of data.
4. Role of Assessment Center.

Figure 6. The Assessment Plan

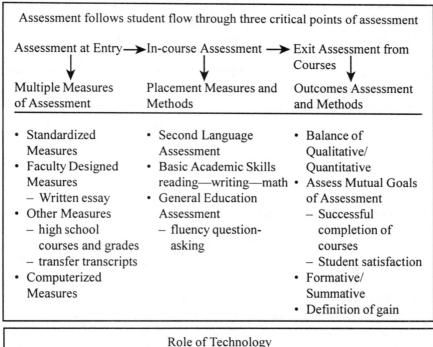

Assessment follows student flow through three critical points of assessment

Assessment at Entry ➤ In-course Assessment ➤ Exit Assessment from Courses

Multiple Measures of Assessment	Placement Measures and Methods	Outcomes Assessment and Methods

• Standardized Measures
• Faculty Designed Measures
  – Written essay
• Other Measures
  – high school courses and grades
  – transfer transcripts
• Computerized Measures
	• Second Language Assessment
	• Basic Academic Skills reading—writing—math
	• General Education Assessment
	  – fluency question-asking
		• Balance of Qualitative/ Quantitative
		• Assess Mutual Goals of Assessment
		  – Successful completion of courses
		  – Student satisfaction
		• Formative/ Summative
		• Definition of gain

Role of Technology

assessment models, the advising element of CAL emerged from "a commonly faulted student service" to a new and well defined activity (Muffo & Bunda in Banta, p. 168). Since the 1960's advising models have proliferated in higher education but with little consistency. Although virtually all institutions of higher education have an advising program in place, no two programs are identical. Some institutions have programs in which faculty provide advising in the major only, whereas career advising and class counseling are centralized. At other colleges and universities, the faculty is responsible for both career and academic advising. At still others, some faculty members are specifically designated as advisers. Some institutions have peer advising in academic as well as personal areas (Muffo & Bunda in Banta, p. 175).

Faculty and Counselors: Co-Providers of Advising

As the use of advising activities expanded and began to involve faculty more, differences were delineated between counselor and faculty roles and perspectives. Who was best equipped to advise on academic programs emerged as a key controversy from perceived faculty and counselor incongruities in providing expert advice on academic programs. A positive result of the involvement of faculty in advising models is that "Assessment activities have provided direction for faculty development experiences that increase faculty members' capacities to contribute to a mission-centered campus climate. Most institutions found that faculty who were involved in the development of assessment models developed a much fuller appreciation of individual differences in the ability of students to profit from various kind of instruction and evaluation approaches (Banta & Associates, pp. 369-370).

The CAL Model specifies a partnership between advising and instruction. Faculty Advising, a necessity in this student focused environment, is enjoying a renewal on college campuses. Typically, college counselors are allocating more or their time to pre-college counseling, pre-college orientation, and follow-up counseling, while faculty assist students with an Individualized Educational plan. Together, counselors and faculty are connecting student development processes to academic advancement.

The goal of the CAL plan for advising is to develop a new focus on advising and the development of advising systems. The two objectives are 1) To provide a significant link between the activities of assessment and instruction and 2) to reduce incongruencies between the following: student expectations and skills competencies, faculty expectations and student self-placement, faculty and counselor perceptions about respective roles in advising. **To define a specific role for technology and acquisitions, to implement collaborative strategies in advising and to implement assessment and advisement centers.**

The CAL Advising Plan

Action one of the Plan involves creating and implementing an extensive series of actions in the Institutional Plan of Advising. The second part of this plan is a check-list of actions which, together, will comprise the collaborative emphasis between counselors and faculty.

Action One of the Advising Plan is to determine the goal which is to develop and implement an advising system featuring collaborative efforts between counselors, faculty and students. The objectives include: 1) Revision of Student publications (Student Handbook) to include broader definition of advising, 2) Development of Orientation System featuring combined counseling-academic advising information, and 3) Delineating Mandatory processes: (a) mandatory counseling session, and (b) mandatory course for advising.

Action Two of the Advising Plan is a check list of actions for collaboration between counselors and faculty in advising:

____ 1. Redefine the Role of Counselor.

____ 2. Define the roles and duties in the Faculty Advisor System.

____   • Plan in-service for faculty advisor

____   • Assign time for advising students

____   • Participate in the evaluation of assessment processes

____   • Assist departments to develop explicit student outcome objectives, developed and agreed to by faculty

____   • Assist departments to align course content and assessment content and context

____ 3. Define the Role of Students in collaborating on assessment strategies with faculty, and as peer advisors.

____ 4. Plan for the role of Technology which will utilize a number of elements:

____   • Computerized Assessment Instruments

____   • Computerized Tracking System able to permit faculty to provide academic advisement, schedule students into classes

____   • On line transcripts

____   • On line assessment results

____   • On line schedule of classes

____ 5. Networked model to Department Offices—Counseling Center—Assessment Center—Faculty offices

____   • On line description of other institutional services: finance, tutoring, library, special assistance

___ 6. Individual Student Tracking System
___   •   Student Tracking Subsystem
___   •   degree monitoring (computerized)
___ 7. Strengthen articulation agreements
___ 8. Track retention and persistence
___ 9. Individualized Communications for student -institutional feedback
        during semester.

Conclusion

Advising with feedback is one of the most important aspects of assessment. The term *co-provider-provider of services* is now used commonly to refer to the partnerships between student services and instruction in overseeing assessment and connecting it to instruction.

System 2—Placement-Instruction. This system consists of two key activities: 1) placement into courses and 2) the instruction in courses. It is important to understand that models of organization for Assessment Models have changed rapidly over a two decade period of intense activity. Basic to all of these models however is the reality that one of the most difficult tasks, which an institution will face, will be to connect the skills deficiencies and proficiencies, uncovered by assessment, to appropriate courses of instruction which, in turn, will be assessed on learning and teaching success.

Learning Skills Instruction—A Key Result of Mandatory Assessment for Placement

Four major student trends still are affecting all colleges and universities:

1. A majority of college students have deficiencies in one or more areas of reading, writing and mathematics.

2. Since the early 1980's the remediation of basic skills has been and still is one of the fastest growing areas of curriculum.

3. Colleges, universities, and industry are requiring increasingly higher levels of competencies, thus expanding the deficiencies of many college students.

4. The growing minority populations in higher education bring even more diversity in learning and teaching needs.

How can educators be proactive instead of reactive in regard to this data? The most promising approach to these challenges is for the institutional practitioners to focus on the four years ahead for the student rather than the twelve years behind him.

The linkage of activities of assessment and instruction is a continuing theme particularly relevant to the continuing growth of learning skills needs. The goals and objectives of collegiate instruction have become increasingly dependent on assessment activities that monitor the growth of students from entrance to exit. The tension between quality and access issues, centered around lack of student readiness for college, involves all of the curriculum in assessment—through *course skills prerequisites*.

Figure 7 depicts the curricular elements which link placement and instruction, primarily through the impact of course skills prerequisites on students and courses.

Figure 7. Curricular Elements Linking Advisement, Placement and Instruction

```
                            Placement
                         • match student
                           proficiency to
                           course prerequisites

Student Profile   Advisement ———————————— Instruction
                  • level of student        • taxonomy
                    proficiency             • gains in learning
                                              skills
                                            • courses exit
                                              standards
```

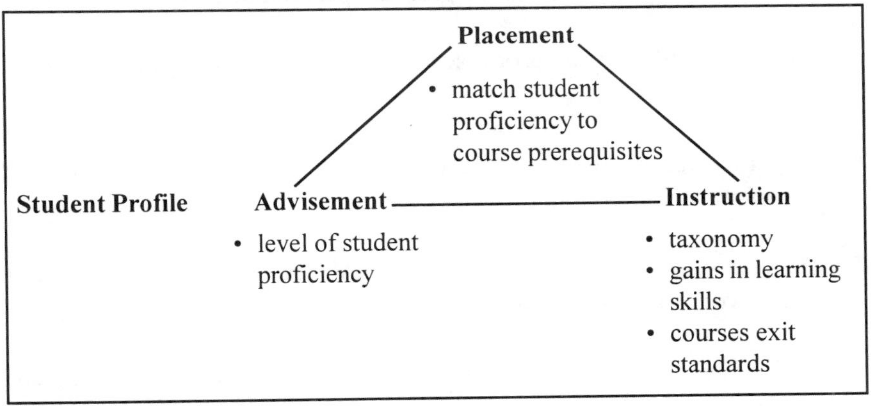

Step Four—Develop Student Placement Plan

The Placement Plan consists of five goals: 1) Utilize assessment information to organize systematic learning skills and academic skills development in college curricula; 2) organize learning-academic skills development as a total program of courses, tutorial services learning assistance labs, policies, etc.; 3) develop, implement, and review specific course prerequisites annually; 4) provide for continual review and reorganization of learning skills programs as necessary to meet emerging student needs; and 5) broaden college participation in learning skills and academic skills development.

Define Conditions to Implement the Placement-Instruction System

Mandatory assessment and placement require a series of actions for implementation. These twelve conditions may be used to implement a Placement-Instruction System:

1. Determine learning skills courses and course levels.

2. Delineate sequence of learning skills development.

3. Have adequate learning skill courses available to accommodate wide range of students.

4. Develop consensus for course/program prerequisites and standards.

5. Involve faculty in all processes and decision-making regarding the model.

6. Organize college teams for a total institutional effort and to minimize the burden on individual faculty.

7. Provide in-service for faculty to work with the assessment systems as a framework to improve learning/retention.

8. Delineate role of assessment center in conducting assessment and advisement.

9. Develop course benchmarks for entry and exit to courses.

10. Specify academic skills required for degree completion.

11. (An institutional emphasis on student performance will result in " full disclosure" of grading criteria.) As faculty grading and evaluation processes become more public, the grading process will need benchmarks as anchors to validate student performance gains.

12. Provide in-service for faculty on grading performance gains.

Much of this information is derived from Bray's *Practicing Assessment in the Community Colleges: A Two Year Scenario from 1988 to 1990.*

Conclusion

Given the reality that the segments of higher education must continue to provide for the learning skills development of a majority of its students, who need to have stronger reading, writing, mathematical, and critical thinking skills to succeed in college, colleges must be proactive rather than reactive.

These conditions reflect a new role for faculty. The prevalent methodology, to deliver instruction as content knowledge in a lecture mode— is not compatible with the conditions of implementing this placement-instruction system. Here faculty must concentrate on parameters of student learning and course benchmarks which will delineate student growth.

The Institution has a changed role also. As often as not, student growth in learning skills can be supported and motivation maintained by the opportunity for students to concurrently enroll in college level courses supported by necessary instruction in learning skills classes.

Research supports these assumptions. Over a decade ago, research in California found that appropriate placement has been shown to significantly increase the student's retention rate, skills growth, and grade point average. This research also concluded that explicit course entry and exit requirements delineated in course outlines are more important for student success than standardized course outlines. Important to student success also is a flexibility in program delivery within a wide array of courses and support services.

Research in California in 1985 found in an evaluation of its (learning skills) remedial services the following: 1. The semester retention rate is as great for the underprepared (remedial student) as it is for students enrolled in degree classes; 2. Average skills growth in reading, writing, and mathematics is, at minimum, twice that expected in a semester growth period and can be as great as four times the expected skills growth in that period; 3. After taking (learning skills) remedial courses, students report a major increase in self confidence and a need to complete college programs; and 4. The majority of students enrolled in (learning skills) remedial programs are enrolled in an average of five to six additional units in college courses (Providers of Remediation, LARC Consortium, October, 1985 Report).

System 3—Outcomes Assessment-Follow-up. The third system in the CAL Model is the Outcomes Assessment-Follow-Up System. A symposium of national experts on assessment met in California in 1988 to define the role of outcomes assessment. Their guidelines predicted the expansive role of outcomes assessment today, a decade later. They defined assessment of outcomes as a formative function. Other key premises were defined by that group: 1) College outcomes assessment is to measure college learning and is a separate function from entry level assessment for placement, and 2) outcomes assessment should measure proficiency, not predict aptitude.

Their definitions reflected the fundamental premise of assessment models: that a primary use of outcomes information is to integrate the findings into institutional change. In the CAL Model, outcomes assessment is used for the improvement of learning and teaching and to collect data for institutional accountability.

The principle of differential outcomes is essential to realize two institutional goals: (l) information used to evaluate institutional accountability does not necessarily have to involve the faculty, (2) information used to guide program improvement must involve faculty. A great challenge for outcomes assessment to measure learning and improvement is the changing demography of our students which will keep institutions focused on changing needs in instruction. Since there is a large amount of information available in outcomes assessment processes, colleges need to determine how to use the data and what types of outcomes information will be used.

Step Five: Delineate How Outcomes Assessment Data Will Be Used:

1. To tell us more about student learning and faculty teaching.

2. To review and adjust curriculum.

3. To impact on student preparation, improve instructor capabilities, and improve institutional capabilities.

Step Six: Develop a Follow-Up Plan For Use of Outcomes Assessment Data

A. *Delineate the desired types of outcomes Information*

Desired Follow-up Information From Outcomes Assessment
1. Retention in Courses, both learning skills and college level.
2. Course Effectiveness.
3. Correlation studies of GPA, Placement Proficiencies levels.
4. Persistence to other courses.
5. Misplacement of students.
6. Correlation of student outcomes to Student Educational Plan

B. Delineate purposes of the follow-up plan

1. Determine student progress.
2. Determine more effective ways to help students be successful.
3. Communicate the effectiveness of institutional programs to appropriate publics.
4. Assist in decision making about instruction and use of resources (LARC Assessment/Placement Model, 1982).

C. Define the Points of Data Collection in Student Flow Cycle

As a component of the Institutional Assessment System, a follow-up plan provides cyclical and on-going information. Figure 8 describes the data collection at various points in the student flow cycle. At each stage in the cycle, data is collected for feedback.

**Figure 8. Data Collection for Outcomes
Assessment/Follow-up Student Flow Cycle**

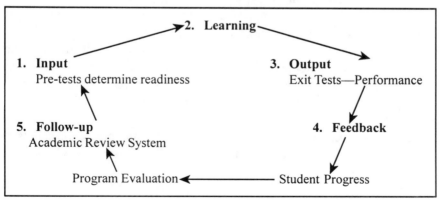

Conclusion

The processes of an outcomes assessment-follow up system, while complex, are as important as the outcomes data itself (Katz, in Banta, p. 58). In the process of selecting and validating the choices of data and goals of collection, an academic department puts its curriculum under a high powered microscope. While this model describes an Outcomes Assessment System, the current dialogue on national standards of competencies requires any assessment model to consider the outcomes results, produced by the model activities. This dialogue on national standards is introducing more issues for assessment models including the issue of equity and equal group outcomes. This model meets the criteria of the expectations of policy makers in three key areas: 1) Assessment primarily should inform teaching, 2) assessment is to be used for accountability, and 3) assessment must bring about curriculum coherence and act as a lever to change instructional content and strategies.

Step Seven: Colleges Must Deal With Implementation Concerns

Assessment is a formative function involving all college consistencies. As well the implementation of models also is a formative function, requiring processes of consultation, information gathering, and planning. Implementation concerns can be critical for effective institutional models. While the college practitioners should provide expert advice and interpretation of learning and teaching processes, they should not be expected to design comprehensive models. However, any model is only a picture unless it is adapted as part of daily processes and practice.

The implementation of comprehensive institutional assessment models requires strong leadership, and a college ethic to support change in the organizational systems as well as innovation in services and instruction. An initial step in the implementation of models is to consider the concerns of those who will be affected by it. The CAL Model requires two stages of assessment to be linked: (1) assessment for placement and (2) assessment for outcomes.

Figure 9 describes some concerns for the two implementation stages of assessment—from three key points of view: (1)administrative, (2) faculty, and (3) student.

Figure 9. Assessment Concerns for Two Implementation Stages

Stage 1: Assessment For Placement	Stage 2: Assessment For Outcomes
Administrative Concerns	
student flow	information gathering systems
student enrollment	multiple methods of assessment
process of assessment	how to follow with program evaluation
budget for system assessment	validation of money spent on assessment
using results in the institution	
realistic do-able plans of assessment	
policies for registration	
coordinating with other institutions	
how to get faculty to participate	
Faculty Concerns	
performance is key issue	adjunct faculty participation
raising standards	making grading policies public
establishing course prerequisites	collaborative grading
maintaining faculty rigor	validating impact of course instruction
evaluating assessment instruments	
Student Concerns	
placement in courses	multiple measures of assistance
availability of learning skills courses	definitions of student success
time to be assessed	movement from learning skills to college level
costs of assessment	split outcomes: those who succeed, don't succeed

Conclusion
Models Have Re-Defined Assessment

The Comprehensive Assessment Learning Model presents an *assessment-learning* process consisting of three integrated systems of actions: 1) The Assessment/Advising System combines two categories of actions, *advising and assessing*; 2) Placement-Instructional System links student placement directly to course instruction, primarily through an emphasis on *course* prerequisites; and (3) an Outcome Assessment—Follow-Up System provides feedback on teaching and learning to the institution for its program evaluation and program review activities.

Together these three systems make up a holistic process which continually provides information to the institution. Key to the implementation of this model is the process of assessment which is as important as *the data collected. Of necessity, the model provides the detail to guide its implementation across the college.*

Incomplete models have resulted in little transformation of college culture. Over the past decade, there has been much activity by higher education institutions in developing assessment processes. However, most of this activity has fragmented into implementing discrete elements of assessment models. A majority of colleges and universities have some pieces of assessment models in place. But, there has been little transformation of the organizational cultures of colleges.

The most desired result of assessment is to improve learning and teaching. This model focuses on a strict institutional-student compact—to improve the success of underprepared students, a majority of the students in colleges. The data from the model is capable of being used for the evaluation of institutional quality and accountability but its primary aim is to initiate changes in campus cultures and systems, which will lead to, improved learning and teaching for student success.

The model stresses a context, which enables educators to develop a competence with assessment—a necessity for educational reform to occur. clearly, performance based assessment can be both part of the solution and part of the problem in effecting institutional change. However, the key change must be when the institution re-directs faculty reluctance to focus on learning instead of teaching style and preferences.

We assume that most colleges and universities have some portions of the model in place. Therefore, the implementation should be guided by using processes which *will make assessment systems last.* All of the constituent groups in the college should be involved in consultation to reach consensus on planning and implementation strategies and timelines. Annual plans with goals and objectives will allow time for pilots, revisions and phasing in the model as desired.

Today's realities must include models which will assist with underprepared students. Colleges and universities have much at stake to motivate them to adopt and implement comprehensive models such as the CAL Model. The enrollment level of an institution is affected directly by its success rate with all of its students. Ideally, colleges and universities should admit only students capable of succeeding in its courses. However, in 1997, higher education institutions cannot disregard the underprepared students, now in a majority, in its admissions cohort.

Many experts predict a clouded horizon for continuing involvement of higher education with assessment. Most are plagued by underfunding, campus politics, and state and national politics. Nevertheless, it is time to move into the next century with institutional models which can guide college transformation, inevitable as the 1990's close out this century of education.

Chapter 16

ℬℭ

Program Evaluation for Remedial, Compensatory, and Developmental Education: Definitional Problems and Design Decisions

Darrel A. Clowes

Introduction

There is an enormous concern today for the problems presented by underprepared students entering higher education, but a restricted vocabulary limits our ability to address the problems. New terms have been coined to describe underprepared students: high-risk, nontraditional, new students and concurrently a series of terms has emerged to describe the programs that serve them. John Roueche has been the Boswell of the movement to serve underprepared students and his use of terms is representative. In his early writings Roueche referred to remedial programs (1968); in his later writings (1977) he refers to developmental programs. A gradual transition in meaning is revealed through his works, but little clear differentiation is drawn in his or the general literature. The vocabulary of this field has developed "like Topsey" to reflect needs of the moment, without systematic plan or definition. This lack of clarity is a problem. Because we use several terms interchangeably, we lose the ability to distinguish among distinctly different approaches to the underprepared student, and this failure to distinguish has led us to gloss over differences and obscure the uniqueness inherent in specific approaches. The purpose of this paper is to describe each of the three dominant terms used in this field and propose more precise uses of them. A more careful distinction among types of developmental programs used with underprepared students should allow us to make better decision about program design and program evaluation.

Remedial Education

Remedial education is the term most commonly associated with the underprepared student. Remedial shares its root with remedy, meaning to heal, cure, or make whole. This curative connotation has the sense of education as a palliative which will "fix" the student or some weakness in the student. Webster's New Collegiate Dictionary (1964) defines remedial as "concerned with the correction of faulty study habits and the raising of a pupil's general competence." In this sense remedial education denotes the activities correcting specific deficiencies in skill areas, improving a student's writing and mathematical skills, and addressing the general area of study skills. In this more restricted definition remedial education applies only to work in subjects taught at a more advanced level in college. The connotation of remedial education in this model is work with academically backward or less able students to bring them up to an acceptable range of competence. This is consistent with the traditional image of higher education as the providence of the elite, where remediation carries serious negative overtones for the college mission. Remedial education focuses on academic skills using a medical model. Specific weaknesses are diagnosed, appropriate treatments are prescribed, and the patient is evaluated to determine the effect of the treatment. If the treatment is inadequate, then the prescription is revised and the process is repeated.

Compensatory Education

The term compensatory education was introduced following World War II and is particularly associated with the Elementary and Secondary Education Act of 1965, and the resulting Office of Compensatory Education within the Office of Education (Chazan 1973). The term is defined by Frost and Rowland as "those efforts designed to make up for the debilitating consequences of discrimination and poverty (1971, p. vii). Compensatory education became associated with efforts toward Aimproving cognitive achievement deficits which are primarily environmentally induced (Ntuk-Iden 1978, p.45). In the dictionary sense compensatory is a noun form of the verb "to compensate" meaning "to make an appropriate and usually counter balancing payment to neutralize the effect of." In practical terms compensatory education implies offsetting a home environment unsupportive of educational attainment. Compensatory education in higher education faces a hostile environment. Because basic attitudes and preferences are well established by the college years, there is little hope and limited evidence that direct intervention at this late stage is successful. Compensatory education includes remediation activities such as preparatory and supplementary work in writing and computational skills, attention to study skill development, and work on reading skills as part of a program to provide an enriching experience beyond the academic environment to counter balance a nonsupportive home environment. Because the model focuses on extracurricular activities, the residential college offers some opportunity to develop strengths that are brought to the institution and represents whatever hope might exist for the compensatory model in higher education. Perhaps the success of historically black colleges can best be explained as an application of a compensatory model where the college assumes a strong in loco parentis role, offers remedial programs, and provides strong support for students' academic endeavors. However, for most students, but especially for nonresidential and commuting students at public community colleges, the compensatory model holds little or no promise.

Developmental Education

The term developmental education has emerged recently as part of efforts to merge the activities of academic and student affairs personnel to support student learning. The mood of the 1970s was congenial to the development of programs that stressed the value and worth of each individual, saw individual differences not as negatives but as unique possibilities, and focused upon the notion of continuing growth and change for the individual. These growth-oriented programs contrast with the more static remedial and compensatory programs designed to bring students "up" to an arbitrary performance level. Developmental education has its genesis in the work of human development theorists who articulated a concept of development meaning "to evolve the possibilities of" or "to promote the growth of" (Webster's New Collegiate Dictionary, 1964). Miller and Prince define this model of education as "the application of human development concepts in postsecondary settings so that everyone involved can master increasingly complex developmental tasks, achieve self-direction, and become interdependent" (1976, p.3). This concept is further expanded by David Drew when he describes developmental education as a process where during the undergraduate years the student also develops and refines his philosophy and value systems, acquires interests which may enrich both his leisure and his work life, and makes decisions about relationships between commitment to work and commitment to family roles (1978, p. vii). Here developmental education is defined as a process through which students must go, extending beyond academic subjects into basic decisions about life direction and purpose. The connotation that all students must proceed through this developmental process establishes developmental education as appropriate for all, as distinct from remedial or compensatory education which are appropriate only for the unfortunate few. Developmental education emphasizes a series of major life choices and processes. These choices and processes are expedited by academic skills but also are dependent upon interpersonal skills and life coping skills, which are equally the province of the academic and nonacademic student. The student development model attempts to bring the student-support and academic functions of a college together to assist students in becoming fully functioning adults.

It is important to distinguish among these various approaches to dealing with the underprepared student. There are at least three distinctly different approaches currently in use in two- and four-year institutions. Yet we tend to lump all these activities under the same imprecise terms and to confuse the situation by treating these different approaches as if they were one. If we can distinguish clearly among at least these three elements in our approaches to the underprepared student, then we will be better able to articulate the precise goals for these programs and to be clearer about the expectations we hold for our students. There has been a constant but unanswered plea for evaluation of remedial/compensatory/developmental programs. Clearer definition of terms could improve our program planning, our evaluation, and ultimately our effect upon the students we strive to serve.

While remedial, compensatory or developmental programs can be evaluated like other academic programs, there are significant areas of difference. These areas of difference provide the basis for proposing a stage model of program evaluation appropriate to remedial, compensatory, or developmental programs. This chapter will lay out the areas in which remedial programs are like other academic programs for evaluation purposes and will then explore the ways remedial programs are unlike other academic programs. With these areas of difference as a starting point, a four-stage model of program evaluation will be proposed.

Standard Features of Remedial/ DevelopmentProgram Evaluation

Evaluations of remedial, compensatory, or developmental programs have the same *primary purposes* as other academic program evaluations: formative evaluation, summative evaluation, and politically-oriented evaluation. Formative evaluation is evaluation to determine the components of the program which need revisions for improved overall effectiveness. Areas of weakness and strength are identified and adjusted to eliminate weaknesses and improve upon strengths. Where goals are known, data are used to assess and revise activities which produce results consistent with goals. Summative evaluation is conducted in order to inform management regarding decisions about the continuance or discontinuance of a particular program. Ideally, the goals of the program can be clearly stated, the data gathered has high reliability and validity, and the evaluation can be designed to provide clear insight into the effectiveness of the program. Academic evaluations are also conducted for political purposes. Politically-oriented evaluations done to involve the appropriate parties in direct consideration of positive and negative aspects of a program can be a good use of evaluation. Political evaluation is a positive activity as part of the institution's process designed to bring about appropriate change by bringing together various people within an institution to assess and share information about a program. Political evaluation done only for cosmetic purposes is a negative or limited use of evaluation.

The evaluation of remedial, compensatory, or developmental programs is similar in many ways to the evaluation of other academic programs; the *data sources* are the same. Quantitative data can be gathered to describe the performance of students within a program; these data are particularly useful in assessing the amount of progress toward clearly stated and generally accepted program goals. Qualitative data may also be gathered and are particularly useful in evaluation where the goals for a program are unclear, unmeasurable, or unstated. All program evaluations face the need to use both qualitative and quantitative data. All programs share the common problem of determining which kinds of data are appropriate to the evaluation at hand, which kinds of data are actually obtainable, and which kinds of data are appropriate.

Remedial, compensatory, or developmental programs share with other academic programs a limited array of *primary audiences*. The most immediate audience of a program evaluation is that body of faculty, staff, and administrators directly involved with the program. Another audience can be those in the institution directly affected by that program. For example, the science faculty of an institution would be the other audience affected by the mathematics program when it functions in a service relationship, preparing students for science programs. A third audience goes beyond the first two to include those individuals in the institution who express a concern about or interest in the academic program being evaluated. The final audience for program evaluation would be the external audiences presented by state, federal, or foundation interests. These interests may have a financial or a legal interest in the performance of a particular academic unit and would be the recipients of evaluation reports.

The *processes* within a program are common across all forms of academic program evaluation including remedial, compensatory, or developmental. Programs have an input phase, in the sense that students come to the program with various characteristics, and a process phase where the institution influences those students through its faculty and programs. The process stage is monitored through the assignment of academic credits, grades, and assessments of the student's persistence in the institution. Concurrently, a variety of opinions are formed by students and faculty about the instructional process and student performance within the process phase. In the output phase, students emerge from the structured activities of the program both as individuals with opinions and feelings about the program and as statistics representative of their progress through the program. Thus there are three basic phases of any evaluation: the input, the process, and the output phases. In summary, there are four components common to all forms of academic evaluation: the *purposes served*—formative, summative or political; the *data sources* used which might be qualitative, quantitative, or both; the *audiences addressed* which might be program staff, all affected staff, all interested staff, or externals and the *program phases*—input, process, and output.

Unique Features of Remedial, Compensatory, or Developmental Program Evaluation

Remedial, compensatory, or developmental program evaluation differs from most other academic program evaluation. The most unique feature is that the students of remedial, compensatory, or developmental do not leave the institution and move into work settings or other academic institutions where little feedback data is available. Instead, students or completers become the input to other academic programs and curricula within the parent institution. The remedial program links basic skills work in remediation to the advanced basic skills coursework provided in the main stream curriculum of an institution. This direct linkage is a unique and important difference between remedial programs and other academic programs in our colleges and universities. Quality measures in academic programs are typically a series of internal indicators having to do with faculty qualifications and activities, with student grade point averages, and with the ability of students to complete the prescribed program of study. These internal measures are the standards for academic quality throughout the college and university world. They are important not because they are particularly valid measures of quality but because they are the best available measures of quality for most programs. Remedial, compensatory, or developmental programs have available to them, in addition to the usual internal measures, a series of external quality measures. The output of remedial, compensatory, or developmental programs is uniquely available and important in program evaluation. Therefore, the standard internal measures of quality are less significant and less important as measures of program quality. These external quality measures for remedial programs come into play as students complete the remedial activities and move into the mainstream curriculum of the institution. The proof of the quality of a remedial, compensatory, or developmental program exists not in the ability of students to survive within that program but rather in the ability of students to complete the program and make a successful transition into the main stream curricula of the institution. This transition occurs first as students complete basic skills courses in the remedial program and move into the advanced basic skills courses (usually the first "college level" math and English course) for which they prepared. Their achievement in these courses is a first measure of the success and quality of the remedial, compensatory, or developmental program. A second measure is the students' ability to move through a curriculum or program with success as measured initially by grade point average (GPA) and ultimately by graduation or program completion. Qualitative data may also be gathered to assess quality through interviews with students and faculty on the appropriateness of the remedial, compensatory, or developmental effort and its assistance to them in the mainstream curriculum. Interview data, observational data of classroom interactions and student academic growth, and selected case study activities can inform evaluation of student or student subgroup progress as they move through the program, into the mainstream curriculum, and to curriculum completion or graduation.

Remedial, compensatory, or developmental program evaluation has much in common with all academic evaluation but also has unique and significant characteristics. The traditional measures and assessments of program quality are less meaningful in the context of remedial programs than in academic programs, and evaluation must focus on events subsequent to program completion. It is this difference that provides the starting point for a four-stage model for remedial, compensatory, or developmental program evaluation.

Further uniqueness can occur through institutional decisions on the purposes of the program or on the design of the program. A remedial program has different goals and a different design than a compensatory or a developmental program, and the same holds for compensatory and developmental programs. If an institution has not worked through its program goals, program design decisions will influence and shape the programs

Table 1. Evaluation of a Remedial, Compensatory, or Developmental Program: A Stage Model

First Stage Evaluation:
Activities within the Remedial, Compensatory, or Developmental Program itself are evaluated.

Second Stage Evaluation: Interface Phase
Students move from the Remedial, Compensatory, or Developmental Program into the mainstream curriculum; the interface is assessed.

Third Stage Evaluation: Normative Phase
Student progress and faculty, staff and administration judgments are used to assess the goals of the program as remedial, compensatory, or developmental. It and goals for mainstream courses and curricula are assessed.

Fourth State Evaluation: Reassessing Measures
Using revised goals, appropriate measures and criteria are identified and fed into first two states.

Table 2. First Stage Evaluation: R/D Program Phase. Activities within the R/D program itself are evaluated.

Evaluation Components

Measures	Primary Purpose(s)			Methods		Primary Audience(s)			
	Formative	Summative	Political	Quantitative	Qualitative	RD Staff	RD and Receiving	All Concerned Staff and Administration	External
Input Phase									
Aptitude scales	X			X		X			
• Aptitude scales	X			X		X			
• Interview/observation data	X				X	X			
Process Phase									
Faculty Data									
1. Qualifications		X	X	X		X			X
2. Activities		X	X	X		X			X
Student Transcript Data									
1. Course grades/competencies	X			X		X			X
2. Persistence in R/D courses	X			X		X			X
3. Hours attempted/earned	X			X		X			
4. Pre-test/pos-test scores	X			X		X			
People Data									
1. Interview/observation data									
Student	X				X	X			
Faculty	X				X	X			
Output Phase									
• R/D Program									
• Completion	X			X	X	X			
• Student satisfaction	X			X	X	X			
• Cumulative G.P.A.	X			X					

outcomes. For each program type, unique data sources and criteria must be developed. In most cases, but especially in compensatory and developmental programs, these would differ from those traditionally used in academic program evaluation.

First Stage

Evaluation for remedial, compensatory, or developmental programs can be broken into four separate stages representing four different levels of activity and points at which evaluation can be conducted. First-stage evaluation involves the remedial, compensatory, or developmental program phase. This is an internal phase of the program where evaluation is concerned with the activities which go on within the program. Evaluation occurs only in that context. The inputs to such a program are the students admitted, identified, and assigned in various ways to a remedial, compensatory, or developmental program or activity. The processes of the program are those instructional activities designed to bring the resources of the institution to bear upon the students in a series of courses and planned instructional activities. The output of such a program are students who have completed the assigned activities of their program, survived the weeding out of those unable to function at the appropriate academic level, and been prepared for movement into the main stream curriculum. Program evaluation at this stage is inappropriate. Evaluation of a particular learning activity or of a particular course within the remedial, compensatory, or developmental program could be accomplished through a series of pretests and posttests or through assessment of students grades or retention rates of students within the course. However, at this stage the program cannot be properly assessed using measures which are only internal to the program. The true test of a remedial, compensatory, or developmental program occurs when its students move into the mainstream curriculum and begin function there.

It is, therefore, the contention of this paper that first stage evaluation is not proper for program evaluation but can be useful as formative evaluation of learning activities and for course revision. Table 2 illustrates first stage evaluation. There ought to be heavy emphasis upon quantitative methodology in this stage and also an emphasis upon formative evaluation. The audience addressed at this stage of the evaluation process is an internal audience made up of the remedial program staff. There are occasional uses of data for reporting to external audiences and occasional (but inappropriate) summative evaluations made by external agencies.

Second Stage

Second-stage evaluation involves assessing the interface phase where students move from a remedial program into the mainstream curriculum of the institution. Here the output of students from the first stage becomes the input to the second stage; thus, the stages within the model are linked. In the second stage of evaluation faculty qualifications and activities again are frequently used as quality measures but are obviously weak and indirect measures of quality. A variety of quantitative data can be gathered about students progressing through the main stream curriculum. These can be measures of the number of curricular courses completed, the kinds of curriculum courses taken, the students' rate of course completion, and student GPA as an index of learning. Qualitative data may also be gathered. These are all process measures of the interface between the remedial program and the mainstream curriculum. The assumption is that a student who completes basic skills work in writing or mathematics should be able to enter the related advanced basic skills activities in the mainstream curriculum and successfully complete those courses. A variety of quantitative data may also be obtained to assess students' movement through the mainstream curriculum. The output of the second stage is the students who complete courses and programs, and who graduate from the institution. Quantitative measures of this output can be supplemented with qualitative data addressing the perceptions of students, faculty, and administration about the preparation provided by the remedial program. This is the stage at which remedial, compensatory, or developmental program evaluation can appropriately be carried forward. The measures appropriate to the second stage are the measures of program success or failure. Most measures are used in formative evaluation, but a great number can also be used appropriately in summative evaluation. Second-stage evaluation typically involves a wider audience than first-stage evaluation, as indirectly affected staff are involved. External people are also involved to serve the demands for external summative evaluation; interested staff are occasionally involved to introduce the evaluation activities to the widest possible range of influential people within the institution.

Third Stage

The third stage of evaluation is a normative phase where student progress and faculty, staff, and administrative judgments are used to reassess the goals of the remedial, compensatory, or developmental program and the goals of mainstream courses and curriculum. This is a truly formative aspect

Table 3. Second-Stage Evaluation: Interface Phase. Students move from the R/D program (activities) into the mainstream curriculum. This interface is assessed.

| | Evaluation Components | | | | | | | | |
| | Primary Purpose(s) | | | Methods | | Primary Audience(s) | | | |
Measures	Formative	Summative	Political	Quantitative	Qualitative	RD Staff	RD and Receiving	All Concerned Staff and Administration	External
Input Phase									
• R/D program completion									
• Student satisfaction									
• Cumulative G.P.A.									
• Registration mainstream courses	X			X			X		X
Process Phase									
Faculty Data									
1. Qualifications		X	X	X			X		
2. Activities		X	X	X			X		X
Transcript Data									
1. Number mainstream courses completed	X	X		X			X		
2. Kind mainstream courses completed	X			X			X		
3. Hours attempted/passed	X	X		X			X		
4. G.P.A. in mainstream	X	X		X			X		
People Data									
1. Interview/observation data									
Student	X				X		X		
Faculty	X				X		X	X	
2. Case Study	X		X		X		X		
Output Phase									
• Graduation rates	X	X		X			X		X
• Program completion rate	X	X		X			X		X
1. Interview/observation data									
Student	X				X			X	
Faculty	X		X		X			X	
Administration	X		X		X			X	
2. Case study data	X		X		X			X	

Table 4. Third Stage Evaluation: Normative Phase. Student progress and staff and administration judgments are used to reassess the goals of the R/D program (activities) and of mainstream courses and curriculum.

Evaluation Components

Measures	Primary Purpose(s)			Methods		Primary Audience(s)			
	Formative	Summative	Political	Quantitative	Qualitative	RD Staff	RD and Receiving	All Concerned Staff and Administration	External
Input Phase									
• Graduation rates									
• Program/completion rates									
• Interview/observation data									
• Students									
• Faculty									
• Case study data									
Process Phase									
Renewal activities	X				X			X	
Output Phase									
Revised goals for									
1. R/D activities/program	X		X	X	X			X	
2. Curriculum courses and programs	X		X	X	X			X	

of the evaluation process. An effort is made to take the data gathered as output from the second stage and use this data about graduation rates, program and course completion, and the qualitative data gathered through interviews, observations and case studies to begin a reassessment of the goals of the program. This is an important and significant step since program goals are typically broader than the operational goal of moving students through the mainstream curriculum. It is important that each institution identify for itself the real goals with which it operates and thus determine meaningful indicators of success for its remedial programs.

This renegotiation of program goals is the most important activity at the third stage. Here the previous decisions (or non-decisions) about whether the goals of a remedial, compensatory, or developmental program are appropriate for the institution need to be affirmed or renegotiated. Indeed, the alternative of no program ought also be considered. This is a significant decision issue with broad institutional ramifications; it warrants the involvement of all audiences (Clowes, 1992; McGrath and Spear, 1991; Richardson, Martens and Fisk, 1981). It is important that the political purposes and broad audiences addressed in the second stage of evaluation be brought to bear on decisions at the third stage and upon subsequent institutional renewal activities. While it is obvious that the goals of the remedial, compensatory, or developmental effort are the primary area of scrutiny, it is also important that the goals for the advanced basics skills courses and for the main stream curriculum also be reassessed in recognition of what the institution can realistically expect from its efforts with underprepared students. The output of this stage should be a series of revised goals for the program for underprepared students in whichever form it takes and for the various main stream curriculum activities.

Fourth Stage

The fourth stage of evaluation is a reassessment phase where the measures used in stages one and two are reconsidered. This stage assumes that goals have been revised through a process of negotiation within the institution represented by the third stage; with revised goals, it is possible to conduct comparative studies. Groups of students using and not using the remedial, compensatory, or developmental program can be compared to develop data useful for reassessing the measures used in the first two evaluation stages. Course grades, student persistence, and the number and kind of courses completed are examples of measures used to track student

Table 5. Fourth Stage Evaluation: Reassessing Measures Phase. Revised goals have been negotiated; comparative studies are now useful to produce data for reassessing the original Phase One and Phase Two measures.

Evaluation Components

Measures	Primary Purpose(s)			Methods		Primary Audience(s)			
	Formative	Summative	Political	Quantitative	Qualitative	RD Staff	RD and Receiving	All Concerned Staff and Administration	External
Input Phase									
Revised goals for									
1. R/D activities/program									
2. Curriculum courses and programs									
Process Phase									
Comparative studies of completers and noncompleters using revised									
goals		X			X			X	
Transcript Data									
course description		X			X			X	
persistence		X			X			X	
achievement		X					X	X	
People Data									
student goals/commitment		X					X	X	
student development		X					X	X	
student perceptions					X		X	X	
Output Phase									
Information on the appropriateness and validity of measures used in Stage One and Two									

progress and provide data on the attainment of the goals of the program. With revised goals in place, these measures need to be reassessed to determine whether they do indeed provide appropriate and useful data for evaluation. The process used here could be comparative studies using qualitative data obtained through interview and case study methodologies, or it could be the quantitative data represented through the transcript data available. Ideally, both methods for data generation would be used. The output of this phase would be information about the appropriateness and validity of measures used. Thus the fourth stage completes the process of evaluation and allows revised measures to be used in the first and second stages. The process continues with a built-in recycling loop as program goals and program measures are brought into a new alignment with the realities of the institution.

Summary

Remedial, compensatory, or developmental program evaluation is unique in academic evaluation, and this uniqueness provides special opportunities. A four-stage model for program evaluation is proposed where the first stage focuses only upon activities internal to the remedial, compensatory, or developmental program and where only formative evaluation is appropriate. The second stage includes an interface between the remedial, compensatory, or developmental program and the mainstream curriculum; evaluation should be conducted in terms of the student's progress through the mainstream curriculum. The argument is made that only at this stage is true program evaluation possible. The measures appropriate for program evaluation are laid out and treated as distinct from the course and learning activity measures used in the first phase. A third stage of evaluation includes a process of goal refinement carried out for the remedial, compensatory, or developmental program and then for other programs and curriculum. Goals for the remedial, compensatory, or developmental program would be negotiated with its own people, the receiving faculty in the mainstream curriculum, and concerned faculty and administrators throughout the institution. These politically revitalized goals are essential for healthy program development and for appropriate subsequent program evaluation. The fourth stage involves a reconsideration of the measures used in evaluation to bring these measures in line with the renegotiated program goals. In summary, the stage model for remedial program evaluation proposes an initial stage of internal assessment only, an interface stage involving remedial program evaluation, and two concluding stages to establish appropriate goals and measures for the next cycle of evaluation.

Note: The above chapter is reprinted with permission from Clowes, D. A. (1980). More than a definitional problem: Remedial, compensatory, and developmental education. *Journal of Developmental & Remedial Education, 4*(1), 8-10; and Clowes, D. A. (1984). The evaluation of remedial/developmental programs: A stage model of program evaluation. *Journal of Developmental Education, 8*(1), 14-15, 27-30. Published by the National Center for Developmental Education, Appalachian State University, Boone, NC. A fuller discussion of the issues addressed here may be found in Clowes, D. A. (1992). Remediation in American higher education. In J. Smart (Ed.) *Higher Education: Handbook of Theory and Research* (Vol. VIII, pp. 460-493). New York: Agathon Press.

Chapter 17

℘℺

Assessment in Developmental Education

Leonard B. Bliss

Using Models in Student Assessment

Planning and carrying out assessment of the results of instruction is a complex process. The fact is that people are complicated animals and the planning and carrying out of any such assessment must, of necessity, involve people. This is further complicated by the fact that assessment is only one part of a dynamic process we can refer to as "instruction." After all, it wouldn't make any sense to assess students' skills, knowledges and attitudes if those students had not had the opportunity to acquire them in the course of what was going on in the school. An exception to the previous sentence is, of course, found during the process of diagnosis where teachers and other helpers are interested in determining what knowledges, skills and attitudes students bring to a learning activity in order to plan future instruction. For the sake of brevity, this chapter will deal primarily with the assessment of instruction which is carried out after instruction is completed and touch only briefly on diagnosis. This is certainly not to denigrate the value of diagnosis; a very important procedure, particularly in programs of developmental education. However, the issue of diagnostic assessment should be treated in depth at another time and place and by someone with expertise in this area. So, models of student assessment can really only be looked at as parts of models of planning and instruction.

If models of assessment are complex, as mentioned above, any model of planning and instruction, of which assessment is a part, must be even more complex. However, we should not let this complexity deter us from looking for useful models of planning on instruction. We must find methods to model human learning as physics allows physicists to model simpler things, such as the universe using the Theories of Relativity. Let's resist the urge to say that, since we do not have a complete model of learning and instruction, teaching must really be an art with each artist, somewhat mystically, supplied with a certain amount of natural talent which can be increased and refined through practice. After all, we did quite well for over two hundred years with Newtonian mechanics as a model of the universe. Models don't have to explain *everything* in order to be useful. It turns out that the theoretical and research bases in education tell us some very important things about models of planning and instruction.

Any model of instruction that presents the process as flowing in a single direction (from teacher to student) and ignores the interaction of what teachers do with characteristics of students and the feedback that teachers are constantly receiving from students during instruction is simply inadequate. The use of such an instructional model is doomed to result in bad feelings among and between teachers and students and to low levels of achievement. Still, it is discouraging to see teachers who vehemently and honestly proclaim their beliefs in the need to begin to teach students from "where they are" and in the idea that every student is an "individual" work with classes of twenty or more students as if they were a homogeneous group; they fail to even informally assess the needs and understandings of individual students until a summative written examination is given at the end of instruction. While we can be somewhat sympathetic to explanations which cite lack of time for reflection and planning of large student-loads, there seems to be little to account for the fact that people who make decisions regarding what happens in schools, from elementary through higher education, often fail to make use of models for the planning of curriculum, including instruction and assessment, which allow them to systematically look at student needs and personality characteristics.

Tyler (1949) suggested such a model for curriculum development which identified four steps in the development of any curriculum. Although the model has been criticized as overly structured and mechanistic (c.f. Darling-Hammond & Snyder, 1992) it remains a popular and respected strategy for curriculum development. The "Tylerian Rationale," as this strategy has come to be known, includes four consecutive procedures which can be described as 1) Determining educational objectives; 2) Determining learning strategies for facilitating students' reaching these objectives; 3) Ordering the learning strategies so they are most likely to facilitate students' reaching the educational objectives; and 4) Assessing the level of acquisition of these objectives after instruction has taken place.

The first of these sets up assessment models since it asks, "What should the student appear like after instruction?" The results of instruction will almost certainly include cognitive outcomes; intellectual subject matter that students "learn," but they may also include physical abilities such as tying shoes, creating written letters by hand or on a keyboard, using a ratchet wrench to unbolt the head of an internal combustion engine, assuming the third position in classical ballet, or replacing the hard drive on a personal computer. The instructional outcomes will also include certain attitudes, feelings and values. After instruction we might expect students to be more tolerant of people with beliefs different from their own. We usually expect them to be willing to do things like bringing the necessary tools to class, following directions given by the teacher, and doing outside of class assignments. Of course, we expect them to come to class. So, indeed, we expect students to have attained a series of knowledges, skills, and attitudes as a result of instruction.

The Tylerian Rationale tells us that instructional objectives do not simply come out of the teacher's head (or out of a textbook). Rather, the rationale suggests that there are three sources of objectives. The first involves studies of the learners themselves. These studies should identify needs of students which can be met through the agency of educational programs. For instance, studies of entering students at a university may indicate that they are unable to read at the level at which most text books at the university are written. This would suggest the need for some developmental reading instruction. Likewise, a study might indicate that a high proportion of these students have racist attitudes, suggesting the need for some type of program dealing with tolerance and the value of diversity.

The second source of objectives suggested by Tyler involves studies of contemporary life outside of the school. A finding of increasing computerization of tasks in all facets of the society, including the world of work, could suggest programs where students learn to integrate this technology into their everyday lives. If students have failed to have reached objectives dealing with this technology prior to entering the institution of higher education, developmental education programs might seriously consider dealing with instructional objectives in this area. Such programs might include objectives such as keyboarding skills, and the use of various tools designed to facilitate the search for information which is available on the Internet and in other computer accessible forms. The fact that people from Latin America are rapidly becoming the largest minority group in the United States might be a good reason to offer classes in Spanish language.

The third and final source of instructional objectives is suggestions from subject matter specialists. Tyler pointed out that this is the sources of most of the objectives used by institutions of elementary, secondary, and higher education. It is certainly the source of most of the objectives in developmental education programs. The question here, we are told, is "What can this subject contribute to the education of young people who are not to specialize in it" (Tyler, 1949, p. 27)? In applying this idea to developmental education we might think of objectives that deal with elementary algebra. Mathematicians and mathematics educators (subject matter specialists within mathematics) tell us that all students should have mastered at least elementary algebra before they graduate from high school. Clearly, if students enter colleges and universities without having mastered these objectives, it is a job for developmental education and we indeed find that most developmental education mathematics programs include instruction in elementary algebra and that our screening procedures test for competence in algebra. So, Tyler would insist that developmental educators confront the questions of whether and how elementary algebra is useful to the students who do not plan to specialize in mathematics.

The list of objectives devised from these four sources will be huge and will consists of many more objectives than any school or program could or should possibly incorporate. Furthermore, it will inevitably be found that some objectives are simply inconsistent with each other. Tyler pointed out that what we need is really a relatively small number of consistent objectives. "An educational program is not effective if so much is attempted that little is accomplished" (p. 33). Finally, all identified objectives may not be appropriate to given students at a particular time and place. Tyler requires us to take the initial set of objectives identified from the three sources above and to screen them through two sets of ideas to come up with a manageable set of consistent objectives. These screens are philosophy, both educational and social, and psychology.

Suppose that we believed in the value of diversity of thoughts and ideas; that the availability of this diversity enriches us and allows us to make well considered choices. Further, suppose that we believed that the "correctness" of an idea depended on the people involved in implementing it and the situations that these people find themselves in. For example, that democracy is a fine idea for the societies of North American and Europe, but might not be appropriate in Asia and the Middle East because of the nature of the cultures of the people living in those areas. Our instructional objectives might differ from those developed and used by people who believed that the basic criteria for judging the "correctness" of ideas and action were literally graven in stone and handed to a man on a mountain over 3,000 years ago by a perfect, omniscient being and that these criteria are applicable through all time, with minor to moderately important changes made by almost equally perfect and omniscient beings, and applicable to all people in all situations. Objectives involving critical thinking might be considered appropriate by the first group of people, but not by the second group. On the other hand, objectives related to obedience to authority and the memorization of rules might be important to the latter group and not seen as appropriate to the former. Battles over educational objectives and programs on the basis of philosophy are continually going on in boards of education and state legislatures. In terms of developmental education programs, issues of philosophy would determine whether our institutions would have programs of developmental education, at all, and what these programs might look like.

The second screen through which objectives should be passed before they are included in the curriculum, psychology, involves what we believe about the nature of learning and how human beings learn. After all, "Educational objectives are educational ends. They are results achieved from learning. Unless these ends are in conformity with conditions intrinsic in learning, they are worthless as educational goals" (Tyler, 1949, p. 38). A knowledge of psychology enables us to determine which objectives are likely to be attained by students and which are likely to take too long a time or not be attained at all by students at a particular age and/or developmental level. Here, too, we must struggle with issues of belief. Just as there are competing philosophies in educational thought, there are competing psychological models of learning and the model we choose to accept will determine the appropriateness of various educational objectives. Adherents of cognitive development models would very likely find it necessary to use various levels of diagnostic screening to determine the readiness of students to deal with certain objectives while those who tend toward behaviorist models might be more concerned with the physical structure of the learning environment, the nature of the learning activities, and the order in which these activities will take place. Activity theorists might not be nearly as concerned about prespecifying educational objectives as they would be in specifying the types of interactions students, teachers, and other persons involved in the educational procedure would experience. Working on objectives concerned with the mathematical manipulation of fractions in the absence of specific uses for this skill in the real life of developmental mathematics, students might be considered appropriate by behaviorists on the basis of the facts that appropriate contingencies for instruction could be set up for these students for the attainment of these objectives, and by cognitive psychologists because students at universities are probably at a stage of cognitive development where they could deal with the abstract concepts involved in these objectives. However, activity theorists might call for holding off efforts to attain these objectives until the student is involved in activities where these skills are necessary, such as taking science or technology courses where manipulation of fractions is required to solve problems. To sum up, instructional objectives can be screened out of a curriculum based on our beliefs about educational psychology.

Once instructional objectives have been established, the Tylerian Rationale tells us that we must determine learning activities that would facilitate students' attainments of these objectives. Clearly, these activities will vary with the nature of the objective and the nature of the student. This chapter is not about curriculum development, but at least a cursory survey of some of the issues involved in making decisions about learning activities is certainly appropriate in light of the fact, pointed out earlier, that it doesn't make sense to assess the acquisition of skills, knowledges and attitudes by students unless the students have had ample instruction directed towards these objectives. With an eye toward effective assessment, when we devise instructional activities we need to take, at minimum, two characteristics of the objective to be acquired into consideration.

The first of these is the nature of the outcome specified by the objective. Objectives generally are concerned with either knowledges, attitudes or skills. Bloom and his colleagues (Bloom et al, 1956; Krathwohl, Bloom, & Masia, 1964) referred to these areas as "domains" and defined the cognitive domain as being concerned with subject matter, intellectual objectives (knowledges), the affective domain as being concerned with attitudes and feelings, and the psychomotor domain as consisting of objectives dealing with physical abilities (skills). Gagné (1985) described three levels of learning dealing with intellectual subject matter (Intellectual Skills; Verbal Information; and Cognitive Strategies) as well as learnings dealing with Motor Skills and with Attitudes. The types of instructional strategies we might consider in trying to facilitate the acquisition of objectives dealing with intellectual subject matter might certainly be different from the ones we would use to facilitate changes in attitudes. The former might be more likely to involve verbal and written presentations combined with activities including opportunities for discovery and for practice while the latter might be more therapeutic in nature. Likewise, objectives dealing with eye-muscle coordination might be more likely to include briefer presentations than those involving cognitive skills and to allow for more supervised practice. This will prove to be very important when we deal with methods for assessing the outcome of these instructional activities. We would not want to assess a students' attitude toward reading by administering a standardized reading test.

The second characteristic of an objective to be considered when devising instructional activities to facilitate the acquisition of that objective is the level at which the student must perform in order to reach the objective. Within Bloom's domains and Gagné's levels of learning are hierarchical levels so that we may classify instructional objectives as either simple or complex or concrete or abstract. Within the Cognitive Domain Bloom defines six main hierarchical levels moving in increasing complexity and abstractness from "Knowledge," the simple recognition or recall of simple facts, to "Evaluation," the ability to determine the usefulness of certain information or concepts in solving a particular problem. Harrow (1972) identified six main categories in the psychomotor domain (with additional sub-categories for each) ranging from "Reflex Movements," actions which occur with conscious will in response to stimuli, to "Non-Discursive Communication," which involves communication through body movements which can be such things as facial movement to very complex choreographies. One thing these hierarchies do is allow us to determine what objectives are prerequisite for the acquisition of others and to define instructional activities based on this knowledge. It should be obvious that we cannot devise instructional strategies to facilitate the acquisition of objectives by students if we do not know the complexity of the objectives we are working with or that our students have reached the objectives which are prerequisite to acquiring the objective we have in mind. For instance, the ability to read at a particular level is probably prerequisite for students attempting to learn to use the library to do literature reviews on research topics. Equally obvious should be the fact that we cannot devise effective and appropriate assessment strategies if we are unclear about the level of complexity an objective contains. For instance, we would not want to assess a students' ability to use the library by asking him or her to write down the Library of Congress cataloging system's two letter code for books on history.

Once learning activities are identified, whether for whole groups of students or for individual students, these learning activities must be ordered. That is, we must decide which activities students should engage in early in the program and what activities should be saved until later. Tyler pointed out that educational objectives are often reached very slowly. "In some respects educational experiences produce their effects in the way water dripping upon a stone wears it away. In a day or a week or a month there is no appreciable change in the stone, but over a period of years definite erosion is noted. Correspondingly, by the cumulation [sic] of educational experiences, profound changes are brought about in the learner" (p. 83). He defined three criteria that need to be considered in setting up an effective set of learning experiences. These are 1) continuity; 2) sequence; and 3) integration.

Continuity refers to the way major content of the curriculum is repeated at various times within the process of instruction in a program. If in a developmental reading program the ability judge whether the author has sufficient information to make a statement he or she has made is considered important, learning activities need to be ordered so that students will have continuing opportunities for this skill to be practiced and sharpened. So, we can see that it is usually not sufficient to simply "cover" an instructional objective. A single set of learning activities without the opportunity for practice and refinement does not present sufficient opportunity for students to achieve important, complex objectives.

Sequence is similar to continuity, but is more complex. Learning activities dealing with a particular instructional objective or set of objects can reoccur in various parts of the program but they may reoccur at the same level so that there is no increasing understanding or ability on the part of the student. In the example in the previous paragraph, the student might simply be asked to repeatedly judge the adequacy of information for making a statement that is at a relatively low level of complexity and is highly concrete. This is certainly a good place to start, but to meet the criterion of sequencing, the statements that must be judged should become increasingly complex and move from the very concrete to the rather abstract. They should move from mere statements of fact to statements that describe opinions and value judgments. Likewise, the amount of information that the author of the statement has should move from a few pieces of declarative information to a large and complex set of data. To adequately sequence, then, requires us to be aware of the level of complexity of the objective the activities are to facilitate. This underscores the importance of taxonomies of educational objectives. The taxonomies allow us to get a good idea of the complexity of the objective. This is not only important for curriculum development, but it is essential for assessment. Many a well meant attempt at assessment has foundered on the problem of attempting to assess a high level objective through lower level tasks. Similarly, some very well intentioned programs have proven to be less than effective when the learning activities meant to deal with complex instructional objectives remained at simple levels instead of gradually moving to an appropriate level of complexity.

Finally, while the continuity and sequence principles refer to vertical organization of instructional activities, the principle of integration refers to the horizontal relationship of instructional experiences. This principle is of particular importance to developmental educators since developmental education does not occur in a vacuum. In fact, where most courses outside of the developmental program are designed to provide students with knowledges, skills and attitudes which have vocational or professional utility, developmental education programs and their courses and other activities exist to prepare students to take these "regular" courses at the college or university. Whereas professors of literature and calculus can determine their objectives and instructional activities based on the traditions and standards of their fields, developmental English and mathematics professors must choose the objectives of their programs with a keen awareness of the curriculum of these "regular" classes. The integration principle tells us that we must plan learning activities across subject areas and individual classes. The learning activities of developmental reading courses must be related to activities involving reading in regular college reading courses and in reading in the content area of sociology and chemistry. The activities presented to students in a developmental mathematics course must relate to the types of activities in a regular college level mathematics course or a course in physics or physical anthropology as well as a research methodology course in psychology. If there is no horizontal connection between the learning activities in developmental education courses and the activities in "regular" college courses, we cannot confidently say that developmental education students have had the opportunity to reach the objectives necessary for them to be successful in "regular" college or university classes. This would make the assessment of the efficacy of any developmental education program or preparation of any developmental education student a mute case.

The fourth and final step of the Tylerian Rationale involves testing the effectiveness of the learning activities. The designers of the curriculum of the class or program may follow the appropriate procedures for identifying instructional objectives and for designing and sequencing learning activities which should facilitate the acquisition of these objectives by students in these programs, and the instructor may see that students engage in these activities under appropriate conditions, but the criterion for evaluating the effectiveness of these learning activities is *not* what curriculum designers and instructors do, but rather what students are like after instruction. To evaluate the effectiveness of a set of learning activities, we need to collect evidence that students have developed, or are in the process of developing, the skills, knowledges and attitudes described in the instructional objectives. This evidence can take many forms from the results of a paper and pencil examination to the items in a portfolio, but, as we shall soon see, this evidence must have certain characteristics before we can accept it as creditable.

In Tyler's model, the first three steps involve inputs which are designed to identify objectives and facilitate the knowledge, skills, and attitudes defined by these objectives. The sources of these inputs may be those traditionally used in higher education, including instructor and various multimedia inputs, or they may include interactions with other students and even a certain amount of introspection by students themselves.

The fourth step involves outputs. That is, things students are able to do as a result of their engaging in the educational process. Since what Tyler described is a coherent process, it makes no sense to look at student outcomes without assessing the level and quality of the inputs if we wish to make useful assessments of students achievement and other programs designed to bring about these outcomes.

Assessing Inputs

Educational inputs in developmental education may be assessed by looking at three types of activities which occur consecutively over time. These are 1) The use of diagnostic procedures; 2) The development of instructional procedures that make available appropriate instruction to deal with diagnosed student needs; and 3) The actual implementation of the planned instructional strategies.

The use of diagnostic procedures. Tyler suggested that the first step in determining a program of instruction is to determine the objectives of instruction. While all students come to colleges and universities with varying knowledges, skills and attitudes, those of developmental education students should be expected to vary more than typical entering students. Keeping in mind that the goal of developmental education is to provide individual students with the skills, knowledges and attitudes that will facilitate their being successful college students, it follows that instructional objectives for these students should be more closely tailored to their individual needs. Incoming students should be assessed for cognitive knowledges and skills as well as for affective characteristics, such as study behaviors and self perception as a student, so that developmental educators working with them can tailor a set of appropriate objectives and determine appropriate instructional strategies to help them reach these objectives.

Developmental education programs have typically done very well in the diagnosis of the cognitive abilities of their students. Even institutions that are openly skeptical concerning the whole idea of developmental education give "placement tests" to their entering students with the purpose of determining course placement in the areas of English, mathematics, and foreign languages. It is curious that such tests are not given for social science and natural science placement, as well, but this is probably not the time nor place to discuss that issue. What institutions of higher education both with and without developmental education programs very often fail to consider is the level of their incoming students in terms of affective objectives or psychomotor skills. In short, they seem to be concerned with diagnostics only at the level of knowledges while they tend to ignore the other two objective types.

One area of affect that is widely neglected in considering necessary diagnostic procedures for students beginning developmental education programs is the area of study behaviors. While it may seem odd to speak of behaviors as affects, the sense of this becomes clearer when we remember that behaviors are often the results of feelings and attitudes. The strategies that students use when studying are more often than not the results of their feelings about and attitudes towards school and academic endeavors. A student who views his or her placement in a developmental program as unfair or as a punishment or simply as another useless hoop to jump through is liable to behave very differently when preparing for developmental education classes than one who perceives of this program as necessary and helpful. Likewise, a student who sees the entire higher educational experience as simply a method of developing vocational skills or obtaining credentials is liable to behave differently than one who views the experience as a time to learn new things and explore new worlds of ideas which may or may not have vocational value. These feelings and attitudes are important. Bliss and

Mueller (1993) found that a measure of study behaviors of freshman students at two and four year institutions of higher education predicted academic achievement better when measured by freshman grade point average than by the Scholastic Aptitude Test (SAT).

So, we may need to assess the diagnostic activities in a developmental education program. To do this we must consider the instructional objectives that students must have successfully attained prior to entering the institution of higher education in order to be successful in the institution. These can be determined only by looking at the objectives in the courses of study of various "regular" university and colleges courses and determining the knowledges, skills and attitudes that professors of these courses assume that their students bring into their programs. Diagnostic procedures in developmental education programs must be capable of determining which of these entering students have already attained. Therefore, there must be a good match between these knowledges, skills, and attitudes and those assessed in the diagnostic procedures. There is a popular diagnostic reading test that essentially measures the speed at which students can read. While being able to read at a high speed is probably a useful skill for any student to have, there is little or no evidence that the ability to read quickly is a requirement for being successful in any university or college class. Therefore, this popular test might not be a particularly useful diagnostic tool. On the other hand, if an examination of the curricula in "regular" college mathematics classes determines that students in these classes would be expected to have mastered objectives involving concepts in elementary algebra, it would important to assess incoming students' knowledges in this area. Hence, we can say that the first step in assessment of developmental education programs is determining whether appropriate diagnoses are being carried out. The first step in the assessment of students is carrying out diagnostic activities and reporting their results to people with a need to know.

Availability of instruction. Further inputs in developmental education programs are the instructional strategies designed for use in these programs and the activities carried out by instructors and students participating in them. Before we can begin assessing the efficacy of these activities we need to establish what these activities will be and this can only be done if we know what skills, knowledges, and attitudes we expect our developmental education students to have attained when they complete our programs. Once we know what these objectives are, we can then look to see if the learning activities are such that students have an opportunity to achieve the instructional objectives. So, there are really two levels at which inputs must be assessed. We can think of these levels as answering two questions.

The first of these is, "Are the learning activities that have been developed and organized into the curriculum likely to facilitate the acquisition of the objectives they were designed to facilitate?" It is not reasonable to expect students to reach instructional objectives if they do not have the opportunity to reach them. For instance, it is unlikely that a developmental education student will develop adequate study skills if the staff of the developmental program does not provide some manner of instruction in the development of study skills and/or if the student does not receive this instruction. The simple offering of a course or some other manner of instruction is not necessarily sufficient to assure availability of instruction. If conflicts with other activities such as work or family obligations make it impossible for a student to obtain instruction, the instruction is not available to that student. It is important to assess the availability of instruction for each student on each objective.

Beyond the simple physical availability of instruction, all educators, including developmental educators are obligated to be confident that the instructional strategies they are using are likely, to the best of their knowledge, to be effective in facilitating the acquisition of instructional objectives. This assessment of this condition is not done simply by appealing to philosophy or ideology. It is not answered by asking students or instructors their feelings about the instructional strategies. While it is certainly a humane thing to be concerned with students' and instructors' feelings of satisfaction, this is not convincing evidence of the likely efficacy of any individual or set of instructional activities. When attempting to make predictions about the likely effectiveness of learning activities, we need to appeal to the theoretical and empirical literature of our profession.

Contrary to common folk wisdom, we now know a great deal about how people learn. There is now a sufficient literature to suggest learning strategies that are likely to be successful with adult learners in general (c.f. Davenport & Davenport, 1985) and with developmental learners, in particular. We have theories of cognitive development with impressive empirical evidence to support them. We also have theories of moral development which, while not as thoroughly investigated as those dealing with cognitive development, still give us some useful ideas about what to expect in this area of human growth. Finally, theories of physical development are even more explanatory than theories of cognitive development. Through research in physiology we know more than ever about the hows and wherefores of physical development in human beings. Any instructional activities we choose to use in facilitating students' acquisition of instructional objectives must be consistent with what we know to be true about how people learn.

In assessing the appropriateness of instructional activities or programs of instructional activities, we must also take into consideration what we know about the subject matter of the objectives. This information is available from subject matter specialists. Often the instructor in a university or college course is the subject matter specialist, but this is not necessarily so. It particularly might not be the case in developmental education where developmental educators may be experts in the teaching of developmental reading or mathematics or study skills, but may not be psychologists or mathematicians, themselves. This is probably as it should be since we need experts in androgogy, not necessarily in advanced subject matter, to work with developmental students. In these cases, it is especially important that curriculum designers consult with subject matter specialists to insure the appropriateness of the instructional strategies they design and organize. Failure to do this can result in some unfortunate outcomes.

During the early 1960's, as it became evident that large groups of elementary school students were not learning to read adequately in the time allowed for reading instruction and that United States society, having finally accomplished a large population shift from the farms to the cities at the same time that the manufacturing and service industries in these cities were becoming more automated, would present less and less opportunity for illiterate or functionally illiterate members to lead productive and prosperous lives. A group of reading specialists diagnosed the problem in the following way. They reasoned that learning to read English requires two main processes. The first is "decoding" where the reader simply translates the word from its written to spoken form. Someone looking at the letters c-a-t would say, "Cat." The second is that the reader obtain meaning from the word or group of words. So, after saying, "Cat," the reader would conjure up in his or her mind a small furry animal that liked to lap up milk from saucers, shred furniture, and say, "Meow!" Of course this is an oversimplification of finding meaning. Very complex meaning requires series of words and are much more difficult to deal with. English differs from, let us say the Romance (French and Spanish, for instance) and Semitic (e.g. Arabic and Hebrew) languages, in that English words are not sounded exactly as they are written. With a small set of rules one can actually sound out words in these languages without having any idea of what these words mean. Words such as "enough" and "read" ("I have read the book" vs "I am going to read the book") make decoding a complex task in English whereas Israeli children are expert decoders of Hebrew by the middle of first grade. The aforementioned group of reading specialists reasoned that young children would have an easier time learning to read and be more successful at it if the two processes (decoding and finding meaning) were decoupled in English very much as it is in the languages mentioned above. In that manner, children learning to read English could handle one of the tasks at a time.

In order to accomplish this, they devised the "Initial Teaching Alphabet" (ITA), a completely phonetic method for writing English. A given letter in the ITA would have one and only one sound. This involved inventing some new vowels, but the new alphabet was not particularly unwieldy. For instance, the little furry animal that shredded furniture was a "kăt." Primers and high interest/low vocabulary books—a whole library—were written using the Initial Teaching Alphabet and students who were first learning to read were taught this alphabet and learned to read using these books. The plan was to gradually switch these students over to the standard alphabet towards the end of second grade or the beginning of third grade. After students had learned to decode using the ITA, they could concern themselves with reading for meaning. Separating the tasks, the advocates of the ITA said, would make the process of learning to read easier and increase the success rate of beginning readers.

Using non-standard notation as an aid for beginning readers is not unknown. The Hebrew language is written using a non-Roman alphabet and without vowels. Beginning readers of Hebrew in Israeli schools are provided with written materials that use a set of vowel points underneath letters which makes written words totally phonetic. Students are gradually weaned off these vowel points so by the time they finish the first grade they are reading standard Hebrew text without the vowel points. The technique is highly successful and Israel enjoys one of the highest literacy rates of any country in the world. This might have boded well for the Initial Teaching Alphabet, but thirty years after its introduction and wide acceptance, there were no schools using the ITA in the United States. Tens of millions of dollars worth of instructional materials bought by school districts to implement the ITA ended up moldering in storerooms or burning on rubbish heaps.

This unhappy occurrence could have been foreseen by decision makers in schools and avoided by the ITA developers if they had tempered their enthusiasm for teaching every child to read with a serious look at the literature. The difficulty with trying to devise a phonetic alphabet to use in English was apparent as long ago as the beginning of the 20th century when George Bernard Shaw attempted the task. To see the problem one merely has to pronounce the following three words: Merry, Marry, Mary. A person who learned to talk in the southeastern region of the United States will pronounce all three words identically. One who learned to speak in the New York City area or in one of the New England states will pronounce them all differently. Midwesterners tend to pronounce two of them alike and one differently from the other two. How would you spell these words using the ITA or any other phonetic alphabet? Would the words be spelled differently for New Yorkers, North Carolinians and Mainers? The psycholinguistic literature is clear on this problem. Years before the Initial Teaching Alphabet was even conceived of, psycholinguists had firmly established the principle which tells us that the sound a vowel has depends on the consonants on either side of it and on *regionalisms*. We could *never* expect to have a truly phonetic alphabet in English. Simply put, while well intentioned, the ITA program was doomed from the start and literally tens of millions of dollars could have been saved for more useful purposes if the designers of the program had simply consulted the literature on reading and language.

So, one type of assessment we must make in assessing the appropriateness of any program is an assessment of whether the instructional activities that have been designed are consistent with what we know about the subject matter and how students learn it. Inappropriate instruction is virtually the same as no instruction at all and we cannot honestly say that students given instruction that is not consistent with what we know about people and how they learn are really given the opportunity to acquire the knowledges, skills, and attitudes that we list as instructional objectives.

Implementation of instruction. The second question regarding inputs that must be asked when assessing inputs in developmental education programs is, "Are the instructional strategies that have been devised to facilitate the acquisition of objections by students actually being carried out in a manner that is likely to be effective?" Unlike the issues dealt with previously, this is not a matter that can be dealt with using scholarship and appealing to the literature of pedagogy, andragogy, or subject matter. This question is an issue of supervision and supervision is fraught with both political and technical components.

Any attempt to discover whether instructional strategies are being carried out appropriately should simply be a matter of observing what is going on in classes and determining whether these things are consistent with the instructional strategies identified during curriculum development. Of course, this is a naïve view of the situation. Supervision involves making value judgments which can lead to internal consequences such as changes in self concept and feelings of worth in the individuals being supervised. The results of supervision can also lead external consequences such as the requirement that the person being supervised attend staff or professional development activities, the loss of promotion or of pay. At its most extreme, supervision can lead to the termination of an employee. Being such a high stake issue, the process is confounded by a host of political, gender, racial and legal issues. Questions of fairness based on group membership abound. Can a male supervisor fairly supervise a female instructor? Can a white supervisor fairly supervise an African-American instructor? The literature is particularly sparse in empirical studies designed to cast light on these questions. The whole issue of whether unbiased supervision is even possible has been called into question by proponents of various post-modern ways of thinking. Proponents of these ideas point to claims that people, particularly people living in the United States of America, are unavoidably racists and sexists. Others suggest that in a society that consists of one struggle for power after another, it is impossible for people to put away their needs to accumulate power at the expense of other people and carry out fair assessments. Still others suggest that what is *correct* or *incorrect*, *true* or *false* is uniquely different for each person and is negotiable, at any rate. This discussion of assessment of inputs (and, in fact, of outputs) will cut through these arguments by making the assumption that there is objective truth. That is, by using clearly articulated criteria and appropriate assessment strategies, it is possible to say whether a statement is correct or incorrect or whether it is true or false and that the assessment will be a fair one. The operative word in the pervious sentence is *fair*. An assessment that is fair is one that is consistent and accurate.

In assessing instructional inputs our judgments must be consistent over two dimensions. The first is within judges. If an assessor is observing what is going on in a classroom and reports that certain instructional activities are being carried out adequately in that classroom, the same assessor, seeing similar activities in another classroom carried out by a different instructor in the same manner, should report that the activities are being carried out adequately in the second classroom. This report should be made regardless of the race, sex, ethnicity, age, socioeconomic status, or any other group membership of the instructors whose performance is being assessed. In short, the same judge, seeing the same thing, should make the same report.

The second dimension is between judges. Two assessors observing the same instructor carrying out instructional activities should both report that the instructor was working at the same level. If one assessor reports the instructor is carrying out the activities adequately, the second should report the same. Likewise, if one assessor reports that the instructor is failing to carry out the instructional activities in an adequate manner, the second should so report. These assessments should be consistent regardless of the assessors' race, sex, ethnicity, age, socioeconomic status, or membership in any other group.

Thorndike (1997) noted that assessments of the adequacy of the behaviors are more likely to be consistent when we can define what the end-product of instructor behavior is supposed to be. When we consider the behavior of instructors when they are carrying out instructional activities, the end-product could be considered the successful carrying out of the activities. Thorndike tells us that the purpose of this definition of end-products is to enable us to develop a list of behaviors and characteristics that would describe adequate carrying out of the instructional activities. So, the next step in evaluating how well instructional activities were carried out would be to develop a list of what we would expect to see if the activity was being carried out adequately. A partial listing of parts of an instructional activity designed to facilitate the acquisition of the objective of using the card catalogue to find materials in a library might include:

1. Lecture on the Library of Congress cataloguing system.

2. Discussion concerning the scope of the card catalogue.

3. Demonstrations of strategies for deriving subject descriptions.

4. Demonstration of the use of the Library of Congress thesaurus.

5. Practice using the Library of Congress thesaurus to find appropriate subject descriptors.

6. Demonstration of the use of cross referenced descriptors.

7. Practice using cross referenced descriptors.

These activities could be included in a check-list for assessors to use when they observed instruction taking place. If the assessment is concerned with making some judgment concerning the quality of components of the instructional activity rather than simply whether the component was present or absent, instruments such as rating scales could be devised for assessing the component.

A second practice that can increase the consistency of assessments of the carrying out of instructional activities is training the assessors. Even when the specifications are carefully defined, differences in judgments between observers can occur. Thorndike (1997) mentioned that, "In one extreme case, a researcher reported the rate of interobserver agreement on the gender of the teacher in classrooms where the observations were taking place to be 95%" (p. 300). In training sessions assessors make observations on the same sample of behavior. They then compare the findings, discuss discrepancies, and reconcile differences, finally agreeing on what has indeed taken place. It is also useful to have previously trained assessors sit in on and participate in the training sessions. This procedure not only aids in enhancing the uniformity of the assessments that are made, but it also tends to increase the probability of the assessor making a correct observation.

It is clear that a set of assessment can be consistent, but be consistently incorrect. Have you ever had a bathroom scale that measured your weight incorrectly by reading five pounds under your true weight? If you weighed 140 pounds, but every time you got on the scale the scale read 135 pounds, the scale would be consistent, but incorrect. This is a simple example, to be sure, but it demonstrates that consistency is not sufficient proof of accuracy. Indeed, the process of providing evidence that assessments are accurate is much trickier than that of providing evidence that they are consistent.

One type of evidence that argues for the accuracy of an assessment is the demonstration that the checklists, scales, and other observational instruments that are used in the assessment include the relevant behaviors necessary to provide evidence that the instructional activity is being carried out adequately. For example, does the list of observable behaviors for the learning activity to facilitate learning to use the library card catalogue incorporate adequate behaviors so that experts in library education will agree that these should facilitate the objective? This literary evidence from subject matter specialists can provide a compelling argument.

A second type of evidence can only be provided as the result of a long term study, but is the most compelling of all. If we can demonstrate that students of instructors who are assessed as having carried out the learning activities adequately are more likely to have reached the objectives the activities were designed to facilitate than are students of instructors who are assessed as failing to carry out the activities adequately, when such things as student abilities and prior achievement are taken into consideration, we have powerful evidence that the assessment is accurate. This is clearly a difficult, long term process, but when it can be carried out it produces the most convincing evidence of all that the results of the assessment are correct.

Space does not permit going into detail about the procedures that will provide evidence for the consistency and accuracy of the assessments of instructional activity inputs described so briefly, above. The reader is referred to one of the many excellent texts and articles on the assessment of instruction and academic programs that are available in our field. In any case, the difficulty of the task of providing evidence that educational inputs are appropriate is vitally important. The inadequate carrying out of instructional activities puts students in virtually the same position they would have been in if there had been no instructional activities at all. Besides presenting us with the usual problems of students not learning because of poor instruction, this situation could also put us in the ethically questionable position of assessing students for the acquisition of objective that they had no opportunity to acquire.

Assessing Outputs

The establishment of objectives and determining the instructional strategies for assessing student attainment of these objectives constitutes the first three of the four steps in the Tylerian rationale. The fourth step, determining whether the instructional objectives have been acquired, involves assessing student outputs.

The criterion problem in assessing individual students. Criteria are standards used when making assessments. Decisions need to be made carefully when choosing criteria for student assessment in developmental education programs. One important decision concerns whether to choose criteria which directly represent student skills, knowleges, and attitudes and to assess students according to the extent to which they exhibit these (criterion referenced assessment) or to assess students by comparing their levels of attainment of objectives to that of other students (norm referenced assessment). Choosing the former poses questions which include determining cutoff scores which define an acceptable level of attainment. Choosing the latter focus brings to the fore questions involving the definition of normative populations and minimum acceptable standings of developmental education students within these populations.

If we choose the first focus, and choose to assess the acquisition of objectives of the developmental program, the issue is rather straight forward.

Figure 1. An Assessment Model for
Developmental Education Programs

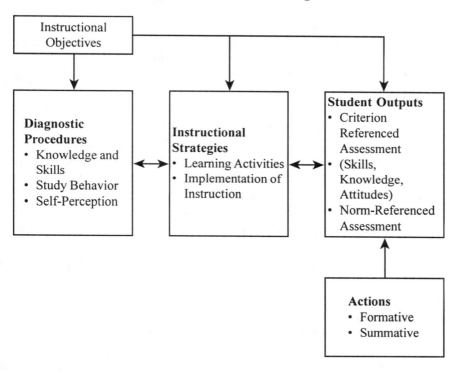

We will simply assess developmental education students in courses and other instructional procedures in the same manner that instructors in regular college and university courses evaluate their students. That is, we will choose criterion referenced tests and other assessment activities such as observations, portfolios and interviews and involve students in these assessment activities so that we can determine whether or not they have reached the various objectives of the course. As we do in most courses and other learning situations, we will decide (or our institutions will decide for us) what proportions of the objectives students must learn in order to receive credit for (pass) the course. In developmental education courses there should at least be a theoretical connection between the objectives of the course and the skills, knowledges, and attitudes students should have in order to be successful in regular college and university courses, of course, but there need be no other differences between how we assess student outputs in developmental or regular courses if we choose to take this focus. Authors of texts in educational evaluation and assessment provide excellent guidelines for developing valid, reliable, and useable criterion referenced assessment. Three that I have found particularly useful are Ebel and Frisbie (1991), Nitko (1996) and Thorndike (1997).

Choosing a norm referenced focus immediately involves us in the choice of a comparison group for the developmental education students who are being assessed. We must keep in mind that by choosing to compare the knowledges, skills, and attitudes that our students have acquired with those acquired by another group, the choice of comparison group will be the key to the whole procedure. If we are assessing developmental education students, it may be reasonable to choose one of two groups of students: Previous developmental education students who succeeded in regular college courses or students who here determined by their institutions' screening policies not to require a developmental education program before they attempted regular college or university courses. In the former case, we need only look at students who had been in the program in previous years and had moved on to take regular college courses. We could observe the scores these students had obtained on the various assessment instruments in the program. We could also look at some measure of those students' success in their first regular college course that was related to the developmental program and determine the minimum standard score on the assessment measure obtained by students who were successful in the regular college course. For instance, most developmental mathematics programs have some type of instrument that they administer to students at the end of a semester or quarter of instruction. At some institutions, students need not wait until the end of a period of instruction, but may choose to "test out" of the program at any time. In either case, it would be relatively simple to follow students who do test out of developmental mathematics and observe their success (however the institution chooses to define it) in the first regular college or university mathematics course. Now suppose that we decide that any student who has less than an 80% chance of succeeding in the first regular mathematics course should continue in developmental mathematics. We can find the standard score on the developmental education test below which the probability of being successful in the first regular course in that area is below 80% and use that standard score as the cutoff for the developmental education program achievement test.

If we choose entering students who did not require developmental education in a particular area as the comparison group we can simply use the same cutoff scores on the screening instrument that we used when students were placed into developmental or regular classes. For instance, if the institution has decided that entering students who score below the fortieth percentile on a nationally normed reading test are in need of developmental reading instruction, it is simple enough to say that students in developmental reading programs are ready to leave these programs when they can score at or above the fortieth percentile on the same nationally normed test or a parallel form of that test.

The criterion problem in assessing developmental programs. The special function of developmental education adds another facet to the task of developing criteria for student assessment. Since the prime purpose of developmental programs is to prepare students to succeed in academic tasks at the college or university level, any assessment of the efficacy of developmental education programs needs to take into account the future performance of clients in regular college and university courses. This future performance can be looked at in two ways.

One option is to decide that we will consider our developmental education programs to be successful when students who successfully pass through these programs cannot be distinguished from students who never needed to participate in programs of developmental education. We could assess this criterion rather simply. We might look at the proportion of former developmental education students in particular areas who pass subsequent regular college courses in those areas and determine whether it is different from the proportion of nondevelopmental students who pass these courses. We could go a step further and actually look at the distribution of grades between the two groups to see if they are different. Another way to compare these two cohorts of students is to look at their graduation rates. We might decide that our developmental education program was a success if the proportion of developmental education students who graduated within a certain period of time was no different than the proportion of nondevelopmental education students who graduated in the same period of time. A final thought on this subject comes to mind. How shall we interpret a finding that former developmental education students actually had a higher pass rate or more A's and B's in regular college courses or graduated at a higher rate than students who were not judged to need developmental education services? The answer to this question is left as an exercise for the reader.

The second option we may use in assessing the effectiveness of developmental education programs is to determine whether former developmental education students are more academically successful that students who needed developmental education but chose not to participate. We could make all the comparisons listed in the preceding paragraph but use a sample of students who needed, but did not participate in developmental education programs as the comparison group. Very often the decision to use one or the other of these option depends on the policies of the institutions where the developmental education programs are housed. For instance, Boylan, Bliss and Bonham (1997) found positive correlations between mandatory screening and placement of developmental students at institutions and the success rates (as measured by grade point averages in regular college courses, success in the first regular college course in specific areas and graduation rates) of students at those institutions. At institutions that have policies of mandatory screening and placement of students into developmental education programs, only the first option is available to assessors since a comparison group of students who should have, but did not take developmental education programs would not be available.

Acting on the Results of Assessment

The Tylerian rationale tells us that, "It is not only desirable to analyze the results of an evaluation to indicate the various strengths and weakness, but it is also necessary to examine these data to suggest possible explanations or hypotheses about the reason for this particular pattern of strengths and weaknesses" (Tyler, 1949, p. 122). This tells us that simply reporting the results of the assessment procedure to stakeholders is not sufficient to assure that assessment will result in improvement in student and program characteristics. To result in positive change assessment also involves using personal and programmatic experience, the experiences of others as represented in the professional literature, and what we know about theories of instruction and learning in order to suggest hypotheses to explain the findings of assessments. Actions taken as a result of the findings of assessment should be design, initially, to test these hypotheses. Payne (1992) suggested that assessment, seen in this way, can be viewed as a research effort. Scriven (1967) referred to this type of evaluation as "formative."

In contrast to the procedures described above, some assessment data are used to simply make overall judgments about the worth or value of something. In developmental education we make decisions like this at the end of a unit of instruction (e.g. a course, a laboratory experience, a unit of self-instruction). These decisions include determining whether a student requires further developmental work, whether or not a student has achieved certain objectives or certifying that a developmental education student is prepared to enter the regular college or university course of study. Scriven referred to this type of evaluation as "summative."

Formative actions. Ebel and Frisbie (1991) tell us that formative evaluation is "to provide feedback to the teacher and to the student about how things are going" (p. 24). This type of assessment takes place on a constant basis throughout the period of instruction. It may include formal testing procedures, but is more likely to consist of frequent, sometimes daily informal observations and the evaluation of assignments. Some of the more qualitative or interpretive methods of the collection of information are often used in good formative assessment. Such feedback provides information to teachers and program administrators to modify instructional techniques and materials for whole classes or individual students if things are not going well. Actions taken in the course of formative assessment allow remediation to take place before the end of classes or other units of instruction and are invaluable in programs of developmental education.

Summative actions. The primary purpose of summative assessment is to determine the level of student knowledges, skills, and attitudes at the end of a unit of instruction and to report this information to the student, instructor, and other stakeholders. They are often used to determine the readiness of developmental education students to progress to more advanced levels of developmental work or to enter regular college and university programs. In the latter case, the issue of prediction comes to the fore. Specifically, whether we realize it or not, allowing a developmental student to pass out of the developmental education program and into the regular college or university program involves our predicting that this student will be successful in subsequent regular courses in our area. Alternatively, it can be thought of as predicting that said student would be at least equally likely to succeed in the regular class as a student who did not need to participate in a developmental education program. Very often developmental education programs base this prediction on the passing of developmental education classes without providing any evidence that the prediction is a valid one. How many faculty members in developmental education writing programs, for example can say, "We can present objective evidence that students who pass courses in our program as likely as non-developmental students to succeed in their first college composition course"?

Other developmental education programs determine readiness of students to leave the program on the basis of a final examination or placement test which the student may take, in some cases, at any time during the program or at the end of a unit of instruction, in others. In these cases an important, but often overlooked, issue is the determination of what Thorndike (1997) referred to as "cut scores" (p. 152). To put it simply, a cut score is the minimum score on an examination that would allow us to confidently say that a student has reached a criterion level of whatever is being tested. To think of it another way, it is the minimum score that would allow us to predict that a student would be successful in a future task that has been defined as the criterion. In terms of screening tests in a developmental education program, it is the minimum score on the screening test that would allow us to comfortably predict that the student would be successful in his or her first regular college or university course in the subject area being tested. Jaeger (1989) and Mehrens and Popham (1992) also provided valuable insight into the idea and process of standards setting.

The uses of summative evaluation are not all instructional. These assessments can be reported to institutional authorities to validate the effectiveness of the developmental program. They also serve as indications of program effectiveness to local, state, and federal authorities as well as to accreditation agencies. Finally, summative assessment results can be used in credibility statements to private and public funding agencies. There is often a political agenda in the use of the results of summative assessment results.

An Admonition

Of all the things that developmental educators do in the course of their professional lives, assessment is probably the least pleasant. Assessment involves anxiety and fear. I remember sitting in a rather small, poorly ventilated room giving a final examination one fine spring day many years ago. I was reading a novel as the students were taking the test and suddenly felt a feeling of intense anxiety which was accompanied by cold sweating and an increased heart rate. After taking my pulse to assure myself that my heart beat was regular, if elevated, I walked over to the window and opened it, taking a few deep breathes of fresh air before I went back to my seat. With the room well ventilated, the symptoms never returned. I suppose that there are a number of alternative explanations for this phenomenon, but I firmly believe that my symptoms were due to pheromones, chemical substance secreted by members of an animal species that alters the behavior of other members of the same species. In this case, I believe my students were so anxious that they were producing chemicals as a result of this fear which affected me. Assessment also involves the necessity of telling some people that they have failed. This is usually an unpleasant task and developmental educators, who tend to be very student oriented, naturally find this task unpleasant.

Finally, assessment takes time that might be used for instruction. Developmental educators, as most college and university faculty, more often than not feel themselves pressed for time. There is never enough time in a semester or quarter to do what really needs to be done. For these and other reasons, it is tempting to overlook the need for high quality assessment in developmental education programs and substitute easily obtained measures of student satisfaction for serious program assessment and the subjective judgments of instructors or low level achievement testing for objective assessment of students. The problems with these practices is that, while possibly meeting the short-range objectives of instructors and institutions, they short-change students by not adequately preparing them to do college level work with the failure and low rates of retention that accompany this lack of preparation and they open the institution to charges of educational malpractice.

Chapter 18

ಬಿೂ

An Assessment and Evaluation Model for Developmental Programs

Darlene A. Thurston and V. Carolyn Craig

Introduction

E manating from the national movements (1) to raise academic standards and (2) to improve the levels of academic achievement, demands have come to document program effectiveness. Fueled by the vast resources expended, society is constantly and loudly requesting accountability from the educational community. These accountability requests have become priorities for educational administrators in general and for developmental education program directors specifically.

Most policy makers view success in college and universities as a realistic expectation for developmental education program participants. Starks (1994) states that in order to fully understand the effects of these developmental interventions upon student retention, one must first review student departure rates and determine how developmental educational programs converge with the other post secondary educational programs offered.

Program evaluation is a necessary but difficult and complex task that will answer questions about effectiveness. Evaluation outcome indicators should become more insightful than current measures such as how many students are in the program, the degrees of the instructors, and the total budget expended. Learning in a developmental education program also includes faculty interactions with students, the maturity and motivational levels of students, and the timing of the academic assessments, in addition to the training and experiences of the professional staff. Consequently, explanatory information on the evaluation design, its implementation, monitoring, and impact of the program should be exhaustively examined.

In the past, program evaluation has been driven by a quantitative or numerical philosophy. However, the trend today is to bring together a combination of both quantitative and qualitative approaches, thus providing a more holistic view of the program as it relates to all the things that make a program successful or unsuccessful. The most fundamental uses of evaluation are to inform, to illuminate, and to educate (Geis & Smith, 1992). The evaluation design should focus on the different aspects of the learning process and how learning can be facilitated through various formal and informal processes. Evaluation should span from the day of program initiation to the day of termination. Evaluation should address formative questions and summative questions. Evaluation should distinguish the inefficient and ineffective developmental education activities from those that are effective and efficient in providing the needed education services.

Defining Evaluation

For purposes of this chapter, the following definition of program evaluation is offered: Program evaluation deals with the systematic gathering of data about existing programs, their students, and the postsecondary institution. The data are collected to make judgments on the value, worth, and benefit of programs within which faculty, students, and administrators participate. The steps used for program evaluation are usually on-going and repetitive. Program evaluation aims to take a specific educational program and provide an exhaustive portrayal of its resources, interventions, and outcomes. Program evaluation aims to find out what is working well and why it is working well. If the program is not working well it aims to determine what can be done to improve the program.

The evaluation of any developmental education program should seek to answer three key questions:

(1) What goals and objectives does the program want to accomplish?

(2) What is the program doing to accomplish those goals and objectives?

(3) Have the stated goals and objectives been actually accomplished?

How is Evaluation Different from Assessment?

Student assessment, program evaluation, and educational research all focus on the collection of empirical data. Program evaluation is considered to be an aspect of research, however, the focus of program evaluation is different from student assessment as well as from educational research. Educational research aims to generalize the findings of a specific study to other similar settings for the advancement of theory or the improvement of educational practice. Student assessment, on the other hand, is designed to determine the cognitive, affective, and psychomotor dimensions of the student for selection, diagnosis, placement, grading, and academic progression. The emphasis of program evaluation is situation specific and holistic in its coverage.

Program evaluation should provide diagnostic feedback to the participating individuals and to the postsecondary educational institution. Evaluations should have utilitarian value and the results should be used to effect change. These evaluations should inform the institution on the need for program revisions and where those revisions are most appropriate. Program evaluation should facilitate decision making that may be of an immediate or long range significance. Enabling staff, faculty, and administrators to make better decisions, is the purview of program evaluation.

Types of Education Decisions

There appears to be ten categories of educational decisions that developmental educators and administrators are responsible for making. Kubiszyn and Borich (1995) have identified eight of them to be: (1) instructional, (2) grading, (3) diagnostic, (4) selection, (5) placement, (6) counseling and guidance, (7) program or curriculum, and (8) administrative policy.

Instructional decisions would involve those activities related to teaching and learning made by the faculty and staff. Grading decisions are those related to the letter or numerical grade assigned and the collection of data that are associated with grading. Faculty and staff who utilize objective data in combination with subjective data will make the more discerning decisions. Diagnostic decisions are made about the students strengths and weaknesses and the reason or reasons for their specific academic performance. Selection decisions involve the use of data for accepting or rejecting students for an educational program. These decisions involve where in the program sequence a learner is best suited to begin his/her academic assignment. For example, students in developmental education are frequently urged to take remedial mathematics before enrolling in a regular college mathematics course. Counseling and guidance decisions use program evaluation data to help recommend programs of study that are appropriate for the developmental education students' career interests and academic strengths.

Choice of program or choice of curriculum decisions are usually made at levels above the faculty and staff. These decisions embrace the directors, the deans, the vice presidents of academic affairs, and any other individuals who have policy making authorities over the program. These decisions are made primarily using the results of program evaluations that compare two or more alternative programs. Administrative policy decisions are also generally made at a level higher than faculty and staff. These decisions are customarily based on the availability of funding to implement the institution's vision, goals, and objectives.

In addition to the decision categories proffered by Kubiszyn and Borich, there are two other decision categories that would logically affect the program and would, therefore, require relevant data. These are decisions related to the culture of the organization and decisions about what are the best responses to the needs and expectations of the community in which the institution exists. The cultural climate of a learning setting is swayed by all ten of these decisions.

The Model

The model for evaluating developmental programs presented in this chapter values students as the "most important product" of an educational service. The model integrates a number of critical elements that contribute to the full evaluation of a developmental educational program. It is a holistic approach to evaluation that combines both quantitative and qualitative measures and both formative and summative evaluation perspectives. The idea and beliefs for this model stem from knowledge gained working in developmental programs, a review of the literature, and work experiences as evaluators.

This model consists of three steps that contribute to the effectiveness of program evaluation. The steps in the evaluation chain are (1) resource evaluation, (2) intervention evaluation, and (3) outcome evaluation. Each of these steps should be investigated from the viewpoints of the student, the program, and the post secondary institution.

Resource Evaluation

The identification of resources is comparable to a needs assessment and answers questions related to perceived and observed problems. Resources identification is also analogous to the input identification that is done in the business/industrial sectors. Resource identification attempts to respond to issues of adequacy—Are the available resources adequate to accomplish the goals and objectives of the developmental education program? When the resources are inadequate, program planners are then able to articulate the gaps and the anticipated consequences of these gaps on program outcomes.

The resources to be identified would include the money, materials, supplies, personnel, buildings, and technology needed to plan and to implement a developmental education program. Resources, by virtue of their intent and function, are diverse and include the information obtained from needs assessments done by the developmental education program and/or by the institution. Resources would also address data on students' weaknesses and strengths and the specific instructional strategies recommended to assist them in their academic development.

The desired outcomes of developmental education programs should be clearly specified at this resources step while identifying goals and objectives. The outcomes should be realistic, obtainable, and measurable.

What are some of the indicators for resource evaluation? Examples of indicators for resource evaluation appear in Table 1. The list, it should be noted, is not inclusive. It is given in order to illustrate the resource possibilities. The selected resource indicators may be used in other steps in the program evaluation sequence. Columns for intervention evaluation and outcome evaluation are included to show the potential relevance of the indicators to those steps.

Intervention Evaluation

Intervention evaluation would describe the **activities** undertaken to accomplish the goals and objectives of the developmental education program. Intervention evaluation would specify **who** is to do **what** to **whom** and **how** it is to be done. The who would be the specific staff member(s) assigned to deliver the activity and a rationale for this assignment. The **what** refers to

Table 1. Resource Indicators

Resource Indicator	Intervention Evaluation	Outcome Evaluation
1. Types & number of student strength.	1. Types & number of student strength.	1. Types & number of student strength.
2. Percent of student centered faculty.		
3. Total Budget		
4. Time allowed for program participation.		
5. Curriculum materials.	5. Curriculum materials.	
6. Faculty/Staff Credentials.		
7. Computer hardware & computer software.	7. Computer hardware & computer software.	
8. Faculty-student ratio.		
9. Number of forums.		
10. Minimum criteria for exit.		10. Minimum criteria for exit.
11. Entry SAT, ACT scores & GPA.		
12. Types & number of student deficiencies	12. Types & number of student deficiencies	12. Types & number of student deficiencies
13. Course offering per semester.	13. Course offering per semester.	
14. Funds for staff development.	14. Funds for staff development.	14. Funds for staff development.
15. The DEP Curriculum.	15. The DEP Curriculum.	
16. Physical space.		
17. Number of group help sessions.	17. Number of group help sessions.	17. Number of group help sessions.
18. Number of individual help sessions.	18. Number of individual help sessions.	18. Number of individual help sessions.
19. Number of seminars.	19. Number of seminars.	
20. Minimum & maximum criteria for admission.	20. Minimum & maximum criteria for admission.	
21. Pretest scores.	21. Pretest scores.	
22. Students demonstrating minimum criteria for exit.	22. Students demonstrating minimum criteria for exit.	22. Students demonstrating minimum criteria for exit.

Table 2. Intervention Indication

Intervention Indicator	Resource Evaluation	Outcome Evaluation
1. Number & nature of out-of class student contacts.		1. Number & nature of out-of class student contacts
2. Faculty description of learning activities, products & students' competencies.		2. Faculty description of learning activities, products & students' competencies.
3. Student presentations		3. Student presentations
4. Student's behavior at social events		4. Student's behavior at social events
5. Test scores in specific areas.	5. Test scores in specific areas.	5. Test scores in specific areas.
6. Self-assessments of competencies & level of confidence.	6. Self-assessments of competencies & level of confidence.	6. Self-assessments of competencies & level of confidence.
7. Student's assessments of courses offering, forums, seminars, orientation & self-help sessions.	7. Student's assessments of courses offering, forums, seminars, orientation & self-help sessions.	7. Student's assessments of courses offering, forums, seminars, orientation & self-help sessions.
8. Videos of student-teacher interactions.	8. Videos of student-teacher interactions.	
9. Unit or mid-semester examination grades.		9. Unit or mid-semester examination grades.
10. Nature & types of student's in-class questions & answers.		10. Nature & types of student's in-class questions & answers.
11. Student's jounals or portfolios.	11. Student's jounals or portfolios.	11. Student's jounals or portfolios.

the specific activity. An activity example would be the planning and implementation of baby-sitting services for an after-class group tutoring session. Other activities could be teaching a course, showing a documentary, and modeling note taking. The heart of the **how** refers to the time, setting, and content of the activity.

Intervention evaluation encourages the program staff to detail all of the intended activities that will accomplish the developmental education program goals. The staff can then specify answers to questions such as: How many of the activities were carried out and with which group of students? Which student was missing? What topics were covered? What activities were not carried out and why ?

Intervention evaluation is an excellent monitoring system for the developmental education program. Student reactions are an important factor in intervention evaluation. Students should be allowed to evaluate activities and suggest changes. Useful questions might be: Was the activity helpful and if yes, reflect on how it prepared you to accomplish a task or develop a skill? Which activities are more significant for student development? If the activity is most viable, is it adequately funded?

Intervention evaluation reflects the formative perspective for this model. The enormous amount of data gathered during the intervention evaluation step are used to monitor and improve activities. This step helps to ensure that planned activities for the developmental education program are not neglected. Intervention evaluation data will aid the program in using resources where they are needed.

Examples of indicators for intervention evaluation appear in Table 2. Again, it should be noted that the list is not intended to be inclusive. Suggestions are given in order to illustrate the intervention evaluation possibilities. The selected resource indicators may inform other steps in the program evaluation sequence. Columns for resource evaluation and outcome evaluation are included to show the potential overlap of the indicators to those steps.

Outcome Evaluation

Outcome evaluation is essential and focuses on effects of the developmental education program on the students. The question to be answered might be: Is the developmental studies program accomplishing its intended goals? It is this step that can most forcefully articulates the effectiveness of the developmental education program. Outcome evaluation forms the nucleus of the summative evaluation perspective.

There are two types of results related to program effects—short term effects and long term effects of the developmental education program. An example of a short term effect would be the computational competencies acquired after a developmental mathematics course is completed. The long term effects of a developmental education program include an increase in the number of participants graduating from the post secondary institution or a decrease in the number of students needing to enroll in the program. Outcome evaluation attempts to collect data on the direct effects of the program.

Table 3. Outcome Indicator

Outcome Indicator	Resource Evaluation	Intervention Evaluation
Short Term Effects		
1. Completion rate for DSP students.	1. Completion rate for DSP students.	1. Completion rate for DSP students.
2. Post program testing scores.	2. Post program testing scores.	2. Post program testing scores.
3. Participation rate in student leadership, activities, social groups & organizations.	3. Participation rate in student leadership, activities, social groups & organizations.	
4. Academic majors pursued & those completed written essays.	4. Academic majors pursued & those completed written essays.	4. Academic majors pursued & those completed written essays.
5. Faculty assessment of student's learning activities, products & competencies.	5. Faculty assessment of student's learning activities, products & competencies.	
6. Number & nature of course passes & course failures.	6. Number & nature of course passes & course failures.	6. Number & nature of course passes & course failures.
7. Comparative statistics on DSP & non-DSP students.	7. Comparative statistics on DSP & non-DSP students.	7. Comparative statistics on DSP & non-DSP students.
8. Grade point average.	8. Grade point average.	8. Grade point average.
9. Students' assessment of their competencies & level of confidence.	9. Students' assessment of their competencies & level of confidence.	9. Students' assessment of their competencies & level of confidence.
10. Faculty assessment of student competencies	10. Faculty assessment of student competencies	10. Faculty assessment of student competencies
Long Term Effects		
11. Percent of students who graduate from the institution.	11. Percent of students who graduate from the institution.	
12. Percent of students who apply and are admitted into graduate program.	12. Percent of students who apply and are admitted into graduate program.	
13. Nature of employment.	13. Nature of employment.	
14. Involvement in civic & fraternal groups.	14. Involvement in civic & fraternal groups.	
15. Pass rate on professional examination.	15. Pass rate on professional examination.	
16. Rates of employment.	16. Rates of employment.	
17. Rating on job by supervisors.	17. Rating on job by supervisors.	

Included at the intervention step is reviewing the desired outcomes stated at the resource evaluation step and looking for the evidence to support the extent that the goals were achieved. The potential sources of information for outcome evaluation include questionnaires, archival data, and ratings by the faculty and students. Long term effects might be measured by examining these measures twice, once before the developmental education program was implemented and years after implementation.

Examples of indicators for outcome evaluation appear in Table 3. Again, it should be noted that the list is not intended to be inclusive. Suggestions are given in order to illustrate the outcome evaluation possibilities. The selected outcome indicators may also be used in other steps of the program evaluation sequence. The table is divided into sections for short term effects and long term effects. Columns for resource evaluation and intervention evaluation are included to show the potential overlap of the indicators in those steps.

The Model

The model, as illustrated in Figure 1, is described as an integrated approach to program evaluation for two complementary reasons. First, it investigates all the components that contribute to a program's success—the students, the program, and the post secondary institution. Each is individually and collectively viewed in terms of the resources, the interventions, and the outcomes performing to benefit the developmental education program's implementation. The successful developmental education program explains its effectiveness through these steps interrelating to one another. Indicators from one step in the model may be used to instruct other steps in the model. Second, the model has combined summative evaluation with formative evaluation.

Integrated Model

When considering this model, the following additional information may add to your understanding and implementation. Resources are what are needed to directly implement the developmental education program. Resources are the instructional materials, the background and characteristics of the learner, and the scope and sequence of the curriculum. Other examples of program resources are the different educational background and experiences of faculty members, the culture of the institution, and the assessment practices.

The importance of the resources required for the implementation of developmental education programs cannot be over emphasized. The delineation of resources start, of course, with the allocation of a sufficient budget to support the educational program. However, sufficient budgets are not always possible and therefore the role of program evaluation is to adequately address all resources as they relate to the implementation of the program's goal. Care must be taken not to allow negative results to be blamed on inadequate resources.

Intervention evaluation is more action oriented than resource evaluation and involves the seminars, actual classroom interactions, forums, and tutoring sessions that the participating students experience. In addition, intervention evaluation would include the advising, the instruction, the counseling, the testing, and the mentoring that students are provided. Just as the resources are evaluated for appropriateness and adequacy, so too, must interventions be evaluated for their relevance in achieving program goals and objectives. Another aspect of intervention evaluation is that of the interactions that students have in the informal context of the post secondary institution. These

Figure 1. An Integrated Assessment and Evaluation Model

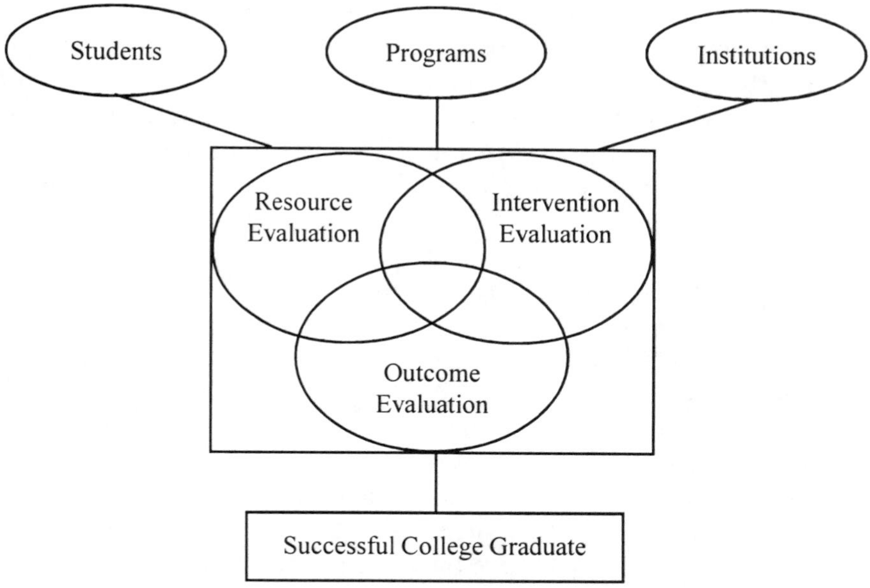

consist of both social and cultural events as well as informal and formal interactions with faculty, other students, and guest presenters.

Outcomes are reflective of the students' academic performance during their matriculation both during students' enrollment in developmental education programs as well as during the regular college course sequence. Outcomes are the short term and long term effects of developmental education programs. Outcomes are the indicators of how much and how well the students have learned the objectives of the developmental education program. Such things as enhanced test-taking skills, improved test performance, and higher levels of competency in problem solving, are all examples of program outcomes. Outcomes may be attendance rates, motivation levels, participation rates, and willingness to complete assignments. Key indicators of the effects of the developmental education program are graduation rates of developmental students, employment rates, and categories of the jobs the students have acquired.

Relating the Model to the Literature

The model presented in this chapter is consistent with the literature on program evaluation. The literature speaks to the need for evaluation to be addressed in three steps. Those steps include the planning of the program, the monitoring of the program, and the accountability of the program.

Resource evaluation can be considered as the planning step. Planning is essentially a managerial task. In an ideal administrative structure, all staff and faculty would be involved in the proposal to initiate a developmental education program. Step one involves the completion of a needs assessment. A useful question may be: Is the program needed and what evidence supports this recommendation?

The second step covers the monitoring purposes. This step involve determining if a program is adhering to the design delineated in step one. This step also has a formative evaluation perspective where information gained during monitoring is used to make necessary program modifications and enhancements.

The third step is outcome evaluation. The information collected at this step is critical to the decision making process on accountability. Helpful questions might be: Will the developmental studies program continue or will it be terminated? What contributions did the coordinator of the program make to the success or failure of the program? If the program continues, will there be changes in the delivery system?

Steps two and three are essential to the legal and budgetary concerns related to accountability. The three steps can occur continuously through out the life cycle of a developmental education program. The three step model presented in this chapter has incorporated these three key convictions.

Who Should Do the Program Evaluation?

Getting started requires that the stakeholders of a developmental education program be identified and an evaluation task force should be formed. Who should be represented on the evaluation task force becomes a critical decision that must be judiciously answered. Suggestions for facilitating the formation of the task force are to:

• Form a discussion group for the purpose of selecting a task force that will be given the responsibility for planning an evaluation study.

• Formulate a rationale for recommending each member on the constituted task force.

The task force becomes a representative body of the individuals involved in a developmental program. The advantage of having a task force is that the perspectives and ideas of all the constituents will be addressed. Decisions this task force may make are: What evaluation model should be used? Will the members of the developmental education program complete the evaluation, will an external person(s) complete the evaluation, or will there be a combination of the two?

Evaluation Points to Remember

The following points are offered to facilitate the use of this model:

1. Program evaluation results should lead to important improvements in the practice of developmental educators.

2. Program evaluation is designed to collect and analyze indicators on the status of the program.

3. Program evaluation measures student, program and college/university characteristics.

4. Program evaluation will collect and describe information on resources, interventions, and outcomes.

5. Program evaluation results are designed to improve decision making regarding the improvement, continuance, discontinuance, or expansion of a developmental education program.

Chapter 19

ഇറെ

A Model for Evaluating Developmental Students' College Persistence

Clara Wilson-Cook

Introduction

If a student fails, should he be shunned as an outcast from our colleges and universities? Should he be allowed a second opportunity to succeed or fail? Is academic failure a terminal disease or only a temporary malady? What is the prognosis for recovery from this condition? Can an institution salvage human potential by readmitting the failed student? (Browne, 1986, p. 90)

These challenging questions which confront educational administrators who are concerned with the reinstatement of academically dismissed students today are not new. Giesecke and Hancock's (1950) research evidenced that the decision whether or when to readmit a student who has been dismissed for unsatisfactory scholastic work is never an easy one.

It is surmised that this decision is made more often than not on the basis of inspired guess work. Specifically, the Committee responsible for making the decision to reinstate or deny a student's reinstatement to the university has limited information. The information is often gathered from the students' reinstatement application along with their written reasons for requesting reinstatement. Often, the Committee must try to secure more information from the admission and records office (i.e., complete transcript) as a part of the reinstatement process. Additionally, the Committee is representative of fulltime faculty and counselors for the student body-at-large; therefore, they find it difficult to commit the needed time to meet individually with the many students who find themselves seeking consideration for reinstatement in a given academic period. These factors (limited manpower and time allowance) usually impede a consistent review process. And, the constraints assuredly challenge the Committee to make an intuitive guess, which ultimately decides the fate of the student seeking a second chance at realizing his/her educational goals in higher education. The Committee rarely realize whether the decision to approve or deny a reinstatement of a student was an accurate one. Surprisingly, some forty years later, the literature does not refute the fact that we, as educators, know little about the outcome of students who are reinstated in institutions of higher education as a result of having experienced academic difficulty.

There is a proliferation of literature on studies of the initial admission to college; however, there are few studies that attempt to identify predictors of college success after academic dismissal. Although a disproportionate amount of administrative time is required to handle reinstated students who have been academically dismissed, little has been published about them or how to deal with them (Elliott, 1973). This population virtually goes unnoticed (unadvised and unmonitored) once they have matriculated back into institutions. Most institutions of higher education do not have tracking systems/programs to determine the persistence of these students (Wilson-Cook, 1990).

The reinstatement of the student who has failed academically [still] poses a serious problem for the university administrator (Lautz, MacLean, Vaughan, & Oliver, 1970). As administrators probe the problem of excessive academic failure, it is natural and proper that they should focus their attention initially on the admissions process. Ideally, students who might experience academic failure or withdrawal would be identified before college entrance. Such identification would certainly avert the personal and institutional difficulties which may result from [academic dismissal] withdrawal prior to graduation (Hansmeier, 1965). Unfortunately, however, it must be realistically acknowledged that certain factors, such as inconsistent admission standards and university requirements as well as the error of measurement relative to prediction of academic success or persistence will always partially negate efforts directed toward the prevention of student failure.

Whether students graduate from college depends on a combination of factors: the ability the students possess when they enter college, the intellectual motivation of the students, the intellectual climate that exists at the college, and the "match" between the needs, interests, and abilities of the students and the demands, rewards, and constraints of the particular setting (Astin, 1971; Feldman & Newcomb, 1970; Hossler, 1984; Hossler, 1985; Noel, 1985).

Tinto (1975) suggested that so many factors have an effect on students' progress toward a college degree that analyzing the "dropout phenomenon" (p. 76) is difficult. But such analysis is vitally important. One way to provide additional information for the ongoing study of the problem of withdrawal from college is to study the reinstated student (Cronklin, 1976). Cronklin suggested that reinstated students fall into two categories: those who withdrew from the college of their own volition and those who were academically ineligible to continue their education without interruption. Moreover, students in both groups share one important aspiration—the desire to resume their formal education. Additionally, Cronklin believes these students have determined for themselves that the college environment they previously abandoned [or were academically dismissed from] does not pose an impossible challenge to their hoped-for achievement in academia.

An Investigation of Students' College Persistence

The purpose of this investigation is to determine the correlation of academic performance and persistence of students reinstated in the College of Education (COE) after academic dismissal at a Midwestern State University. Specifically, this investigation examined selected characteristics (age, sex, college academic history, motivational data, marital status, ethnic background, and composite ACT scores) of reinstated students from January, 1980 - January, 1990 to determine whether there is a relationship between these characteristics and the academic persistence of the reinstated students. The relationship between the selected characteristics and the persistence of reinstated students, as indicated by matriculation for the semester of reinstatement, was also investigated. The high point of this investigation was to determine why some reinstated students persisted and why some did not persist through personal stratified interviews. It is presupposed that when selected characteristics of reinstated students are identified and examined in isolation and in multiples, relationships between their characteristics and academic persistence will be revealed.

This information will add to the existing body of knowledge concerning college retention and contribute to the development of viable policies and guidance practices to assist reinstated students in realizing their academic potential. The development of the purpose and the delineation of the reinstated students' characteristics to be investigated has led to the following research objectives:

1. To determine the number of reinstated students who were academically successful, as indicated by a grade point average reflected of University's Scholastic Deficiencies Chart or at least a 2.0 grade point average.

2. To determine if reinstated students by sex achieved a higher grade point average for the semester of reinstatement than the cumulative grade point average achieved at the time of dismissal.

3. To determine if reinstated students who stated academic difficulty as the reason for the discontinuance of their studies achieved lower grade point averages for the semester of reinstatement than their counterparts who gave non-academic reasons for the discontinuance of their studies.

4. To determine if reinstated students matriculating in the same major achieved a higher grade point average than reinstated students selecting a different major for the semester of reinstatement.

5. To determine the correlation of the ACT score to the grade point average achieved by the reinstated students for the semester of reinstatement.

6. To determine whether the longer reinstated students matriculated at the time of academic dismissal, as indicated by the number of semester hours completed, the higher the grade point average they will achieve for the semester of reinstatement.

7. To determine whether the older the students were upon reinstatement, the higher the grade point average they achieved for the semester of reinstatement.

8. To determine if reinstated students who were married upon reinstatement achieved a higher grade point average than reinstated students who were unmarried.

9. To determine if nonminority students persisted in their studies more than minority students during the semester of reinstatement.

10. To determine why some reinstated students did not persist in their educational objective(s).

11. To determine why some reinstated students continued with their educational objective(s).

12. To determine those characteristics, prior to academic dismissal, that distinguished those who persisted from those who did not.

13. To determine how many reinstated students continued to persist in their studies, dropped out, academically dismissed again, transferred to another college or university, or graduated after reinstatement.

The research objectives were based on the assumption that variables which have been proven empirically to be related to college student achievement and persistence in general may also be related to student achievement and persistence after reinstatement.

Definition of Terms

The following definitions of selected words and terms are used in this investigation:

Academic Dismissal - denotes a student who did not meet the University's academic requirements; for example, "had been on probation the previous semester and received a GPA more than 12 points below a 2.0 or as determined by scholastic requirements.

Academic Success - the degree of achievement in the academic course work as measured by a grade point average of 2.00 or higher.

Dropout or Voluntary Withdrawal - refers to a regularly matriculated student in a four-year degree granting program who, by her/his own decision, had terminated her/his college experience prior to the completion of a program of study. Students withdrawing from all courses prior to the completion of a semester were considered academically unsuccessful.

Grade Point Average (GPA) - a measure of scholastic performance. A GPA is obtained by dividing the number of grade points by the hours of work attempted. For the purpose of GPA, an A = 4 points, a B = 3 points, a C = 2 points, a D = 1 point, and a F = 0 point.

Grade Point Average After (GPAAFT) - the semester grade point average earned the semester of reinstatement.

Grade Point Average Prior (GPAP) - the cumulative grade point average earned prior to reinstatement.

Reinstatement - a process of readmitting students who had been academically dismissed.

Reinstated Student - a matriculated student who had sought and had been granted reinstatement to the COE after having been dismissed from the University for a period of at least one semester. There were two types of reinstated students: (1) new student - a student who was academically dismissed in another college and, subsequently, was reinstated in the COE, and (2) returning student - a student formerly enrolled in the COE. The reinstated students secured approval through the Academic Standards Committee in the COE.

Transfer Student - a student who was granted reinstatement in the COE, yet later decided to transfer to another college at the University.

Procedures

This investigation was restricted to 92 students who were reinstated in the COE from January, 1980–January, 1990. Of this number, 9 students were omitted from the investigation because the Student Information System (SIS) data source as well as an assessment of the transcripts showed that these students had not been dismissed but, instead, they requested reinstatement due to a break in matriculation. Minus this group, there were 83 students reinstated during the researched years.

Given the small number of reinstated students in the COE during the specified years, the total sample of reinstated students (83) was used initially in this investigation. Of that population, 55 were females and 28 were males; the ethnicity of this population represented 75 nonminorities and 8 minorities; the age ranged from 20 to 48 years old, and 71 were unmarried and 12 were married.

Much of the information required for making inferences could not be gathered from a single source. Therefore, several related methods were used in the investigation. These included survey procedures - the COE application for reinstatement, University Catalog, interviews, and the use of the University's Student Information System (SIS). The files of the identified reinstated students were examined to verify that they met the following criteria: (1) had been previously enrolled as a full-time student before academic dismissal; (2) had discontinued their studies for at least one semester; and (3) had attempted at least twelve credit hours during the semester of dismissal. The researcher developed one (1) instrument and three (3) interview questionnaires in order to gather the information needed for this investigation. This combination of methods and sources allowed for a greater synthesis of ideas concerning the persistence of reinstated students.

Sample and Sampling Procedure for Interviews

The population for the study (n = 83) was subdivided into 4 groups as follows (Figure 1): (1) 30 Persisters; (2) 29 Nonpersisters; (3) 11 Persisters/nonpersisters; and 13 Reinstated/No Shows. For the interview, 27 students were stratified from the first three groups (9 reinstated students in each group), then a predetermined quota (Isaac & Michael, 1987) of five females and four males were drawn at random from each group. A primary concern of this investigation was to determine what happened to the students who were reinstated and matriculated the semester of reinstatement during

Figure 1. Definition of the Reinstated Student

Persisters (n=30)	Nonpersisters (n=29)	Persisters/ Nonpersisters (n=11)	Reinstates/No Shows (n=13)
• Reinstated students enrolled with a 2.0 or better • Graduates • Students who were enrolled with a "continued probation" status (less than a 2 gpa)	• Students who failed to achieve a 2.0 gpa and were dismissed again	• Students who achieved at least a 2.0 gpa the semester of reinstatement, yet chose not to matriculate the following semester of reinstatement	• Students who were granted reinstatement but decided not to return to the University

Note: Successful reinstated students are classifed as Persisters. Unsuccessful reinstated students are classified as Nonpersisters, Persisters/Nonpersisters, and Reinstated/No Shows.

researched years; therefore, the reinstated/no show students were not considered for the interview. However, data were analyzed for this group. The sample for the interviews was taken from the University community.

Sex, age, ethnicity, marital status, composite ACT scores, academic history, and motivational data of reinstated students in the COE were the selected variables examined (Figure 2). Motivational data were obtained from the application for reinstatement. In order to assess the motivational data, the researcher developed an instrument to categorize the reinstated students' self-reported responses. The other selected variables (e.g., age, academic history, ACT scores) were obtained through the Student Information System (SIS). To determine whether the reinstated students' educational objectives were met, scheduled interviews were held with a randomly selected group of reinstated students.

Based on the kinds of responses assessed from the application for reinstatement, the reinstated students' explanation for their dismissal was classified under three headings: (1) academic, (2) nonacademic, and (3) other. An 'other' category was needed because of the varied responses. The reinstated students' primary reason for requesting reinstatement was classified under four headings: (1) personal, academic, (3) occupational, and (4) external (See Table 3).

Results

T-tests, Pearson correlation coefficients, frequency distributions, contingency tables, and LSD multiple comparisons were the statistical procedures used to analyze the seven variables of the reinstated students. In research objective 1, it was found that 41 (58.6%) of the 70 students who matriculated the semester of reinstatement were academically successful as indicated by a grade point average reflective of the Table 1. University's Deficiencies Chart or at least a 2.0; 3 of the 41 students who were identified as academically successful, achieved less than a 2.0 grade point average. These students were deemed academically successful because the university permitted them to matriculate with a "continued probation" status (See Table 1).

In response to objective one, the data shown in Table 1 indicate that 41 of the 70 students who reinstated the semester of reinstatement were academically successful by a grade point average of 2.0 or more. Four point three percent (4.3%) of the persisters (reinstated students enrolled and/or graduated) were permitted to re-enroll, although these students made less

Figure 2. Listing of Variables on Reinstated Students

• Male • Female	• Traditional students (20-22 years.) • Nontraditional students	• Nonminority (Caucasian - code 1) • Minority (African American - code 4, Asian American - code 6)	• Married • Unmarried	• Composite scores	• Cumulative GPA at dismissal • Cumulative semester hours at dismissal • GPA achieved at reinstatement • Semester hours achieved at reinstatement • Whether student transferred from another college/university • Whether student changed curriculum	• Primary reason for academic dismissal • Primary reason for requesting reinstatement

than a 2.0 and did not fall within the University's Scholastic Deficiencies Chart; they were permitted to continue their matriculation status by "continued probation." Therefore, these students were defined as successful; 41.4% were unsuccessful.

In research objective 2, it was found that there is no significant difference at the .05 level in the mean grade point average prior to reinstatement (GPAP) or by sex among the reinstated students (p = .553). However, there is a significant difference in means for the grade point average the semester of reinstatement (GPAAFT) among reinstated students (p = .001). Therefore, the reinstated students did achieve a higher GPAAFT.

In research objective 3, it was found that there are no significant differences in the means of GPAP and GPAAFT between academic and nonacademic reasons for dismissal, given by reinstated students. To determine research objective 4, three (3) categories of major selection were analyzed: (1) students who changed their majors within the COE, (2) students who did not change their major, and (3) students who changed their major outside of the COE. There was no significant difference at the .05 level (p = .678) between reinstated students who changed their major at reinstatement to those students who changed their major to another college, with respect to means GPAP and GPAAFT (p = .691 and p =.678).

For research objectives 5 and 6, there was a weak positive correlation (p = .270) between the reinstated students' composite ACT score and GPAAFT as well as a weak positive correlation (p = .124) between reinstated students' cumulative hours and GPAAFT.

For research objective 7, age was computed for 2 subgroups: (1) traditional students (20-22 years old) and (2) nontraditional students (23 years and older). There were weak positive correlations between age and

Table 1. GPAs of Reinstated Students (Persisters and Nonpersisters)

Group	GPA Less Than 2		GPA 2 or More		Total	
	n	%	n	%	N	%
Persisters	3	4.3	27	38.6	30	42.9
Nonpersisters	29	41.4	0	0	29	41.4
Persisters/ Nonpersisters	0	0	11	15.7	11	15.7
Total	32	45.7	38	54.3	70	100.0

GPAAFT of both groups (respectively, p = .058 and p .120). However, the literature infers that age (or maturation) does impact the grade point average positively.

For research objective 8, the results showed that there is a significant difference at the .05 level (p = .001) in GPAAFT between reinstated unmarried students and reinstated married students. In research objective 9, it was found that there was no significant difference at the .05 level (p=.324) in GPAAFT between nonminority students and minority reinstated students.

In research objectives 10 and 11, interviews were held with reinstated students in an attempt to understand why they persisted or were persisting after reinstatement and/or to understand why they did not persist. A summary of the interviews follows:

The responses of the reinstated students were reflective of the analysis of the motivational data taken from the application for reinstatement. Their reasons for academic dismissal varied from not being knowledgeable of the academic process to employment interference. Educational aspirations and maturation were the commonalities for requesting reinstatement. The counselor/advisor was named as the contact person sought when academic difficulty was experienced before dismissal. The professors and tutors were the contact persons seen after reinstatement.

The reinstatement process was described most favorably. The Academic Standards Committee (ASC) was viewed as being helpful in that it showed genuine concern for their (the reinstated students) welfare. An observation of a reinstatement meeting evidenced the ASC to be sensitive to the many extenuating circumstances shared by the students requesting reinstatement. The ASC made a conscientious effort to review the students' academic history. It is presupposed that the ASC wanted the students to understand the seriousness of their past performance and the reality of the conditions that they must realize in order to improve their existing grade point averages as well as to chart the routes to successful retention in the College of Education. The one thing that stood most in the minds of the students regarding the reinstatement process was that the ASC made them feel relaxed, thereby reducing their level of anxiety and stress. The recommendations made by the ASC regarding course retakes and study skills labs were agreeable to the students who had not retaken failing grades. There was one student who disagreed with the recommendations of the ASC; this disagreement went unknown to the ASC. The consensus of the students who did retake the failed courses and/or enrolled in the study skills labs believed that there was improvement in their grade point averages.

The students expressed much apprehension when sharing their feelings about the COE entrance requirements. Only one student was familiar with the entrance requirements to the Teacher Education Program in its totality. All except one student believed that certain provisions should be made for students who were reinstated with a grade point average of less than 1.00. This student believed that such a grade point average indicate that the students are not really serious about being in college and they are merely attending for the 'social life.' A probationary period (pre-reinstatement) to allow all reinstated students the chance to improve an existing low grade point average was the most focused provision the students believed should be instituted. Although all the students were adamant about what provision should be instituted, their feelings varied as to the advice the ASC should give to students with extremely low grade point averages. The most coherent response was that the Committee should make the students more responsive to them (e.g., make the students prove that they are following their recommendations before the probationary period for reinstatement is removed). More support programs that would enhance the reinstated students' skill development and awareness of the COE requirements were felt to be an essential role that the college could assume in helping their students meet entrance requirements. There were mixed feelings as to whether the University assumes an active role in helping students prevent academic dismissal and whether the University help reinstated students prevent future dismissals. The need to organize support groups for reinstated students was a main concern.

All the students expressed empathy and compassion for the students who would assumably be reinstated in the College. They strongly recommended that reinstated students take study skills courses seriously and to seek help immediately when experiencing academic difficulty. A program designated specifically to monitor and track reinstated students was believed to be the most needed of academic support services.

The advice for students seeking reinstatement in the COE regarding time management, employment, and extracurricular activities equated to "be careful." The students related that the diverse backgrounds (e.g. low grade point averages) as well as economical needs of reinstated students make it difficult to "just" be a student. Yet, they all felt that the reinstated students must also find ways to balance their personal responsibilities and course requirements.

In response to the general information after reinstatement, over 50% of the students changed their major during the reinstatement process. All except one said they interacted more with professors when experiencing academic difficulty and that they were visiting with their advisors more often. There were two students who felt they could not manage employment and academic requirements and, therefore, chose not to remain employed. Most students had reduced their involvement with extra-curricular activities. Perseverance, determination, and the restoration of self-esteem were factors they attributed to their success. Although the nonpersister did not matriculate after reinstatement, it was expressed that projected educational goals and objectives would be realized at another university. The discontinuance of academic studies was clearly opted by the persister/nonpersister because of personal problems. All students were very optimistic about their future graduation date. Data shown in Table 2 indicate that the persisters gave more academic reasons for their dismissal. The nonpersisters gave more nonacademic reasons. The breakdown of academic and nonacademic reasons are shown Table 3.

In response to research objective 12, the mean GPAP, composite ACT score, and cumulative semester hours at dismissal were the three pre-reinstatement variables used to make the comparison of the two groups. The results found the composite ACT score as the most distinguishable characteristic between the two groups. There was a weak positive linear correlation (respectively, p=.113) between the reinstated students' composite ACT scores and GPAAFT.

In research objective 13, it was found that of the 83 reinstated students, there were 30 (36.1%) persisters (inclusive of the 10 graduate students), and 53 (63.9%) students did not persist (nonpersisters-29 (34.9%), 11 (15.7%) students who were deemed academically successful by at least 2.0 or by continued probation status, but dropped after the semester of reinstatement; and 13.3% reinstated/no shows students who chose not to matriculate the semester of reinstatement. These percentages are based on the number of students (83) who were approved for reinstatement during the researched years. The reported persistence results represent the 70 students who actually matriculated the semester of reinstatement. Of the 70 students, 41 (58.6%) were successful and 29 (41.4%) were unsuccessful. Additionally, there were 10 graduates (minus this group from the 30 persisters, there were 20 students persisting in their studies at the time of this research). Six of the 83 students transferred to another college at the University after reinstatement in the COE.

Table 2. Motivational Data by Academic and Nonacademic Percentages of Reinstated Students

Subgroups	Academic		Nonacademic		Total	
	n	%	n	%	N	%
Persisters	17	20.5	13	15.7	30	36.1
Nonpersisters	9	10.8	20	24.1	29	34.9
Persisters/ Nonpersisters	4	4.8	7	8.4	11	13.3
Reinstated/ No Shows	4	4.8	9	10.8	13	15.7
Total	34	41.0	49	59.0	83	100

Discussion

A great number of students dismissed from other colleges within the University petition for reinstatement in the College of Education (COE) based on the notion that the curricula are easier "because of the de-emphasis on quantitative skills" (Yoder, 1963, p. 65). While the assumption here is debatable, most education majors believe the admission requirements to the COE are quite rigorous. Namely, the students are required to earn a cumulative GPA of 2.5 and completion of 90 hours before they are accepted into the teacher education program. Once the students meet the required GPA and hours, a pre-professional skills test (PPST) must be taken. Aside from the prerequisites, the students must satisfy other college requirements to graduate, such as completion of early field experience, and the Professional Knowledge section of the National Teachers Examination (NTE).

Students who have been academically dismissed are eligible to apply for reinstatement to any of the University's colleges instead of being limited to applying only to the college where they were dismissed. Dismissed students are reinstated only when approved for reinstatement by the Academic Standards Committee (ASC) of the college they are trying to enter. Normally, students must wait, or "sit out," at least one semester before they are considered for reinstatement. Students who earn a semester grade point average (GPA) of at least 2.0 but less than 2.2 for 12 or more credits hours during the semester they are dismissed can be considered for immediate reinstatement. However, for the College of Education, as mentioned, a 2.5 is the required grade point average for admission to the teacher education program (University General Catalog, 1988-90), whereas the required grade point average to enter most colleges is less than 2.5.

Until recently, there was a "knowledge void" about what happens to reinstated students. Very little was known as to how these students performed after reinstatement. Were they dismissed again? Did they leave the University? Or did they graduate? Compounding the problem is the fact that students are reinstated with considerable variation about the requirements needed to succeed (in the College of Education). Some students have three (3) years to go (before graduation), some have one (1) year. Also, some students are reinstated with a low GPA while "some are barely below the standard for dismissal" (L. Enochs, personal communication, February 28, 1990). Although the University has a retake policy which allows students to repeat up to five (5) courses (as a means of enabling the students to raise their cumulative grade point average), it does not have an academic forgiveness or bankruptcy policy. Perhaps, not having such a policy in place for aspiring education majors who have experienced academic dismissal often bleakens the reality of raising an existing low GPA.

Recommendations, Conclusions and Summary

The sex of a student is not significantly related to persistence after reinstatement. Also, this study found that sex differences in persisters and nonpersisters can be accounted for largely by differences in motivation and marital status. Cross (1971) and Pantages and Creedon (1978) reported that sex of the student has been found to have an equivocal relationship to academic failure with differences in the relationship between sex and attrition by the type of institution and by each institution having differing ratios of men and women.

There is a weak positive correlation between age and the persistence of reinstated students. The findings of this research are consistent with researchers who found that age, when considered alone does not seem to contribute significantly to the prediction of who will or will not persist after academic dismissal. However, Summerskill and Darling (1955) found that older students were less likely to graduate (i.e., because of the added responsibilities). The findings of this study do not confirm this presupposition. Also, for further analysis, the age of the students who were reinstated was divided into two categories: (1) 20-22 years old (traditional students), and (2) 23 and older (nontraditional students). The mean age of the traditional students was 21.27 (10) and the mean age of the nontraditional students was 27.04 (60).

Ethnicity was not significantly related to the persistence of the reinstated students. While this finding is consistent with Ott's (1988) research, the results are not consistent with Astin's (1972, 1982) reports that being black has a significant negative correlation with all measures of persistence. Although this study did not control for high school grades of the minority students (e.g., African American), the findings are consistent with Cronklin (1976), Sanford (1979), and Atkinson et al (1990) that if abilities and past achievement were comparable, minority students are less likely to drop out or experience academic dismissal than nonminority students. Further, the findings of this study do not indicate as does Preer (1981) that blacks are most likely to withdraw while whites and Asians are least likely to do so.

For marital status there is a significant difference between unmarried and married students' grade point averages for the semester of reinstatement. However, this study could not conclude that marrying tends to increase men's chances of persistence to women's chances of persistence until graduation (Cope & Hannah, 1975; Lenning, Beal & Sauer, 1980; Lenning, Sauer & Beal, 1980; Pantages & Creedon, 1978; Ramist, 1981). In fact, the analysis of the 10 graduates in this study show that married women persisted (4) over married men (0). Moreover, there were more single men (4) who graduated than single women (2). There is a weak positive correlation between the composite ACT scores and the grade point average the semester of reinstatement (GPAAFT). The findings indicate that this predictor variable should not be used in isolation when assessing measurements of persistence (Cope, 1971; Lautz, et al., 1970; Tinto, 1975).

For Academic History this investigation found there was a weak positive correlation between the cumulative semester hours at dismissal and the grade point average achieved the semester of reinstatement (GPAAFT). Also, there was a weak positive correlation between the grade point average prior to reinstatement (GPAP) and the (GPAAFT). As with the composite ACT scores, researchers caution using academic history as a predictor for persistence (Hansmeier, 1965; Ott, 1988; Tinto, 1975).

There was no significant difference between grade point average prior to reinstatement (GPAP) and grade point average the semester of reinstatement (GPAAFT) of those students who gave academic reasons for their dismissal to those students who gave nonacademic reasons. Although

Elliott's (1973) findings showed that men give more academic reasons for dismissal and women give more nonacademic reasons, this study found the opposite (women gave more academic reasons than men). The difference in the sex ratio, for this study, may account for the difference.

Interviews

The results of the interviews indicate that the students identified as persisters attributed their success to being more knowledgeable of campus resources, self-determined, interacted with faculty/advisors, and attended classes regularly. The students identified as nonpersisters attributed their lack of success to family problems (i.e., day care, budget constraints, illness). These findings correlated to the self-reported reasons taken from the application for reinstatement (See Table 3).

Data shown in Table 3 indicate the most frequent academic reason given by the 83 reinstated students for dismissal was poor study habits (37.3%). Employment interference (21.7%), not attending classes (19.3%), emotional problems/health (19.3%), lack of discipline (13.3%) and family problems (10.8%) were the most frequent nonacademic reasons given for dismissal. The category for "other" was the most dispersed (42%). Some examples given under this header were: "lack of interest in courses," "impersonal environment," "extracurricular activities," "University was too large," "drinking and partying," "undecided about major," "being away from home and peers," "transportation problem," and "was not mature enough." Data shown in Table 3 also indicate that 41.0% of the reinstated students gave personal reasons for requesting reinstatement (e.g. educational aspirational, self-awareness), 19.3% gave academic reasons (e.g. a desire to remove the existing low grade point average), 15.7% gave occupational reasons (e.g. job related), and 16.9% gave external reasons (e.g. a commitment made to family and/or peers).

**Table 3. Motivational Data of Reinstated Student
by Percentages and Self Reported Reasons**

Category	n		%
N = 83	No Response	Yes Response	
Academic Reasons for Dismissal			
Poor Advising	81		97.6
		2	2.4
Major Too Hard	81		97.6
		2	2.4
Poor Study Habits*	52		62.7
		31	37.3
Nonacademic Reasons for Dismissal			
Not Attending Classes*	67		80.7
		16	19.3
Lack of Discipline*	72		86.7
		11	13.3
Family Problems*	74		89.2
		9	13.3
Dating Problems	81		97.6
		2	2.4
Roommate	79		94.0
		5	6.0
Employment Interference	65		78.3
		18	21.7
Financial Aid Needed	80		96.4
		3	3.6
Emotional Problems*	67		80.7
		16	19.3
Death/Illness in Family	79		94.0
		5	6.0
Other*	41		49.4
		42	50.6
Reasons for Requesting Reinstatement			
Personal	49		59.0
		41.0	
Academic	67		80.7
		19.3	
Occupational	70		84.3
		15.7	
External	69	16.9	83.1

* indicates the most frequent responses

Conclusions

Motivational data (the students' self-reported reasons for dismissal) are not significant in predicting academic persistence among reinstated students. However, Figure 3 shows the recurring responses shared by nonpersisters during the personal interview. The researcher evidenced that the self-reported responses taken from the application for reinstatement were inconsistent with the responses given during the interview session. There was time lapse since their dismissal after reinstatement, and as a result, maturation could have made the difference in the responses.

Figure 3. Predictors of the Unsuccessful Reinstated Student*

less goal directed	daydreamer in class
more married males	fewer family problems
more single females	less active in classroom
bleak outlook on life	never changed major
more "D's and F's" courses	commutes to campus by city transit
more personal problems	poor health
involved in too many extracurricular activites	poor class attendance
poor time management	lower ACT scores (e.g., English, Math)
does not utilize support services	works fulltime (often holds two jobs)
lower gpa at reinstatement	lives off campus with peers
little interaction with faculty, advisor or peers	unfamiliar with scholastic requirements
unfamiliar with university environment	completed less hours prior to reinstatement
enrolled in more than one(1) remedial course	negative attitudes toward faculty
lower self-esteem	disruptive classroom behavior

* Much research has been done to determine the predictable variables for the successful students; however, this investigation determined the correlates of interviews to yield with students' self-reported responses and personal interviews to yield the predictors for the unsuccessful students. There is no descending order to the list.

Implications

Based on these conclusions, the following implications are drawn:

Low ACT scores should signal those students who will likely experience academic difficulty. The number of semester hours that students do not successfully complete the first semester of matriculation warrants immediate attention from significant persons (i.e., counselors, office of records, student affairs professionals). A change of major should signal those students who will likely experience academic difficulty.

The first probation status is a very strong indicator that the student is experiencing academic difficulty. The number of returning nontraditional students requesting reinstatement is an indicator that more support services (monitoring and tracking systems) are needed to assist in the retention rate of this population. The Academic Standards Committee should establish a check and balance system (through the appropriate offices) to determine whether the students remain committed to the conditions of reinstatement. The Academic Standards Committee seems to be paying too much attention to deciding reinstatement. The reinstated students might be better served by more careful monitoring and support after reinstatement.

Recommendations

As a result, of the findings of this study, the following recommendation is made:

A replication of this study in the College of Education (COE) for the purpose of determining:

a.   the persistence of reinstated students who live on campus to those who live off campus. The literature indicates that about 68% of the full time undergraduates in public universities are students who live off campus. Upcraft (1985) and Stewart et al. (1985) postulate that students who live off campus (commuters) may be particularly high attrition risks, in part because they have less time on campus to engage in activities and thus, they have reduced opportunities for social and academic integration. These researchers question the issue of retention, and specifically academic failure, of off campus students. Therefore, it would be interesting to find out how many reinstated students lived on/off campus and their persistence;

b.   what happened to the students who were denied reinstatement in the COE. This investigation did not look at the students who were denied reinstatement. Did the students transfer to another university to complete their educational objectives? Or did the students attempt to be reinstated in another college? Such a knowledge base could enhance strategic planning for recruitment of dismissed students;

c.   the characteristics of those students who graduated after reinstatement. This investigation examined the graduates with the persisters. It did not look at the graduates in isolation, therefore, an attempt to establish patterns or traits of the graduates should be distinguished (e.g. Did they change their major? Were they transfer students from another university? Did they have higher grade point averages at dismissal? Did they have higher composite ACT scores?;

d.   the persistence of students who are reinstated on continued probation status (i.e., students who are permitted to matriculate with less than a 2.0 grade point average, after reinstatement). This investigation determined there were 3 students identified as continued probation students. Although that is a small number, such knowledge would add further clarity to this population. The continued probation students were defined as persisters;

e.   a replication of this study at the University to determine the percentage of dismissed students who have been reinstated and their persistence, specifically minority students. Approximately 10,000 students were dismissed from the University during the researched years, which averages about 1,000 students per year. Determining what happened to these students should be a quest of the university's retention and attrition efforts; and

f.   interview more reinstated students to ascertain why some students persisted to those who did not. Interviewing this population was a high point of this investigation. It allowed the opportunity to hear these students' concerns and needs. As far as this investigation could determine, this was the first study that incorporated interviews as factors for understanding the persistence of reinstated students.

In addition to the subareas of this recommendation, the following steps for designing a retention model is suggested.

Designing a Model for the
Retention of Reinstated Students

1. Employ personnel to work specifically with this population.

2. Establish a database for students who have been reinstated at the university. For example, the database should detail the academic history prior to reinstatement, the bi-semester academic performance, break in matriculation, and whether the student matriculated the semester of reinstatement. Establishing a database could also differentiate those students who are reinstated into the colleges as a result of a break in matriculation from those who were academically dismissed. During the process of identifying reinstated students, it was realized that some students were erroneously identified as dismissed students whereas in fact, these students had only experienced a break in matriculation (i.e., had discontinued their studies for at least one semester). Interestingly, these students went before the Academic Standards Committee (ASC) and were granted reinstatement. This mode of operation of the ASC is certainly questionable.

3. Establish a monitoring and tracking system to target those reinstated students who may be experiencing early academic difficulty after reinstatement. "…[S]uch a system allows for immediate feedback about the students' academic performance and their likelihood of succeeding" (Smittle, et al.1989, p. 44). It also allows for networking with the faculty/ advisor and establishing interaction with student. This process will minimize the predictors as outlined (Figure 3).

4. Establish a support group with students who have been reinstated. This support group should consist of formal (academically dismissed) reinstated students. Such a group can bolster self-esteem and decrease anxiety levels which reinstated students experience (Bers & Rubin, 1989; Boyer, 1986, 1987; Brown & DeCoster, 1982; House & Wohlt, 1990; Sanford, 1979). The reinstated students who were interviewed expressed that their low self-esteem and high stress levels were most prevalent at dismissal and then again at reinstatement. This support group can also assist in the awareness and use of university resources (e.g. labs, child care, financial assistance, study groups, rap session).

5.   At reinstatement, the personnel should have students commit to a written "contract" after explaining reinstatement conditions (e.g. students should evidence that they are honoring their conditions for reinstatement such as planned class schedules and recommended as well as use of support services). The signed contract is a commitment by the reinstated students to show improvement in their academic performance (Akridge & Ross, 1987; Chapman, 1982; Pervin, 1966). The Committee should communicate the conditions of the student's reinstatement to the appropriate offices and thus, request at least bi-monthly follow-up on the reinstated students for the semester of reinstatement. And monthly follow-up should be made for at least the next three (3) semesters or until graduation—whichever comes first.

6.   Students with extremely low grade point averages (below 1.50) should be placed on probationary reinstatement. This was one of the concerns strongly expressed by the reinstated students who were interviewed. A probationary period would allow a student a substantial opportunity to achieve a significant improvement in their grade point average. In addition, this period would likely reduce the stress of having to achieve a 2.0 grade point average the semester of reinstatement or become academically dismissed again (after an extended absence from school). It is recommended that the conditions of the probationary period should allow the students 2 semesters to bring the semester grade point average up to a 2.0. It is believed that such a policy would encourage more reinstated students to remain hopeful in their educational endeavors. Additionally, this student should not be permitted to take remedial and academic courses concurrently. Giesecke and Hancock (1950) most eloquently stated "…That it is unrealistic to expect every student to overcome in the first term following readmission those factors which caused his/her failure" (p. 72). It is believed that such institution of a probationary policy could decrease the percentage of reinstated/no show students as well as to retain more of the students constituted as nonpersisters. The presupposition regarding the nonpersisters who refused the interview is based on their comments made by telephone. Namely, they believed that it would be too difficult to bring their grade point average up to the required 2.5 for the COE, thus expressing that they had nothing else to share before declining the requested interview.

7. An academic bankruptcy policy should be implemented in an attempt to salvage the academic potential of students desiring a "fresh" start (Browne, 1986, 1987; Masat, 1984; Winchell, 1987). The implementation of this policy could mainly assist (1) those students who have less than a 1.50 grade point average at reinstatement and or less than 25 semester hours, and (2) those students who have had an extended absence from the university, particularly for poor scholarship. It is realized that the University has a retake policy which allows the student the opportunity to repeat up to 5 failing grades, however, for the latter population there is no relief system or virtually no programs in place specifically for retention. Namely, these students matriculate back into the university with unwarranted excess baggage that was perhaps generated because of immaturity or lack of college adjustment, yet they have to attend to those grades that will no doubtedly hinder them from being able to enroll in their area of desired specialty. It is also realized that the Faculty Senate at the University has recently "tabled" the discussion of the implementation of an academic bankruptcy policy; however, it is concurred with the author of the proposal that we should seriously look at the implications of not instituting such a policy. In the words of Browne (1986), "by expunging a previous record, an individual may re-enter without a millstone from the past. Should not a democratic institution that encourages individuals to succeed also allow them to an unfettered right to try again (p. 91)?"

8. The point is that those students with grade point averages below a 1.50 should be considered for the proposed probationary reinstatement period rather than being subjected to the "specified minimum period" of one semester. "The wisdom of the practice of allowing reinstatement to all students alike for a specified minimum period of time is open to serious question" (Giesecke & Hancock, 1950, p. 78). Unfortunately, this practice still persists at most institutions of higher education some forty years later. It is evidenced that there are extenuating circumstances rather than nonacademic ability that lead a great number of dismissed students to academic failure. Therefore more often than not, reinstated students with extremely low grade point averages find it impossible to raise their semester grade point average to a 2.0 as required by the University for the semester of reinstatement. Of particular concern is the 2.5 barrier that students must achieve in the COE before they can petition for admission to the core education program. This investigation found that

only 10 of the 83 reinstated students had graduated over a ten-year period. Given this data, the 2.5 barrier is certainly a questionable cause as correlated to the earned grade point averages after the semester of reinstatement and/or effect as to why these students are not ascertaining their educational goals in the COE. Note: this recommendation can be generalized to other colleges.

9. Establish more minority support groups or role models for morale building. Research show that students tend to perform better academically when they have role models of the same ethnic group to share their concerns. This recommendation can be generalized to the minority students at either predominant ethnic university.

10. The Academic Standards Committee (ARC) and the College of Education (COE) may wish to review its efficacy in light of these findings and recommendations.

Summary

Although it is clearly recognized that there is a paucity of research on the reinstated student in higher education, the increased numbers of dismissed students from the University is an indicator that more intervention strategies for the retention of students who are experiencing academic difficulty should be implemented. It is theorized that we cannot begin to effectuate change or improve the retention rates of reinstated students until we have programs designed to track and monitor these students. Several studies posited the question as to whether the academically deficient student is at risk (e.g., Taylor, et al, 1987). Based on the literature, the answer is postulated, "yes!"

Granted, institutions of higher education are beginning to show ingenuity in developing programs and curricular to help remediate students who may experience academic difficulty (Anliot & Oncley, 1989; Blanchette, 1994; Fogel & Yaffe, 1992; Gillespie & Noble, 1992; Hall, 1994; Han & Ganges, 1995; Hood, 1992; Krotseng, 1991; Noel, 1985; Roueche & Roueche, 1994; Slith & Russell, 1994; Tatum & Rasool, 1992; Windham, 1995); however, there is little evidence that personnel are in place to work specifically with this population. Given that more students are entering college who read below the eighth-grade level (Rouche, Baker, & Rouche, 1984), Cross (1985) suggested "we have no more right to expect a student without reading [or academic] skills to be an effective learner than we do to expect a carpenter without a hammer to be effective at pounding nails" (p. 124). The literature shows that these are the same students who are placed on academic probation and later on academic dismissal; and thus, who often return to the university by reinstatement. These students are re-entering the University with the same academic deficits. Unless the institutions of higher education are prepared to assist this population with special programming and guidance designed specifically for them, then these students are being reinstated with "inflated" hope.

Chapter 20

ℰⱺℭℛ

Developing a Perspective for an Institutional Assessment Model for Developmental Education Program Evaluation

Vernon L. Farmer, Neari F. Warner and Raymond A. Hicks

Introduction

During the past three decades increasing rhetoric has been devoted to educational quality, a dimension that is difficult to measure in any educational program. Previous commitment to greater access in higher education, however, may be in conflict with increasing emphasis on educational quality and accountability. The egalitarian philosophy (greater access) of educational programs resulted not only in an increase in student enrollment, but also of institutional function in higher education. Some argued that the egalitarian philosophy of educational programs may be out of synchronization with current concerns about student learning outcomes and program quality. Tomlinson (1989) stated that "In some systems, future changes in the profile of the developmental population will, no doubt, be a function of recent changes in policy related to efforts to improve quality" (p. 80). However, as higher education institutions make these changes in policies in their attempt to improve educational quality, they must be careful not to create new inequalities for the new student clientele on college campuses. Keimig (1983) argued that "Institutions can turn their backs neither on academic standards nor on countless students who have been a product of inferior [public school systems] schooling" (Forward to *Raising Academic Standards: A Guide to Learning Improvement*). In the new millennium the student population in higher education will become increasingly more diverse in race, ethnicity, and age which suggests that the traditional measure of student success may be far less significant than in the past millennium. Rendon (1994) reported that the 1990s ushered in a changing student demography: (a) the majority of college students were women, (b) a new wave of immigrants entered school and colleges, (c) adult students over 25 constituted a sizeable proportion of the student body, (d) African American, Mexican American, Puerto Rican, American Indian, and Asian students emerged as a new student majority on some campuses, (e) sizeable numbers of first-generation students (first in their family to attend college) enrolled in college, (f) many students from families with poverty level incomes seeded a college degree as a means to a better life, and (g) non-racial student minorities such as disabled students, gays and lesbians, and Jewish students demanded colleges and universities respond to their needs. Many of these students will undoubtedly need support from effective developmental education programs if they are to be successful.

Meanwhile, in this period of educational accountability we can expect tremendous pressure on higher education institutions to provide evidence of developmental education programs' value and long-range effect (Maxwell, 1979). With this in mind, public policy must therefore focus much more on student assessment outcomes rather than the magnitude of the student population and the prestige of academic programs in higher education institutions. Kerschner (1987) insisted that "...student outcomes assessment is not a single matter; rather, it is rife with a whole series of public policy questions that must be answered before it can be used appropriately" (p. 30). A large number of higher education institutions have already begun to initiate changes in institutional policies in order to place more emphasis on student assessment outcomes in developmental education programs. Halpern (1987) maintained that with student outcomes assessment, "...institutions can refocus priorities so that educational quality is based on what and how much students learn..." (p. 6). This would show that when student gains serve as the focal point of assessment in higher education institutions, educational quality and student learning outcomes are improved.

A Review of the Literature

Related Research

What does the research say about developmental education programs in higher education institutions? Some of the earlier studies showed that both positive and negative relationships between GPA gains and developmental student participation in developmental education programs were commonplace, making a definitive assessment of developmental students' learning outcomes for the most part, difficult to achieve (Cross, 1975, 1976; Gordon, 1975; Grant & Hoeber,1978; Halpern, 1987; Jacobi, Astin & Ayala 1987; Raygor, 1974; Richardson, 1981; Roueche & Snow, 1977; Santeusanio, 1974; Sherman & Tinto 1975; Snow 1977; Summers, 1979; Tilman, 1973; Tomlinson, 1989; Trillin 1980). Nevertheless, a number of well designed studies during the same period did show more consistently positive results (Allarie, 1979; Bellucci,1981; Carter,1976; Donovan, 1975; Moore, 1977; Sutherland & Sutherland,1982; Whimbey, Boylan, & Burke, 1979).

Tomlinson (1989) asserted that assessments of the validity and reliability of some of the earlier developmental program evaluations caused some concern as to the adequacy of the research designs used to evaluate the effectiveness of developmental education programs in higher education institutions. She further explained that

> ...program effectiveness has been based on varying criteria for measuring improvement, ranging from specific skill performance to grade point average, matriculation, and persistence; applied to a variety of types of schools, selective and public; within the various regions of variables from program to program confounds systematic comparative assessments. (p. 55)

The research showed that most of the earlier research designs used for institutional assessment and program evaluation prior to the 1960s were deficient (Raygor, 1974). Keimig (1983) argued that the widespread use of these deficient research designs may have depressed the results and obscured the relative strengths and weaknesses of various types of developmental programs and practices during this period.

In an attempt to determine the extent to which comprehensive systematic institutional assessment and evaluation programs were employed earlier in higher education institutions to evaluate developmental education programs, several nationwide studies were reviewed for inclusion in this chapter (Ball & Anderson, 1975; Hodgkinson, 1975; Roueche, Baker & Roueche, 1984). Ball and Anderson's survey of 200 developmental education programs showed that higher education institutions for the most part had implemented few systematic assessment and evaluation studies to determine the effectiveness of developmental education programs. Meanwhile, Hodgkinson's (1975) study of 375 colleges and universities provided similar evidence that vigorous, analytical assessment procedures were frequently present in higher education institutions, and even when assessments were implemented, they consisted mainly of survey questionnaires designed primarily to obtain information about students' and faculty's perception of developmental programs effectiveness. Finally, Roueche's et al. (1984) nationwide survey of 1,452 two- and four-year colleges provided further evidence that systematic assessment procedures were not in place to evaluate basic skills programs in higher education institutions during this period. Roueche's findings showed that data collected for assessment purposes were limited to students' performance in developmental studies and did not show the application of basic skills acquired in these courses to regular college studies. Finally, lack of emphasis on systematic assessment and program evaluation was clearly evident throughout the research literature.

Meta-Analyses Studies

In an attempt to determine developmental students' learning outcomes in developmental programs in higher education institutions, we must not only consider the findings of single evaluation studies, but also must the findings of meta-analyses studies. Therefore, this chapter consists of a review of the findings of several studies that employed meta-analysis techniques. Meta-analysis has been used in a number of areas in higher education during the past two decades (Boylan, 1983; Burley, 1994; Johnson, Maruyama, Johnson, Nelson, & Skon, 1981; Kulik, Kulik, & Bangert-Drowns, 1990; Kulik, Kulik, & Cohen, 1979; Kulik, Kulik, & Shwalb, 1983; Whitener, 1989; Wise & Okey,1983). Glass (1976) developed the meta-analysis statistical method to help researchers draw more reliable conclusions from the data. He defined meta-analysis as the statistical analysis of a large collection of results from single research studies with the objective of integrating the findings. The goal of meta-analysts is to use multivariate techniques to describe research findings and to relate characteristics of studies to outcome. Glass argued that this method allows for more reliable and valid conclusions because of the multivariate techniques used to analyze the data and make sense out of the research. Glass, McGaw and Smith (1981) view meta-analysis as an important quantitative technique since it uses numbers and statistical methods for organizing and extracting information from large masses of data that are nearly incomprehensible by other methods. They also point out that the findings of studies are not ignored *a priori* by imposing what may be arbitrary and non-empirical criteria of research quality.

A meta-analysis computes standard scores for various treatments' gains or losses by dividing the difference between pretest scores by the pooled standard deviation of posttest scores for all groups in the study. The resulting score, referred to as effect size, reports a given treatment gain or loss in terms of standard score units. Consequently, a given treatment might be said to have an experimental effect size of .5 standard deviation, meaning that the gain for the average student in the experimental group is .5 standard deviations greater than the gain for the average student in the control group.

Effect sizes can be accumulated across studies. The meta-analysis techniques developed by Hedges (1981) weights each effect size by the reciprocal of its variance so that the accumulation is not simply an average of raw effect sizes, but a mean effect size dependent on the variance of its constituents. He goes on to argue that the major goal of this technique is to explain the variability among the characteristics of the treatments in relation to the variability of their effect sizes. This technique involves categorizing the treatments along various dimensions (e.g., instructional mode, focus of instruction, duration), comparing mean effect sizes of treatments grouped together, and testing the studies grouped together for homogeneity (Hedges, 1982). Finally, the simple comparison of mean effect sizes provides useful information about the effectiveness of treatments.

This chapter includes meta-analyses studies and research concerned specifically with the evaluation of developmental education programs in higher education institutions (Boylan, 1983; Burley, 1994; Kulik, Kulik & Shwalb, 1983). Kulik, Kulik and Shwalb employed the meta-analysis techniques of Glass (1976) and Glass, McGaw and Smith (1981) to analyze 60 evaluation studies. The meta-analysis showed that developmental programs tended to have positive effects on developmental students. For instance, developmental students who enrolled in developmental programs tended to remain in college longer than traditionally admitted students and earned higher grades in regular college courses. The meta-analysis showed that program effects were statistically reliable. Although small in size the effects ranged in magnitude from high positive to moderate negative in the 60 studies. The findings also showed that effect size varied as a result of the type and the age of the developmental program being evaluated.

The 60 studies investigated in Kulik, Kulik and Shwalb's (1983) meta-analysis showed developmental program effects in both student achievement and student persistence in college. Achievement was measured by a student's grade-point average (GPA) in subsequent college courses after completing developmental courses. Meanwhile, persistence was measured by the proportion of developmental students who were initially admitted and remained enrolled during the evaluation period. In several of the studies, the evaluation period was one or two semesters, which was also the timeframe for the treatment period. However, in most studies the evaluation period for developmental programs was much longer than one or two semesters.

All but 3 of the 60 studies in Kulik, Kulik and Shwalb's (1983) meta-analysis reported GPA and college persistence results for students in both developmental and regular college programs. In 13 studies, students in regular courses had higher GPAs than students in developmental courses, while students in developmental courses had higher GPAs than students in regular courses in 44 studies. Meanwhile, 17 of the 57 studies showed a significant difference in GPAs for students in developmental courses while only one study showed a significant difference in GPAs for students in regular courses. In other words, a positive effect for students in developmental courses was identified in 16 of the 17 studies. The meta-analysis of Kulik, Kulik and Shwalb also showed dissimilarity in GPAs for students in developmental and regular college courses corresponding to an effect size of .27; the standard deviation of effect size was .31, and the standard error was .04. The results showed that in the typical study, GPAs for students in developmental courses were 2.03 and 1.82 for students in regular courses for the previous semester enrolled, respectively.

Meanwhile, 30 of the 60 studies in Kulik, Kulik and Shwalb's (1983) meta-analysis focused on the effectiveness of developmental programs on developmental students' college persistence. Persistence was defined as the ratio of admitted students who remained in the developmental education programs during the duration of the study. The rate of persistence was higher for students in 9 of the 30 studies that evaluated the effectiveness of developmental programs. Meanwhile, the persistence rate was higher for students in regular programs in 5 of the 30 studies and statistically significant in 11 of the studies. The findings for both GPA and persistence indicated positive effects for developmental education programs.

Finally, Kulik, Kulik and Shwalb's meta-analysis (1983) showed that the effect size on college students' persistence varied in effect size similar to GPA. These researchers suggested that this variation raised the question that different categories of studies may possess different average persistence rates. Comparative analysis of average persistence rates in various courses identified three factors related to persistence outcomes, including classification of students upon entry into developmental programs, the type of higher education institutions in which developmental programs are offered, and the time period in which the study is implemented. The results showed that effect sizes were larger for developmental programs that began in high school compared to those that began in the freshman year of college, while persistence rates effect size was smaller for developmental programs that began after the freshman year. Overall, Kulik, Kulik and Shwalb's meta-analysis found developmental education programs to be moderately effective in enhancing learning outcomes of developmental learners in higher education institutions.

Burley (1994) employed the meta-analysis techniques of Glass (1976) and Hedges and Olkin (1985) to determine the effects of developmental student achievement, attitude, and persistence in a subset of 27 developmental studies programs. Burley sought answers to several vital questions: What are the effects of developmental studies on college student achievement? What are the effects of developmental studies on college student attitude? and What are the effects of developmental studies on college student persistence? These questions are particularly important when one considers the high attrition rate of developmental learners attending higher education institutions.

In Burley's (1994) meta-analysis, 27 surveys of developmental studies programs produced 40 effect sizes as a result of the meta-analysis technique. The effect size for achievement was the smallest (ES = .134, K = 23). Meanwhile, the effect size for attitude (ES = .27, K = 5) and for persistence was larger (ES = .30, K = 12), respectively. Although the effect sizes for attitude and persistence were larger, the effect sizes were still small. Of the 40 effect sizes produced from the 27 studies, the overall effect size was small (ES = .20). Nevertheless, these effects of developmental studies on developmental students' learning outcomes were positive. Even though 60% of these effect sizes were positive, strong negative effects of developmental studies' achievement effects significantly moderated the overall effect size.

Burley's (1994) meta-analysis further showed that when achievement effects were considered, the percentage of positive effect sizes dropped to

52% of the total. Studies that reported achievement results, posttests, final course grades, next course grades, or GPA had the majority of negative effect sizes. The overall effect size for student achievement was .134. The majority of these studies did not specify a particular methodology other than a developmental studies program; therefore, they were categorized as simply remediation. The overall effect size for student achievement-remediation was .07.

Only five studies considered student attitude toward remedial programs. The overall effect size was .27. Twelve studies focused on student persistence; the overall effect size for these studies was .30. The persistence statistics are all effect size estimates that are derived from percentages of students who returned to the college during the final semester of the treatment period.

The purpose of Boylan's (1983) nationwide study was to test three research assumptions based on his analysis of 51 evaluation studies. The study assumed that developmental education activities might be judged as effective if evidence showed that developmental education program activities (a) improved the basic skills of students participating in developmental education programs, (b) resulted in higher grades for students participating in developmental education programs when compared to students who did not participate, and (c) resulted in higher rates of retention for students who participate in developmental education programs when compared to students who did not participate. Boylan's research, although not described as a meta-analysis study, employed many of the meta-analysis techniques developed by Glass (1976), Glass, McGaw, and Smith (1981), Hedges (1981), and Hedges and Olkin (1985). Boylan conducted a survey of developmental education research and evaluation studies and reports that employed several sources to identify information relevant to his research assumptions. His analysis examined evaluation studies and reports (journal articles, books, monographs, and unpublished reports) identified from a manual, computer and DIALOG online literature search. The survey also included evaluation studies and reports identified from a call for papers in the National Association for Remedial and Developmental Studies in Postsecondary Education (NARDSPE) Newsletter. Of the 73 evaluation studies and reports reviewed using these sources, 51 were considered eligible for analysis in Boylan's study. To be eligible, evaluation studies and reports selected for analysis in this study must have possessed quantifiable outcomes and a reasonably sound methodology that employed appropriate statistical methods. The selected evaluation studies and reports had to meet the following criteria, including the suitability of setting, the suitability of subjects, the nature and recency of the data for this period, the method of study, and the relevance of information.

The findings of 51 evaluation studies and reports of the 73 reviewed were selected to test Boylan's (1983) research assumptions. Boylan pointed out that it was difficult to test these assumptions empirically due to the fact that many of the evaluation reports' measures were indirect and suffer from a number of limitations. He argued that the general findings of the 51 evaluation studies and reports did, however, provide valuable information in determining developmental education program effectiveness in enhancing students' learning outcomes in higher education institutions.

An analysis of research on the effectiveness of developmental education programs concerned with basic skills development, GPA improvement, and retention rates is presented by Boylan (1983). In his analysis of studies concerned with basic skills development, the findings revealed that: "(a) underprepared students who participate in basic skills courses tend to show measurable gains in skill development as assessed by a variety of standardized and locally-developed instruments, (b) underprepared students who participate in basic skills courses tend to show greater measurable gains in skill development than similar students who do not participate in such course, and (c) developmental programs offering credit for participation in basic skills courses tend to show greater gains from pre-test to post-test in those courses than programs which do not offer credit" (pp. 30-35). However, the degree of basic skill improvement varied from developmental program to developmental program and from student to student. Moreover, underprepared students' basic skill improvement after enrollment in skill development courses tends to be consistent apart from the instructional methods or the measurements used to determine gain.

A second major finding of Boylan's (1983) study indicated that developmental education programs improved underprepared students' grade point averages (GPAs). For example, "(a) students with low grade point averages tend to improve their GPA's following participation in the developmental program, and (b) underprepared students who participate in developmental programs tend to obtain higher grades than similar students who do not participate" (pp. 28-29).

A third major finding of Boylan's (1983) study demonstrated, without question, that underprepared student participation in developmental programs lead to higher rates of retention. In reviewing the data on retention in developmental programs, it appears that: (a) underprepared students who participate in developmental programs are retained to a greater extent than would be expected based on admissions credentials, (b) underprepared students who participate in developmental programs are more likely to be retained than those who do not, (c) underprepared students who participate in developmental programs are frequently retained at higher rates than better prepared students with superior admissions credentials" (pp. 29-30). When considering all the measures used to confirm the idea that developmental education produces a positive effect on higher education, the record of developmental education is perhaps the strongest in increasing underprepared students' retention rates.

Finally, Boylan (1983) cautions us that some of the techniques used in these studies were subject to limitations of validity and reliability. He further argued that the use of gain scores is subject to limitations, possibly as a result of the interactive effect of pretesting. The use of grade point averages as a measure of the effect of a particular treatment does not take into account intervening variables that may have an impact on student GPAs. Meanwhile, retention data is subject to an even greater number of intervening variables that may affect the persistence rates of developmental college students.

In summary, the overall findings of Boylan (1983), Burley (1994), and Kulik, Kulik, and Shwalb's (1983) studies presented in this chapter showed that developmental education programs, for the most part, have been effective in raising students' GPAs, in increasing students' basic skills, in improving students' attitudes, in enhancing students' academic achievement, and in increasing the overall persistence and retention rates of developmental students in higher education institutions.

A Perspective for an Institutional Assessment Model

The research and related literature reveals that educators now recognize that many of the developmental education programs established prior to the 1970s were shaped by policies and practices of previous decades. This research led to an increased interest in a nationwide effort to clarify institutional assessment policies and practices in higher education. However, more research is needed to examine past policies and practices in order to provide educators with the data needed for building the conceptual framework critical to developing a perspective for an institutional assessment model to evaluate developmental education programs effectiveness in higher education institutions. Some of the goals to guide this research are (a) to determine the extent to which commonalties exists in success measures as defined by developmental education programs in higher education institutions, (b) to determine the extent to which assessment data are available to evaluate developmental education programs effectiveness, in improving students' learning outcomes, and (c) to determine the flexibility of alternative methods for evaluating the effectiveness of developmental education programs and developmental students' learning outcomes.

Research Problems

The primary research problems that must be examined when developing an institutional assessment model for developmental education program evaluation to determine student learning outcomes, however, are broader than a straight-forward query of whether these programs are effective. The delivery system as well as the terminology used to describe these programs are basic to understanding program focus and assessment concerns necessary for developing a perspective for an institutional assessment model. However, the terminology used to define these special programs prior to the mid 1980s presented a major problem for educators conducting research in developmental education. Higher education institutions have used various labels or terms (compensatory, basic skills, remedial, developmental, preparatory etc.) to describe their special programs with little or no consensus on which term or terminology should be employed. Meanwhile, depending on the type of higher education institution and the time period, students with skill deficiencies have been described and special programs designed to resolve these problems utilizing a variety of labels (See Table 1). The authors have slightly revised Table 1 by adding student labels used since 1989.*

The absence of a common definition of terminology to describe these special programs and special needs students has been a major problem for researchers in their attempt to identify appropriate criteria for developmental education program evaluation. The research by far has shown that there have been few attempts to distinguish between the various definitions of terminology, but rather reveal that the definitions have been used in tandem to reflect similar usage among higher education institutions.

Although the field of developmental education is relatively new, it is clearly evident that it has not been adequately defined in the research literature. Much of the research literature has focused on the issue of remedial education versus developmental education. Roueche and Wheeler (1973) described remedial education programs as being designed to remove student deficiencies so that they may enter a college program for which they were previously unprepared. Cross (1976) and Maxwell (1979) called attention to distinctions between remedial and developmental education. Remedial

Table 1. Labels Used for Developmental Programs and Their Student Populations from 1860 to Present (Tomlinson, 1989)

Time Span	Program Labels	Student Labels
1860s to 1890s	college preparatory preparatory studies	special students
1900s to 1940s	remedial assistance learning assistance how-to-study	underachievers underprepared students
1950s to present	compensatory special studies academic skills services basic skills college reading academic rehabilitation college study skills academic support learning assistance remedial developmental	low ability underachievers disadvantaged underprepared deficient high risk nontraditional *remedial *developmental

education, Cross and Maxwell agreed, involved bringing underprepared students, especially those with the weakest preparation, up to the levels of skills required for success at their institutions. However, Cross believes that developmental education was a broader term signifying the goal of talent development for typical students at any given institution. Maxwell maintains, in contrast, that the term developmental education came into use to avoid the stigma of remedial education. Indeed, many states would not fund remedial programs while they would subsidize developmental education (Maxwell, 1979). However, Maxwell pointed out that when waves of underprepared students entered higher education in the 1960s and 1970s, they became the more typical students. Although remedial and developmental education are sometimes used synonymously, with developmental education preferred as an ameliorative designation, there are many other terms that have been associated with developmental education throughout its history.

During the mid 1980s and the 1990s some real distinction in terminology began to evolve making it more possible to develop effective institutional assessment models for developmental education program evaluation. The

Illinois Association for Personalized Learning Programs (1985) states that "Developmental education is an umbrella term for a variety of instructional programs and individualized services that are unified by basic educational assumptions about variation of learning style being greater than ability to learn, variation of age for the achievement of educational potential, and the ability of those with varied cultural or environmental backgrounds or physical or economic handicaps to learn-given the appropriate conditions and strategies" (Tomlinson, 1989, pp.8-9).

Grambling State University (GSU) (home of the nation's only doctoral degree program with a major in developmental education) defines developmental education as the umbrella for services ranging from remediation to enrichment. It recognizes that even though a student might be intellectually capable, the absence of successful linking experiences and/or the preference for a certain academic area play a major role in how well the student performs academically in a given area. Assessments of student performance may yield prescriptions which call for remediating or enriching responses from developmental personnel. In large measure, and based upon the definition of developmental learners, remediation and enrichment differ only in the degree to which there is an absence of experience or intellectual preference in an area on the part of the learner. This philosophical viewpoint permeates the educational programs at all graduate degree levels in developmental education at Grambling State University and serves to guide faculty in the development of curriculum and instruction.

Who are the developmental learners or students as described by Grambling State University? They are those students who for various reasons: (a) perform poorly or unevenly on standardized achievement tests, (b) need preparatory or review work in basic skills subjects before pursuing regular degree programs, (c) undertake enriching experiences to improve average and below average academic performance, (d) require non-instructional support that leads to self-awareness, academic responsibility and "careerwiseness," (e) need remediation in areas where academic growth fails to occur at an acceptable rate, and/or (f) require additional training to meet changing job demands.

Grambling's graduate faculty is the belief that developmental learners need assistance in achieving growth in one of a combination of academic, social-emotional areas. They might have such needs as entrants, or their needs may emerge throughout their academic careers. Thus developmental education personnel must be prepared to render services at all levels of the academic ladder. They must be prepared to examine the developmental learner from a holistic perspective and utilize this perspective to)a) create supportive learning climates, (b) provide appropriate curriculum and instruction, and (c) help students adjust to the changes in life-style demanded by postsecondary studies and environments.

Grambling State University's advanced degree programs in developmental education are designed to train developmental educators to specifically assist adult learners to improve their study skills and academic performance in areas such as reading, English and mathematics through the delivery of instruction in regular classroom settings, distant learning, tutorial programs, counseling activities, and related support services. Because developmental education is a relatively young. Grambling prepares not only practitioners for the areas cited above, but also managers, program developers, administrators and researchers to facilitate the work of developmental practitioners (Handbook for Advisors and Students: Graduate Programs in Developmental Education, 1986).

Finally in 1996, a national definition along with a set of goals was developed by the National Association of Developmental Education (NADE) with significant input from the graduate programs in developmental education at GSU. The definition begins with the acknowledgment that the field of developmental education is a professional specialty within the field of higher education. The definition is threefold: First, developmental education is defined as a field of practice and research within higher education with a theoretical foundation in developmental psychology and learning theory. It is described as promoting the cognitive and affective growth of postsecondary learners at all levels of the learning continuum. Secondly, developmental education is viewed as being sensitive and responsive to the individual differences and special needs among learners. Finally, developmental education programs and services are viewed as commonly addressing academic preparedness, diagnostic assessment and placement, affective barriers to learning, and development of general and discipline-specific learning strategies.

The following goals have been put forward to guide the field of developmental education by NADE (1996): "(1) To preserve and make possible educational opportunity for each postsecondary learner, (2) To develop in each learner the skills and attitudes necessary for the attainment of academic, career, and life goals, (3) To ensure proper placement by assessing each learner's level of preparedness for college course work, (4) To maintain academic standards by enabling learner to acquire competencies needed for success in mainstream college courses, (5) To enhance the retention of students, and (6) To promote the continued development and application of cognitive and affective learning theory" (Higbee & Dwinell, 1996, Back Cover).

Research Concerns

A number of research concerns must also be clarified prior to developing a perspective for an institutional assessment model for evaluating the effectiveness of developmental education programs. These concerns are: (1) To what extent have higher education institutions identified success measures other than student enrollment data? (2) What policies, plans, techniques or strategies are evolving to specifically address program quality and course effectiveness? (3) Are the levels of student deficiency addressed in institutional assessment models designed to evaluate developmental education program outcomes? (4) Can existing programs be described in terms of program components, entrance criteria, exit criteria? (5) How many students are currently enrolled in developmental programs? (6) What percentage of students in developmental studies are successful and go on to be successful in regular college courses? (7) What is the average number of semesters students participate in developmental education activities? (8) How do success rates of developmental and regular college students who have gone on to enroll in regular programs compare? and (9) What is the estimated program cost per semester/academic year? The answers to these questions are critical to developing an institutional assessment model for evaluating the effectiveness of developmental education programs in higher education institutions.

The research literature showed that assessment procedures tended to be more present than were standards of success in institutional assessment models in higher education institutions. Therefore, the evaluation of a specific developmental program frequently lacks the basis for a comparison to a college-wide standard since standards for program evaluation were often not included in institutional assessment models. Consequently, a major concern of researchers conducting earlier evaluation studies was how to measure the effectiveness of a developmental education program against an unknown college-wide expectation. However, given the increased emphasis on educational quality and accountability, efforts to improve institutional assessment models for developmental education program evaluation with a focus on student assessment outcomes are on the increase.

There is not much chance that a program will be developed and put into place without educators having opinions and feelings about it. The only question is whether these opinions and feelings are based upon systematically collected data and are consciously arrived at using some planned process or whether they are simply ad hoc and unconsciously developed. The research provided evidence that institutional assessment models designed for developmental education program evaluation can yield pertinent information for making decisions to enhance student learning outcomes. However, this becomes extremely difficult in the absence of a sound conceptual framework critical for developing an appropriate evaluation strategy.

Student Outcomes Assessment

Before beginning the discussion of student outcomes assessment within the context of an institutional assessment model, it seems appropriate to first define assessment. Assessment is defined for the purpose of this chapter as a process of collecting and organizing information or data that makes it possible for educators to effectively evaluate developmental education programs to determine student learning outcomes. In other words, assessment is the process of gathering the data and fashioning them into an interpretable form so evaluation can be made. Assessment then, precedes the final decision-making stage in evaluation.

Institutional assessment models that are designed for developmental education program evaluation in higher education institutions must do more than simply identify students whose skills deficiencies hinder their chances of being successful, but instead focus on student assessment outcomes. Bray (1987), Clowes (1992), Cohen (1985), Farmer and Barham (1996) and Walvekar (1981) have developed models focusing on student assessment outcomes. For example, Walvekar urged a three-stage approach to program evaluation: assessment of students' skills at entrance, ongoing assessment of students' skills to determine whether instructional programs need to be modified to meet student needs, and follow-up evaluations to document student learning on program or course completion. Second, Cohen (1984-85) argued that assessment should be viewed as part of an overall student retention effort, not simply as an initial placement mechanism. He draws on the research literature to show how student orientation, tutorial activities, and other supplemental support services complement entry testing in an overall retention program that starts with recruitment and ends with follow-up activities. Third, Bray (1987) in her three assessment steps links assessment outcomes to instructional improvement and student retention by using test results as a guide to course development and student services.

She illustrates this linkage by describing the student flow model designed by Sacramento City College (California) and the assessment and placement model developed by the Learning, Assessment, and Retention Consortium of the California Community College System. Fourth, Clowes (1992) developed a four-stage model of program evaluation. His model was built to evaluate remedial/developmental programs effectiveness, proposing an initial stage of internal assessment only, an interface stage involving remedial program evaluation, and two concluding stages to establish appropriate goals and measures for the next cycle of evaluation. Finally, Farmer and Barham (1996) designed a comprehensive developmental model of integrated services, consisting of three major components: assessment and placement of students upon admission, curriculum and academic support services designed to enhance students' basic skills, and an evaluation component designed to determine student assessment outcomes. This comprehensive model connects program evaluation, student outcomes assessment and institutional assessment, teaching and learning to program evaluation.

As the outcomes assessment movement begins to spread into the higher education systems in America, institutional assessment is becoming an increasingly controversial issue. Although interest is widespread, progress in designing institutional assessment models that focus on student learning outcomes has been slow. Halpern (1987) argued that many of the controversial issues concerning assessment in higher education are really issues of values, philosophy, and theory, rather than practical, nuts-and-bolts issues. At the heart of these philosophical issues is our sense of what the purpose of higher education is or should be and what is meant by educational quality.

Astin (1987) stated that "...in trying to design an effective program of assessment based on value-added, perhaps the most important thing to keep in mind is the necessity of basing that program on some coherent philosophy of the institution's mission. In particular, the assessment program should reflect some conception of what constitutes effective performance of that mission. A philosophy of the institution's purpose and mission is not just an abstract intellectual exercise, it has concrete implications for how one views the assessment problem" (Astin, p. 95). Moreover, the institutional mission statement is frequently referred to as the statement of purpose for an institution. The goals then, which are supported or derived from the institutional mission statement, constitute the action plan which gives direction to the overall operation of the higher education institution and clearly identifies its intentions. The process of assessing institutional effectiveness is based on the degree of accomplishment of the institution's stated purpose as reflected in its mission or purpose statement. In order to make sense of the research then, a common and consistent framework of definitions, values, and criteria is critical. This type of framework would provide us with a more consistent method for evaluating developmental programs and student assessment outcomes in higher education institutions. It would also provide us with a basis for comparing the findings of the various studies that investigated developmental education programs effectiveness (Richardson et al. 1981; Walvekar, 1981). The absence of a consistent framework of terminology regarding the objectives, goals, methods, structure, and evaluation of developmental education programs further compound the problem when trying to compare, understand, and apply developmental findings. Therefore, without an institutional assessment model to systematically collect, synthesize, and analyze data, developmental education program evaluations will continue to show inconsistent and contradictory results.

The first step in the institutional assessment design should be to know the purpose of your assessment: What do you plan to use the results for? What aspects of student performance do you want to know about? Is your primary purpose to assess student accomplishment; for instance, how well have students learned to write essays, to communicate verbally, to synthesize research? If so, you will be most interested in assessing the status or level of student accomplishment for purposes of grading, special placement, and progress monitoring, or for the institution and other purposes of evaluation and accountability. Because the primary intent is to describe the extent to which students have attained particular knowledge and skills, your assessment should focus on student learning outcomes.

But, if your purpose is diagnosis and improvement, such as diagnosing a student's strengths and weaknesses, prescribing the most appropriate instructional programs, or identifying strategies students use well and those they need help with, you'll want an assessment that gives you information about the process as well as the outcome. What have the students achieved and how did they do it?

Whatever is the case, the type of institutional assessment model that is designed for developmental program evaluation should be based on answers to a number of critical questions. The primary questions that should be resolved early in the process of developing a perspective for an institutional assessment model are: 1) Who should be assessed? 2) What do you want to know? and 3) Why do you want to know it? Comprehensive and precise answers to these primary questions will provide direction to the secondary questions: 4) What should be measured? 5) How should it be measured? and 6) When should it be measured? (See Figure 1).

These questions are addressed in a growing body of research literature on assessment practices in developmental education programs in higher education institutions. The resolve of these questions are essential to developing an institutional assessment model for effective developmental program evaluation. Deciding the answers to all of these questions is an essential first step in planning the assessment process.

Tomlinson (1989) argued that although "Program evaluation provides a monitoring system with which to assess effectiveness and facilitate improvement; it is by no means a panacea in terms of serving to ameliorate all of the many problems that a program may experience" (p. 53). However, a sound institutional assessment model may be the key to effective program evaluation.

Figure 1. Questions for Developing a Perspective for an Institutional Assessment Model

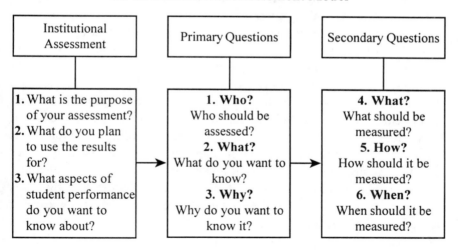

Summary, Conclusions, and Recommendations for Further Research

Without question, the research literature has provided evidence of a nationwide concern for improvement in educational quality. Higher education institutions appear to be genuinely committed to developing and improving institutional assessment models to evaluate developmental education programs effectiveness. There is also widespread recognition of the existing problems and issues that have resulted from poorly planned developmental education programs of the past. However, additional research is needed to help clarify a number of research questions that have evolved from this situation: (1) To what extent should higher education institutions establish college-wide success standards to serve as the basis for evaluating specific programs? More germane to developmental/remedial programs, can performance standards be set which would be politically, socially, and academically acceptable? (2) To what extent are questions related to effectiveness of developmental programs merely reflective of questions appropriate to all programs regardless of content? (3) Are developmental/remedial/basic skill programs expected to evaluate more systematically and more critically than other programs? If so, why should they? (4) Are there problems in reconciling the access mission of colleges and universities with emerging priorities of quality and excellence? (5) To what extent should developmental education programs be expected to overcome extreme student basic skill deficiencies? In view of the range of these deficiencies, are placement procedures and policies and entrance criteria valid as predictors of student needs? Is what's being taught appropriate to student needs? (6) To what extent can some consensus be reached regarding terminology? If so, how would such consensus facilitate response to related issues (such as credit status, structure, philosophy, and evaluation)? (7) What is the feasibility of systematically collecting data that indicate the extent to which the skills taught in developmental education are used as tools for facilitating learning in regular college courses? What role do these skills play in the achievement of individual student goals?

Finally, the research literature has provided evidence that higher education institutions are beginning to respond to these research problems and concerns from the perspective of their campus involvement, students, human and financial resources. The institutional responses have several common threads: (a) a more comprehensive assessment of developmental education programs would be conducted if financial and human resources were available, and (b) success could be improved by more selective admissions, but this is not an acceptable solution. While success criteria are generally agreed upon by higher education institutions, it is also agreed that no one criterion is sufficient given the range of factors impacting success. The research literature clearly demonstrates that consensus among colleges and universities on common standards of program success does not currently exist. Some educators believe, however, that such common standards would be inappropriate given the differences among institutions, their programs and particularly their students. It is agreed upon by educators that higher education institutions differ in how they view various standards for success and therefore must establish their own threshold level for success. Nevertheless, many of them agree that there must exist some elements of standards common among all higher education institutions.

Note: Small portions of the above chapter are reprinted with permission from Farmer, V. L. (1992). Developing a perspective on assessment of effectiveness in developmental education. *Educational Research Quarterly, 16*(1), 25-33. Published by Grambling State University, Grambling, LA 71245.

Part V:
Integrating Developmental Programs
in a Comprehensive Developmental
Education Model

Chapter 21

℘℘℘

An Integrated Developmental Education Model: A Comprehensive Approach

Vernon L. Farmer and Wilton A. Barham

In postsecondary institutions, faculty are responsible for the personal growth of learners, for their social development, and for their mastery of academic subjects, including the basic skills, communicative and quantitative, that are so essential to success in college. To perform multiple responsibilities, faculty as well as other professional educators often engage in a number of developmental education activities designed to help facilitate student learning and development. To achieve this objective, educators draw upon a variety of models to organize and deliver learning experiences to developmental learners in these institutions.

We have recently completed an examination of the literature concerned with selected models of Assessment and Placement, Curriculum and Instruction, and Evaluation and Research for developmental learners in postsecondary institutions. In our review, it is clear to us that college and university administrators and faculty have been attempting for decades to respond effectively to the increasing number of students entering their institutions with deficiencies in both communication and quantitative skills areas. Educating the developmental student is more than simply a matter of providing a few isolated support activities. Institutional priority must be given to the development of a comprehensive program of integrated services. It is towards this end that our discussion focuses on a comprehensive developmental education model (see Figure 1) with three major components: (a) Assessment and Placement of Students in the College Curriculum, (b) Curriculum and Academic Services, and (c) Evaluation and Research: Internal and External. This comprehensive model is proposed as an effective approach to promote the integration of teaching, learning, and evaluation models that are essential to developmental learners' success in these institutions. It approaches the needs of developmental students in a comprehensive and holistic manner.

Because an increasing number of students have been entering institutions with deficiencies in both communication and quantitative skills areas, hundreds of institutions of higher learning have implemented assessment programs to determine the competency of students in these skills areas. The results of these assessments are then used by some of these institutions to place students into either developmental studies or regular college courses. Other institutions have simply provided tutorial instruction, academic advising, and counseling services to these students, (who will be referred to from this point on in this chapter as developmental students). Most colleges and universities however, have fallen short of providing a comprehensive program of developmental education for developmental students (Tomlinson, 1989). Moreover, the research shows that for a variety of reasons developmental education programs vary from college to college (Abraham, 1990). As was indicated, we must understand that educating the developmental student is more than simply a matter of providing a few isolated support activities, but rather institutional priority must be given to the development of a comprehensive program of integrated services. These services must be fully integrated into the mainstream of the institution's mission to improve student retention. This comprehensive model must be designed with a clearly defined philosophy, goals, and objectives. In other words, this model must be high-powered, highly visible and consistent with the institution's mission to improve student retention. The operational definition of developmental education in this model is that developmental education programs are organized educational efforts providing a wide-range of learning experiences intended to improve educational skills, attitudes and deficiencies of students.

This comprehensive developmental education model is designed to identify the special academic needs of college freshmen, to develop and

Figure 1. A Comprehensive Developmental Education Model

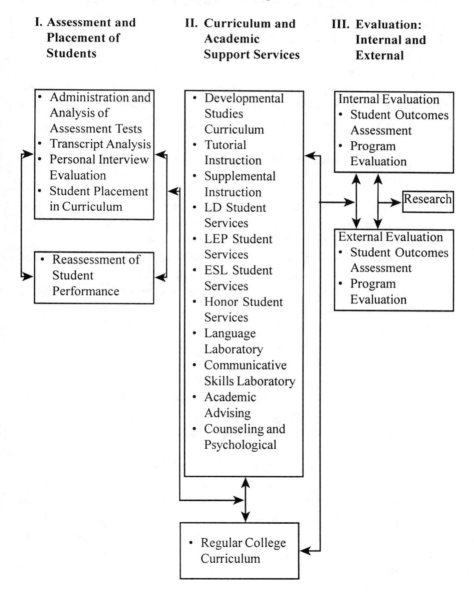

I. Assessment and Placement of Students

- Administration and Analysis of Assessment Tests
- Transcript Analysis
- Personal Interview Evaluation
- Student Placement in Curriculum

- Reassessment of Student Performance

II. Curriculum and Academic Support Services

- Developmental Studies Curriculum
- Tutorial Instruction
- Supplemental Instruction
- LD Student Services
- LEP Student Services
- ESL Student Services
- Honor Student Services
- Language Laboratory
- Communicative Skills Laboratory
- Academic Advising
- Counseling and Psychological

- Regular College Curriculum

III. Evaluation: Internal and External

Internal Evaluation
- Student Outcomes Assessment
- Program Evaluation

Research

External Evaluation
- Student Outcomes Assessment
- Program Evaluation

prescribe an appropriate course of study and to enhance the opportunity for developmental students to acquire the skills and behavior necessary to help them be successful in college. This model approaches the needs of developmental students in a comprehensive and holistic manner. The model integrates developmental studies courses, tutorial instruction, learning laboratories, academic advising and counseling, as well as special academic accommodations for students with learning disabilities and those who speak English as a second language. This model includes three major operational phases: Phase 1) Assessment and Placement; Phase 2) Curriculum and Academic Services; and Phase 3) Evaluation and Research: Internal and External. A brief overview of the components follows:

Assessment and Placement of Students in the College Curriculum

Our model identifies the activities at this first stage as the administration and analysis of assessment tests, transcript analysis, personal interview evaluation, and student placement in the curriculum. Research studies concerned with assessment and placement of students into the college curriculum demonstrate that no one success measure is considered to be sufficient given the range of variables impacting student success (Ewell, 1987). The development of an effective assessment program should be guided by the following questions: Who will be assessed? What basic skills will be assessed and used to determine placement? How will cutoff scores be determined?

In Figure 2, we present a more detailed list of some questions that relate to assessment, guidance and placement, program delivery, and research evaluation. The program developer's/manager's goal should be the provision of answers to these questions at every level of this proposed comprehensive model.

Assessment and Placement may be the link to each student's right to have a chance to succeed. Since many students enter college lacking the skills necessary to be successful, it is mandatory that all institutions of higher learning require entering freshmen to participate in a college Assessment and Placement Program designed to determine their strengths and weaknesses. Information from this type of program will be used then to place these students in an appropriate program of study to enhance their chances for academic success.

It must be understood however, that successful placement of students into the appropriate program of study is not without problems. As was mentioned before, research studies concerned with assessment and placement of students into the college curriculum demonstrate that no one success measure is considered to be sufficient given the range of variable impacting student success (Callas, 1985). In other words, no one assessment technique or method or experience has guaranteed academic success in higher education. Nevertheless, the first indicator of academic success may be previous achievement in high school but no one predictor or combination of predictors can fully measure the strengths and weaknesses of a student (Ewell, 1987). Therefore, in order to minimize this problem this model requires that a combination of assessment techniques be used, including the assessment test battery, the high school transcript, and the personal interview. In Astin's Input-Environment-Output (I-E-O) model in developmental education (Boylan, 1999), this assessment and placement phase is referred to as input. Astin indicates that examples of input data are student characteristics which include demographic and academic factors. Specifically, demographic data include age, ethnicity, gender, socio-economic status and part/full-time enrollment. Academic factors may include ACT/SAT scores, other assessment information, study strategies, learning styles and program participation. When information from this combination of assessment materials are used, a more accurate placement decision will then be possible.

The assessment tests must be carefully chosen. Research demands that each institution make an effort to make its local student placement decisions (Tomlinson, 1989). Assessment tests must be designed or tailored to meet the unique needs of the institution in which it is to be used. The assessment instrument must have proven to be an effective means of assessing the communication and quantitative skills of entering freshmen. It is extremely important that the assessment tests chosen by institutions of higher learning be designed so that they can be used as pre-test and post-test instruments. Assessment tests that are composed of a form A and a form B equated with each other, where scores on both forms have the same meaning, can be especially useful in evaluating student progress. Results from pre- and post-tests will provide evidence of student success or failure in developmental studies courses. Cut-off scores to be used in an assessment and placement program must be determined after a thorough review of test scores and grades earned after a period of at least two years. Careful monitoring of students placed into developmental studies courses during this period will provide institutions with the necessary data to determine cut-off scores. Once these data have been analyzed, cut-off scores on assessment tests must then be cooperatively determined by faculty members both in the regular and Developmental Studies curriculum. This model also requires that the institution's assessment program have a retest policy that would allow for retesting wherever appropriate.

For many years colleges and universities have used the high school transcript as a major assessment instrument to place students into appropriate college courses. High school academic records may be the first indicator of academic success, however reliance on the results of a transcript analysis as an indicator of student potential has obvious problems. Callas (1985) in his research study strongly suggested that previous grades in high school must not be considered sole predictors of success or failure in college. Since high schools vary in the content and quality of instruction, in the quality of teachers, in grading practices, etc., the placement of students in college courses based solely on high school transcripts must be prohibited. This is not to suggest that the results of a transcript analysis provides no useable data. Roueche and Pitman (1972) argued in their research study that previous grade may indicate, for example, which students are verbal and which students are independent learners. Although the results drawn from a transcript analysis as well as assessment tests scores may provide valuable information to the placement process, they frequently contradict each other. What should happen when this contradiction occurs? This model requires that a number of activities be conducted to examine this contradiction. First, a student must be re-tested, and secondly, the high school record must again be thoroughly examined to determine a student's overall academic performance. An analysis of the high school transcript may reveal a pattern of strengths and weaknesses similar to those demonstrated on the college assessment test. It is unlikely that many students will do poorly or well in every course by chance. In what area do a student's strengths and weaknesses fall? An examination of weaknesses and strengths identified by placement tests may reveal a pattern similar to that demonstrated on the high school transcript. Knowledge of the various program requirements will help to determine whether a student seeking a particular program has the appropriate background to be successful. For example, a student who seeks to enter a program requiring a strong quantitative skills background but was placed into a basic mathematics course, should not be placed in a college course requiring this type of content. This should only occur when the student has demonstrated competency in the quantitative skills area.

This model demands that a personal interview be conducted for students whenever appropriate. The personal interview must be designed to gather

Figure 2. Guidelines for the Development of an Assessment and Placement System

Systems	Who?	What?	How and Where?
Assessment	Who will be assessed? Who will do the assessing? Who will be administratively responsible?	What basic skills will be assessed and used to determine placement? How will cutoff scores be determined? What alternatives to standardized tests will be available?	How will an assessment and placement system differ from a diagnostic system? How will an assessment and placement system be used? How will the system be able to screen large numbers rapidly and inexpensively? How and where will testing take place?
Guidance and Placement	Who will do the advising? Who will be administratively responsible?	What are advising needs? What is the relationship of the advisory system to other support services?	How should advisory services be delivered? How should advisers be selected and trained? How are placement and information to be unified?
Program Delivery	Who will determine available programs? Who will be administratively responsible?	What courses will be available for skills placement? What minimum skill competencies are needed to succeed in course?	How many courses and levels will be available? How will staff be trained?
Research and Evaluation	Who will conduct follow-up studies? Who will be administratively responsible?	What type of program evaluation will be conducted? What student progress information will be available?	How will research results be used to adjust placement as needed?

pertinent information which may be valuable in helping to resolve contradictions between assessment tests scores and results of a transcript analysis. For this reason the personal interview must be required of some students prior to making course placement decisions. For instance, the personal interview may reveal how a student perceives a discrepancy between his or her assessment tests scores and high school transcript. Often-times a student may reveal his or her own areas of strengths and weaknesses and the reasons for such. Students can tell us how much time was spent on coursework outside of high school, and whether they were employed during this period. They can also tell us whether or not tutorial assistance, as well as advising and counseling were available while they were in high school. There is obviously, other pertinent information that can be brought to the assessment and placement process through the personal interview. The personal interview can serve as a valuable assessment instrument for helping to make more accurate course placement decisions.

It must be understood that this model requires institutions to develop a mandatory policy to guide the placement of students into appropriate college courses. The placement of students into the college curriculum must be based on their performance on the college assessment program, which includes assessment tests scores, high school background (including transcripts), information suggested by Astin (1998) and Boylan (1999), and the personal interview when required. This model requires that students be placed into one of four curriculum plans. The four curriculum plans are as follows:

First, a student with the basic skills necessary to do college-level work must be allowed to pursue his or her chosen plan of study; secondly, a student possessing borderline skills should be required to enroll in a special section (extended hours) of Freshman Composition and/or Elementary Algebra or College Algebra. The designated sections of English and mathematics would meet for five hours (rather than the normal three hours) per week so that students may move at a slower pace and benefit from individualized instruction. This type of course structure should be expanded to other courses as this model evolves; thirdly, a student required to take two or fewer developmental courses as a result of deficient skills may be allowed to take several courses within his or her chosen field (the regular college curriculum) depending upon program requirements and the area(s) of student needs. For example, a student requiring a course in basic writing skills should not be allowed to enroll in a college course requiring extensive writing, neither should a student required to take a basic mathematics skills course be allowed to enroll in a course that requires a quantitative skills foundation. Moreover, a student required to take a basic reading course must not be placed in a college course requiring extensive reading; and fourthly, a student with serious deficiencies in all of the basic skills areas must be required to enroll in all Developmental Studies courses.

The research demonstrates that a large number of developmental students have taken more than two years to complete their degree at two-year colleges, while many other students have taken more than four years to complete their degree at senior institutions (Farmer, 1988). In some cases, developmental students have taken even more time than mentioned to complete their plan of study. However, this is expected. It simply will take time to help these students to acquire the necessary skills to be successful in college. This model requires that "a letter of understanding" be signed by developmental students and their parents so that they will be aware from the beginning that it may require them more than the usual amount of time to complete a college degree. An extended-time program of study will give all developmental students more time to acquire the basic skills necessary for them to be successful. The models of assessment presented in Part IV of this book are other examples of models that could be adopted and utilized at the first phase of our comprehensive developmental model. For example, Farmer and Barham's, Bray's, Bliss', Clark's, et al., and Thurston and Craig's chapters present excellent information that can be used in addressing the assessment issue. Developmental education administrators should always seek effective assessment techniques for implementation within this comprehensive format.

Curriculum and Academic Services

Once the cognitive and affective needs of the students have been assessed, a variety of curriculum and academic services should be developed, including any of the following instructional and support approaches: developmental studies curriculum, tutorial instruction, supplemental instruction, learning disabled (LD) student services, limited English proficient (LEP) student services, English as a second language (ESL) student services, honor student services, language laboratory, quantitative skills laboratory, communicative skills laboratory, academic advising, and counseling and psychological services. Students who meet the standards of learning can then move into the regular college curriculum. They may move back into any of the remedial-enhancement programs, if necessary.

Several Developmental Studies courses included in this model are designed to assist developmental students in acquiring the basic skills and cognitive behavior that are essential to their success in college. These courses are: 1) Basic Writing Skills; 2) Basic Mathematics Skills; 3) Basic Reading Skills; 4) Basic Speaking Skills; 5) Scientific Reasoning Skills; 6) Basic Library Skills; 7) Critical Thinking and Problem Solving Skills; and 8) Study Skills. Each of these courses are designed to address key skill areas that can determine a students' success or failure in higher education. Let use briefly describe several of these courses.

Basic Writing Skills course is designed to develop a student's ability to write complete, grammatically correct sentences and to combine them into unified, coherent, complete paragraphs using a variety of syntactic and paragraph-level structures. If student numbers warrant it, a special section of this course may be designated for students whose first language is not English. This section would need to be taught by an English faculty member with ESL credentials and experience.

Basic Mathematics Skills course is designed to developed a student's computational skills through intensive coverage of such arithmetic concepts as operations on whole numbers and the use of fractions, decimals, percents and square roots.

Basic Reading Skills course is designed to develop a student's ability to read critically in different formats, to expand his or her vocabulary, and to adjust his or her reading rates to fit specific needs.

Basic Library Skills course is designed to develop a student's ability to effectively use the library by acquainting him or her with the functions of the college library, the arrangement of library materials, the use of reference materials and on-line databases, and to instruct the student in research methods and techniques.

Basic Study Skills course is designed to improve a student's chances in college courses by increasing his or her awareness of the need for regular study habits as well as providing the student with specific strategies on how to study.

Personal Development course to help increase a student's ability to understand the processes involved in making rational decisions regarding educational, career and personal matters. Several counseling principles are used to help the student accomplish this objective.

There are several other Developmental Studies courses that can be included in this model, however, we will not be exhaustive in this chapter. It is important to understand nevertheless that all of these courses must be designed to specifically answer the following questions if they are to be effective. How does the curriculum content match the defined academic deficiencies of developmental students assigned to a given level of instruction? What skills do the students need in order to exit from the course? What skills do the students need to demonstrate in order to earn a college degree and so on?

In order to supplement the Developmental Studies curriculum, a number of Skills Laboratories must also be designed and implemented to assist students with improving their skills in communications and qualitative areas. However, it is not our goal to discuss these laboratories in this chapter. Nevertheless, these Skills Laboratories are essential and must be designed to assist students enrolled in Developmental Studies courses and for those who simply need reinforcement and review in the basic skills areas.

The Comprehensive Developmental Education Model also includes as indicated earlier, tutorial instructions, programs for Learning Disabled (LD) students and those who speak English as a foreign language (ESL). In addition, this model mandates that an academic advising and counseling support network be an integral component of the program. Astin (1998), and Boylan (1999) indicated that Astin's I-E-O includes courses and services at the environment stage which is similar to our second stage. In addition to courses, types of faculty, types of staff, faculty and staff characteristics, course and program structure would constitute quantitative factors to be included. They also suggested the inclusion of qualitative factors such as surveys of students, faculty and staff and case studies.

We have attempted to provide the reader with several examples of possible curriculum and academic services that may be useful at the second phase of our comprehensive model. The models presented in Part III by the various authors are also effective ones that are worthy of adoption. However, the appropriate model for implementation depends on the students' needs. These models of curricula and instruction and others should be seriously considered by those who are responsible for the development and delivery of academic support services for developmental learners.

Evaluation and Research: Internal and External

We are usually interested in using the data generated to assess student outcomes within the context of program evaluation and research that can be conducted by internal and external evaluators. Ewell (1987) recommended that assessment programs examine a number of important outcomes such as knowledge, skills, attitudes and values, and behaviors. Various program evaluation models could be adopted by administrators and faculty based on particular needs (Boylan, 1999; Clowes, 1984; Scriven, 1972; Somers, 1987; Stufflebeam & Shinkfield, 1985). Research questions and hypotheses may be developed around program goals and institutional mission and then subjected to validation using appropriate research design and multivariate statistical techniques. Astin (1998) and Boylan (1999) suggested that the quantitative measures that may be evaluated at the output stage of the I-E-O model include number of students served, number/hours of contact generated, gain scores, completion rates in courses, grades in courses, attempts required to pass courses, credits attempted/credits earned ratio, grades in post-developmental education courses, retention from term to term, and graduation rates. Qualitative measures could include surveys of students and faculty, case studies, testimonials, and interviews.

Program evaluation and research is an integral part of this Developmental Education Model. The major focus of program evaluation must be based on retention. A student database must be devised which will allow a cumulative record of pertinent information, including test scores, courses taken, course grades, time to complete program, and those suggested by Astin and Boylan. The development of a student database is increasingly viewed as an effective strategy for monitoring individual students throughout their college experience and is considered a positive step in the assessment process. The student database will provide much of the raw data essential for effective program evaluation. However, a standard of success must be made clear for a specific institution so that the Developmental Education program will have a basis for comparison to a college or university-wide standard.

Student Outcome Assessment

Based on the data that are generated, we are usually interested in using them to assess specific student outcomes (i.e., to answer specific research questions) and/or to evaluate a particular program. Halpern (1987) has reminded us that the determination of many potential outcomes of the developmental student's experiences are most important and must be an institution's decision. But what are some of the student outcomes that are of importance? Ewell (1987) recommended in his research study that assessment programs should examine a number of important areas which may include the following:

1. Knowledge Outcomes
   A. Experimental Inquiry
   B. Historical or Documentary Inquiry
   C. Technological Inquiry
   D. Esthetic Inquiry

2. Skills Outcomes
   A. Basic Skills: reading comprehension, writing and computational skills
   B. Higher-order cognitive skills: critical thinking, problem-solving, other complex applications of information and learned techniques.
   C. Knowledge-building skills: locating through library research, planning and executing independent intellectual projects, familiarity with computers, etc.
   D. Skills required for effective practice in particular occupations or professions: certification or licensure examinations, both cognitive recall and simulated application.

3. Attitudes and Value Outcomes
   A. Tolerance for diversity and recognition of the value and contributions of other cultures.
   B. Development of a workable array of personal values that help define identity.
   C. Social values: taking responsibility for personal action, etc.
   D. Action-oriented attitudes: persistence, motivation, task consciousness, etc.

4. Behavioral Outcomes
   A. Persistence and program completion
   B. Choice of major field and persistence within major field
   C. Course selection and completion

Other data of importance to evaluation and research are program standards or standards of success. Some important questions offered by Fadle (1985) that may be of great importance to an institution when considering program standards or standards of success are:

1. How does evaluation of developmental education programs relate to division, department or college assessment?

2. Does definition of program effectiveness exist in sufficient specificity to guide an evaluation effort? Are there identifiable standards for the developmental education program?
3. What decisions need to be made or what questions are being asked about the developmental program by faculty, administration, and students?

Obviously, one set of program standards will not be applicable throughout higher education. Therefore, standards should be determined locally in terms of the college's mission, clientele and priority given to serving developmental students.

Since Carter and Skinner (1987) and Callas (1985) indicated that more than one success criteria are needed to sufficiently evaluate their impact, several success measures were identified as essential to program evaluation and research:

1. Successful completion of exit requirements for developmental studies courses (See Phase 2 of model).

2. Successful completion of the entry level course in sequence after completing the developmental education course.

3. Grade point average at the conclusion of each semester subsequent to the completion of developmental education courses.

4. Graduation from the institution.

5. Achievement of goals held by developmental students. The developmental education student's goal for success may be determined by what he or she anticipated accomplishing when entering the institution.

The determination of student outcomes and success are important for both *internal and external evaluation*. External evaluators may or may not confirm internal evaluators' findings and certain generalizations may be made based on the external validity (i.e., the validity of the research method) of the evaluation or research.

Program Evaluation

What are some characteristics or elements of evaluation studies? Or what do we know about evaluation studies? The following are some characteristics (Gredler, 1996):

1. Evaluation studies are concerned with improving a program or product (Formative evaluation) or determining its value or worth (Summative evaluation).

2. Formative evaluation is used in the development stage to guide the evolutionary process.

3. Summative evaluation determines the worth of a more mature program or process.

4. Evaluation as an aspect of research had been developing for years but it blossomed in the 1970s.

5. Evaluation methods are borrowed from all the social sciences.

6. Different points of view with respect to the evaluation process emphasize *product, process, stakeholder rights, administrator concerns, and client rights*. Some examples are:

    *   Knowledge resulting from evaluation is seen as a tool for more effective program management.

    *   Knowledge resulting from evaluation is seen as a means of empowerment for the people affected by those programs (House, 1976, 1980; Cronbach, 1982).

    *   Evaluation is seen as being directed by a highly competent professional opinion.

    *   Evaluation is seen as a transactional endeavor in which professionals and stakeholders together sought the answers (Rippey, 1973).

    *   Evaluation is seen as a means to conclusions and recommendations.

- Evaluation is seen as a process of negotiation with and among stakeholders, the product being an agenda for further negotiation (Lincoln & Guba, 1986; Argyris, Putman & Smith, 1985).

- Evaluation is seen as an effort to be responsive to the concerns of the stakeholders (Stake, 1991).

- Evaluation is seen as embedded in measurement and experimentation.

- Evaluation is seen as a place for connosseurial judgments by an area's experts (Eisner, 1981).

- A systematic evaluation is based on a plan, includes all components of developmental education, involves quantitative and qualitative evaluation, is used for program improvement, is widely disseminated, and takes place at regular intervals (Boylan, 1999).

7. Evaluation uses research methods but is decision-driven.

8. Utilization is a prime criterion of a successful evaluation.

9. Faith in the product is sufficient for decision-making (i.e. building a consensus around the proper interpretation of the data.). Faith in the product means having faith in the process by which it was derived.

10. The process may be as important as the product.

11. Consensus must be built among the stakeholders, as they are defined by the sponsor and the evaluator (Krathwohl, 1993, pp. 526, 528, & 529).

Various Approaches to Evaluation

There are various approaches to the conduct of evaluation studies:

1. Goal-based approaches — the evaluation concentrates on the intended goals of a program; a major question is whose version of intended goals is used, that of a sponsor, administrator, staff, clients, etc? (Tyler & Waples, 1930; Tyler, 1934).

2. Goal-free approaches — the evaluator looks at what occurred and compares that with the intended changes (Scriven, 1972).

3. Management-oriented approaches — evaluations are designed to assist managers in the administration of projects, often concerned with efficiency and effectiveness (Rossi & Freeman, 1985; Stufflebeam & Shinkfield, 1985).

4. Consumer-oriented approaches — evaluations are intended to help consumers decide what programs to use, what product to buy, etc. (Scriven, 1974; Tyler, Klein, & Associates, 1976).

5. Expertise-oriented approaches — evaluators employ experts to judge what has occurred (Eisner, 1976, 1981).

6. Adversarial approaches — evaluators prepare cases to represent the two or more alternative solutions to a problem and present their cases as in a court of law (Wolf, 1975, 1979).

7. Naturalistic approaches — evaluators use qualitative methods to describe what occurred and seek to be responsive to the stakeholder audience (Stake, 1975; Stake & Easley, 1978a, 1978b).

8. Participant-oriented approaches — the stakeholders are taught how to carry out the evaluations themselves (Rippey, 1973; Guba & Lincoln, 1981). The following is an evaluation model that could be adopted by developmental education program administrators or evaluators.

Application of Stufflebeam's Management-oriented Approaches Model (CIPP)

According to Stufflebeam's model, **Context evaluation** involves planning decisions such as identifying the target audience and determining the needs. This would include information at phase one (1) of the Comprehensive model (e.g., testing, transcript analysis, interview, and placement) and results of subsequent needs assessment.

The **Input evaluation** step would include information at phase step two (2): Curriculum and academic services. Here, the resources that can be used, the alternative strategies to be considered, and the best plans and techniques to be utilized to respond to the needs assessment, are determined.

Process evaluation determines how well the plan or support strategies were implemented. Were there implementation problems? How can they be resolved?

Product evaluation examines the kind of results that were obtained and determines whether the needs were met or reduced. The research process discussed below can help evaluators at this step.

Some Examples of Evaluations of Educational Programs

1. Perry Preschool Program: attempted to show what could be done with preschool programs such as Head Start. The evaluation extended longitudinally, following the students to age 19, and included causal models of what contributed to both positive and negative long-term outcomes (Berrueta-Clement, Barnett, & Weikart, 1985).

2. Educational Vouchers: voucher programs gave parents and children freedom to use a tuition voucher to choose any school they wished-initial discouragement was misleading, as found in later evaluations (Wortman, Reichardt, & St. Pierre, 1978).

3. Outward Bound: designed to expose participants to the physical challenges of the wild and help them learn more self-reliance (Krathwohl, 1993, p. 527; Smith, Gabriel, Schott, & Padia, 1976).

Research

What are some characteristics of research studies? Most research studies are hypothesis-driven instead of decision-driven (such as evaluation), and they seek consensus from experts around the proper interpretation of data.

Problem Statement/Research Questions

Once an institution has implemented a Comprehensive Developmental Education Model and it begins to evolve, a number of research questions will have to be answered. Some of these research questions may be:

1. What is the relationship between developmental education students' learning and the elements of the developmental studies curriculum?

2. What is the relationship between the teaching styles of the faculty and the learning styles of developmental students?

3. How is the cognitive behavior of developmental education students related to their learning?

4. What are the effective teaching strategies that can enhance developmental education students' academic performance and persistence?

These questions should be generated from the **goals** of the program and **research hypotheses** should then be developed and subsequently validated.

Research Design and Analysis

Longitudinal study designs such as Time Series, Equivalent Time Samples and the Separate-Sample Pretest-Posttest designs (Campbell & Stanley, 1963; Kerlinger, 1986) are appropriate for the collection and analysis of outcome assessment data. For instance, in the Time Series design a group of students are tested with the same (or comparable) measures at different times so that measures can be provided to determine growth and change over time. Jacobi, Astin, and Ayala (1987) argued that for any of these longitudinal designs, a researcher can use objective tests (standardized tests), essays, interviews, departmental examinations and any other assessment instruments depending on the content and objectives of the curriculum or program being assessed. A major question that longitudinal research will be able to answer in this effort is: Are placement procedures and admission criteria valid as predictors of student needs?

Multiple levels of analysis can also be undertaken in areas of cognitive development, character development and personal growth, attitude, values, etc. Both internal and external evaluators can utilize univariate and multivariate statistical techniques such as correlations, one-way or two-way analysis of variance, simple and multiple linear regression, path analysis, factor analysis, multivariate analysis of variance, or linear structural equation modeling (with or without latent factors) to assess relationships among variables essential to the academic success of developmental students.

Notes About Lead Authors

Vernon L. Farmer is acting dean of the School of Graduate Studies and Research and acting assistant vice president for Academic Affairs at Grambling State University. He is also professor in the Department of Educational Leadership in the College of Education. He earned the A.B. in sociology, the A.M. in counselor education, and the Ph.D. in higher education from the University of Michigan at Ann Arbor.

Wilton A. Barham is acting head of the Department of Educational Leadership and Director of Doctoral Studies in the College of Education at Grambling State University. He is also professor in the Department of Educational Leadership in the College of Education. He earned his B.S. in education (statistics and research methods) from the State University of New York, the M.P.H. in biostatistics, and the Ph.D. in educational research methods and statistics from the University of Michigan at Ann Arbor.

Notes About Other Contributing Authors

Leonard B. Bliss is a professor in the Department of Leadership and Policy Analysis in the College of Education at Florida International University. He earned his Ph.D. degree in educational research and statistics from Syracuse University.

Hunter R. Boylan is a professor in the Department of Leadership and Educational Studies and Director of the National Center for Developmental Education at Appalachian State University. He earned his Ph.D. degree in higher education administration from Bowling Green State University.

Dorothy Bray is the former vice president of Educational Services at the College of the Desert in California. She earned her Ed.D. degree in educational psychology from the University of Southern California at Los Angeles.

A. Phillip Butler is a professor in the Department of Educational Leadership and Principal/Director of Grambling High School in the College of Education at Grambling State University. He earned his Ph.D. degree in education from George Peabody College of Vanderbilt University.

Lorraine Page Cadet is an assistant professor of developmental English in the Academic Skills Center in the College of Education at Grambling State University. She earned her Ph.D. degree in curriculum and instruction from Kansas State University.

Carol A. Callahan is an assistant professor and chair of the Division of Academic Support at Floyd College in Rome, Georgia. She earned her M.Ed. degree in education from The University of Georgia.

Augusta A. Clark is an associate professor in the Department of Educational Leadership in the College of Education at Grambling State University. She earned her Ph.D. degree in adult education from Florida State University.

Darrel A. Clowes is an associate professor of education emeritus in the Division of Curriculum and Instruction in the College of Education at Virginia Polytechnic Institute and State University. He earned his Ph.D. degree in higher education administration from the University of Texas at Austin.

William Collins is an adjunct associate professor of psychology and Director of the Comprehensive Studies Program at The University of Michigan. He earned his Ph.D. degree in psychology from the University of Michigan at Ann Arbor.

Nannette E. Commander is an associate professor in the Department of Learning Support Programs in the College of Arts and Sciences at Georgia State University at Atlanta. She earned her Ph.D. degree in educational psychology from Georgia State University.

V. Carolyn Craig is an assistant professor in the Department of Educational Foundations and Leadership in the College of Education at Jackson State University. She earned her Ph.D. degree in educational administration from the University of Southern Mississippi.

Nelson DuBois is a former professor of educational psychology in the College of Education at the State University of New York College at Oneonta. He earned his Ph.D. degree in special education and child development from the University of Maryland at College Park.

Gabriel O. Fagbeyiro is an assistant professor of computer science and Director of Information Technology and Telecommunications at Southern University at Shreveport. He earned his Ed.D. degree in developmental education from Grambling State University.

Thomas J. Grites is an assistant to the vice president for Academic Affairs at The Richard Stockton College of New Jersey. He earned his Ph.D. degree in student personnel and higher education from the University of Maryland at College Park.

Ada Harrington-Belton is an assistant professor in the Department of Curriculum and Instruction in the College of Education and Psychology at the University of Southern Mississippi. She earned her Ph.D. degree in curriculum and instruction from Fordham University.

Andolyn B. Harrison is a professor and acting dean in the Department of Educational Leadership in the College of Education at Grambling State University. She earned her Ph.D. degree in educational administration from Bowling Green State University.

Raymond A. Hicks is a professor in the Department of Educational Leadership in the College of Education at Grambling State University. He earned his Ph.D. degree in educational administration from Southern Illinois University at Carbondale.

Martha Maxwell is a former lecturer of education in the College of Education and academic coordinator of the Student Learning Center at the University of California at Berkeley. She earned her Ph.D. degree in educational psychology from the University of Maryland at College Park.

B. Runi Mukerji is a professor of psychology in the Department of Psychology at the State University of New York, College at Old Westbury. She earned her Ph.D. degree in psychology from State University of New York at Stoney Brook.

Olatunde A. Ogunyemi is a professor of Educational Leadership in the College of Education at Grambling State University. He earned his Ed.D. degree in instructional systems and technology from Northern Illinois University.

Ernesta Parker Pendleton is a program analyst in the Office of Academic Affairs in the Division of Academic Programs and Research at the University of District of Columbia. She earned her Ed.D. degree in developmental education from Grambling State University.

Peggy R. Porter is the department chair of Developmental English, Reading, English for Foreign Speakers, and Foreign Languages at Houston Community College System Northwest. She is a candidate for the Ed.D. degree in developmental education in the College of Education at Grambling State University.

Evelyn Shepherd-Wynn is an instructor in the English Department in the College of Liberal Arts at Grambling State University. She earned her Ed.D. degree in developmental education from Grambling State University.

Brenda D. Smith is a former professor in the Department of Educational Foundations at Georgia State University, Atlanta, Georgia. She earned her Ed.D. degree in curriculum and instruction from Georgia State University.

Cheryl B. Stratton is an assistant professor in the Division of Academic Assistance at the University of Georgia in Athens, Georgia. She received her Ed.D. degree in curriculum development and instructional leadership from the University of Alabama at Tuscaloosa.

Darlene A. Thurston is an associate professor in the Department of Educational Foundations and Leadership in the College of Education at Jackson State University. She earned her Ph.D. degree in educational policy, planning and analysis from Florida State University.

Kathleen G. Velsor is an assistant professor in the College of Education at the State University of New York College at Old Westbury. She earned her Ed.D. degree in curriculum evaluation and research from the University of Cincinnati.

Loretta Walton-Jaggers is a professor in the Department of Teacher Education in the College of Education at Grambling State University. She earned her Ed.D. degree in curriculum and instruction from the University of Houston at University Park.

Neari F. Warner is the provost and vice president for Academic Affairs at Grambling State University. She is also a professor in the College of Education at Grambling State University. She earned her Ph.D. degree in curriculum and instruction from Louisiana State University at Baton Rouge.

Clara M. Wilson-Cook is an associate professor in the College of Education and dean of the Junior Division at Southern University at New Orleans. She earned her Ph.D. degree in higher education administration and student personnel services from Kansas State University.

References

Chapter 1

Krathwohl, D.R. (1993). *Methods of educational and social science research: An integrated approach.* New York: Longman.

McCray, J. H. & Farmer, V. L. (In Progress). *Logical thinking and scientific reasoning.* Bristol: Wyndham Hall Press.

Chapter 2

Abraham, A. A. (1991). *They came to college? A remedial/development profile of first-time freshmen in SREB States.* Issues in Higher Education No. 25. Southern Regional Education Board, Atlanta, GA.

American Council on Education (1996). *Campus trends: 1996.* Washington, DC: American Council on Education.

Boylan, H., & White, W. (1988). Educating all the nations' students. *Research in Developmental Education, 5*(1), 1-4.

Boylan, H., Bonham, B., & Bliss, L. (1992). *Report of the National Study of Developmental Education.* Presented at the National Conference on Research in Developmental Education, Charlotte, NC, November.

Boylan, H., Bonham, B., & Bliss, L. (1992). The impact of developmental education programs. *Research in Developmental Education, 9* (5), 1-4.

Boylan, H., Bonham, B., & Bliss, L. (1992). *The state of the art in developmental education.* Presented at the National Association for Developmental Education Conference, Washington, DC, March.

Boylan, H. Bonham, B. & Bliss, L. (1994a, March). *The national study of developmental education: Profile of developmental educators.* Paper presented at the National Association for developmental Education Conference, Chicago, IL.

Boylan, H. (1995). The scope of developmental education: Some basic information on the field. *Research in Developmental Education, 11*(2), 1-4.

Breneman, D. W. (1998). *Remediation in higher education: Its extent and cost, in Brookings papers on educational policy 1998*, 359-383. Washington, DC: The Brookings Institute.

Breneman, D., & Haarlow, W. (1998). *Remedial education: Remedial education: Costs and consequences.* Unpublished paper. Charlottesville, VA: University of Virginia.

Cohen, A., & Brawer, F. (1989). *The American community college.* San Francisco: Jossey-Bass.

Hodgkinson, H. (1993). *Southern crossroads: A demographic look at the Southeast.* Tallahassee, FL: southeastern Regional Vision for Education.

Knopp, L. (1996). Remedial education: An undergraduate student profile. *ACE Research Briefs. 6* (8), 1-11.

Maxwell, M. (1985). *Improving student learning skills.* San Francisco: Jossey-Bass.

National Center for Education Statistics (1985). *The condition of education.* Washington, Office of Educational Research and Improvement.

National Center for Education Statistics. (May, 1991). *Survey report: College level remedial education in the fall of 1989.* Washington, DC: U.S. Department of Education, Office of Educational Research and Improvement.

The Nation: Average scores on the scholastic assessment test (1994, September 1). *The Chronicle of Higher Education,* p. 13.

Tinto, V. (1987). *Leaving college: Rethinking the causes and cures of student attrition.* Chicago: University of Chicago Press.

South Carolina Commission on Higher Education (1992). *Standard information on developmental education programs, 1992 report.* Columbia, SC.

Chapter 3

Abraham, A. A. (1987). *A report on college level remediation/developmental programs in SREB states.* Atlanta, GA: Southern Regional Education Board.

Bandura, A. (1986). *Social foundations of thought and action: A social-cognitive theory.* Englewood-Cliffs, NJ: Prentice Hall.

Bandura, A. (1991). Self-regulation of motivation through anticipatory and self-regulatory mechanisms. In R. A. Dienstbier (Ed.), *Nebraska symposium on motivation: perspectives on motivation* (vol. 38, pp. 69-164). Lincoln: University of Nebraska Press.

Borkowski, J. G., Carr, M., Rellinger, E. A., & Pressley, M. (1990). Self-regulated strategy use: Interdependence of metacognition, attributions, and self-esteem. In B. F. Jones (Ed.), *Dimensions of thinking: Review of research* (pp. 53-92). Hillsdale, NJ: Earlbaum & Associates.

Borkowski, J. G., Weyhing, R. S. & Carr, M. (1986). Effects of attributional retraining on strategy-based reading comprehension in learning-disabled students. *Journal of Educational Psychology, 80,* 46-53.

Broadbent, D. E. (1958). *Perception and communication.* London: Pergamon Press.

Butler, D. L. & Winne, P. H. (1995). Feedback and self-regulated learning: A theoretical synthesis. *Review of Educational Research, 65,* 245-281.

Carr, M. & Borkowski, J. G. (1989). Attributional training and the generalization of reading strategies with underachieving children. *Learning and Individual Differences, 1,* 327-341.

Carr, M., Borkowski, J. G., & Maxwell, S. E. (1991). Motivational components of underachievement. *Developmental Psychology, 27,* 108-118.

Claxton, C. S. (1990). Learning styles, minority students, and effective education. *Journal of Developmental Education, 14,* 6-7; 35.

Corno, L. (1986). The metacognitive control components of self-regulated learning. *Contemporary Educational Psychology, 11,* 333-346.

Corno, L. (1994). Student volition and education: Outcomes, influences, and practices (pp. 229-254). In D. H. Schunk & B. H. Zimmerman (Eds.), *Self regulation of learning and performance: Issues and educational applications.* Hillsdale, NJ: Lawrence Earlbaum Associates.

Corno, L. (1995). Working toward foresight and follow-through. *Midwesterner Educational Researcher, 8,* 2-10.

Dempster, G. N. (1992). The rise and fall of the inhibitory mechanism: toward a unified theory of cognitive development and aging. *Developmental Review, 12,* 45-75.

Dweck, C. S. (1986). Motivational processes affecting learning. *American Psychologist, 41,* 1040-1048.

Elliot, E. S., & Dweck, C. (1988). Goals: an approach to motivation and achievement. *Journal of Personality and Social Psychology, 54,* 5-12.

Fingeret, A. (1983). Common sense of book learning: Culture clash? *Lifelong Learning, 6,* 22-24.

Flavell, J. H. (1985). *Cognitive development.* Englewood Cliffs, NJ: Prentice Hall.

Garcia, T., & Pintrich, P. R. (1994). Regulating motivation and cognition in the classroom: The role of self regulatory strategies. In D. H. Schunk & B. J. Zimmerman (Eds.), *Self-regulation of learning and performance: Issues and educational applications* (pp. 127-153). Hillsdale, Lawrence Earlbaum Associates.

Gernsbacher, M. & Faust, M. E. (1991). The mechanism of suppression: A component of general comprehension skill. *Journal of Experimental Psychology, 17,* 245-262.

Heckhausen, H., & Kuhl, J. (1985). From wishes to action: the dead ends and short-cuts on the long way to action. In M. Frese & J. Sabini (Eds.), *Goal-directed behavior: Psychological theory and research on action* (pp. 134-159). Hillsdale, NJ: Lawrence Earlbaum Associates.

Jonassen, D. H., Beissner, K. & Yacci, M. (1993). *Structural knowledge: Techniques for representing, conveying, and acquiring structural knowledge.* Hillsdale, NJ: Earlbaum.

Kanfer, F. H., & Grimm, L. G. (1978). Freedom of choice and behavioral change. *Journal of Consulting and Clinical Psychology, 46,* 873-878.

Kiewra, K. (1988). Cognitive aspects of autonomous note taking: Control processes, learning strategies, and prior knowledge. *Educational Psychologist, 23,* 39-56.

King, A. (1992). Comparison of self-questioning, summarizing, and note taking-review as strategies for learning from lectures. *American Educational Research Journal, 29,* 303-323.

King, A. (1989). Effects of self-questioning training on college students' comprehension of lectures. *Contemporary Educational Psychology, 14,* 366-381.

King, A. (1991). Effects of training in strategic questioning on children's problem solving performance. *Journal of Educational Psychology, 83,* 307-317.

Knott, E. S. (1991). Working with culturally diverse learners. *Journal of Developmental Education, 15,* 14-18.

Larkin, J. H., & Simon, H. A. (1987). Why a diagram is (sometimes) worth ten thousand words. *Cognitive Science, 11,* 65-99.

Locke, E. A., Frederick, E., Lee, C., & Bobko, P. (1984). Effect of self-efficacy, goals, and task strategies on task performance. *Journal of Applied Psychology, 69,* 241-251.

Locke, E. A., & Latham, G. P. (1990). *A theory of goal setting and task performance.* Englewood Cliffs, NJ: Prentice Hall.

Mandler, J. M. (1984). *Stories, scripts, and scenes: Aspects of schema theory.* Hillsdale, NJ: Lawrence Erlbaum Associates.

Marshall, S. (1995). *Schemas in problem solving.* New York, NY: Cambridge University Press.

Mayer, R. (1989). Models for understanding. *Review of Educational Research, 59,* 43-64.

McDaniel, M. A., & Einstein, G. O. (1989). Material appropriate processing: A contextualist approach to reading and studying strategies. *Educational Psychology Review, 1,* 113-145.

McGraw, K. (1987). *Developmental psychology.* NJ: Harcourt Brace Jovanovich.

McKeachie, W. J., Pintrich, P. R., & Lin, Y. (1985). Teaching learning strategies. *Educational Psychologist, 20,* 153-161.

Miles, C. (1990). The fourth "R": Teaching more or teaching better. *Journal of Developmental Education, 14,* 34.

Moates, D., & Schumacher, G. (1980). *An introduction to cognitive psychology.* Belmont, CA: Wadsworth.

Mossholder, K. W. (1980). Effects of externally mediated goal setting on intrinsic motivation: A laboratory experiment. *Journal of Applied Psychology, 65,* 202-210.

Nicholls, J. G. (1984). Conceptions of ability and achievement motivation. In Ames, R. E. A. C. (Ed.), *Research on motivation in education. Vol. 1: Student motivation:* Academic Press, New York.

Nicholls, J. G. (1989). *The competitive ethos and democratic education.* Cambridge, MA: Harvard University Press.

Noel, L., Levitz, R., & Saluri, D. (1985). *Increasing student retention.* San Francisco: Jossey-Bass.

Nolen, S. B. (1988). Reasons for studying: Motivational orientations and studying strategies. *Cognition and Instruction, 5,* 269-287.

Nolen, S. B. (1996). Why study? How reasons for learning influence strategy selection. *Educational Psychology Review, 8,* 335-355.

Nolen, S. B. & Haladyna, T. M. (1990). Personal and environmental influences on students' beliefs about effective study strategies. *Contemporary Educational Psychology, 15,* 116-130.

Palinscar, A. S. & Brown, A. L. (1984). Reciprocal teaching of comprehensive-fostering and monitoring activities. *Cognition and Instruction, 1,* 117-175.

Paris, S. G., Lipson, M. Y., & Wixson, K. K. (1983). Becoming a strategic reader. *Contemporary Educational Psychology, 8,* 294-316.

Pintrich, P. R., & DeGroot, E. V. (1990). Motivational and self-regulated learning components of classroom academic performance. *Journal of Educational Psychology, 82,* 33-40.

Pintrich, P. R. & Garcia, T. (1991). Student goal orientation and self-regulation in the college classroom. In M. L. Maehr & P. R. Pintrich (Eds.), (Vol. 7, pp. 371-402). Greenwich, CT: JAI Press.

Pressley, M., Borkowski, J. G., & O'Sullivan, J. T. (1984). Memory strategy instruction is made of this: Metamemory and durable strategy use. *Educational Psychologist, 19,* 94-107.

Pressley, M., Borkowski, J. G., & Schneider, W. (1989). Good information processing: What it is and what education can do to promote it. *International Journal of Educational Research, 13,* 857-867.

Pressley, M., Ghatala, E. S., Woloshyn, V., & Pirie, J. (1990). Sometimes adults miss the main ideas and do not realize it: Confidence in responses to short-answer and multiple choice comprehension questions. *Reading Research Quarterly, 25,* 233-249.

Pressley, M., McDaniel, M. A., Turnure, J. E., Wood, E. & Ahmad, M. (1987). Generation and precision of elaboration: Effects on intentional and incidental learning. *Journal of Experimental Psychology: Learning, Memory, Cognition, 13,* 291-300.

Pressley, M., Yokoi, L., van Meter, P., Van Etten, S., & Freebern, G. (1997). Some of the reasons why preparing for exams is so hard. What can be done to make it easier? *Educational Psychology Review, 9,* 1-38.

Robinson, D., & Kiewra, K. (1995). Visual argument: Graphic organizers are superior to outlines in improving learning from text. *Journal of Educational Psychology, 87,* 455-467.

Rumelhart, D. E., & Ortony, A. (1977). The representation of knowledge in memory. In R. C. Anderson, R. J. Spiro, & W. E. Montegue (Eds.), *Schooling and the acquisition of knowledge.* Hillsdale, NJ: Earlbaum.

Schommer, M. (1993). Epistemological development and academic performance among secondary students. *Journal of Educational Psychology, 85,* 406-411.

Schunk, D. H. (1991). Self-efficacy and academic motivation. *Educational Psychologist, 26,* 207-231.

Schunk, D. H. (1994). Self-regulation of self-efficacy and attributions in academic settings. In D. H. Schunk, & B. J. Zimmerman (Eds.) *Self-regulation of learning and performance: Issues in educational applications* (pp. 75-99). Hillsdale, NJ: Earlbaum.

Schunk, D. H., & Schwartz, C. W. (1993). Goals and progress feedback: Effects on self-efficacy and writing achievement. *Contemporary Educational Psychology, 18,* 337-354.

Seligman, M. E. P. (1975). *Helplessness: On depression, development, and death.* San Francisco: W. H. Freeman.

Shriffrin, R. M., & Schneider, W. (1977). Controlled and automatic human information processing: Perceptual learning, automatic attending, and general theory. *Psychological Review, 84,* 127-190.

Simpson, M. L., Hynd, C. R., Nist, S. L., & Burrell, K. I. (1997). College reading and learning strategy programs and practices. *Educational Psychology Review, 9*(1), 39-87.

Spann, N. G. (1990). Student retention: An interview with Vincent Tinto. *Journal of Developmental Education, 14,* 18-24.

Tennyson, R. D., & Cochiarella, M. J. (1986). An empirically based instructional design theory for teaching concepts. *Review of Educational Research, 56,* 40-71.

Weiner, B. (1979). A theory of motivation for some classroom experiences. *Journal of Educational Psychology, 71,* 3-25.

Weiner, B. (1990). History of motivational research in education. *Journal of Educational Psychology, 82,* 616-622.

Weinstein, C. & Mayer, R. (1986). The teaching of learning strategies. In M. C. Wittrock (Ed.). *Handbook of research on teaching.* 3rd ed. (pp. 315-327). New York: Macmillan.

Zimmerman, B. J. (1986). Development of self-regulated learning: Which are the key sup processes. *Contemporary Educational Psychology, 16,* 307-313.

Zimmerman, B. J. (1989). Self-regulated learning and academic achievement: An overview. *Educational Psychologist, 25,* 3-18.

Zimmerman, B. J., Bandura, A., & Martinez-Pons, M. (1992). Self-motivation for academic attainment: The role of self-efficacy beliefs and personal goal setting. *American Educational Research Journal, 29,* 663-676.

Zimmerman, B. J., Greenberg, D., & Weinstein, C. (1994). Self-regulating academic study time: A strategy approach. In D. H. Schunk, & B. J. Zimmerman (Eds.), *Self-regulation of learning and performance: Issues in educational applications* (pp. 181-199). Hillsdale, NJ: Earlbaum.

Zimmerman, B. J. & Schunk, D. H. (1994). *Self-regulated learning and academic achievement: Theory research and practice.* New York, NY: Springer-Verlag.

Chapter 4

Abraham, A. A. (1987). *A report on college-level remedial/developmental programs in SREB states.* Atlanta, GA: Southern Regional Education Board. (ERIC Document Reproduction Service No. ED 280 369)

American College Testing Program. (1992). *ACT institutional data file.* Iowa City: Author.

Arendale, D. R. (1996). *Survey on remedial education in higher education institutions.* [Online]. Available: www.umkc.edu

Astin, A. (1993). *What matters in college.* San Francisco: Jossey-Bass Publishers.

Boylan, H. R., Bliss, L. B., & Bonham, B. S., (1997). Program components and their relationship to student performance. *Journal of Developmental Education, 20*(3), 2 - 8.

Callas, D. (1985). Academic placement practices: An Analysis and proposed model. *College Teaching, 33*(1), 27-32.

Commander, N.E., & Smith, B.D. (1995). Developing adjunct reading and learning courses that work. *Journal of Reading, 38*(5), 352-360.

Dimon, M. G. (1988). Why adjunct courses work. *Journal of College Reading and Learning, 21,* 33-40.

Hart, L. & Najee-ullah, D. (1995). *Studying for mathematics.* New York: Harper Collins.

Henry, T. C. (1986). Needed: Comprehensive evaluation of education program efforts. *Community College Review, 14*(2), 46-52.

Keimig, R. T. (1983). *Raising academic standards: A guide to learning improvement.* (ASHE-ERIC Higher Education Report No. 4). Washington, D.C.: Association for the Study of Higher Education.

Kleupfel, G. (1994). Developing successful retention programs: An interview with Michael Hovland. *Journal of Developmental Education, 17*(3), 28-33.

Kulik, C. C., Kulik, J. A., & Schwalb, B. J. (1993). College programs for high-risk and disadvantaged students: A metaanalysis of findings. *Review of Educational Research, (53),* 397-414.

Levine, J. H. & Tompkins, D. P. (1996). Making learning communities work. *American Association of Higher Education Bulletin, 40*(10), pp. 3-6.

Martin, D. C. (1980). Learning centers in professional schools. In K. V. Lauridsen (Eds.), *New directions for college learning assistance: Examining the scope of learning centers.* San Francisco: Jossey-Bass.

Martin, D. C. & Arendale, D. R. (1990). *Supplemental instruction: Improving standards and performance, increasing student persistence.* Kansas City, MO: University of Missouri Center for Academic Development. (ERIC Document Reproduction Service. ED 327103. MF-1; PC01).

Maxwell, M. (1979). *Improving student learning skills.* San Francisco: Jossey-Bass.

Noel, L., Levitz, R., & Saluri, D. (1985). *Increasing student retention.* San Francisco: Jossey Bass.

Pascarella, E., & Terenzini, P. T. (1991). *How college affects students.* San Francisco: Jossey-Bass Publishers.

Roueche, S. D. (1985). *Basic skills: Dealing with deficiencies.* (ERIC Document Reproduction Service No. ED 271 087).

Simpson, M. L., Holschah, J. H., Nist, S. L., & Hynd, C. (1994, April). *Adjunct seminars: A viable form of supplemental instruction.* Paper presented at the 19th Annual Developmental Studies Conference, Jekyll Island, GA.

Simpson, M. L., Hynd, C. R., Nist, S. L., & Burrell, K. I. (1997, March). College academic assistance programs and practices. *Educational Psychology Review, 9*(1), 39-87.

Stahl, N. A., Simpson, M. L. & Hayes, C. G. (1992). Ten recommendations from research for teaching high-risk college students. *Journal of Developmental Education, 16*(1), 2-10.

Stone, K. R.(1995). *Annual report: Division of developmental studies.* Unpublished manuscript, Georgia State University, Atlanta.

Stratton, C. B. (1996). Effects of learning support on college algebra. *Defining developmental education: Theory, research, & pedagogy.* Cold Stream, IL: National Association for Developmental Education.

Tinto, V. (1996). *Building learning communities for new college students: A summary of research findings of the collaborative learning project.* National Center on Postsecondary Teaching, Learning and Assessment, Syracuse University School of Education.

Tinto, V. (1987). *Leaving college: Rethinking the causes and cures of student attrition.* Chicago: The University of Chicago Press.

Tinto, V. (1993). *Leaving college: Rethinking the causes and cures of student attrition.* Chicago: The University of Chicago Press.

Visor, J. M., Johnson, J. J., & Cole, L. N. (1992). Relationship of supplemental instruction to affect. *Journal of Developmental Education, 16*(2), 12-18.

Visor, J. M., Johnson, J. J., Schollaet, A. M., Good Majab, C. A., & Davenport, O. (1995). *Supplemental instruction's impact on affect; A follow-up and expansion.* Proceedings from the 20th Annual Conference on Developmental Education, Chicago, IL.

Wyatt, M.(1992). The past, present, and future need for college reading courses in the U.S. *Journal of Reading, 36,* 10-20.

Chapter 5

Adelman, C. (1995). *The new college course map and transcript files.* Washington, DC: U.S. Department of Education, Office of Educational Research and Improvement, National Institute on Post-secondary Education, Libraries and Lifelong Learning.

Anderson, E. (1978). A retention design applied to an equal opportunity program. In L. Noel (Ed.). *Reducing the Dropout Rate.* San Francisco: Jossey-Bass, Inc.

Beal, P. E. & Noel, L. (1980). *What works in student retention.* Iowa City, Ioqa and Boulder, CO: American College Testing Program and National Center for Higher Education Management Systems.

Beckett, G. (1995). *Developmental education goals and definition.* Chicago, IL: National Association for Developmental Education.

Berryman, S. E. (1983*). Who will do science?* New York: Rockefeller Foundation.

Busser, J. A. et al., (1992). Balancing the rigors of academic study: A summer enrichment program for minority students. *Journal of Physical Education, Recreation and Dance, 63,* 32-35.

Collins, W. (1981). Developing basic skills through learning center summer programs. In L. Noel (Ed.) *Serving Academically Underprepared Students.* Iowa City, Iowa: American College Testing Program.

Collins, W. (1982). Affective development as a foundation for college adjustment. In K. Lauridsen & C. Myers (eds.) *New Directions for College Learning Assistance, No. 10,* San Francisco: Jossey-Bass, December.

Coppola, B. P. & Daniels, D. S. (1996). Structuring the liberal (Arts) education in chemistry. *The Chemical Educator, 1*(2).

Davis, J. (1986). *The effects of mathematics course enrollment on minority students' achievement in secondary school mathematics.* Princeton, NJ: Educational Testing Service.

Gardner, A. J. & Jewler, J. A. (1992). *Your college experience: Strategies for success.* Belmont, CA: Wadsworth Publishing Co.

Gordon, V. N. (1984). *The undecided student.* Springfield, IL: Charles C. Thomas.

Grites, T. J. (1977). Student development through academic advising. A 4 x 4 model. *NASPA Journal, 4,* 33-37.

Gurthrie, L. F., et al., (1991). *Minority achievement and retention: Evaluation of the California State University Summer Bridge and Intensive Learning Experience Program (1985-1991): Final report.* San Francisco: Far West Laboratory for Educational Research and Development.

Hardy, D. G. & Karanthanos, D. (1992). A bridge course for high-risk freshmen: Evaluating outcomes. *NASPA Journal, 29*(3), 13-21.

Johnson, D. W., Johnson, R. T., & Smith, K. A. (1991). *Cooperative learning: Increasing college faculty instructional productivity.* ASHE-ERIC Higher Education Report No. 2, Washington, DC: George Washington University, School of Education and Human Development.

Johnson, L. (1965, June 4). *Commencement Address.* Presented at Howard University, Washington, D.C.

King, N. S. (1993). Partnerships and collaboration and new student success. *College Student Affairs Journal, 13*(1), 44-47.

Kulik, C., Kulik, J., & Schwalb, B. (1983). College programs for high-risk and disadvantaged students: A meta-analysis of findings. *Review of Educational Research, 53,* 397-414.

Levine, A. (1993). *Higher education in America: 1980-2000.* Baltimore: The Johns Hopkins University Press.

Martin, D. & Arendale, D. R. (Eds.). (1994). Supplemental instruction: Increasing achievement and retention. *New Directions in Teaching and Learning.* San Francisco: Jossey Bass, No. 60, Winter.

Massey, W. E. (1992, Nov.) A success story amid decades of disappointment. *Science, 258*(13), 1177-1180.

Matlock, J. (1992). *The Michigan study.* Ann Arbor, MI: The University of Michigan, Office of Academic Multicultural Initiatives.

Maxwell, M. (1979). *Improving student learning skills.* San Francisco: Jossey-Bass Publishers.

Rudenstine, N. L. (1996, April 19). Why a diverse student body is so important. In *The Chronicle of Higher Education, XLII,* 32.

Sullivan, L. L. (1978). *A guide to higher education learning centers in the United States and Canada.* Portsmoth, NH.: Entelek.

Thomas, G. E. (1987). Black students in U. S. graduate and professional schools in the 1980s: A national and institutional assessment. *Harvard Educational Review, 57*(3) Aug, 1988, 261-282.

Weinstein, C. E., Goetz, E. T. & Alexander, P. A. (1988). *Learning and study strategies.* NY: Academic Press.

Chapter 6

American Council of Education. (January 22, 1996). ACE Report Provides Data on Students in Developmental Courses, *Higher Education & National Affairs, 45,* II., pp. 3 & 6.

Astin, A. W. *What matters in college.* (1993). San Francisco: Jossey-Bass.

Black, M., Mansfield, W., & Farris, E. (May 1991). *College level remedial education in the fall of 1989., Survey Report.* Washington, DC: U. S. Department of Education.

Bandura, A. (1982). Self efficacy mechanism in human agency. *American Psychologist, 37*(2), 122-147.

Boylan H.R., Bonham, B.S., & Bliss, L. B. (1994). Characteristics components of developmental programs. *Research in Developmental Education, 11*(1).

Boylan, H.R., & Bonham, B.S. (1992). The impact of developmental education programs. *Research in Developmental Education 9*(2).

Brookfield, S. *The skillful teacher.* San Francisco: Jossey-Bass, 1990. York: Bronx Community College.

Donovan, R. A. (1976, July). The Southwest Institution of National Project II. *Alternatives to the Revolving Door Newsletter #2,* pp. 1-6.

Fleming, J. (1984). *Blacks in college: A comparative study of students' success in black and white institutions.* Iowa City, IA: American College Testing Program, National Center for Advancement of Educational Practices.

Fletcher, M. A. (May 10,1997). Xavier's desk-side manner is prescription for med school: Small black college nurtures achievement. Wash., DC: *The Washington Post.*

Hardin, C. J. (Fall 1988). Access to higher education: Who belongs? *Journal of Developmental Education, 12(1),* 2-6. Reprinted in M. Maxwell, (Ed.) *From Access to Success,* Clearwater, FL: H&H Publishing Co. 1994.

Johnson, C. S. (1989). Mentoring programs. In M. L. Upgraft & J. N. Gardner & Associates. *The Freshman Year Experience: Helping Students Survive and Succeed in College,* San Francisco: Jossey-Bass., pp.118-128.

Kirk, B. A. (1965). Test versus academic performance in Malfunctioning Students. In M. Kornrich (Ed.) *Underachievement.* Springfield, IL: Thomas.

Lester, V. & Johnson, C. S., (1981).The learning dialogue: Mentoring. In J. Fried, (Ed,) *Education for Student Development, New Directions for Student Services, no. 15.* San Francisco: Jossey-Bass,

Maxwell, M. (1997). *Improving student learning skills.* Clearwater, FL: H&H Publishing Company.

National Center for Education Statistics. (October 1996). *Remedial education at higher education institutions in Fall 1995,* Statistical Analysis Report NCES 97-584 Washington, DC: National Center for Education Statistics. Office of Educational Research and Improvement, U.S. Department of Education.

Noel, L., Levitz, R., & Saluri, D. (Eds.). 1987. *Increasing student retention: Effective programs and pracitices for reducing the dropout rate.* San Francisco: Jossey-Bass.

Perry, R. P. & Penner, K S. (1990). Enhancing academic achievement in college students through attributional retraining and instruction. *Journal of Educational Psychology, 92*(2), 262-271.

Petit, J. M. & White, W. G., Jr. (1996). *The impact of underprepared students on regular college faculty.* Paper presented at the Second National Conference on Research in Developmental Education, Charlotte, NC.

Rayman, J. R. & Garis, J. W. (1989). Counseling, In M. L. Upgraft & J. N. Gardner & Associates. *The Freshman Year Experience: Helping Students Survive and Succeed in College,* San Francisco: Jossey-Bass, 129-141.

Rotter, J. B. (1966). Generalized expectancies for internal versus external control of reinforcement. *Psychological Measurements, 80,* 1-28.

Roueche J. E. & Snow, J. J. (1977). *Overcoming learning problems.* San Francisco: Jossey-Bass.

Roueche, J. E. & Roueche, S .D. (1993*). Between a rock and a hard place: The at-risk student in the open-door college.* Washington, DC: The American Association of Community Colleges.

Silverman, S. & Juhasz, A. M. (1993). A developmental interpretation of help rejection. *Journal of Developmental Education, 17*(2), 24-26, 28, 30-31.

Whimbey, A. E. & Whimbey, L. S. (1975). *Intelligence can be taught.* New York: Dutton.

Chapter 7

Brown, T. & Rivas, M. (1995). Pluralistic advising: Facilitating the development and achievement of first-year students of color. In Upcraft, M. L. and Kramer, G. L. (Eds.). *First-year academic advising: Patters in the present, pathways to the future.* Columbia, SC: University of South Carolina National Resource Center for the Freshman Year Experience and Students in Transition.

Chickering, A. W. (1969). *Education and identity.* San Francisco: Jossey-Bass

Crookston, B.B. (1972). A developmental view of academic advising as teaching. *Journal of College Student Personnel, 13,* 12-17.

Fidler, P. P. & Fidler, D. S. (1991). *First national survey on freshman seminar programs: Findings, conclusions, and recommendations.* Columbia, SC: University of South Carolina National Resource Center for The Freshman Year Experience.

Frost, S. H. (1991). Academic advising for student success: A system of shared responsibility. *ASHE-ERIC Higher Education Report No. 3.* Washington, D.C.: The George Washington University, School of Education and Human Development.

Glennen, R.E. (1976). Intrusive college counseling. *School Counselor, 24,* 48-50.

Glennen, R.E. & Vowell, F.N. (Eds.) (1995). *Academic advising as a comprehensive campus process.* Manhattan, KS: National Academic Advising Association.

Gordon, V.N. (1992). *Handbook of academic advising.* Westport, CT: Greenwood Press.

Gordon, V. N. (1988). Developmental advising. In Habley, W. R. (Ed.). *The status and future of academic advising: Problems and promise.* Manhattan, KS: National Academic Advising Association.

Gordon, V. N. & Grites, T. J. (1984). The freshman seminar course: Helping students succeed. *Journal of College Student Personnel, 25,* 315-320.

Habley, W.R. (1981). Academic Advisement: The critical link in student retention. *NASPA Journal, 18*(4), 45-50.

Habley, W.R. (1993*). Fulfilling the promise? Final report ACT fourth national survey of academic advising.* Iowa City, IA: American College Testing.

Higbee, J. L. (1996). Defining developmental education: A commentary. In Higbee, J. L. & Dwinell, P. L. (Eds.). *Defining developmental education: Theory, research, & pedagogy.* Cold Stream, IL: National Association for Developmental Education.

National Association for Developmental Education (NADE). Cold Stream, IL.

Payne, E. M. & Lyman, B. G. (1996). Issues affecting the definition of developmental education. In Higbee, J. L. & Dwinell, P. L. (Eds.). *Defining Developmental Education: Theory, Research, & Pedagogy.* Cold Stream, IL: National Association for Developmental Education.

Patrick, J., Furlow, J. W., & Donovan, S. (1988). Using a comprehensive intervention program in the retention of high-risk students. *NACADA Journal, 8*(1), 29-34.

Simmons, G., Wallins, J., & George, A. (1995). The effects of a freshman seminar on at-risk under-, over-, and low achievers. *NACADA Journal, 15*(1), 8-14.

Spann, N. G., Spann, M. G., Jr., & Confer, L. S. (1995). In Upcraft, M. L. & Kramer, G. L. (Eds.). *First-year academic advising: Patterns in the present, pathways to the future*. Columbia, SC: University of South Carolina National Resource Center for the Freshman Year Experience & Students in Transition.

Tinto, V. (1987). *Leaving college*. Chicago: The University of Chicago Press.

Winston, R. B., Jr., Miller, T.K., Ender, S.C., Grites, T. J., & Associates (1984). *Developmental academic advising*. San Francisco, CA: Jossey-Bass.

Chapter 8

Abrams, H. G., & Jernigan, L. P. (1984). Academic support services and success of high risk college students. *American Educational Research Journal, 21*(2), 261-274.

American Council on Education. *Minorities on campus: A handbook for enhancing diversity*. Madeleine F. Green (Ed.) Washington, DC: no date given.

Boylan, H. R. (1988). The historical roots of developmental education. *Research in Developmental Education, 5*(3), 1-3.

Chauncey, H. (1961). *Educational Testing Service Annual Report*, 1960-61, p. 25.

Chauncey, J. & Dobbins, J. E. (1963). *Testing: Its place in education today*. New York: Harper and Row.

Chenoweth, K. (1997, Sept. 4). A measurement of what? *Black Issues in Higher Education, 14*(14), 18-25.

Cross, K. P. (1974). *Beyond the open door*. San Francisco: Jossey Bass.

Cross, K.P. (1976). *Accent on learning: Improving instructions and reshaping the curriculum*. San Francisco, CA: Jossey-Bass.

Crouse, J. & Trusheim, D. (1988). *The case against the SAT*. Chicago: The University of Chicago Press.

Educational Testing Service, "Statement of Educational Testing Service on Certain Key Issues in None of the Above: Behind the Myths of Scholastic Aptitude" by David Owen. p. 1.

Elifson, J., Pounds, M. L., & Stone, K. R. (1995). Planning for and assessment of developmental programs. *Journal of Developmental Education, 19*(1), 2-11.

Gardner, H. (1993). *Multiple intelligences: The theory into practice*. New York: Basic Books.

Gardner, H. (1983). *Frames of mind: The theory of multiple intelligences*. New York: Basic Books.

Grafton, C. L., & Michael, W. B. (1983). The predictive validity of cognitive and affective measures in a small religiously oriented liberal arts college. *Educational and Psychological Measurement, 43*, 865-872.

Hanford, G. H. (1991). *Life with the SAT*. New York: College Entrance Examination Board, p. 29.

Hasit, C. & DiObilda, N. (1996). Portfolio assessment in a college developmental reading class. *Journal of Developmental Education, 19*(3), 26-31.

Havighurst, R. J. (1960). *American higher education in the 1960s*. Columbus, Ohio: Ohio State University Press.

Hess, J. H., Grafton, C. L., & Michael, W. B. (1983). The predictive validity of cognitive and affective measures in a small religiously oriented liberal arts college. *Educational and Psychological Measurement, 43*(3), 865-872.

Hiss, W. (1990). Optional SATS: Six years later. *Bates: The Alumni Magazine*, 15-19.

Hiss, W. (1990). Optional testing: The emperor's new clothes? *Journal of College Admission*, 9-11.

Jencks, C. & Crouse, J. (1982). *Should we relabel the SAT or replace it?* New Directions for Testing and Measurement, no. 13, 13-49.

Larose, S. & Roy, R. (1991). The role of prior academic performance and nonacademic attributes in the prediction of the success of high risk college students. *Journal of College Student Development, 32*(2), 171-177.

Maxwell, M. (1981). *Improving student learning skills*. San Francisco, CA: Jossey-Bass.

Nisbet J., Ruble, V. E., & Schurr, K. T. (1982). Predictors of academic success with high risk college students. *Journal of College Personnel, 23*(3), 227-235.

Owen, D. (1985). *None of the above: Behind the myth of scholastic aptitude*. Boston: Houghton Mifflin.

Paulson, F. L., Paulson, P. R., & Meyer, C. A. (1991). What makes a portfolio a portfolio? *Educational Leadership, 48*(5), 60-63.

Ratitch, D. (1996). *New SAT score validate mediocrity*, The Miami Herald. p. 25A August 26, 1996.

Rose, M. (1989). *Lives on the boundary*. New York: The Free Press.

Schaffner, P. E. (1985). Competitive admission practices when the SAT is optional. *Journal of Higher Education, 56*(1), 55-72.

Scott, K. J., & Robbins, S. B. (1985). Goal instability: Implications for academic performance among students in learning skills courses. *Journal of College Student Personnel, 26*(2), 129-133.

Shabazz, M. (1985). Competitive admission practices when the SAT is optional. *Journal of Higher Education, 56*(1), 55-72.

————. (1995). Testing: Education's necessary evil. *Black Issues in Higher Education, 11,* 24-29

Stemmer, P., Brown, B., & Smith, C. (1992). The employability skills portfolio. *Educational Leadership, 49*(6), 32-35.

Test free admissions. (1997, Sept. 4). *Black Issues in Higher Education*, 26-27.

Tomlinson, L. M. (1989). *Postsecondary developmental programs*. ASHE ERIC Higher Education Report 3. Washington, DC: The George Washington University.

Unger, H. G. (1995). *A student's guide to college admissions*. New York: Facts on File, Inc.

Wechsler, H. S. (1977). *The qualified student: A history of selective college admission in America*. New York: John Wiley and Sons.

White, T. J. & Sedlacek, W. E. (1986). Noncognitive predictors: Grade retention of specially admitted students. *The Journal of College Admissions,* no. 111, 20-23.

Young, R. E. (1997). *Cognaffective thinking: An integrated approach to facilitating cognitive and affective problem-solving skills.* Ruston, LA: The Word Publishing Company.

Chapter 9

American College Testing Program. (1996). *Institutional data file, 1996.* Iowa City: Author.

Arons, A. B., & Karplus, R. (1976). Implications of accumulating data on levels of intellectual development. *American Journal of Physics, 44,* 386.

Astin, A. W. (1987, September/October). Competition or cooperation? Teaching teamwork as a basic skill. *Change, 19:* 12, 14, 16-19.

Beckett, G. (1989, June 14). In Response to "Admitting and Retaining Underprepared Students." (Letter to the Editor). *The Chronicle of Higher Education,* p. B3.

Blanc, R. A., DeBuhr, L., & Martin, D. C. (1983). Breaking the attrition cycle: The effects of supplemental instruction on undergraduate performance and attrition. *Journal of Higher Education, 54(1),* 80-90.

Bloom, B. et al. (1956). *Taxonomy of educational objectives: The classification of educational goals.* Handbook 1. Cognitive domain. New York: McKay.

Boylan, H. R. (1988). The historical roots of developmental education. *Review of Research in Developmental Education, 5(3),* 1-3.

Boylan, H. (1985). Effectiveness of developmental programs. *Research in Developmental Education, 2,* 1-6.

Boylan, H. R., Bingham, E. L., & Cookman, D. C. (1988). Organizational patterns for developmental education programs. *Review of Research in Developmental Education, 5 (4),* 1-4.

Clayton, D. (1995). *Supplemental instruction vs. peer tutoring—What works for math.* Paper presented at the annual conference of the National Association for Developmental Education (NADE), Chicago, Illinois, February 23, 1997.

Cross, K. P. (1971). *Beyond the open door.* San Francisco: Jossey-Bass Publishers.

Dale, E. (1969). *Audiovisual methods in teaching.* New York: The Dryden Press.

Davis, A. (1995). *Collaborative learning-peer/faculty.* Paper presented at the annual conference of the National Association for Developmental Education (NADE), Chicago, Illinois, February 23, 1997.

Denton, P. H., Seybert, J. A., & Franklin, E. L. (1988). Ideas in practice: A content-based learning strategies program. *Journal of Developmental Education, 11* (3), 20-24.

Dimon, M. G. (1994). Why adjunct courses work. In Martha Maxwell (Ed.)., *From access to success: A book of readings on college developmental education and learning assistance programs, pp. 201-207.* Clearwater, FL: H & H Publishing Company, Inc.

Fjortoft, N., Bentley, R., Crawford, D. & Russell, J. C. (1991). *Evaluation of the Supplemental Instruction Program at the College of Pharmacy, Fall 1990.* Chicago, IL: The University of Illinois at Chicago.

Fuller, R. G. (Ed.). (1984). *Piagetian programs in higher education.* Lincoln, NB: ADAPT.

Greenburg, D. E. (1983). College basic skills: A national survey. *Journal of Developmental and Remedial Education, 6 (3)*, 2-31.

Grimes, H. (1989). *The Supplemental Instruction Model-Testing Program in the College of Pharmacy: Some Preliminary Results.* Chicago, IL: The University of Illinois at Chicago.

Hardin, C. J. (1988, September). Access to Higher Education: Who Belongs? *Journal of Developmental Education, 12 (1)*, 2-6, 19.

Hawthorne, J., & Hawthorne, J. W. (1987, March). *Separating the wheat from the chaff: finding the unique effect of supplemental course instruction.* Paper presented at the 11th Annual Conference of the National Association for Developmental Education, New Orleans, LA.

Heiman, M., & Slomianko, J. (1986). *Methods of inquiry: The learning to learn thinking improvement system.* Cambridge, MA: Learning Skills Consultants.

Hines, S. M. (1989, December 7). Are we fostering dependence in minority students? *Black Issues in Higher Education*, p. 112.

Karplus, R., Lawson, A. E., Wollman, W., Appel, M., Bernoff, R., Howe, A., Rusch, J. J., & Sullivan, F. (1976). *Science teaching and the development of reasoning: A workshop.* Berkeley, CA: Regents of the University of California.

Kearney, G. W. (1990, June 14). In response to "Admitting and Retaining Underprepared Students." (Letter to the Editor). *The Chronicle of Higher Education*, p. B3.

Keimig, R. T. (1983). *Raising academic standards: A guide to learning improvement.* ASHE-ERIC Higher Education Report No. 4. Washington, D. C.: Association for the Study of Higher Education. ED 233 669.

Kelly, J. (1989, May 17). Colleges shouldn't waste their resources on students who aren't qualified to be there in the first place. *The Chronicle of Higher Education*, p. B2.

Kulik, C. C., Kulik, J. A., & Schwalb, B. J. (1983, Fall). College programs for high-risk and disadvantaged students: A meta-analysis of findings. *Review of Educational Research, 53 (3)*, 397-414.

Light, R. J. (1990). *The Harvard assessment seminars: Explorations with students and faculty about teaching, learning, and student life.* Cambridge, MA: Harvard University.

LoCascio, B. S. (1991). Supplemental instruction: An integrative approach to help high risk students. In Johanna Dvorak (Ed.), *Breaking Barriers To Learning: Proceedings From The Fifth Annual MCLCA Conference* (pp. 37-38). Milwaukee, WI: Midwest College Learning Center Association.

Luvaas-Briggs, L. (1984). Integrating basic skills with college content instruction. *Journal of Developmental and Remedial Education, 7(2)*, 6-9, 31.

Martin, D. C., & Arendale, D. A. (Eds.). (1994, Winter). *Supplemental Instruction: Improving student achievement and persistence.* New Directions for Teaching and Learning. San Francisco: Jossey-Bass.

Martin, D. C., & Blanc, R. (1981, Spring). The learning center's role in retention: integrating student support services with departmental instruction. *Journal of Developmental Instruction, 4*, 2-4, 21-23.

Martin, D. C., Arendale, D. A., & Associates. (1992). *Supplemental Instruction: Improving first-year student success in high risk courses.* Columbia, SC: National Resource Center for The Freshman Year Experience, University of South Carolina, Division of Continuing Education.

Martin, D. C., Blanc, R. A., & DeBuhr, L. (1982). Supplemental Instruction: A model for increasing student performance and persistence. In L. Noel & R. Levitz (Eds.), *How to succeed with academically underprepared students.* Iowa City, IA: The ACT National Center for the Advancement of Educational Practices.

Martin, D., Blanc, R., DeBuhr, L., & Associates. (1983). *Retention with integrity through supplemental instruction.* Kansas City, MO: University of Missouri-Kansas City.

Martin, D., Blanc, R., DeBuhr, L., Alderman, H., Garland, M., & Lewis, C. (1983). *Supplemental Instruction: A model for student academic support.* Kansas City, MO: University of Missouri-Kansas City and ACT National Center for the Advancement of Educational Practices.

Maxwell, M. (1990). Does tutoring help? A look at the literature. *Research in Developmental Education, 7 (4),* 1-5.

Maxwell, M. (1979). *Improving Student Learning Skills.* San Francisco: Jossey-Bass Publishers.

McKeachie, W. J., Pintrich, P. R., & Lin, Y. (1985). Teaching learning strategies. *Educational Psychologist, 20 (3),* 153-160.

Morante, E. A. (1986). The Effectiveness of developmental programs: A two-year follow-up study. *Journal of Developmental Education, 9 (3),* 14-15.

National Center for Supplemental Instruction. (1996). *Supplemental Instruction: Review of research concerning the effectiveness of SI from The University of Missouri-Kansas City and other institutions from across the United States.* Kansas City, MO: Author.

Noel, L. (Ed). (1978). *Reducing the dropout rate.* San Francisco: Jossey-Bass Publishers.

Noel, L., & Beal, P. E. (1980). *What works in student retention.* Iowa City, IA: American College Testing Program.

Noel, L., Levitz, R., Saluri, D., & Associates. (1985). *Increasing student retention: Effective programs and practices for reducing the dropout rate.* San Francisco, CA: Jossey-Bass, Publishers.

Pascarella, E. T., & Terenzini, P. T. (1991). *How college affects students: Findings and insights from twenty years of research.* San Francisco, CA: Jossey-Bass Publishers.

Perry, W. G. (1970). *Forms of intellectual and ethical development in the college years.* New York: Holt, Rinehart and Winston.

Piaget, J. (1964). Development and learning. *Journal of Research in Science Teaching, Vol. 2*, pp. 176-186.

Piaget, J., & Inhelder, B. (1958). *Growth of logical thinking.* New York: Basic Books.

Rumelhart, D. (1980). Schemata: The building blocks of cognition. In R. Spiro, B. Bruce, & W. Brewer (Eds.), *Theoretical issues in reading comprehension* (pp. 33-58). Hillsdale, NJ: Erlbaum.

Sternberg, R. (1984, September). How can we teach intelligence? *Educational Leadership, 42*, 38-50.

Sternberg, R. (1985a). Critical thinking: Its nature, measurement, and improvement. In F. Link (Ed.). *Association for Supervision and Curriculum Development: Essays on the intellect*, 45-66.

Sternberg, R.. (1985b, November). Teaching critical thinking, Part I: Are we making critical mistakes? *Phi Delta Kappan, 67,* 194-198.

Thompson, C. G. (1988). Equal opportunity—past and present: An interview with Harold Howe II. *Journal of Developmental Education, 11(3)*, 16-19.

Tinto, V. (1987). *Leaving college: Rethinking the causes and cures of student attrition.* Chicago, IL: The University of Chicago Press.

Upcraft, M. L., Gardner, J. N., & Associates. (1989). *The freshman year experience: Helping students survive and succeed in college.* San Francisco, CA: Jossey-Bass Publishers.

Van, B. (1992). College learning assistance programs: Ingredients for success. *Journal of College Reading and Learning, 24(2)*, 27-39.

Watkins, B. T. (1989, June 14). Many campuses now challenging minority students to excel in math and science. *Chronicle of Higher Education,* p. A13, 16.

Weinstein, C. (1984, April). *Comprehension monitoring: The neglected learning strategy.* Paper presented at the annual meeting of the American Educational Association, New Orleans, LA.

Whimbey, A. (1984, September). The key to higher order thinking is precise processing. *Educational Leadership, 42,* 66-70.

Whimbey, A., & Lockhead, J. (1982). *Problem solving and comprehension: A short course in analytical reasoning.* Philadelphia: Franklin Institute.

Yates, J. F., Barham, W. A., Shure, P. , & Story, R. D. (1984). *Guidelines and suggestions for teachers of CSP Intensive Course sections.* 1984-85 Edition. Ann Arbor, MI: The Comprehensive Studies Program.

Chapter 10

Bandura, A. (1977). *Social learning theory.* Englewood Cliffs, NJ: Prentiss Hall.

Dick, W., & Carey, L. (1996). *The systematic design of instruction.* New York NY: Harper Collins.

Gagne, R. M. (1972). *The conditions of learning* (2nd ed.). New York, NY: Holt, Rinehart & Winston.

Gagne, R. M., & Briggs, L. J. (1979). *Principles of instructional design* (2nd ed.). New York, NY: Holt, Rinehart & Winston.

Gentry, C. G. (1994). *Introduction to instructional development.* Belmont, CA: Wadsworth Publishing Company.

Gooler, D. D. (1980). Formative evaluation for major instructional design projects. *Journal of Instructional Design, 3,* 7-11.

Haas, G., & Parkay, F. W. (1993). *Curriculum planning: A new approach* (6th ed.). Needham Heights, MA: Allyn & Bacon.

Keller, J. M. (1987). Strategies for stimulating the motivation to learn. *Performance and Instruction, 26*(9), 1-7.

Kemp, J. E., Morrison, G. R., & Ross, S. M. (1996). *Designing effective instruction.* Upper Saddle River, NJ: Prentice-Hall, Inc.

Mager, R. F. (1962). *Preparing instructional objectives.* Palo Alto, CA: Fearon.

Markle, S. (1969). *Good frames and bad: A grammar of frame writing.* New York: Wiley.

McNeil, J. (1996). *Curriculum: A comprehensive introduction* (5th ed.). New York: HarperCollins College Publishers.

National Association for Developmental Educators. (1996). *Developmental education: Goals and definition* [Poster]. Cold Stream, IL: Author.

Ornstein, A. C., & Hunkins, F. (1993). *Curriculum: Foundations, principles, and theory* (2nd ed.). Needham Heights, MA: Allyn & Bacon.

Romiszowski, A. J. (1988). *The selection and use of instructional media* (2nd ed.). New York, NY: Kogan Page.

Seels, B., & Glasgow, Z. (1990). *Exercises in instructional design.* Columbus, OH: Merrill Publishing Company.

Smith, P. L., & Ragan, T. J. (1983). *Instructional design.* New York: Macmillan Publishing Company.

Stamas, S. (1973). *Instructional design models.* Division of Instructional Development Occasional Paper. Washington DC: Association for Educational Communications and Technology.

Walker, D. (1990). *Fundamentals of curriculum.* Orlando, FL: Harcourt Brace Jovanovich, Inc. Curriculum Design for Developmental Learners.

Chapter 11

Applebee, A. N., Langer, J. A., & Mullis, I. V. S. (1986). *The writing report card: Writing achievement in American schools.* Princeton, J: Educational Testing Service.

Banks, J. A. (1981). *Multiethnic education theory and practice.* Boston, MA: Allyn and Bacon, Inc.

Berkenkotter, C. (1983, May). *Student writers and their audiences: Case studies of the revising decisions of three college freshman.* Paper presented at the

16th Annual Meeting of the Canadian Council of Teachers of English, Montreal, CA.

Berkenkotter, C. (1984). Student writers and their sense of authority over texts. *College Composition and Communication, 35*(3), 312-19.

Bleich, D. (1995). Collaboration and the pedagogy of disclosure. *College English, 57* (1), 43-61.

Bloom, B. S. (1956). *Taxonomy of educational objectives.* New York: McKay.

Bruffee, K. A. (1984). Collaborative learning and the "conversation of mankind." *College English, 46* (7), 635-652.

Bruffee, K. A. (1993). *Collaborative learning: Higher education, interdependence and the authority of knowledge.* Baltimore: The Johns Hopkins University Press.

Clifford, J. P. (1977). An experimental inquiry into the effectiveness of collaborative learning as a method for improving the experiential writing performance of college freshmen in a remedial writing class. (Doctoral dissertation, New York University, 1978). *Dissertation Abstracts International,* 38-12A, AAI7808455.

Coleman, E. (1987, Mar.). *Response groups as a source of data for classroom based research.* Paper presented at the 38th Annual Meeting of the Conference on College Composition and Communication. Atlanta, GA. (ERIC Document Reproduction Services No. ED 281 192)

Connors, R. & Lunsford, A. (1993, May). Teachers' rhetorical comments on students papers. *College Composition and Communication, 44* (2), 200-223.

Davidman, L. & Davidman, P. T. (1994). *Teaching with a multicultural perspective: A practical guide.* New York: Longman Publishing Group.

DeWine, S., et al. (1977). *Modeling and self-disclosure in the classroom.* Paper presented at the Annual Meeting of the International Communication Association, Berlin, Germany. (ERIC Document Reproduction Services No. ED 141 848)

Dobie, A. B. (1992, Mar.). *Back to school: Adults in the freshman writing class.* Paper presented at the Annual Meeting of the Conference on College Composition and Communication, Cincinnati, OH. (ERIC Reproduction Document Services No. ED 345 283)

Durrani, N. et al. (1981). *Emotional and personality development: Symposium III C.* Prepared in Preparation for Adulthood. Third Asian Workshop on Child and Adolescent Development. (ERIC Reproduction Document Services No. ED 273 368)

Dyson, A. H. & Freedman, S. W. (1991). *Critical challenges for research on writing and literacy: 1990-1995.* Technical Report No. 1B. Center for the Study of Writing, Berkeley, CA; Center for the Study of Writing, Pittsburgh, PA.

Flynn, E. A., McCully, G. A. & Gratz, R. K. (1982, November). *Effects of peer critiquing and model analysis on the quality of biology student laboratory reports.* Paper presented at the Annual Meeting of the National Council of Teachers of English. Washington, D. C. (ERIC Document Reproduction Services No. ED 234 403).

Freeman, M. (1997). *Math and science on a personal level.* (ERIC Reproduction Document Services No. ED 415 936)

Henry, G. B. (1986). *Cultural diversity awareness inventory—Inventario Sobre el reconocimento de diversas cultures.* Special Education Programs, Washington D.C. (ERIC Document Reproduction Services No. ED 282 657)

Hernandez, H. (1989). *Multicultural education: A teachers guide to instruction.* Columbus, OH: Merrill.

Jourard, S. M. (1964). *The transparent self.* Princeton, NJ: D. Van Nostrand.

Lewes, U. E. (1981). *Peer-evaluation in a writing seminar. Guides-classroom.* (ERIC Document Reproduction Services No. ED 226 355)

Locke, D. C. (1992). *Increasing multicultural understanding.* Newbury Park, CA: Sage Publications, Inc.

Matthews, J. (1997, December 27). Peer teaching makes the grade in many schools. *The Washington Post.* A1, A7

Mead, D. G. (1994). *Celebrating dissensus in collaboration: A professional writing perspective.* Conference on College Composition and Communication. Nashville, TN. (ERIC Document Reproduction Service No. ED 375 427)

Morganthau, T. (1997, January 27). Demographics: The face of the future. *Newsweek,* 58-60.

Nieto, S. (1992). *Affirming diversity: The sociopolitical context of multicultural education.* White Plains, NY: Longman.

Noel, R. C., & Smith, S. E. (1996). Self-disclosure of college students to faculty: The influence of ethnicity. *Journal of College Student Development, 37*(1),88-94.

O'Connor, R. E. & Jenkins, J. R. (1993, April 12-16). *Cooperative learning as an inclusion strategy: The experience of children with disabilities.* Paper presented at the 74th Annual meeting of the American Educational Research Association, Atlanta, GA. (ERIC Document Reproduction Service No. ED 360778)

Perry, W. G., Jr. (1971). *Forms of intellectual and ethical development in the college years: A scheme.* New York: Holt, Rinehart and Winston.

Prather, D. L. & Bermu'dez, A. B. (1993). Using peer response groups with limited English proficient writers. *Bilingual Research Journal, 17*(1-2), 99-116.

Saunders, M. A. (1986, Feb.). *The collaborative description paper.* Paper presented at the Annual Meeting of the Southeastern Conference on English in the Two-Year College, Memphis, TN. (ERIC Reproduction Document Services No. ED 272 894)

Scott, A. M. (1995). Collaborative projects in technical communication classes: A survey of student attitudes and perceptions. *Journal of Technical Writing and Communication, 25*(2) 181-200.

Sharan, S. (1980). Cooperative learning in small groups: Recent methods and effects on achievement, attitudes, and ethnic relations. *Review of Educational Research 50,* 241-271.

Shepherd-Wynn, E. (1999). *The effects of collaborative learning on English composition students' writing anxiety, apprehension, attitude and writing quality.* Unpublished doctoral dissertation, Grambling State University, Grambling, Louisiana.

Sleeter, C. E. & Grant, C. A. (1988). *Making choices for multicultural education: Five approaches to race, class, gender.* Columbus, OH: Merrill.

Wood, J. B. (1992, Oct.). *The application of computer technology and cooperative learning in developmental algebra at the community college.* Paper presented at the Annual Computer Conference of the League for Innovation in the Community College. Orlando, FL. (ERIC Reproduction Document Services No. ED 352 099)

Ziv, W. C. (1983). Peer groups in the composition classroom: A case study. Paper presented at the 34th Annual Meeting of the Conference of College Composition and Communication. Detroit, MI. (ERIC Document Reproduction Service No. ED 229 799)

Chapter 12

Altwerger, B., Edelsky, C., & Flores, B. M. (1987). Whole language: What's new? *The Reading Teacher, 41,* 144-154.

Altwerger, B. & Resta, P. E. (1985). *Miscue analysis profile.* Albuquerque: University of New Mexico.

Aweiss, S. (1993). *Verbal protocol data as a reliable source of information about reading behavior and cognitive processes: The case of reading Arabic as a foreign language.* Paper presented at the Annual Meeting of the Central State Conference on the Teaching of Foreign Languages.

Baines, L. (1997). Future schlock: Using fabricated data and politically correct platitudes in the name of education. *Phi Delta Kappan, 78* (7).

Bernitz, J. G. (1997). Dialect barriers to reading comprehension revisited. *The Reading Teacher, 50*(6), 454-459.

Belenky, M., Clinchy, B., Goldberger, N., & Tarule, J. (1986). *Women's ways of knowing.* New York: Basic Books.

Boyer, E. (1990). *Campus life: In search of community.* Princeton, NJ: Carnegie Foundation for the Advancement of Teaching.

Brown, A. L. (1980). Learning how to learn from reading. In Langer, J. A., & Smith-Burke, M.T. (Eds.), *Reader meets author/Bridging the gap.* Neward, Del.: International Reading Association.

Caverly, D. C., Mandeville, T. F., & Nicholson, S. A. (1995). PLAN: A study reading strategy for informational text. *Journal of Adolescent, & Adult Literacy, 39* (3), 190-199.

Chai, D. T. (1967). *Communication of pronominal referents in ambiguous English sentences for children and adults.* Michigan University, Ann Arbor: Center for Human Growth. U. S. Department of health, Education & Welfare. Office of Education.

Chomsky, N. (1965). *Aspects of a theory of syntax.* Cambridge, MA: MIT Press.

Christensen, K. E. (1990). *A study of teachers' viewpoints on whole language.* (ERIC Document Reproduction Service No. ED 329 907)

Cooper, J. & Mueck, R. (1990). Student involvement in learning. Cooperative learning and college instruction. *Journal of Excellence in College Teaching, 1*(1), 68-76.

Daiute, C. A. (1981). Psycholinguistic foundations of the writing process. *Research in the Teaching of English, 15* (1), 5-22.

Dewey, J. (1936). *Democracy in education.* New York: Macmillan.

Dewey, J. (1910). *How we think.* Boston: D.C. Heath and Co.

Dillon, R. (1996). Learning and leading with technology. *Team problem-solving activities, 24* (1).

Dixon-Krauss. L. (1996). *Vygotsky in the classroom: Mediated literacy instruction and assessment.* New York: Longman.

Ehri, L. C. (1971). *Sentence learning in children and adults: The production of forms and transforms.* Paper presented at the Annual Meeting of the American Educational Association, New York, NY: U. S. Department of Health, Education & Welfare. Office of Education.

Goodman, K. S. (1989). Whole-language research: Foundation and development. *Elementary School Journal, 90* (2), 207-221.

Goodman, K. S. (1989). Whole language is whole: A response to Heymsfeld. *Educational Leadership, 46,* 69-70.

Goodman, K. S. (1986). *The psycholinguistic nature of the reading process.* Detroit: Wayne State University Press.

Goodman, K. S. (1971). Decoding—from what? *Journal of Reading.* Newark, Delaware: International Reading Association Press.

Goodman, K. S. & Burke, C. L. (1972). *Theoretically based studies of patterns of miscues in oral reading performance.* (USOE Project 9-0375 Tech. Rep.).

Goodman, K. S. & Goodman, Y. M. (1981). *A whole-language, comprehension-centered reading program.* Program in Language and Literacy Occasional Paper Number 1. Washington, D.C. (ERIC Document Reproduction Service No. ED 210 630)

Grossack, M. (1954). Some effects of cooperation and competition upon small group behavior. *Journal of Abnormal and Social Psychology, 49,* 341-348.

Hornstein, S., Heine, D., & Heine, P. (1992). *Whole language goes to college.* (ERIC Document Reproduction Service No. ED 341960)

Johnson, D. W., Johnson, R. T. & Holubec, E. J. (1994). *Cooperative learning in the classroom.* Alexandria, VA: Association for Supervision and Curriculum Development.

Johnson, D. W., Johnson, R. T. & Holubec, E. J. (1990). *Circles of learning: Cooperation in the classroom.* Edina, MN: Interaction Book Company.

Kaufman, N. & Randlett, A. L. (1983). *The use of cognitive and metacognitive strategies of good and poor readers at the college level.* (ERIC Document Reproduction Service No. ED 239 243)

Kress, G. R. (1976). *Halliday: System and function in language*. London: Oxford University Press.

Malik, A. A. (1990). A psycholinguistic analysis of the reading behavior of EFL-proficient readers using culturally familiar and culturally nonfamiliar expository texts. *American Educational Research Journal, 27*(1), 205-223.

Maller, J. B. (1929). *Cooperation and competition*. New York, NY: J. J. Little and Ives.

Meiklejohn, A. (1932). *The experimental college*. New York: Harper and Row.

Mergendoller, J. R. (1997). Sifting the hype: What research says about technology and learning. *Principal, 76*(3), 12-14.

Mikulecky, L. & Adams, S. M. (1986). *The relationship of extreme attributional styles (learned helplessness) to metacognitive reading behaviors of college students on academic probation*. (ERIC Document Reproduction Service No. ED 280 014)

Monson, R. J., & Pahl, M. (1991). Charting a new course with whole language. *Educational Leadership, 48* (6), 51-53.

Moorman, G. B., Blanton, W. E., & McLaughlin, T. (1994). The rhetoric of whole language. *Reading Research Quarterly, 29* (4), 309-329.

Newman, J. (1991). *Interwoven conversations*. Portsmouth, NH: Heineman.

Nist, S. L. & Mealey, D. (1991). Teacher-directed comprehension strategies. In R. F. Flippo & D. C. Caverly (Eds.), *Teaching reading, & study strategies at the college level (*pp. 42-85). Newark, DE: International Reading Association.

Palij, M. (1987). *Assessing language background differences. Working papers in Psycholinguistics*. NY. (ERIC Document Reproduction Service No. ED 299 814)

Piaget, J. (1950. *The psychology of intelligence*. New York, NY: Harcourt Brace.

Piper, S. G. (1992). *A metacognitive skills/reading comprehension intervention program for sixth grade social studies students*. (ERIC Document Reproduction Service No. ED 350 561)

Ransom, R. E. & Wisenbach, E. L. (1994). *Perceptions of pre-service elementary education students after a reading course and following student teaching*. (ERIC Document Reproduction Service No. ED 376 452)

Roos, M. C. et al. (1993). *The effect of an introductory reading course on pre-service teachers' theoretical orientation to the teaching of reading*. (ERIC Document Reproduction Service No. ED 356 470)

Rosenbaltt, L. M. (1938). *Literature as an exploration*. New York, NY: D. Appleton Century.

Sammon, S. (1988). *A correlation study: The New Jersey college basic skills placement test and degrees of reading power test*. (ERIC Document Reproduction Service No. ED 296 288)

Scholten, B. & Whitmer, J. (1996). *Hypermedia projects-metastacks increase content focus. vol. 24. no. 3.*

Schorr, F. (1982). *Comprehending procedural instructions: The influence of metacognitive strategies.* (ERIC Document Reproduction Service No. ED 214 130)

Slavin, R. E. (1987a). Cooperative learning: Where behavioral and humanistic approaches to classroom motivation meet. *Elementary School Journal, 88* (1), 29-37.

Smith, B. L. & MacGregor, J. T. (1992). What is collaborative learning? *Collaborative learning: A sourcebook for higher education.* National Center on Postsecondary Teaching, Learning and Assessment, (ERIC Document Reproduction Service Project No. R117G10037)

Smith, F. (1973). *Psycholinguistics and reading.* (ERIC Document Reproduction Services No. ED 071 031)

Smith, F. & Goodman, K. ed. (1971). On the psycholinguistic method of teaching reading. *Elementary School Journal, 71.*

Smith, F. & Miller, G. A. (Eds.) (1965). *The genesis of language: A psycholinguistic approach.* Proceedings of the Conference on Language Development in Children, Old Point Comfort, Virginia.

Smith, K. A., Johnson, D. W. & Johnson, R. T. (1992*). Cooperative learning and positive change in higher education.*

Stallworth-Clark, R. M., Scott, & Nist, S. L. (1996). *The teaching-learning process and postsecondary at risk students: Cognitive, metacognitive, affective, and instructional variables explaining academic performance.* Paper presented at the Annual Meeting of the American Educational Research Association, New York, NY. (ERIC Document Reproduction Service No. ED 394 419)

Thompson, K. L. & Tayman, J. (1997). Taking chaos out of cooperative learning: The three most important components. *Clearinghouse.* pp. 81-84.

Tyrel, L. & Parnell, D. (1988). *Building communities: A vision for a new century.* Washington, D. C.: American Association of Community and Junior Colleges.

Whimbey, A. et al. (1980). Teaching critical reading and analytical reasoning in Project SOAR. *Journal of Reading, 24*(1), 5-10.

Wise, B. et al. (1993). *Putting the pieces together: Whole language and the minority developmental student.* (ERIC Document Reproduction Service No. ED 372 362.)

Wong, B. Y. L., Wong, R., Perry, N., & Sawatsky, D. (1989). The efficacy of a self-questioning summarization strategy for use by underachievers and learning disabled adolescents in social studies. *Learning Disabilities Focus, 2,* 20-35.

Classroom References

Walton-Jaggers, L. (1997). *The talking box activity.* Grambling State University, Grambling, LA.

Chapter 13

Brown, J. S., Collins, A. & Duguid, P. (1991). Situated cognition and the culture of learning. In M. Yazdani, R. W. Lawler, R. W. et al. (Eds.), *Artificial intelligence and education,* Vol. 2. (pp. 245-268). Norwood, NJ: Ablex Publishing Corp.

Carroll, J. M. (1990). The Copernican plan: Restructuring the American high school. *Phi Delta Kappan, 71*(5), 358-65.

Chaffee, J. (1992). Critical thinking skills: The cornerstone of developmental education. *Journal of developmental Education. 15*(3), 2-6.

Greene, M. (1993). The passions of pluralism: Multiculturalism and expanding community. *Educational Researcher, 22*(1), 13-18.

Kay, Alan. (1991) Computers, networks and education. *Scientific America, 265*(3), 138-48.

Kiesler, S., Seigel, J., & McGuire, T. W. (1984). Social psychological aspects of computer-medicated communications, *American Psychologist, 39*(10), 1123-1134.

Knowles, M. (1984a). *Andragogy in action.* San Francisco, CA. Jossey-Bass.

Knowles, M. (1984b). *The adult learner: A neglected Species.* (3rd ed.) Houston, Texas. Gulf Publishing.

Lave, J. (1988). *Cognition in practice: Mind, mathematics, and culture in everyday life.* Cambridge U. K.: Cambridge University Press.

McLellan, H. (1994). Situated learning: Continuing the conversation. *Educational Technology, 34*(8), 7-8.

Murray, D. R., & Graham, T. (1996). *Teaching systematic thinking and problem solving through database searching, synthesis and analysis.* (ERIC Document Reproduction Service No. ED 399 251)

O'Neill, I. J., Perez, B. L., & Velsor K. (1994) Constructing a language of action: The literacy experience. In D. Sayers (Ed.). *Bilingual/multicultural handbook.* New York: Kraus.

Papert, S. (1987). Computer criticism versus technocentric thinking. *Educational Researcher, 16* (1), 22- 30.

Rogers, C. R. & Freiberg, J. (1994). *Freedom to learn.* (3rd). Columbus, Ohio: Merrill/Macmillan.

Rogers, C. R. (1974). Can learning encompass both ideas and feelings? *Education, 95*(2), 103-114.

Ross, S. M. (1994). From ingredients to recipes...and back: It's the taste that counts. *Educational Technology Research and Development, 42*(3), 5-6.

Sagor, R. (1988). Teetering on the edge. *Learning,* April, 29-33.

Seifert, C. M., McKoon, G., Abelson, R. P. & Ratcliff, R. (1986). Memory connections between thematically similar episodes. *Journal of Experimental Psychology Learning Memory and Cognition, 12*(2), 220-231.

Seifert, C. M., Robertson, S. R., & Black, J. B. (1985). Types of inferences generated during reading. *Journal of Memory and Language, 24*(4), 405-422.

Sticht, T. (1988). Adult literacy education. *Review of research in education.* Vol.15. Washington. D.C.: American Education Research Association.

Van der Meij, H. & Carroll, J. M. (1995). Principles and neuristics for designing minimalision. *Technical Communications, 42* (2), 243-261.

INTERNET Quality Education Data,qedinfor@qeddata. Com.1997.

Chapter 14

Bangert-Drowns, R. L., & Kozma, R. (1989). Assessing the design of instructional software. *Journal of Research on Computing in Education, 1,* 241-262.

Bardwell, R. (1981). Feedback: How does it function? *Journal of Experimental Education, 50,* 4-9.

Belland, J., Taylor, W., Canelos, J., Dwyer, F., & Baker, P. (1985). Is the self-paced instructional program via micro-computer based instruction, the most effective method of addressing individual learning differences? *Education and Communication Technology, 25,* 39-43.

Carrier, C. (1984). Do learners make good choices? *Instructional Innovator, 29*(2), 15-17.

Cohen, V. B. (1985). A reexamination of feedback in computer-based instruction: implications for instruction. *Educational Technology, 25,* 33-37.

Fagbeyiro, G. O. (1995). *The Effects of Learner Characteristics and Computer Feedback Strategies on Learning Achievement of Developmental Students in Familiar and Unfamiliar Mathematics Lessons.* A published UMI Dissertation, Grambling State University, Grambling, LA.

Finnegan, R., & Sinatra, R. (1991). Interactive CAI with adults. *Journal of Reading, 35,* 108-119.

Gagne, R. M. (1980). Learnable aspects of problem solving. *Educational Psychologist, 15,* 84-92.

Gagne, R. M., Briggs, L. J., & Wager, W. W. (1988). *Principles of instructional design.* New York: Holt, Reinhart & Winston.

Gore, P. M., & Rotter, J. B. (1963). A personality correlate of social action. *Journal of Personality, 31,* 58-64.

Hannafin, M. J. (1984). Guidelines for using locus of instructional control in the design of computer-assisted instruction. *Journal of Instructional Development, 7,* 6-10.

Hull, C. H., & Nie, N. H. (1981). *SPSS update 7-9.* New York: McGraw-Hill.

Keedy, M. L., & Bittinger, M. L. (1991). *Introductory algebra* (4th ed.). Reading, MA: Addison-Wesley Publishing Company.

Kulik, C. C., Schwalb, B. J., & Kulik, J. A. (1982). Programmed instruction in secondary education: A meta-analysis of evaluation findings. *Journal of Educational Research, 75,* 133-138.

Parker, C. S. (1990). *Understanding computers and information processing: Today and tomorrow* (3rd ed.). Chicago, IL: The Dryden Press.

Phares, E. J. (1965). Internal-external control as a determinant of amount of social influence exerted. *Journal of Personality and Social Psychology, 2,* 642-647.

Reid, D. W. (1977). Locus of control as an important concept for interactionist approach to behavior. In D. Magnusson & N. S. Endler (Eds.), *Personality at the crossroads: Current issues in interactional psychology* (pp. 185-915).

Hillsdale, NJ: Lawrence Erlbaum.

Rotter, J. B. (1966). Generalized expectancies for internal versus external control of reinforcement. *Psychological Monographs: General and Applied, 80*(1, Whole No. 609).

Schmeck, R. R., Ribich, F., & Ramanaiah, N. (1977). Development of a self-report inventory for assessing individual differences in learning processes. *Applied Psychological Measurement, 1*, 413-431.

Seeman, M., & Evans, J. W. (1962). Alienation and learning in a hospital environment. *American Sociological Review, 27*, 772-783.

Sloanne, H. N., Gunn, C., Gordon, H. M., & Mickelson, V. (1989). *Evaluating educational software: A guide for teachers.* Englewood Cliffs, NJ: Prentice Hall.

Steinberg, E. R. (1984). *Teaching computers to teach.* Hillsdale, NJ: Lawrence Erlbaum.

Stewart, W. J. (1983). Meeting learning styles through the computer. *Journal of Educational Technology Systems, 11*, 291-296.

Tobias, S. (1982). When do instructional methods make a difference? *Educational Researcher, 11*, 4-9.

Tobias, S. (1976). Achievement treatment interactions. *Review of Educational Research, 46*, 61-74.

Weinstein, C. E. (1987). *LASSI user's manual.* Clearwater, FL: H & H Publishing.

Chapter 15

Angelo, T. A. (1995, November). Reassessing (and defining) assessment, *AAHE Bulletin.* American Association For Higher Education, Vol.48, No.3. Washington, DC.

Banta, T. (1993). Summary and conclusion: Are we making a difference. Banta, Trudy and Associates. *Making a difference: Outcomes of a decade of assessment in higher education.* San Francisco, CA: Jossey-Bass.

Belcher, D. & Strickland, B. J. (Mar.-Apr. 1995). Service mapping: Blueprint for positive change. *Assessment Update, Progress, Trends, and Practices in Higher Education, 7.*

Bray, D. (1985, October). A guide to assessment in six steps. *Unpublished Presentation.* National Conference On Assessment, American Association of Higher Education, Columbia, South Carolina.

Bray, D. (1986). Providing for academic skills and remediation in the California community colleges, recommendations for campus and state roles, *draft statement for the LARC Consortium,* Sacramento City College, Sacramento, California, 1986.

Bray, D. (1988, February). Practicing assessment in the community colleges: A two year scenario for 1988-1990. *Unpublished Presentation:* Workshop, McKinney, Texas.

Bray, D. (1987). Assessment and placement of developmental and high-risk students.

Teaching the Developmental Education Student, Kenneth M. Ahrendt, Editor, Jossey-Bass Inc, San Francisco, CA: Jossey-Bass.

Bray, D. & Kanter, M. J. (1993). Accountability through assessment in community colleges. *Making A Difference, Outcomes Of A Decade Of Assessment In Higher Education,* Trudy Banta and Associates. San Francisco, CA: Jossey-Bass.

Bray, D. (1987, March). *Core curriculum: Report of the task group for the commission on instruction, California association of community colleges,* Sacramento, CA.

Bray, D. (1995, July). *Assessment in a multicultural interdisciplinary environment.* Presentation at the Seventh International Conference on Assessing Quality in Higher Education, Tampere, Finland.

Darling-Hammond, L., Einbender, L., Frelow, F. & Ley-King, J. (1997). *Authentic assessment in practice: A collection of portfolios, performance tasks, exhibitions, and documentation.* National Council For Restructuring Education, Schools, and Teaching, Teachers College, Columbia University, New York, NY.

Ewell, P. (1993). *The role of states and accreditors in shaping assessment practice.* Banta and Associates.

Faculty advising program questionnaire for faculty. (1988, Jan.). College of the Desert, Palm Desert, CA.

Goals 2000, National Education Goals and Goals Panels Reports, 1994.

Historical trends: State Education Facts 1969-1989. (1993). *120 Years of American Education: A statistical portrait education in states and nations.* U.S. Department of Education, Office of Educational Research and Improvement, National Center For Educational Statistics.

Katz, A. M. (1993). *Helping a campus in transition.* Banta and Associates.

Learning Assessment Retention Consortium of the California Community Colleges. (1985, October). California Community Colleges, Providers of Remediation, *Field Draft.*

Learning Assessment Retention Consortium of the California Community Colleges. (1985, November). *Academic Standards: Profiles of Practices In California Community Colleges, Parts I, II, and II.* Sacramento CA.

Muffo, J. A., & Bunda, M. A. (1993). *Attitude and opinion data.* Banta and Associates.

Report on joint committee activities. (1995). *The Joint Committee On Standards For Evaluation.*

Symposium: Outcomes assessment for the future. (1988). Laguna Beach, CA.

Chapter 16

Chazan, M., (Ed.), (1973). *Compensatory education.* London, England: Butterworth.

Clowes, D. A. (1979). More than a definitional problem. *Journal of Developmental and Remedial Education, 4,* 8-10.

Clowes, D. A. (1984). The evaluation of remedial/developmental programs. *Journal of Developmental Education, 8,* 14-15, 27-30.

Clowes, D. A. (1992). Remediation in American higher education. In J. Smart (Ed.), *Higher Education: Handbook of Theory and Research* (Vol. VIII, pp. 460-493). New York: Agathon Press.

Drew, D. E., (Ed.) (1978). *Competency, careers, and college.* New Directions for Education, Work, and Careers, No. 2, pp. 1-18.

Frost, J., and Rowland, G. (1971). *Compensatory education: The acid test of American Education.* Dubuque, Iowa: William C. Brown.

McGrath, D. & Spear, M. B. (1991). *The academic crisis of the community college.* Albany, N.Y.: State University of New York Press.

Miller, T., & Prince, J. (1976). *The future of student affairs.* San Francisco: Jossey-Bass.

Ntuk-Iden, M. (1978). *Compensatory education.* Westmead. England: Teakfield Limited,.

Richardson, R., Martens, K. & Fisk, E. (1981). *Literacy in the open-access college.* San Francisco: Jossey-Bass.

Roueche, J. (1968). *Salvage, redirection or custody? Remedial education in the community and junior college.* (ERIC Document Reproduction Service No. ED 019 077)

Roueche, J. & Snow, J. (1977). *Overcoming learning problems.* San Francisco: Jossey-Bass.

Webster's New Collegiate Dictionary. (1964). Cleveland: World Publishing Company.

Chapter 17

Bliss, L. B. & Mueller, R. J. (1993) An instrument for the assessment of study behaviors of college students. *Reading Research and Instruction, 32*(4) 46-52.

Bloom, B. S., Englehart, M. D., Furst, E. J., Hill, W. H., & Krathwohl, D. R. (1956). *Taxonomy of educational objectives: The classification of education goals. Handbook I: Cognitive domain.* White Plains, NY: Longman.

Boylan, H. R., Bliss, L. B., & Bonham, B. S. (1997). Program components and their relationship to student performance. *Journal of Developmental Education, 20*(3), 2-8.

Darling-Hammond, L. & Snyder, J. (1992). Scientific study of learning as a basis for curriculum. In P. Jackson (Ed.). *Handbook of research on curriculum* (pp. 432-476). New York: Macmillan.

Davenport, J. & Davenport, J. H. (1985). Andragogical- pedagogical orientations of adult learners: Research results and practice recommendations. *Lifelong Learning, 9,* 6-8.

Ebel, R. L. & Frisbie, D. A. (1991). *Essentials of educational measurement* (5th ed.). Englewood Cliffs, NJ: Prentice-Hall.

Gagné, R. M. (1985). *The conditions of learning and theory of instruction.* New York: Holt, Rinehart and Winston.

Harrow, A. J. (1972). *A taxonomy of the psychomotor domain; a guide for developing behavioral objectives.* New York, D. McKay Co.

Jaeger, R. M. (1989). Certification of student competence. In R. L. Linn (Ed.), *Educational Measurement* (3rd ed.) (pp. 485-514). Englewood Cliff, NJ: Prentice-Hall.

Krathwohl, D. R., Bloom, B. S., & Masia, B. B. (1964). *Taxonomy of educational objectives: Book II: Affective Domain.* White Planes, NY: Longman.

Mehrens, W. A. & Popham, W. J. (1992). How to evaluate the legal defensibility of high-stakes tests. *Applied Measurement in Education, 5* (3), 265-283.

Nitko, A. J. (1996). *Educational assessment of students* (2nd ed.). Englewood Cliffs, NJ: Prentice-Hall.

Payne, D. A. (1992). *Measuring and evaluating educational outcomes.* New York: Merrill.

Scriven, M. (1967). The methodology of evaluation. In R.W. Tyler (Ed.), *Perspectives of curriculum evaluation.* AERA Monograph Series on Curriculum Evaluation (No. 1). Skokie, IL: Rand McNally.

Thorndike, R. M. (1997). *Measurement and evaluation in psychology and education* (6th ed.). Upper Saddle River, NJ: Merrill.

Tyler, R. W. (1949). *Basic principles of curriculum and instruction.* Chicago.

Chapter 18

Geis, G. & Smith, M. (1992). The function of evaluation. In H. Stolovitch & E. Keeps (Eds.). *Handbook of human performance technology: A comprehensive guide for analyzing and solving performance problems in organizations.* San Francisco, CA: Jossey- Bass Publishers.

Kubiszyn, T. & Borich, G. (1996). *Educational Testing and Measurement: Classroom application and practice.* New York: Harper Collins.

Starks, G. (1994). Retention and developmental education: What the research has to say. In M. Maxwell (Ed.). *From access to success: A book of readings on college developmental education and learning assistance programs.* Clearwater, FL: H & H Publishing Company.

Chapter 19

Akridge, S. A., & Ross, P. (1987). *CCC's success program: counseling, caring and campus involvement.* (ERIC Document Reproduction Service ED No. 289 545).

Anliot, R. & Oncley, L. (1989, Fall). Admission, enrollment, financial aid and attrition at Pennsylvania institutions of higher education. *Journal of Black Conference on Higher Education, 7,* 12-20.

Astin, A. W. (1971). *Predicting academic performance in college.* New York: American Council on Education.

Astin, A. W. (1972). *College dropouts: A national profile.* Washington, DC: American Council on Education (ERIC Document Reproduction Service No. ED 221 078).

Astin, A. W. (1982). *Minorities in American higher education.* San Francisco: Jossey-Bass.

Atkinson, D. R., Jennings, R. G., & Liongson, L. (1990, July). Minorities students' reasons for not seeking counseling and suggestions for improving services. *Journal of College Student Development, 31,* 342-350.

Bers, T. H. & Rubin, A. M. (Ed.). (1989). Using student tracking systems effectively: The unreported challenges. *New Directions for Community Colleges,* 66, 3-9.

Blanchette, C. (1994*). Higher education grants effective at increasing minorities' chances of graduating.* A Testimony before the Subcommittee on Education, Arts, and Humanities, Committee on Labor and Human Resources, U.S. Senate. General Accounting Office, Washington, DC (ERIC Document Reproduction Service No. ED 370 505).

Boyer, E. L. (1986, December). Smoothing the transition from school to college. *Phi Delta Kappan,* (pp. 139-144).

Boyer, E. L. (1987). *College: The undergraduate experience in America.* New York: Harper & Row.

Brown, R. D., & DeCoster, D. A. (Eds.). (1982). *Mentoring - transcript systems for promoting student growth: New directions for student services no. 19.* San Francisco: Jossey-Bass.

Browne, A. D. (1986). Academic bankruptcy by design. *College and University, 61,* 290-293.

Browne, A. D. (1986-1987). Academic bankruptcy: Who can afford it? *The College Board Review,* (pp. 32-38).

Chapman, B. S. (1982). *Academic retention and talent retrieval.* Paper presented at the Annual Convention of the American Personnel and Guidance Association. Detroit, MI. (ERIC Document Reproduction Service No. ED 221 821)

Cope, R. G. (1971). *An investigation of entrance characteristics related to types of college dropouts.* Washington, DC: U. S. Department of Health, Education, and Welfare.

Cope, R. G., & Hannah, W. (1975). *Revolving college doors: The causes and consequences of dropping out, stopping out, and transferring.* New York: Wiley.

Cross, K. P. (1985). Education for the 21st century. *NASPA Journal, 23*(1), 7-18.

Cronklin, D. D. (1976). *An investigation of the academic performance and persistence of readmitted students as related to selected student characteristics at two community colleges.* Unpublished doctoral dissertation, New York University.

Elliott, T. R. (1973). *A study of academically suspended students whose petitions for readmittance were reviewed by the Auburn University committee on admission during 1979*. Unpublished doctoral dissertation, Auburn University.

Feldman, K. A., & Newcomb, T. H. (1970). *The impact of college on students*. San Francisco: Jossey-Bass.

Fogel, J., & Yaffe, J. (1992). *Ethnic minority and caucasian student experiences at the university of Utah and recommendations for institutional response*. Paper presented with the Annual Forum of the Association for Institutional Research 32nd, Atlanta, GA. (ERIC Document Reproduction Service No. ED 349 874)

Giesecke, G. F., & Hancock, J. W. (1950). Rehabilitation of academic failures. *College and University, 26,* 72-78.

Gillespie, M., & Noble, J. (1992). *Factors affecting student persistence: A longitudinal study*. ACT Research Report Series, P.O. Box 168, Iowa City, IA 52243. (ERIC Document Reproduction Service No. ED 347 056)

Hall, K., & Gahn, W. (1994, Spring). Predictors of Success for Academically Dismissed Students Following Readmission. *NACADA Journal, 14* (1),8-12.

Han, T., & Ganges, T.W. (1995). *A discrete time survival analysis of the education path of specially admitted students*. A paper presented at the Annual Meeting of the American Research Association. San Francisco, CA. (ERIC Document Reproduction Service No. ED 387 033)

Hansmeier, T. W. (1965). Factors related to the success of college students academically dismissed. *College and University, 40,* 194-202.

Hood, D. W. (1992). Academic and noncognitive factors affecting the retention of black men at a predominantly white university. *Journal of Negro Education, 61* (1), 12-23.

Hossler, D. R. (1984). Enrollment management: A paradigm for student affairs professional. *NASPA Journal, 23*(2), 2-8.

Hossler, D. R. (1985). *Enrollment management, an integral approach*. New York: College Entrance Examinations Board.

House, J. D., & Wohlt, V. (1990, July). The effect of tutoring program participation on the performance of academically underprepared college freshmen. *Journal of College Student Development*, 31, 365-370.

Isaac, S., & Michael, W. B. (1987). *Handbook in research and evaluation: A collection of principles, methods, and strategies useful in the planning, design, and evaluation of studies in education and the behavioral sciences* (2nd ed.). San Diego: Edit. Kansas State University General Catalog (1988-90). Manhattan, Kansas: University Relations.

Krotseng, M. V. (1991). *Predicting persistence from the student adaptation to college questionnaire: Early warning or siren song?* A paper presented at the Annual Forum of the Association for Institutional Research. (31st, San Francisco, CA, May 26-29, 1991). (ERIC Document Reproduction Service No. ED 336 036).

Lautz, R., McLean, G. D., Vaughan, A. T., & Oliver, T. C. (1976). Characteristics of successful students readmitted following academic suspension. *College and University, 51,* 192-302.

Lenning, O. T., Beal, P. E., & Sauer, K. (1980). *Attrition and retention: Evidence for action and research.* Boulder, CO: National Center for Higher Education Management Systems.

Lenning, O.T., Sauer, K. & Beal, P. (1980). *Student retention strategies.* Higher Education Research Reports, No. 8. Washington, DC: ERIC Clearinghouse on Higher Education.

Masat, F. E. (1984). *Restarting voluntary leave and academically dismissed students.* (ERIC Document Reproduction Service No. ED 249 858)

Noel, L. (1985). Increasing student retention: New challenges and potential. In L. Noel, R. Levitz, D. Saluri & Associates (Eds.), *Increasing student retention,* (p. 1-26). San Francisco: Jossey-Bass.

Ott, M. D. (1988). An analysis of predictors of early academic dismissal. *Research in Higher Education, 28,* 34-48.

Pantages, T. J., & Creedon, C. F. (1978). Studies of college attrition: 1950 - 1975. *Review of Educational Research, 48,* 49-101.

Pervin, L. A. (Ed.). (1966). *The college dropout and the utilization of talent.* Princeton: Princeton University Press.

Preer, J. L. (1981). *Minority access to higher education.* AAHE-ERIC Higher Education Research Reports No. 1. Washington, DC: American Association for Higher Education.

Ramist, L. (1981). *College student attrition and retention.* The Board Report, No. 81-1. New York: The College Entrance Examination.

Rouche, J. E., Baker, G. A., & Rouche, S. D. (1984). *College responses to low-achieving students: A national study.* San Diego: Harcourt Brace Jovannovich Media Systems.

Roueche, J.E. & Roueche, S.D. (1994). Climbing out from between a rock and a hard place: Responding to the challenges of the at risk student. *Journal of Leadership Abstracts, 7* (3), 4.

Sanford, T. R. (1979). *Non-academic factors influencing the "withdrawal" of academically ineligible black students.* Paper presented at the Annual Meeting of the Southern Association for Institutional Research, Orlando, FL. (ERIC Document Reproduction Service No. ED 180 362).

Smittle, P., LaVallee, M. R., & Carman, W. E. (1989, Summer). Computerized tracking system for underprepared students. In T. H. Bers (Ed.), *Using student tracking systems effectively* (pp. 39-46). San Francisco: Jossey-Bass.

Stewart, S. S., Merrill, M. C., & Saluri, D. (1985). Students who commute. In L. Noel, R. Levitz, D. Saluri & Associates (Eds.), *Increasing student retention,* (pp. 162-182). San Francisco: Jossey-Bass.

Stith, P. L., & Russell, F. (1994). *Faculty/student interaction: Impact on student retention.* A paper presented at the 34th Annual Forum of the Association for Institutional Research. New Orleans, LA. (ERIC Document Reproduction Service No. ED 373 650).

Summerskill, J. & Darling, C.D. (1955). Sex differences in adjustment of college. *Journal of Education Psychology, 56,* 79-84.

Tatum, T. & Rasool, J. (1992, Winter). Reassessing retention courses: The need to empower students. *Journal of Equity and Excellence, 25* (2-4), 16-21.

Taylor, D. V., Powers, S. M., Lindstrom, W. A., & Gibson, T. S. (1987, Spring). Academically deficient readmitted students: Are they really a high risk? *NACADA Journal,* 7(1), 41-47.

Tinto, V. (1975). Dropout from higher education: A theoretical synthesis of recent research. *Review of Educational Research, 45*(1), 89-125.

Upcraft, M. L. (1985). *Residence halls and student activities.* In L. Noel, R. Levitz, D. Saluri, & Associates (Eds.), Increasing student retention (pp. 319-344). San Francisco: Jossey-Bass.

Wilson-Cook, C. (1990). *A quantitative and qualitative investigation of the persistence of a select group of reinstated students at a four-year institution of higher education.* Unpublished doctoral dissertation, Kansas State University.

Winchell, A. (1987). *New start program: September 1985 - June 1986.* Brooklyn, NY: Kingsborough Community College. (ERIC Document Reproduction Service No. ED 278 442)

Windham, P. (1995). *The importance of work and other factors to attrition: A comparison of significancy and odds ratio for different outcomes.* A paper presented at the 24th Annual Conference of the Southeastern Association for Community College Research. Asheville, NC. (ERIC Document Reproduction Service No. ED 385 312)

Yoder, F. A. (1963). *A follow-up study of students readmitted by the Purdue committee on scholastic delinquencies and readmission.* Unpublished doctoral dissertation, Purdue University.

Chapter 20

Allaire, S. (1979). *Course and program development department report on Literacy 1977-78.* Office of Course and Program Development. Edmonton, Canada. Grant MacEwan Community College.

Astin. A. (1987). Assessment, value-added, and educational excellence. In Halpern, D. Student outcomes assessment: What institutions stand to gain. *New Directions for Higher Education, No. 59.* San Francisco: Jossey-Bass.

Ball, S. & Anderson, S. (1975). *Practices in program evaluation: A survey and some case studies.* Princeton, N. J.: Educational Testing Service.

Bellucci, B. N. (1981, June). *Report on the evaluation of developmental education.* Unpublished Consulting Report. Wilkes-Barre, PA: Kings College.

Boylan, H. R. (1979). *Student development program evaluation report.* Bowling Green, OH: Student Development Program, Bowling Green State University.

Boylan, H. R. (1983). Is developmental education working? An analysis of research. (ERIC Document Reproduction Service No. ED 238 471)

Bray, D. (1987). Assessment and placement of developmental and high-risk students.

In K. M. Ahrendt (Ed.). *Teaching the Developmental Education Student New Directions For Community Colleges*, No. 57. pp. 33-48

Burley, (1994, April 4-8). *A meta-analysis of the effects of developmental studies programs on college students achievement, attitude, and persistence.* Paper presented at the Annual Meeting of the American Educational Association. New Orleans, LA:

Carter, L. G. (1976). *Developmental studies project, final report.* Canadiagua, NY, Community College of the Finger Lakes.

Clowes, (1992). The evaluation of remedial/developmental programs: A stage model. *Journal of Developmental Education, 88*(1), 14-15, 27-30.

Cohen, P. A. (1985). Responding to criticism of developmental education. In K. M. Ahrendt (Ed.). *Teaching the Developmental Education Student Directions For Community Colleges*, No. 57. 3-10.

Cole, A. M. (1985). Mathematics instruction at the two-year college: An ERIC review. *Community College Review, 12*(4), 54-61.

Cross, K. P. (1976). *Accent of learning*: Improving instruction. San Francisco: Jossey -Bass.

Cross, K. P. (1975). Years of change for community colleges: 1970 to 1974. *Findings, 2*(2), 5-8.

Donovan, R. A. (1975). *National project II: Alternatives to the revolving door.* New York: Networks, Bronx Community College.

Farmer, V. L. & Barham. W. A. (1996). *NADE selected conference papers volume 2.* 10-11. Paper presented at the 20th Annual Conference, Little Rock, Arkansas. Carol Spring, Illinois. National Association of Developmental Education.

Glass, G. V. (1976). Primary, secondary, and meta-analysis of research. *Educational Researcher, 5,* 3-8.

Glass, G. V., McGaw, B. & Smith, M. L. (1981). *Meta analysis in social research.* Beverly Hill, CA: Sage.

Gordon, E. W. (1975). Opportunity Programs for the disadvantaged in higher education. AAHE-ERIC/Higher Education Research Report No. 6. Washington D.C.: American Association for Higher Education. (ERIC Document Reproduction Service No. ED 114 028)

Grant, M. K. & Hoeber, D. R. (1978). Basic skills programs: Are they working? AAHE-ERIC/Higher Education Research Report No. 1. Washington, D. C.: American Association for Higher Education. (ERIC Document Reproduction Service No. ED 150 918)

Halpern, D. (1987). Student outcomes assessment: What institutions stand to gain. *New Directions for Higher Education, No. 59.* San Francisco: Jossey-Bass.

Handbook for Advisors & Students: Graduate Programs in Developmental Education, (1986). College of Education, Grambling State University, Grambling, LA.

Hedges, L. V. (1981). Distribution theory for glass's estimator of effect size and related estimators. *Journal of Educational Statistics, 6,* 107-28.

Hedges, L. V. (1982). Estimating effect size from a series of independent experiments. *Psychological Bulletin 92*, 490-99.

Hedges, L. V., & Olkin, I. (1985). *Statistical methods for meta-analysis.* New York: Academic Press.

Higbee, J. L. & Dwinell, P. L. (Eds.) (1996). *Defining Developmental Education: Theory, Research, and Pedagogy.* Cold Stream, IL: National Association for Developmental Education.

Hodgkinson, H. L. et al. (1975). Current evaluation practices in innovative colleges and universities. *The Research Reporter, 9*(1).

Jacobi, M., Astin, A., & Ayala, Jr. (1987). *College student outcomes assessment: A talent development perspective.* (ASHE-ERIC Higher Education Research Report #7).

Johnson, D. W., Maruyama, G., Johnson, R. T., Nelson, D., & Skon, L. (1981). Effect of cooperative, competitive, and individualistic goal structures on achievement: A meta-analysis. *Psychological Bulletin, 89*, 47-62.

Keimig, R. (1983). *Raising academic standards: A guide to learning improvement.* (ASHE-ERIC Higher Education Research Report #4).

Kerschner, L. P. (1987). Outcomes assessment in the California Master Plan. In Halpern, D. (Ed.). Student outcomes assessment: What institutions stand to gain. *New Directions for Higher Education, No. 59.* San Francisco: Jossey-Bass.

Kulik, C. C., Kulik, J. A. & Bangert-Drowns, R. L. (1990). Effectiveness of mastery learning programs: A meta-analysis. *Review of Educational Research, 60*(2), 265-299.

Kulik, C., Kulik, J., & Schwalb, B. (1983). College programs for high-risk and disadvantaged students: A meta-analysis of findings. *Review of Educational Research, 53*, 397-414.

Kulik, J. A., Kulik, C.-L. & Cohen, P. A. (1979). A meta-analysis of outcome studies of Keller's personalized System of Instruction. *American Psychologist, 34*, 307-318.

Maxwell, M. (1979). *Improving student learning skills.* San Francisco: Jossey-Bass.

Moore, C. A. (1977). *Teaching writing to the underprepared: The three R's.* Paper presented at the Annual Meeting of the Conference on English Education, Knoxville, TN.

Raygor, A. L. et al. (1973). *Review of research in college-adult reading.* 23rd Yearbook of the National Reading Conference.

Rendon, L. I. (1994). Validating culturally diverse students: Toward a new model of learning and student development. *Innovative Higher Education, 12* (1), 33-51.

Richardson, R., Jr. (1981). *Functional literacy in the college setting.* (ASHE-ERIC Higher Education Research Report #3).

Roueche, J. E. (1968). *Salvage, redirection or custody? Remedial education in the community college.* Washington, D.C.: American Association of Community and Junior Colleges. (ERIC Document Reproduction Service No. ED 019 077)

Roueche, J. E., Baker, G. A. & Roueche, S. D. (1984). College responses to low-achieving students: A national study. (ERIC Document Reproduction Service No. ED 248 924)

Roueche, J. E. & Snow, J. (1977). *Overcoming learning problems.* San Francisco: Jossey-Bass.

Roueche, J. E. & Wheeler, C. L. (1973, Summer). Instructional procedures for the disadvantaged. *Improving College and University Teaching, 21,* 222-225.

Santeusanio, R. P. (1974). Do college reading programs serve their purpose. *Reading World, 13,* 258-271.

Sherman, R. & Tinto, V. (1975). *The effectiveness of secondary and higher education intervention programs: A critical review of research.* Paper presented at the annual meeting of the American Educational Research Association, Washington, D.C. ED 106 378.

Snow, J. J. (1977). Counseling the high-risk student. In John E. Roueche (Ed.). *Increasing Basic Skills by Developmental Studies New Directions for Higher Education, No. 20.* San Francisco: Jossey-Bass. pp. 1-22

Summers, E. G. (1979, October). Doctoral dissertation in college reading. *Journal of Reading, 24,* 9-14.

Sutherland, B. J. & Sutherland, D. (1982). Read Writers: A sensible approach to instruction. *Journal of Developmental and Remedial Education 16* (1), 2-6.

Tilman, C. E. (1973). Four year college reading programs and grades. An annotated review, *Reading Behavior*

Tomlinson, L. (1989). *Post-secondary developmental programs: A traditional agenda with new imperatives.* (ASHE-ERIC Higher Education Research Report #3).

Trillin, A. S. et. al. (1980). *Teaching basic skills in college.* San Francisco, CA: Jossey-Bass.

Walvekar, C. C. (1981). *Assessment of learning assistance services.* San Francisco: Jossey-Bass.

Whimbey, A., Boylan, H. R., & Burke, R. (1979). Cognitive skill-oriented psi for developmental students. *Journal of Developmental and Remedial Education, 2*(2), 7-10.

Whitener, E. M. (1989). A meta-analytic review of the effect on learning of the interaction between prior achievement and instructional support. *Review of Educational Research, 59,* 65-86.

Wise, K. C. & Okey, J. R. (1983). A meta-analysis of the effects of various science teaching strategies on achievement. *Journal of Research in Science Teaching, 20,* 419-435.

Chapter 21

Abraham, A. A. (1990). *Racial issues on campus: How students view them?* Southern

Regional Education Board, Atlanta, GA. (ERIC Document Reproduction Service No. ED 328 180)

Argyris, C., Putman, R., & Smith, D. M. (1985). *Action science: Concepts, methods, and skills for research and intervention.* San Francisco, CA: Jossey-Bass.

Astin, A. W. (1998, January). *Evaluating remedial programs is not just a methodological issue.* Paper presented at the Conference on Replacing Remediation in Higher Education, Palo Alto, CA: Stanford University.

Berrueta-Clement, J. R., Barnett, W. S., & Weikart, D. P. (1985). Changed lives: The effects of the Perry Preschool Program on youths through age 19. In L. H. Aiken and B. H. Kehrer (Eds.), *Evaluation studies review annual* (Vol. 10, pp. 257-279). Beverly Hills, CA: Sage.

Boylan, H. R. (1999). *Evaluation and assessment of developmental education.* Lecture presentation at the Kellogg Institute, National Center for Developmental Education, Appalachian State University, July 19-23.

Callas, D. (1985). Academic placement practices: An analysis and proposed model. *College Teaching, 33*(1), 27-32.

Campbell, D. T., & Stanley, J. C. (1963). *Experimental and quasi-experimental designs for research.* Boston, MA: Houghton Mifflin Company.

Carter, S., & Skinner, E. (1987). *A second for Texans: Remedial education in two-year colleges.* Arizona State University: National Center for Postsecondary Governance and Finance.

Clowes, D. A. (1984). The evaluation of remedial/developmental programs: A stage model of program evaluation. *Journal of Developmental Education, 8*(1), 14-30.

Cronbach, L. J. (1982). *Designing evaluations of educational and social programs.* San Francisco, CA: Jossey-Bass.

Eisner, E. (1981). On the differences between scientific and artistic approaches to qualitative research. *Educational Researcher, 10*(4), 5-9.

Eisner, E. (1976). Educational connoissuership and criticism: Their form and functions in educational evaluation. *Journal of Aesthetic Education, 3-4*(1), 135-150.

Ewell, P. T. (1987). Establishing a campus-based assessment program. In D. F. Halpern (Ed.), *Student outcomes assessment: What institutions stand to gain.* New Directions for Higher Education, no. 59. San Francisco, CA: Jossey-Bass.

Fadle, L. M., & Winter, G. M. (1977). *Assessing the effectiveness of developmental/remedial programs in two year colleges.* Paper presented at the Annual Meeting of the American Educational Research Association. Chicago, IL. (ERIC Document Reproduction Service No. ED 254 542)

Farmer, V. L. (1988). *A comprehensive developmental education program.* Report submitted to the State University of New York, College of Technology, Delhi, New York.

Gredler, M. E. (1996). *Program evaluation.* Englewood Cliffs, NJ: Merrill/Prentice Hall.

Guba, E. G., & Lincoln, Y. S. (1987). The countenance of fourth-generation evaluation: Description, judgment and negotiation. In D. S. Cordray and M. W. Lipsey (Eds.), *Evaluation studies review annual* (Vol. 11). Newbury Park, CA: Sage.

Halpern, D. F. (1987). *Student outcomes assessment: What institutions stand to gain.* New Directions for Higher Education, no. 59. San Francisco: Jossey-Bass.

House, E. R. (1976). Justice in evaluation . In G. V. Glass (Ed.), *Evaluation studies review annual* (Vol. 1). Beverly Hills, CA: Sage.

House, E. R. (1980). *Evaluating with validity.* Beverly Hills, CA: Sage.

Jacobi, M., Astin, A., & Ayala, F. (1987). *College student outcomes assessment: A talent development perspective.* ASHE-ERIC Higher Education Report No. 7. Washington, D. C.: Association for the Study of Higher Education.

Kerlinger, F. N. (1986). *Foundations of behavioral research (3rd ed.).* New York: Holt, Rinehart and Winston.

Krathwohl, D. R. (1993). *Methods of educational and social science research: An integrated approach.* New York: Longman.

Lincoln, Y. S., & Guba, E. G. (1986). But is it rigorous? Trustworthiness and authenticity in naturalistic evaluation. In D. D. Williams (Ed.), *Naturalistic evaluation.* (New Directions for Program Evaluation, No. 30). San Francisco: Jossey-Bass.

Rippey, R. M. (1973). *Studies in transactional evaluation.* Berkeley, CA: McCutcheon.

Rossi, P. H., & Freeman, H. E. (1985). *Evaluation: A systematic approach* (3rd ed.). Beverly Hills, CA: Sage.

Rouche, J. E. in collaboration with J. C. Pitman, (1972). *A modest proposal: Students can learn.* San Francisco: Jossey-Bass.

Scriven, M. (1972). Pros and cons about goal-free evaluation. *Evaluation Comment, 3,* 1-4.

Scriven, M. (1974). Standards for the evaluation of education program and products. In G. D. Borich (Ed.), *Evaluating educational programs and products.* Englewood Cliffs, NJ: Educational Technology Publications.

Smith, M. L., Gabriel, R., Schott, J., & Padia, W. L. (1976). Evaluation effects of Outward Bound. In G. V. Glass (Ed.), *Evaluation studies review annual* (Vol. 1, pp. 400-421). Beverly Hills, CA: Sage.

Somers, R. L. (1987). *Issues, problems, and techniques in program evaluation.* Boone, NC: The Telementoring Project, Reich College of Education, Appalachian State University.

Stake, R. E. (1991). Excerpts from program evaluation, particularly responsive evaluations. *Evaluation Practice, 12,* 63-77.

Stake, R. E. (1975). To evaluate an arts program. In R. E. Stake (Ed.), *Evaluating the arts in education: A responsive approach.* Columbus, Ohio: Merrill.

Stake, R. E., & Easley, J. A., Jr. (Eds.). (1978a). *Case studies in science education,*

Vol. 1: Design, overview and general findings. Washington, D. C.: U. S. Government Printing Office.

Stufflebeam, D. L., & Shinkfield, A. J. (1985). *Systematic evaluation: A self-instructional guide to theory and practice.* Boston: Kluwer Mijhoff.

Tomlinson, L. (1989). *Postsecondary developmental programs: A traditional agenda with new imperatives.* Report no. 3. Washington, D. C.: School of Education and Human Development, The George Washington University. (ASHE/ERIC Higher Education Report Series).

Tyler, L. L., Klein, M. G., & Associates. (1976). *Evaluating and choosing curriculum and instructional materials.* Los Angeles: Educational Resource Associates.

Tyler, R. W. (1934). *Constructing achievement tests.* Columbus: Ohio State University.

Tyler, R. W., & Waples, D. (1930). *Research methods and teacher's problems: A manual for systematic studies of classroom procedure.* New York: Macmillan.

Wolf, R. L. (1975). Trial by jury: A new evaluation method. I. The process. *Phi Delta Kappan, 57*(3), 185-187.

Wolf, R. L. (1979). The use of judicial evaluation methods in the formation of education policy. *Educational Evaluation and Policy Analysis, 3*(1), 19-28.

Wortman, P. M., Reichardt, C. S., & St. Pierre, R. G. (1978). The first year of the education voucher demonstration. *Evaluation Quarterly, 2,* 193-214.

Author Index

Subject Index